Stress, Risk, and Resilience in Children and Adolescents recognizes the complexity of the developmental processes that impact on coping and resilience and the importance of sociocultural factors. In this respect, the relation between a stressor and an outcome depends on many factors, including the individual's previous experience, perception of the event, coping skills, and social supports. In turn, each of these factors displays meaningful variation by developmental status, social background, and cultural context.

The examination of individual differences in vulnerability to stress and risk factors has grown substantially over the past decade as it has become clearer that some children do, in fact, "beat the odds." In order to understand why some children succumb to even modest stress whereas others remain resilient in the face of what appear to be overwhelming stressors, research has increasingly examined the processes and mechanisms by which children of different ages deal with adverse life experiences, rather than merely studying the stressors themselves. Many problem behaviors have multiple causes, and most children with one problem behavior also have others. The co-occurrence and/or interrelatedness of risk factors and problem behaviors is, therefore, an important area of research.

Stress, risk, and resilience in children and adolescents

Stress, risk, and resilience in children and adolescents

Processes, mechanisms, and interventions

Robert J. Haggerty
University of Rochester

Lonnie R. Sherrod
William T. Grant Foundation

Norman Garmezy
University of Minnesota

Michael Rutter
Institute of Psychiatry, London

CAMBRIDGE
UNIVERSITY PRESS

Published by the Press Syndicate of the University of Cambridge
The Pitt Building, Trumpington Street, Cambridge CB2 1RP
40 West 20th Street, New York, NY 10011-4211, USA
10 Stamford Road, Oakleigh, Melbourne 3166, Australia

First published 1994

Printed in the United States of America

Library of Congress Cataloging-in-Publication Data
Stress, risk, and resilience in children and adolescents : processes,
  mechanisms, and interventions / Robert J. Haggerty . . . [et al.].
      p.   cm.
  Includes bibliographic references and index.
    ISBN 0-521-44146-3
      1. Stress in children.   2. Stress in adolescence.   3. Adjustment
  (Psychology) in children.   4. Adjustment (Psychology) in
  adolescence.   5. Resilience (Personality trait) in children.
  6. Resilience (Personality trait) in adolescence.   I. Haggerty,
  Robert J.
  BF723.S75S79   1994
  155.4'18 – dc20   93-42814
                                                                CIP

A catalog record for this book is available from the British Library.

ISBN 0-521-44146-3 hardback

Although the senior editor has fully shared editorial responsibilities with the other three editors, we along with the contributors to this volume wish to dedicate this book to Dr. Robert J. Haggerty. Bob Haggerty has devoted his life to the scholarly and clinical study of children, to examination of their life stresses, of the effects on their physical and psychological health, and to the design and evaluation of programs to assist children in coping with stress. It is fully appropriate that this lifetime of work should culminate in his 12 years as president of the William T. Grant Foundation, where he was able to maximize the scope of his impact in fields relevant to stress and coping in children and adolescents. This volume represents one example of the fruition of these 12 years. This volume and much of the research on which it is based would not have been possible without Bob Haggerty's leadership. In addition to his important editorial contribution, this volume is truly a *Zeitschrift* for Bob, and a recognition of his national role in seeking to assure the well-being of children.

Contents

Contributors

Ronald Barr
McGill University
Montreal Children's Hospital
2300 Tupper Street
Montreal, Quebec
Canada H3H 1P3

W. Thomas Boyce
University of California, San
    Francisco
Division of Behavioral and
    Developmental Pediatrics
Department of Pediatrics
400 Parnassus Avenue
    A 203/Box 0314
San Francisco, California 94143

David C. Clark
Center for Suicide Research and
    Prevention
Rush Presbyterian St. Luke's
    Medical Center
1725 West Harrison Street
Chicago, Illinois 60612

Bruce Compas
University of Vermont
Department of Psychology
Burlington, Vermont 05405

John Eckenrode
Cornell University
College of Human Ecology
Department of Human
    Development and Family Studies
Ithaca, New York 14853

Robert Emery
University of Virginia
Department of Psychology
Gilmer Hall
Charlottesville, Virginia 22903

Rex Forehand
University of Georgia
Department of Psychology
Athens, Georgia 30602

Norman Garmezy
University of Minnesota
Department of Psychology
N419 Elliott Hall
75 East River Road
Minneapolis, Minnesota 55455

Ann E. Goebel
Center for Suicide Research and
    Prevention
Rush Presbyterian St. Luke's
    Medical Center

1725 West Harrison Street
Chicago, Illinois 60612

Susan Gore
University of Massachusetts,
 Boston
Center for Survey Research
100 Morrissey Boulevard
Healey Library, 10th Floor
Boston, Massachusetts 02125-3394

Robert J. Haggerty
University of Rochester
School of Medicine and Dentistry
Department of Pediatrics
601 Elmwood Avenue
Rochester, New York 14642

Constance L. Hammen
University of California, Los
 Angeles
Department of Psychology
Los Angeles, California 90024

Saundra Murray Nettles
Johns Hopkins University
Center for Social Organization of
 Schools
3505 North Charles Street
Baltimore, Maryland 21218

Joseph H. Pleck
Wellesley College
Center for Research on Women
Wellesley, Massachusetts
 02181-8259

I. Barry Pless
Montreal Children's Hospital
2300 Tupper Street

Room C538
Montreal, Quebec
Canada H3H 1P3

Robert S. Pynoos
University of California, Los
 Angeles
Neuropsychiatric Institute
Division of Child Psychiatry
760 Westwood Plaza
Los Angeles, California 90024

Michael Rutter
Institute of Psychiatry
DeCrespigny Park
Denmark Hill
London, England SE5 8AF

Lonnie R. Sherrod
William T. Grant Foundation
515 Madison Avenue
New York, New York 10022-5403

Ruth E. K. Stein
Albert Einstein College of
 Medicine
Department of Pediatrics
Bronx Municipal Hospital Center,
 Room 1N17
Pelham Parkway and Eastchester
 Road
Bronx, New York 10461

Lonnie K. Zeltzer
UCLA School of Medicine
Pediatric Pain Program
Department of Pediatrics
10833 Le Conte Avenue
Los Angeles, California 90024

Tables and figures

Tables

Figures

Preface

Stress and coping: A unifying theme

Perhaps no construct in psychosocial research has been more difficult to define than stress. At the same time, the prevalence in research as well as in public usage of the term *stress* is testimony to its importance.

In 1981, when first author Robert Haggerty came to the William T. Grant Foundation as president, an umbrella term was needed to cover the research areas that the foundation would support under his leadership. The requirements for the label were that it be descriptive of several broad fields of research, but not without boundaries. The rubric *stress and coping in school-age children* was chosen as an umbrella term meeting these criteria. Studies by the first author and others on the relation between stressful life events and infections in children supported this choice (Meyer & Haggerty, 1962). But the lay public's recognition of stress and coping as a meaningful idea was equally important. Additionally, stress and coping expressed the interactive nature of the environment (or context) with the individual's response – in contrast to much child developmental research at that time that focused mainly on the individual. In terms of the criteria used for its choice, the concept of stress and coping has served well as a defining and unifying label for research and for the foundation's program across the past decade. This volume reviews that work.

A brief history of the foundation's program

The William T. Grant Foundation is a private, independent foundation established more than 50 years ago, in the words of its founder, William T. Grant, to "provide, through research, understanding of how people can learn to live more useful and happy lives." From its inception, the foundation has supported research on human development, having undertaken a series of different program efforts to understand factors that impair development. Its first grant was the Grant Study, a longitudinal investigation of four freshman classes at Harvard University, designed to examine how "the best and brightest" failed or succeeded as they moved through life. In the 1950s and 1960s the foundation pioneered in supporting studies of human infancy; and during the last 12 years its focus has been on school-age children and youth. Mr. Grant understood that although human services were of obvious importance, he did not believe that we had then (and we must concur that we still do not have) enough knowledge about what services are effective to justify expending all of the foundation's limited resources on providing direct services. Consistency in the support of research on human development has been the primary characteristic of the foundation: to understand how to assist young people to achieve their full potential. The general rubric of stress and coping has proved to be a useful means for pursuing the objectives established by Mr. Grant for the foundation.

During the past decade, research on stress and coping has flourished, in large part because this general rubric provided a perspective for examining a range of problems dealing with "the seamless whole of childhood." A book that has become a landmark publication, *Stress, Coping, and Development in Childhood*, edited by Norman Garmezy and Michael Rutter, presented one of the first systematic efforts to assemble what was known about the experience of stress and the development of coping during the childhood years. This volume was based upon a series of seminars and a conference led by Rutter and Garmezy at the Center for Advanced Study of the Behavioral Sciences at Stanford during the 1979–1980 academic year. These activities were one of the first projects supported by the William T. Grant Foundation under its then new focus on stress and coping in school-age children: Dr. Garmezy describes the planning of the 1983 volume in his introductory chapter (Garmezy & Rutter, 1983).

At about the same time, the Grant Foundation began supporting a number of research projects in the general area of stress in children. One new type of support begun by the foundation at this time was for consortia. Early in Dr. Haggerty's tenure at the foundation, a group of scholars requested a small grant in order to continue some of the work begun by a national commission to examine the psychological consequences of physical disease during childhood. These scholars were interested in continuing to meet in order to collaborate on the development of measurement and other aspects of research in this field. A Consortium on Chronic Illness in Childhood was funded by the foundation in 1982 and continues to the present day, having recently received a multiple-year award following scientific and foundation board review. In 1983 the foundation's board approved a separate annual appropriation specifically for consortia projects, and in that same year, a second consortium was funded, the Consortium on Research Involving Stress Processes.

The early work of these two consortia was successful and became known, and scholars began to approach the foundation, identifying other areas where this type of activity would be useful to one or more specific subfields of research on stress and coping in childhood. In 1986 three new consortia were funded by the foundation, dealing with adolescent suicide and bereavement, school-based programs to promote social competency, and the adolescent transition in black children. In 1987 a consortium was formed to examine the impact of divorce on children, and in 1988 one funded to address the psychobiology of stress. An eighth and final consortium, focusing on depression in children and adolescence, was funded in 1990. Each of these consortia consisted of 8 to 15 scholars who came together two or three times per year to address the needs of research in these specific areas. Some discuss their research at its earliest phases, plan joint research projects, or conduct multisite collaborative research. Others write papers, edit books, or develop new research instruments. Through exposure to the multiple disciplines that make up each consortium, the research interests of members are also broadened. In sum, the consortia have functioned similarly to committees of the

National Academy of Science, the Institute of Medicine, and the Social Science Research Council, but have somewhat more specific foci.

The existing eight consortia of the foundation cover a broad range of topics. Some are defined by topics that represent major stressors in children's lives – chronic physical disease, divorce, bereavement, or growing up as a disadvantaged, minority adolescent. Others examine specific coping skills or supports, such as social competence or social support networks. As is true for the majority of its awards, the foundation responded to investigator-initiated applications in funding consortia. The decisions about which consortia to fund were based on a strategy to cover a good deal, but not all, of the fields and topics relevant to the research on stress and coping that was being supported by the foundation during the 1980s. As a result, the consortia offer a logical base for reviewing what we have learned after 12 years of foundation-funded research on stress and coping in children. Reviews of their work, therefore, provide the core content of this volume.

A decade of research: What have we learned?

We have learned a great deal across the past decade from research on stress and coping during childhood. Research during the 1960s was focused primarily on demonstrating that there was a relation between stressful life events and illness. In the mechanistic view of health and illness that was then prevalent, the association between stress and illness was questioned. Now the association between a variety of different stressors and various outcomes of poor health is well documented. The amount of variance shown to be attributable to such associations is, however, small. The reason for small effect sizes is that the relationship between stress and illness is more complicated than merely a direct association.

For example, some individuals are more susceptible or vulnerable than others, due both to physiological and psychological differences (either inborn or acquired very early), and to the degree of prior success they have enjoyed (or not) in coping with life experiences. Furthermore, there may well be vulnerable periods of life when difficult experiences are more likely than during other times to overwhelm the individual. The timing and sequencing of experiences is also important. We now know that it is more damaging to suffer adverse life events close in time than over an extended period. We have also learned that the ability to cope with adverse life events generally resides in part outside of the individual's control. In addition to the factors mentioned already that are inherent to the organism, family, peer, and community supports or risks determine a good deal of the outcome.

Thus, over the years as we have learned more about the complexities of the relationship between experienced stress and psychological or physical outcomes, the label stress and coping has become a less useful guide to research. Stress has proved to be very difficult to measure (despite the acknowledged observation that most people can tell you when they feel stressed). Additionally, the complex relation between a stressor and an outcome depends on many factors, and each of these factors displays variation according to developmental status, social background, and cultural context. Thus, in order to understand why some children succumb to even modest stress, whereas others remain resilient in the face of what appear to be overwhelming stressors, future research should increasingly examine the processes and mechanisms by which children of different ages deal with adverse life experiences, rather than merely studying the stressors themselves.

Research across the past decade has also increasingly demonstrated that stressors are rarely single events, but instead are parts of complex environmental and transitional influences. Many problem behaviors have multiple causes or risk factors, and most children with one problem behavior also have other problem behaviors. The co-occurrence and/or interrelatedness of risk factors and problem behaviors is, therefore, a second promising direction for current research; one specific instance is the increasing attention to co-morbidity in psychiatric research on mental illness.

At the same time, however, investigators have also come to realize that certain behaviors (such as unprotected sex with its complications of pregnancy and/or sexually transmitted diseases, substance abuse, and other risk-taking behaviors) that are problematic for long-term developmental outcomes may, in fact, represent young people's attempts to cope with difficult life circumstances. As a result, research on the basic developmental processes of stress and coping during childhood must move to a level allowing careful attention to intervention and prevention. Interventions can now be based on theory and research on causes, outcomes, and mechanisms, so that rigorous evaluations of interventions can become standard. Unifying aspects of interventions have already emerged: helping youth to become masters of their own fate, giving them skills to manage their own problems, and linking them to social supports and comprehensive services. There has been a coming together of the research on multiple causes, multiple outcomes, and understanding of process that has led to the building of comprehensive, coordinated services that help young people deal with the multiple causes of multiple problems. Prevention has become a recognizable goal.

The present volume

One direct implication of research across the past decade is that the label stress and coping is too general and too simplistic to continue to serve as a useful framework for research. Instead, concepts of risk, resilience, and development must guide investigations of processes, mechanisms, and interventions, and this new framework structures the content and organization of this volume. The goal of this book is to illustrate how, across the past decade, research has demonstrated the importance of four rather complex themes that demand both a broadening and a specification of the label stress and coping. (1) Both risk factors and problem outcomes show an *interrelatedness* – at a minimum, they co-occur. Substantial, important and developmentally meaningful individual variability has been demonstrated. (2) Inter- as well as intraindividual variation exists in the factors responsible for *resilience* and susceptibility to stress. There may well be cohort variability as well. Hence, these other forms of variability must be given equal attention, and not treated as error variation. (3) It is critical to examine the *processes and mechanisms* that link multiple stressors to multiple outcomes. It is not sufficient to describe stressors or outcomes. (4) The recognition of interrelatedness and individual variability, and the careful examination of processes then allows the design and evaluation of *interventions and prevention programs* to break the links between stress and adverse outcomes. The most general and explicit purpose of this volume is to update the 1983 book, *Stress, Coping, and Development in Childhood,* by summarizing research illustrating these four themes.

Despite the emergence of these several integrative themes, research during the past decade has continued to focus for the most part on single stressors (such as family conflict and parental divorce or chronic physical illness) and single problem outcomes (such as depression). As a result, this volume is also organized around specific problem areas, including depression in children, children's experience of divorce, and psychosocial consequences of chronic disease. These chapters present state-of-the-art reviews of these fields, but with the additional goal of addressing how research in this area has pursued the four themes just described. One theme is highlighted in each chapter; for example, the chapter on childhood depression pays particular attention to the interrelatedness of risks and problem behaviors because of the specific focus in the field of developmental psychopathology on comorbidity. Similarly, the chapter on research involving stress processes examines the interrelatedness of both risk factors (or stressors) and problem behavior outcomes. Papers both on divorce and black adolescence emphasize the theme of resilience, whereas chapters on adolescent bereavement and on the psychobiology of stress each pursue different approaches to the assessment of processes and mechanisms. Two chapters describe approaches to interventions in quite different areas: school-based social competence training and prevention of psychological problems in chronically ill children.

At the same time that these four themes are highlighted, it is also critical to emphasize that these four areas are also interrelated. For example, one cannot discuss the interrelatedness of problems without considering resilience or the implications for interventions. Although the usual strategy in research is to isolate and study as few variables as possible, it is now clear that this approach is frequently inadequate. To understand how children can be helped to lead productive, happy lives, research must include the whole child, his family, peers, school, and the culture in which the child lives. This holistic view of research is brought to the fore in Garmezy's introductory chapter, focusing on risk, resilience, and development; and we hope that this holistic, integrative view is one of the major contributions made by this volume across all the chapters. The final chapter by Rutter highlights several unifying ideas that have emerged from the research across the past decade, reported in this volume and elsewhere, and helps to spell out an agenda for future research.

This volume, like its predecessor, is based in part on a conference supported and/or organized by the William T. Grant Foundation. The current volume was planned at a conference held at Kiawah Island, South Carolina, on May 28–31, 1992. Each core review chapter in the current volume was prepared by one of the foundation's eight consortia. In some cases, all members of the consortium contributed to the preparation of the chapter; in others, a subset of members took full responsibility. In all cases, the multiple-year deliberations of consortia provided the basis for the organization and content of the chapters. At the conference, two consultants reviewed each of the eight consortia chapters and made integrating and critical comments. Additionally, chairpersons of sessions at the conference reviewed the chapters and offered integrative comments. These deliberations over the eight core papers before, during, and following the conference capture the depth and quality of attention available only through extensive peer review of manuscripts, as might be more typical for a journal publication. Much of the content and quality of the specific and general discussions at the meeting is captured and included by the editors in the opening and concluding chapters (by Garmezy and Rutter respectively). Across all these various meeting and writing activities, a general and thorough review of *Stress, Risk, and Resilience in Children and Adolescents* with attention to processes, mechanisms, and intervention has been achieved and is represented in this volume. As a result, this volume and the conference on which it is based contribute directly to the objectives Mr. Grant set for the foundation more than 50 years ago.

Helping children and their families become masters of their own fate and giving them skills and access to social supports and comprehensive services are clearly in the mainstream of research in this area today. The emphasis can now be on prevention, not just on the treatment of problems already developed. Risk factors and protective factors have now emerged as two separate issues, which are not necessarily reciprocal.

Special acknowledgments

As staff of the foundation as well as coeditors of this volume, we owe a debt of thanks and appreciation to many individuals. First, our coeditors Norman Garmezy and Michael Rutter have been very generous with their time and expertise. Members of the foundation's Program Committee from 1990–1992, Martha Minow, Harvard University, Richard Price, University of Michigan, and Henry Riecken, University of Pennsylvania, were also helpful to us as staff of the foundation during the planning of the conference and volume; Beatrix A. Hamburg, M.D., as a member of the foundation's Program Committee and in her new role as president of the foundation has been especially helpful. And last, but not least, foundation staff members, Sharon Brewster and Linda Newman, have been invaluable behind the scenes in all aspects of the work supporting this book.

ROBERT J. HAGGERTY, M.D.
Professor Emeritus, University of Rochester
President (1980–1992)
William T. Grant Foundation

LONNIE R. SHERROD, PH.D.
Vice-President for Program
William T. Grant Foundation

References

Garmezy, N., & Rutter, M. (1983). *Stress, coping and development in childhood.* New York: McGraw-Hill.

Meyer, R. J., & Haggerty, R. J. (1962). Streptococcal infections in families: Factors altering individual susceptibility. *Pediatrics, 29,* 539.

Acknowledgments

In addition to the persons acknowledged in the Preface, the four editors also wish to mention several groups and individuals who were especially important to the preparation of this volume.

Each of the authors in the volume has contributed much more than is typical for preparing a chapter in an edited volume. And each of these authors, hence we as well, is indebted to the membership of the consortia, listed in Appendix A. The consultants who read, critiqued, and wrote extensive discussions of the eight core papers are: Robert Cairns, Ph.D., University of North Carolina; Donald Cohen, M.D., Yale University; Emory Cowen, Ph.D., University of Rochester; E. Mavis Hetherington, Ph.D., University of Virginia; Richard Jessor, Ph.D., University of Colorado; Ann S. Masten, Ph.D., University of Minnesota; Richard Price, Ph.D., University of Michigan; and Emmy Werner, Ph.D., University of California, Davis; we owe a tremendous debt to these scholars because their contributions substantially improved this volume. The chairpersons of sessions at the conference, James P. Connell, Ph.D., University of Rochester (now Public/Private Ventures, Philadelphia); Jacquelynne Eccles, Ph.D., University of Michigan; Frank Furstenberg, Ph.D., University of Pennsylvania; and Anne Petersen, Ph.D., University of Minnesota, also served as critical resource people.

Because this volume reflects the multiyear deliberations of the William T. Grant Foundation's eight multidisciplinary consortia, each consortium membership has made a contribution to this volume. In some cases, the preparation of the paper involved the full membership of the group; in others, a subset of members, and in others only the authors designated on the paper. Nonetheless, even in the later cases, the paper includes ideas and points of discussion from consortia meetings. Hence, it is appropriate that the full membership of each of the eight consortia be listed and acknowledged (see Appendix A.).

1

Reflections and commentary on risk, resilience, and development

Norman Garmezy

Introduction

Coeditors Haggerty and Sherrod have been gracious in describing the volume *Stress, Coping, and Development in Children* (Garmezy & Rutter, 1983) as a forerunner of the subsequent expansion of research on children's reactions to stressful events and varied disorganizing circumstances. It is appropriate to acknowledge that without Dr. Haggerty's support, that volume may never have reached fruition.

Because there is perceived continuity of the early volume with this one, it may be of historical interest to describe briefly how 12 researchers representing multiple scientific disciplines, and varied orientations and research styles found themselves sharing joint ownership in a volume that sought to describe the status of an emergent research area – one seemingly not ready for an interdisciplinary thrust.

The base for the enterprise was the Center for Advanced Study in the Behavioral Sciences and its director, Gardner Lindzey, who provided strong support for the project. The invited Fellows for the year 1979–1980 included Garmezy, Rutter, Kagan, Lipsitt, Patterson, Segal, and Wallerstein. The center fosters collaborations created out of dissimilar pairings. In this instance one could readily locate within the research programs of these seven individuals ties that made for a communal effort to integrate harmoniously their ongoing research interests with the then comparatively unexplored literature of multiple

Norman Garmezy is Professor of Psychology Emeritus at the University of Minnesota.

stressors that influenced the development of children and adults. Garmezy and Rutter had focused on risk and protective factors in children under stress. Kagan and Lipsitt, developmental psychologists, had long-term research commitments to infants and young children, largely in the context of normative developmental patterns but with a concern for the effects of deviant circumstances. Patterson, who is clearly identified with children at risk, focused on the antecedents to antisocial behavior with an emphasis on the contributory role of coercive family practices. Segal, the director of the Division of Scientific and Public Information for the National Institute of Mental Health, had been recurrently called on to facilitate the protection of various groups that had been exposed to the acute stressors of displacement, war, and devastation. Wallerstein added clinical sophistication in her role as director of a clinic focused on the treatment of children and families under stress. At midyear, psychiatrist Herbert Liederman joined the group, bringing his wide-ranging research interests that traversed infant, child, and adult psychiatry viewed from a cross-cultural perspective. His was a long-term interest in attachment and bonding with particular reference to the impact of the families of infants born with congenital physical handicaps. The group's search for understanding was enhanced by 14 visiting lecturers, including Richard Lazarus, Emmy Werner, and Paul Baltes.

As the format of the projected volume began to emerge it became evident that a more definitive volume on stress, coping, and development required additional contributors. Roland Ciaranello and Seymour Levine of Stanford University's Department of Psychiatry added chapters on the neurochemical and psychobiological aspects of stress. Eleanor Maccoby provided a chapter that emphasized factors of social and emotional responsiveness of children that are keys to developmental change. Lee Robins added her methodological sophistication regarding sociological and epidemiological predictors of successful interventions following exposure to stress.

The status of stress research at the time of the volume invited caution. In the introduction to the text we wrote:

Do they [the contents of the volume] provide a coherent answer to the complex problems of the effects of stress and the quality of different patterns of coping in childhood? The conservative and appropriate answer must be "no." We now stand at the starting point for studying stress and its vicissitudes in children. Perhaps this volume will contribute one solid step into that future. (p. xviii)

The Grant Foundation and stress research

Now, fourteen years later the influence and support of the William T. Grant Foundation during Dr. Haggerty's tenure in the presidency is summarized in this new volume. Haggerty chose an unusual approach to advance the study of stress in children. Initially, research grant support was forthcoming for investigators working in the various stress-related areas, but the brush was a wide one. In their preface to this volume, Haggerty and Sherrod have described the critical linkage that was made between initial grants to investigators and the subsequent formation of consortia focused on specific areas. In making a grant to an investigator engaged in the study of chronic illnesses in children, Haggerty perceived that the area was of such great significance that it was important to expand the boundaries of the research on the interaction of illness and adaptation by forming a consortium that could serve as the structure for a collective of active investigators, all focused jointly on the critical problem of children's adaptations to chronic illness. The purpose of this initial consortium would be to share ideas, initiate collaborations, train young investigators, and so forth. One cannot overvalue the significance of this major step by a distinguished foundation.

For the Grant Foundation, 1982–1983 saw the formation of two consortia – the initial one focused on chronic illness in children and the second on research on stress processes. The latter correctly captured the critical importance of coming to grips with the processes and mechanisms underlying the diversity of children's responsiveness when exposed to stressful circumstances.

There followed a 3-year hiatus, but then in 1986 three new consortia were formed that focused on adolescent bereavement; risk and resilience factors influencing development in black adolescents; and school-based promotion of social competence. The bereavement consortium focused on one of the major stressors for children – the specificity of significant loss. The developmental data on black adolescents, accompanied by a search for *both* risk and resilience factors, tapped into the critical area not only of survivorship in black youths but of their resilience under stress. The Consortium on School-Based Promotion of Social Competence constituted another advance namely by fostering research on how to promote within schools social competence as a potential protective factor in youths exposed to stress. Here the focus was on creating environmental supports and a formal program within the schools to enhance the acquisition of competencies critical to advancing children's adaptability to stressful life events. In 1987 the foundation turned to a critical stressor in the lives of the nation's children – divorce and the trauma induced by family dissolution. This critical area of research is evident by the striking finding reported in the Emery–Forehand chapter that 38% of white children and 75% of black children in the United States will witness their parents' divorce by age 16. Thus a large body of children in the United States will know intimately the trauma of family dissolution and the economic threat subsequently posed by a mother's income loss and the cumulation of stressors that follow.

In 1988 the foundation moved to support a consortium focused on the psychobiology of stress, and in 1989 the consortium on depression in childhood and adolescence was initiated. These two provided support for a growing presence in the literature of the psychobiological correlates of stress exposure, and a recognition of the broad sweep of the incidence and prevalence of depression in young people. These last consortia in the sequence provide a continuity with the earlier volume on *Stress, Coping, and Development in Children.*

Support for the concept of a consortium of researchers to investigate critical problem areas appears to be a strong wave of present planning and likely an even stronger one in the future. Along with the Grant Foundation's interdisciplinary program of support was the decision of the then newly founded John D. and Catherine T. MacArthur Foundation to focus on adaptive and maladaptive patterns of behavior in development. In the latter case the effort began to focus on the structure of a consortium of scientists that would generate new collaborations in the fields of health, illness, and development. "Networks" of scientists were formed to initiate research that would reflect interdisciplinary collaboration on such problem areas as the psychobiology of depression, risk and protective factors in the major mental disorders, early childhood transitions in development, and health and behavior. Subsequently, a longitudinal view of development under stressful circumstances took form in groups focused on the periods of adolescence, midlife, and aging. Additional networks have now included human development and criminal behavior, human development and healthy organizations, and mental health and the law. These forms of support from two major foundations accentuated the future significance of (1) interdisciplinary collaboration, for (2) the longitudinal study of development, with (3) a focus on healthful and maladaptive patterns of response to stress.

The structure of this volume with its multiple authorships is a recognition that an overarching integration of the diverse literature of children under stress currently cannot be definitive. In many ways the task, if anything, has become more difficult as the literature on stress has expanded. Stress continues to invite diversity as is evident in the current volume. In a sense, that resolution may have seemed easier 13 years ago when the coauthors of the multiple chapters that made up *Stress, Coping, and Development in Children* first met and began to map the contents of a comparatively unintegrated area of research. Looking back to that volume reveals that integration was not achieved. The best one could find then were partial integrations that crossed over specific chapters.

There was in the earlier volume some effort at constructing a developmental chain that incorporated social ecology and childbirth, stress in infancy, stress and coping in early development, stress and family process, stress and the developmental tasks associated with divorce, and a review of psychobiological and neurochemical aspects of stress and coping, along with a general review of some of the stressors that accompany the childhood years. Topping this survey were two underlying themes – one methodological and the other focused on public policy implications of the early research on children under stress.

Clearly the content of the chapters of the current volume reflects a broader arc: physical and mental disorders are treated; protective factors and a training protocol for enhancing such potential is provided; issues surrounding minority adolescents are discussed; depression in the young is recognized and described; divorce is again in evidence but treated more systematically.

Each of these areas and others have a contemporary cast and represent some new modes for broadening the focus of collaborative research on stress by bringing able investigators together, and formalizing the concept of the consortium by providing a communal focus on specific topics implicating stress and adaptation through the earlier years of the life cycle. This conception, created by Robert Haggerty, enhances the task of mapping designated areas of stress research more thoroughly by bringing together able researchers who, while focusing on a common problem, can provide a diversity of theoretical and conceptual schemata in a research environment marked by support, open exchange, and collaboration.

In the earlier volume the individualization by chapter authors made more difficult the amalgamation of content on some focused topic. *Stress, Coping, and Development in Children* reflected a composition of chapters formed by individuals who differed in their views of the field, tempered, in small part, by the exchange of viewpoints held by participating colleagues in the course of a year-long seminar. In the current volume representatives of the consortium present their views with, one hopes, a certain degree of concordance with the participating members of their groups.

The current consortium structure suggests a boundedness that may be more apparent than real, for the various authors were not invited to write a chapter summarizing their group's views. I suspect that, had this been made a requirement, the effort to resolve differences may have made the task infinitely more difficult than is currently evident in the individual chapters that follow. However, the authors have lived with their colleagues' thinking for several years, and one can assume that through a process of exchange and absorption some degree of a collective commentary is likely to be reflected in the individual chapters. In effect, the individualization of a specific content area by a single author in the earlier volume has now been supplanted by the collective contributions over time of multiple investigators drawn from different laboratories.

Finally, I want to comment on the foci of the various consortia that have been established by the Grant Foundation. Contentually, these tap into some of the major problems that now confront the nation: depression as a widespread mental disorder, the breakup of the American family, racial disharmony, the limitations of our treatment of chronic childhood illnesses, the effects of social class variations on behavior, and problems of our schools in insuring the later well-being of our children via education and social learning.

We live in a complex world marked by deep-seated problems and many troubled families who share a multitude of risk factors that extend from genetic and biological influences to negative psychosocial factors. The danger to children lies in the *cumulation* of adversities that exist in many families but are evident disproportionately in the poor (Garmezy & Masten, 1994). In poverty there is a heightened possibility of poor parenting, family discord and breakup, inadequate health care, chronic unemployment, welfare status, and inadequate housing. Despite these cumulated effects, there are, at the same time, many impoverished families that give evidence of an effective struggle to escape from poverty.

A focus on specific stressors as antecedent to disordered behavior now has an old-fashioned ring to it. The magnitude of *cumulated adversities* is the key to heightened negative behavioral patterns in parents and children (Garmezy & Masten, 1994; Rutter, this volume). This is the heartland for research on interventions and it requires our immersion in the *multiple* stressors to which a substantial portion of our population is now subjected.

In the chapters that follow, representatives of each of the eight consortia present segments of the concerns of their respective research groups. The range of these chapters makes evident that the editors and authors of *Stress, Coping, and Development in Children* had a narrower task than did the editors of the current volume. Stress has now been embraced by biological, psychological, and sociocultural researchers. In a society under stress there is an abundance of examples to which one can turn for investigation.

Recent significant volumes on stress (Goldberger & Breznitz 1982, 1993) have focused primarily on the vicissitudes of adulthood: sensory deprivation and overload; occupational stress; job loss and unemployment; social disability; stability and change in adulthood; stress and coronary disease; stress and alcohol, headaches, psychiatric disorders, war and terrorism, and so on. Children inevitably get caught up in these familial and environmental stressors too, but there is not the focus on stress contents more directly affecting children – thus the significance of the current volume.

In these consortia scientists were brought together who shared common interests, but often dissimilar orientations. Yet the Grant Foundation's consortia of scientists who have engaged in the collective venture began to evidence a joint spirit that can only enhance the scientific enterprise through collaboration rather than competition.

I had the good fortune earlier in my career to assist in the formation of a consortium that played, unbeknownst to its members at the time of its formation, a critical role in creating the climate for work on a developmental psychopathology that was to follow. This venture, supported initially by a small grant from the National Institute of Mental Health, came to be known as the Risk Research Consortium, because its emphasis was on the adaptation over time of children at risk for schizophrenia by virtue of schizophrenic parentage (Watt, Anthony, Wynne, & Rolf, 1984). Its formation and context bore a striking parallel to Haggerty's efforts to lay the foundation for a broader approach to research on children at risk by virtue of a variety of predisposing conditions. In that earlier volume, however, there was additional parallel to the Grant Foundation's research efforts on behalf of children. This was expressed by Professor Manfred Bleuler, distinguished psychiatrist, scientist, and humanitarian, who became the godfather of the group. In his foreword to the volume *Children at Risk for Schizophrenia: A Longitudinal Perspective*, published in 1984 by Cambridge University Press, Bleuler wrote:

> If one didn't know the members of the Risk Research Consortium, one could be concerned about a . . . danger inherent in their work: that in observing they could forget to help, that in their commitment to science, humanity would be neglected. The experience of their warmth and openness banishes any fear that they might only observe passively when a child might be helped. Active intervention will make the scientific interpretation of their observations more difficult, but not impossible. To intervene and to observe the impact of the intervention may have greater scientific value than to chronicle passively the decline into psychosis. (p. xvii)

In the chapters that follow the scientific enterprise takes precedence, but the contents of these chapters also provide a focus for the types of interventions needed to alleviate the distress manifested by children exposed to mental disorder, family dissolution, racism, chronic illness, bereavement, and the many other disturbing events to which children are exposed in contemporary society.

In this sense the consortia developed by the Grant Foundation meet the hopes that Professor Bleuler had for all whose concern remains focused on the children who are at risk whether because of biological, psychological, or societal disadvantage.

Finally, I note that Michael Rutter has again demonstrated in the final chapter his extraordinary ability to bring together the current status of a field – in this case the effects of contemporary stressors on children – while also providing a vision of research needs and the direction of future research on stress and its vicissitudes.

Risk, resilience, and development: Opportunity and danger

It remains now only to comment briefly on the three constructs that form the essence of this volume. The first is the emerging power of *risk* as a factor in research on adaptation. Risk research has its roots in epidemiology and hence in medicine as well. It is concerned with the identification of factors that accentuate or inhibit disease and deficiency states, and the processes that underlie them. The words *accentuate* or *inhibit* are carefully chosen despite their seemingly contradictory meanings. For they point to the far-reaching range of risk research, which embraces a broad band of risk factors to which children and adults can be exposed – some may eventuate in disease or disorder (which identifies *vulnerability*), but others, in many instances, may be overcome and lead to positive adaptive behavior (which identifies *resilience*).

Studies of risk run a gamut of methods ranging from individual case histories (Comer, 1988; Goertzel & Goertzel, 1962; Illingworth & Illingworth, 1966; MacLeod, 1987; Yin, 1989), to cross-sectional, short-term (Schulz, 1969) and lengthier longitudinal investigations (Lefkowitz, Eron, Walder, & Huesman, 1977). Further, the studies traverse the entire life-span from birth to adulthood (Hunter, 1990) and old age with foci that can include a broad range of risk factors (Pittman, 1987). These include etiological studies emphasizing potential biological and behavioral precursors; personality predispositions of both positive and negative attributes, including genetic and environ mental predisposing factors; the actualizing power of stressful experiences via the ameliorating force of identifiable "protective factors"; the study of coping patterns, including their origins and developmental and situational contexts; and the evaluation of outcomes ranging from signs of severe biobehavioral and social deficits to patterns of resilience and adaptation amid disadvantage.

This is a tall order indeed for any discipline. Fortunately this range is not the exclusive concern of any single profession; rather it embraces multiple biological and behavioral sciences.

The range of inquiry is the life-span. A large number of studies have focused on the identification and screening of infants and children who are defined by biological, cognitive, or sensory factors as being at risk (Abel, 1989; Anthony & Chiland, 1988; Brown, 1988). In many instances, correlates of such vulnerabilities as prematurity, poor nutritional status, low birth weight, organic brain damage, and physical handicap (Birch & Gussow, 1970; Riley & Vorhees, 1986) often implicate a variety of both biological and psychosocial stressors (Brown, 1988; Kopp, 1983a, 1983b, 1987). These include the disadvantaged socioeconomic status of many at-risk children (Rutter & Madge, 1976) whose mothers are often young, unmarried, and poor, or they may come from disorganized urban or rural families (Caton, 1990; Davidson, 1990; Hampton, 1987; Hunter, 1990; Williams & Kornblum, 1985).

From a historical perspective, the emphasis on infants and young children with developmental disabilities reflects a pioneering era in risk studies that has clearly retained vitality from research on screening and intervention efforts. In recent years there has been an expansion in risk research accompanied by a broadening of the groups of children included in research studies and the types of research conducted with them. In years past the foci of our research programs have ranged from prenatal stress and its consequences for subsequent growth and well-being in infants and children, to delinquent adolescents and the instability posed by family conflict, inadequate parenting, and debilitating environments. Genetic concerns too have been reflected in longitudinal studies of delinquent and criminal careers (Lefkowitz et al., 1977), others of children whose at-risk status includes parental schizophrenia (Sameroff, Seifer, & Zax, 1982; Watt et al., 1984), affective disorders (Weissman et al., 1987; Yarrow, 1990), prior signs of antisocial disorder (Farrington et al., 1990; Patterson, 1990; Robins, 1966), hyperactivity and attention deficit disorder (Barkley, 1990; Hinshaw, 1987), and socially isolative behavior (Wanlass & Prinz, 1982). Another direction, of more recent origin, has been the attempt to identify so-called stress-resistant or resilient children, as reflected in signs of retained competence despite the presence of adverse circumstances in which adversity takes the form of biological, psychological, or societal shortcomings (Anthony & Cohler, 1987; Luthar & Zigler, 1991; Werner & Smith, 1982, 1992).

An awareness of the power of chronic and cumulative adversities (Garmezy & Masten, 1994) has now become evident in at-risk studies. To provide a more in-depth awareness of the magnitude of adversities that people are forced to cope with, it is apparent that future studies must seek to focus on a more intensive examination of co-occurring adversities, as opposed to single-stressor observations. To some extent the popular life events scales have provided a cumulated index of stress exposure, but the absence of in-depth inquiries negates the potential power of such instruments (Cohen, 1988; Dohrenwend & Dohrenwend, 1984; Thoits, 1983).

In studying risk in the offspring of mentally disordered parents or criminal families, many investigations have involved the selection of older children as opposed to infants and toddlers. There are good reasons for such age selectivity. The search for precursors to later mental disorders has involved complex behavioral processes such as deficits in attention and information processing, subdeviant social-emotional behavior, poor peer interaction, disturbed parent–child relationships, school performance deficits, and states of psychophysiological arousal. Such procedures, some successful differentiators, others less so, require a level of cooperation and maturity that only older children can muster. There is, however, an emerging series of significant longitudinal research programs that take pregnant women with a known history of psychopathology as their starting point and follow the "at-risk" offspring from birth onward. In some long-term studies these former infants have now reached early or late adolescence or adulthood, thus permitting a more adequate evaluation of the power of risk factors as contributory to heightened risk for deficit behaviors (Sameroff, Seifer, Baldwin, & Baldwin, 1993; Sameroff et al., 1982); follow-up studies have also contributed evidence of continuities and discontinuities in the development of the child at risk (Robins, 1966).

In the Rochester Risk Program headed by Sameroff, 10 risk factors were tabulated and histories and interviews were used to determine the degree of exposure (0–10) to which the at-risk child had been subjected. In a recent discussion Sameroff indicated that children exposed to all 10 negative factors had poor adaptational histories – hence resilience was absent and thus the construct may be found wanting. I strongly disagree with that view. Examples of children and adults in extremis are not the most appropriate tests for rejecting resilience. If a child or an adult is subjected to stressor upon stressor, negative consequences will follow (Garmezy & Masten, 1994). There are few "giants" in the land. What we do know is that competencies once obtained can serve as powerful protective factors. This brings us to the construct of "resilience."

Resilience: The promise and the danger in the concept

History is dotted with images of survivorship despite the most horrendous events. We need go no further than the studies of Holocaust victims to realize that even under the most dreadful circumstances – observing the murder of one's parents, children, siblings, and friends – people can and do actualize their aspirations into adulthood. Moskovitz (1983) noted that these victims were not free of the terror, they neither forgave nor forgot, but they continue even in their occasional personal despair to marry, raise children, work constructively in the community, and build anew a family marked by clear evidence of responsible parenting.

Can one find a greater stressor than that of children reared in a concentration camp and bereft of the support of family and caregivers who had been murdered in the camps? Sarah Moskovitz (1983) decided to search for these survivors, now grown to adulthood, and to learn of their adult lives. She reported on their "affirmation of life," "the quality of stubborn durability," and the reality that none had given up and surrendered via suicide or drugs or psychiatric disorder. She noted that "their hardiness of spirit and their quiet dignity are part of this persistent endurance." She adds:

Despite the severest deprivation in early childhood, these people are neither living a greedy, me-first style of life, nor are they seeking gain at the expense of others. None express the idea that the world owes them a living for all they have suffered. On the contrary; most of their lives are marked by an active compassion for others. (p. 233)

We witness similar behaviors in people in poverty who strive to save their children from the threats posed by high-crime neighborhoods, drugs, gangs, and the dissolution of family. What we have also witnessed, however, has been a politicization and dramatization of the problems associated with poverty. Data are needed to undo the harm so evident in newspaper and television reports pointing to the ghetto as the unregenerate environment for crack, crime, illegitimacy, heightened murder rates, and community threat.

Here then is the nature of the research opportunity that presents itself. We have sufficient knowledge of development to create the types of studies that will bring clarity to the basic issues that surround the concepts of *risk* and *resilience*. Where then is the "danger" that I implanted in the heading of this section? It lies in the sudden popularity of the concept of resilience. Risk has its base in epidemiology; resilience has its base in drama. The drama is that of the "American dream," the Horatio Alger legend – the mistaken view that any and all could succeed were they to work hard.

These are myths that need rejection. They are accompanied by the journalistic exercise of seeking a dramatic case from the researcher and the insistence that this will engage the readership. That is not our primary concern. The construct of resilience is potentially valid but research proof is needed to substantiate its meaning. This will require the heavy demand of short- and long-term research commitments and theoretical constructions that provide a context when opening up any area of neglected study. Only with a solid research background behind it can the construct of resilience gain legitimacy and a place in the sun.

On development

Adaptive and maladaptive behaviors are inextricably linked. To understand the latter we must be conversant with the former; the two are not dichotomous but truly overlapping. Achenbach (1990) stated this interrelatedness:

Many behavioral/emotional problems for which professional help is sought are not qualitatively different from those most individuals display to some degree at some time in their lives. Instead, many problems for which help is sought are quantitative variations on characteristics that may normally be evident at other developmental periods, in less intense degree, in fewer situations or in ways that do not impair developmental progress. (p. 4)

The keys to the differentiation lie in both the individual and the situational context. On the side of the former are those "protective" factors that have now become the focus of study (Masten, Best, & Garmezy, 1990); among these are: (1) stable care; (2) problem-solving abilities; (3) attractiveness to peers and adults; (4) manifest competence and perceived efficacy; (5) identification with competent role models; (6) planfulness and aspiration. These protective factors, some evident within the person, and others dependent upon the external world, are quite heterogeneous. It is evident that "protectiveness" extends to genetic-constitutional variables, personality dispositions, supportive milieus within the family and beyond, and the availability to some degree of societal supports. The role of development, both from an internal as well as an external perspective, is clearly evident in these listings (Masten & Garmezy, 1985). What is perhaps less evident has been the critical role now focused on the emergence of developmental psychopathology as an investigative area. Specifically, this field recognizes the need for the integration of both normative and nonnormative behaviors during transitional periods of development and the major influencing factors that are operative during those periods.

In a seminal article on "The Domain of Developmental Psychopathology," Sroufe and Rutter (1984) provided both a definition and the boundaries of this new field of developmental psychopathology:

The very name of the discipline provides a starting point for defining the scope and particular quality of this field. First, it is concerned with development and is therefore closely wedded to the whole of developmental psychology. The methods, theories, and perspectives of developmental psychopathology are important tools of inquiry. Second, the focus is on pathology, that is, developmental deviations. Developmental psychopathology may be defined as *the* study of the origins and course of individual patterns of behavioral maladaptation, whatever the age of onset, whatever the causes, whatever the transformations in behavioral manifestation, and however complex the course of the developmental pattern may be. (p. 18)

It is this greater outreach of developmental psychopathology as opposed to clinical psychology or clinical psychiatry that provides hope that the study of developmental processes will now finally be integrated into research on both adaptation *and* maladaptation.

This potential is evident in the chapters that follow. It is a significant beginning and, more than that, a hopeful augury of a major integration of disciplines that have hitherto stood apart to the detriment of our efforts to understand the interrelatedness of *risk, resilience,* and *development.*

References

Abel, E. L. (1989). *Behavioral teratogenesis and behavioral mutagenesis.* New York: Plenum.

Achenbach, T. M. (1990). Conceptualization of developmental psychopathology. In M. Lewis & S. M. Miller (Eds.), *Handbook of developmental psychopathology* (pp. 3–14). New York: Plenum.

Anthony, E. J., & Chiland, C. (Eds.). (1988). *The child in his family: Perilous development child raising and identity formation under stress.* New York: Wiley Interscience.

Anthony, E. J., & Cohler, B. J. (Eds.) (1987). *The invulnerable child.* New York: Guilford Press.

Barkley, R. A. (1990). *Attention deficit hyperactivity disorder.* New York: Guilford Press.

Birch, H. G., & Gussow, J. D. (1970). *Disadvantaged children: Health, nutrition and school failure.* New York: Harcourt, Brace, and World.

Bleuler, M. (1984). Foreword. In N. F. Watt, E. J. Anthony, L. C. Wynne, & J. E. Rolf (Eds.), *Children at risk for schizophrenia: A longitudinal perspective* (p. xvii). Cambridge: Cambridge University Press.

Brown, S. S. (Ed.). (1988). *Prenatal care.* Washington, DC: National Academy Press.

Caton, C. L. M. (1990). *Homeless in America.* New York: Oxford University Press.

Cohen, L. H. (Ed.). (1988). *Life events and psychological functioning.* Newbury Park, CA: Sage.

Comer, J. P. (1988). *Maggie's American dream*. New York: New American Library.

Davidson, O. G. (1990). *Broken heartland: The rise of America's rural ghettos*. New York: Free Press.

Dohrenwend, B. S., & Dohrenwend, B. P. (Eds.). (1984). *Stressful life events and their contexts*. New Brunswick, NJ: Rutgers University Press.

Farrington, D. P., Loeber, R., Elliott, D. S., Hawkins, J. D., Kandel, D. B., Klein, M. W., McCord, J., Rowe, D. C., & Tremblay, R. E. (1990). Advancing knowledge about the onset of delinquency and crime. In B. B. Lahey & A. E. Kazdin (Eds.), *Advances in clinical child psychology* (Vol. 13, pp. 283–342). New York: Plenum.

Garmezy, N., & Masten, A. (1994 pp. 191–208). Chronic adversities. In M. Rutter, L. Hersov, & E. Taylor (Eds.), *Child and adolescent psychiatry* (3rd ed.). Oxford: Blackwell Scientific Publications.

Garmezy, N., & Rutter, M. (Eds.) (1983). *Stress, coping, and development in children*. New York: McGraw-Hill.

Goertzel, V., & Goertzel, M. G. (1962). *Cradles of eminence*. Boston: Little, Brown.

Goldberger, L., & Breznitz, S. (Eds.). (1982). *Handbook of stress: Theoretical and clinical aspects*. New York: Free Press.

Goldberger, L., & Breznitz, S. (Eds.). (1993). *Handbook of stress: Theoretical and clinical aspects* (2nd ed.). New York: Free Press.

Hampton, R. L. (Ed.). (1987). *Violence in the black family: Correlates and consequences*. Lexington, MA: Lexington Books.

Hinshaw, S. P. (1987). On the distinction between attentional deficits/hyperactivity and conduct problems/aggression in child psychopathology. *Psychological Bulletin, 101*, 443–463.

Hunter, M. (1990). *Abused boys*. Lexington, MA: Lexington Books.

Illingworth, R. S., & Illingworth, C. M. (1966). *Lessons from childhood*. Edinburgh: E. and S. Livingstone.

Kopp, C. B. (1983a). Risk factors in development. In P. Mussen (Ed.), *Handbook of child psychology: Vol. 2. Infancy and developmental psychobiology* (pp. 1081–1188). New York: Wiley.

Kopp, C. B. (1983b). The developmentalist and the study of biological risk. *Child Development, 54*, 1086–1108.

Kopp, C. B. (1987). Developmental risk: Historical reflections. In J. D. Osofsky (Ed.), *Handbook of infant development* (2nd ed., pp. 881–912). New York: Wiley Interscience.

Lefkowitz, M. M., Eron, L. D., Walder, L. O., & Huesman, L. R. (1977). *Growing up to be violent*. Oxford: Pergamon Press.

Luthar, S. S., & Zigler, E. (1991). Vulnerability and competence: A review of research on resilience in childhood. *American Journal of Orthopsychiatry*, *61*, 6–22.

MacLeod, J. (1987). *Ain't no making it: Leveled aspirations in a low-income neighborhood*. Boulder, CO: Westview Press.

Masten, A., Best, K. M., & Garmezy, N. (1990). Resilience and development: Contributions from the study of children who overcome adversity. *Development and Psychopathology*, *2*, 425–444.

Masten, A. S., & Garmezy, N. (1985). Risk, vulnerability and protective factors in developmental psychopathology. In B. B. Lahey & A. E. Kazdin, *Advances in clinical child psychology* (Vol. 8, pp. 1–52). New York: Plenum.

Moskovitz, S. (1983). *Love despite hate*. New York: Schocken Books.

Patterson, G. R. (Ed.). (1990). *Depression and aggression in family interaction*. Hillsdale, NJ: Erlbaum.

Pittman, F. S., III (1987). *Turning points*. New York: W. W. Norton.

Riley, E. P., & Vorhees, C. V. (1986). *Handbook of behavioral teratology*. New York: Plenum.

Robins, L. M. (1966). *Deviant children grown up*. Baltimore: Williams and Wilkins.

Rutter, M., & Madge, N. (1976). *Cycles of disadvantage*. London: Heinemann Educational Books.

Sameroff, A. J., Seifer, R., Baldwin, A., & Baldwin, C. (1993). Stability of intelligence from preschool to adolescence: The influence of social and family risk factors. *Child Development*, *64*, 80–97.

Sameroff, A. J., Seifer, R., & Zax, M. (1982). Early development of children at risk for emotional disorder. *Monographs of the Society for Research in Child Development*, *47* (7, Serial No. 199).

Schulz, D. A. (1969). *Coming up black: Patterns of ghetto socialization*. Englewood Cliffs, NJ: Prentice-Hall.

Sroufe, L. A., & Rutter, M. (1984). The domain of developmental psychopathology. *Child Development*, *55*, 17–29.

Thoits, P. A. (1983). Dimensions of life events that influence psychological distress: An evaluation and synthesis of the literature. In H. B. Kaplan (Ed.), *Psychosocial stress: Trends in theory and research* (pp. 33–103). New York: Academic Press.

Wanlass, R. L., & Prinz, R. J. (1982). Methodological issues in conceptualizing and treating childhood social isolation. *Psychological Review*, *91*, 39–55.

Watt, N. F., Anthony, E. J., Wynne, L. C., & Rolf, J. E. (Eds.). (1984). *Children at risk for schizophrenia: A longitudinal perspective*. Cambridge: Cambridge University Press.

Weissman, M. M., Gammon, G. D., John, K., Merikangus, K. R., Warner, V., Prusoff, B. A., & Sholomskas, D. (1987). Children of depressed parents. *Archives of General Psychiatry, 44,* 847–853.

Werner, E. E., & Smith, R. S. (1982). *Vulnerable but invincible.* New York: McGraw-Hill.

Werner, E. E., & Smith, R. S. (1992) *Overcoming the odds.* Ithaca, NY: Cornell University Press.

Williams, T. M., & Kornblum, W. (1985). *Growing up poor.* Lexington, MA: Lexington Books.

Yarrow, M. R. (1990). Family environments of depressed and well parents and their children: Issues of research methods. In G. R. Patterson (Ed.), *Depression and aggression in family interaction* (pp. 169–184). Hillsdale, NJ: Erlbaum.

Yin, R. K. (1989). *Case study research: Design and methods.* Newbury Park, CA: Sage Publications.

2

Context and process in research on risk and resilience

Susan Gore and John Eckenrode

A decade ago, in setting an agenda for future research on stress, Rutter (1983a, pp. 33–34) called for three major lines of study. First, arguing that the concept of stress is too global to be useful, he characterized the need for better discrimination among types of stress processes and the mental health implications of each. Second, he saw need for continued study of individual differences in responses to stress, the person–environment interactions that make for vulnerability or resilience. And, finally, he called for research on the interplay between stress and development, with attention to the various sets of indirect linkages between important events and later functioning.

Several research trends have provided an important infrastructure for achieving these goals. First, the 1980s marked major changes in the approaches used to study stress, human development, and mental health, changes marked by the new fields of developmental psychopathology and life course studies. Research on stress in child populations has greatly increased during this period. However, an increased focus on the adolescent and early adult years has served as a "bridge"

Susan Gore is Professor of Sociology at the University of Massachusetts at Boston and John Eckenrode is Associate Professor of Human Development and Family Studies at Cornell University.

An earlier version of this chapter was presented at the Conference on Risk, Resiliency, and Development: Research and Interventions, May 28–31, 1992, Kiawah Island, South Carolina. We benefited greatly from the stimulation and support of our colleagues in the Consortium for Research Involving Stress Processes (CRISP). We wish to thank Anstis Benfield and Jolan Balog for manuscript preparation, and Robert Aseltine, Jr., and Urie Bronfenbrenner for constructive comments. This work is supported by the NIH grant No. MH42909.

between child- and adult-centered concepts, frameworks, and data. This new research activity has fostered needed cross-fertilization between the largely adult-centered epidemiologic research on stress and child-focused developmental studies.

Second, research in the 1980s has involved study of large community samples, in addition to treatment populations, which allowed researchers to examine a wide spectrum of stress and developmental processes in both normal and distressed populations. The more frequent use of representative community samples has been essential for studies of variation in stress and mental health processes. This change has also been important for identifying processes conducive to resilience. At the same time, it has raised concerns about the adequacy of measurement tools, and subgroup differences in the nature and effects of stressful experiences. For example, studies of heterogeneous populations have underscored the chronicity of stressful experiences and disorder in some subgroups, leading us to reexamine our prevailing models of life crisis and acute stress and develop new frameworks for dealing with issues of chronicity.

Finally, building upon a foundation of earlier studies that examined the predictive relationship between childhood experiences and adult functioning, there has been an increased emphasis on the processes and mechanisms that may explain this linkage.

In this chapter we consider some developments in research on stress and mental health that reflect the paradigmatic changes just described. Specifically, we consider two broad issues. A first concerns the features of a more differentiated view of the three major components of the stress process: stressors, stress-mediating and -moderating mechanisms, and adaptive outcomes. In particular, considerable progress has been made toward identifying the diverse character of stressful experiences, including normative or scheduled transitions, nonnormative acute life events, chronic or ongoing life problems, and daily microstressors. There have been significant advances in theory as well, such as in conceptions of how diverse stressors combine to constitute significant mental health risk.

The second broad issue we address pertains to the dynamic processes that link stressors, mediating or moderating factors, and adaptive outcomes. There is now more attention in the literature to long- and short-term sequences of person–environment transactions that help explain the relationship between stressful experiences and health outcomes, and which may also reveal continuities and discontinuities in mental health over the life course. Research on risk and resilience has been guided in recent years by a concern with *stress-moderating* processes, a dynamic through which harmful effects of stress are offset by various coping resources. Although this remains a powerful investigatory model, alternative views of process have recently been advanced, notably the idea of *stress mediation* whereby stressors may also function to erode environmental and personal coping resources.

We organize our discussion of these issues by considering each of the three major constructs that have guided our studies – risk, protective factors, and mental health or social functioning. In each case, we review theoretical developments that have led to increasing complexity in conceptualization, and the analytic strategies this complexity has necessitated. Consistent with the conference theme of *interrelatedness*, we detail the different ways of studying the covariation among the diverse assessments of related concepts, and how these more complex and holistic representations of key concepts lead to better understanding of the contexts and processes of risk and resilience. Because our own research has spanned adult and child populations, we provide examples and insights from a broadly defined field of stress studies, which holds promise for investigations of all age groups.

Models of stress processes: Problems of context, transaction, and development

Early models of risk processes

A point of departure for examining developments in the conceptualization of stress and its linkage to mental health is briefly to consider the three major ways in which the idea of risk has been considered to date. Early investigations of child mental health and development relied upon broad indicators of family socioeconomic and mental health disadvantage for assessing risk status. This is exemplified in Werner's (Werner & Smith, 1982) classic life course study of biological and psychosocial risks among Hawaiian youth. Children identified as high risk were those who were born into poverty, or reared by parents with little education, or who were alcoholic or mentally ill. More recently, there has been a focus on the single-parent environment (Kellam, Brown, Rubin, & Ensminger, 1983), also a global indicator of environmental disadvantage.

Although the relationship between environmental risk and child disorder is strengthened when aggregate risk indicators are used, there has been a general dissatisfaction with reliance on these global measures for several reasons. Foremost is an issue increasingly noted by researchers (Masten, Best, & Garmezy, 1990; Richters & Weintraub, 1990) that these indicators pose problems for the study of resilience because the exact nature and extent of life stressors remain unknown. For example, in characterizing research on parental psychiatric disorder and child's mental health, Richters and Weintraub (1990) have argued that the concepts of "protective factors" and "resilience" have often been prematurely invoked in the relative absence of information regarding the specific stressors that are present in high-risk environments.

There are two reasons for this concern. First, in many such studies it is unclear whether variables, such as family cohesion, should be construed as resilience factors, that is, as protecting the child from the effects of the parental psychiatric risks, or whether it is more appropriate to view the absence of the resilience factor (e.g., family disorganization) as an additional risk for disorder. An additional problem with a reliance on markers of complex social structural processes is that this level of analysis generally fails to address the diverse nature of individual experiences that exist within a general climate of adversity. Within any group of persons considered at risk, there will be variability in their exposure to stressors that are the more proximal causes of disorder. For example, children of schizophrenic parents are not all exposed to abusive or neglectful parenting to the same degree (Walker, Downey, & Bergman, 1989).

A final problem with remaining at this structural level of analysis is that because the indicators of disadvantage are so highly correlated, there is the danger of falsely attributing the effects of low socioeconomic conditions to family structure or parental mental health, thus serving to "blame the victim," namely mothers and families. In addition, although risk factors such as poverty and lack of education tend to go together, it would be a mistake to assume that they influence important outcomes, such as childrens' academic success, in the same ways. Recognition of the fact that problems tend to cluster should go hand in hand with an appreciation of the differences between these risk factors. In this respect, cross-societal studies on the risk–mental health relationship can be useful.

A second approach to risk research is characteristic of epidemiologic studies of acute life events and mental health in adult populations. Life events have also been assessed in child and adolescent populations, and this method continues to be widely employed as a vehicle for assessing the more proximal social role and situational stressors that are associated with physical and mental health status. Early studies of life events explored two major models of stress process. The first sought to determine whether an accumulation of life events might explain the effects of social structural and family background variables on mental health. In this case, effects of the more global social structural variables might be understood in terms of the undesirable life changes these conditions set in motion. A second model stipulated that the association between measures of disadvantage and individual mental health might be accounted for by the greater vulnerability of disadvantaged persons to undesirable life events. Indeed, there is evidence from both adult and child studies that persons occupying lower socioeconomic status are more reactive to environmental stressors, although these status differentials are not fully explained (Kessler & Essex, 1982; Turner & Noh, 1983).

Findings of this nature indicate an important role for the study of life events in relation to more global measures of disadvantage. In addition, the literature on gender and mental health suggests that differential exposure and reactivity to environmental stressors may also be shaped by socialization processes that occurred well in the past. For example, Nolen-Hoeksema (1990) has argued that the higher rates of depression among women may be due to women's tendency to dwell on depressive experiences, a ruminative copying style acquired through gender role socialization in the childhood and adolescent years. In either case, whether through current stressors or vulnerable coping styles shaped in childhood, there appear to be significant differences in exposure and responses to stress across sociodemographic categories such as gender and class. In this regard, the research by Kessler and McLeod (1984) has been particularly insightful in accounting for the higher levels of depressive symptomatology among adult women. Their studies indicate that women become more distressed than men only when they experience stressors affecting social network members outside the immediate family. Thus, to the extent that women's response style enhances vulnerability to depression, this disadvantage appears to operate in a limited number of situations. These findings also call attention to responsibilities outside the immediate family as posing a distinctive arena of vulnerability for women, and contribute to an increasing literature on problematic features of caregiving relationships, again, a gender-related theme.

Another research strategy that has played a major role in studies of child and adolescent mental health and development has focused on critical singular events such as the transition to puberty or specific family stressors, including parental divorce or family illness. Intensive study of individuals experiencing a single, significant event would seem key to redressing two issues raised by the first two paradigms noted earlier, namely the issue of "coping with what," and the need for microsocial detail on processes leading to disorder versus resilience.

In chronicling the development of divorce research over the past decade, however, Wertlieb (1991, p. 37) has argued that the study of singular events offers only the illusion of simplicity due to the complex nature of the divorce experience. He suggests, "Rather than using the traditional static notion of 'divorce' as an 'event' in the life course of an individual or family, consider divorce as a marker for a range of constellations or patterns that include numerous 'events' or linked contingencies." Thus, while research on singular stressors calls attention to special populations and the risks they experience by virtue of major normative and nonnormative life stresses and transitions, these stressors occur in the context of other life conditions often overlooked in single stressor studies, and the singular stressors themselves are in fact markers for the diverse experiences and transitions that make up an event such as divorce.

The need to consider stressors as complex experiences is also evident in policy-centered research on problems such as teenage pregnancy. The work of Furstenberg, Brooks-Gunn, and Morgan (1987), for example, has established that there is considerable variability in the life course of teenage parents. However, there is also variability in the nature and meaning of the event itself – unwed pregnancy. Descriptive data are needed to portray the diverse situations and their personal meanings that are subsumed under the general category of premature parenthood. There are, for example, important distinctions between those for whom pregnancy is the accidental consequences of teenage dating, those who expected but failed to have a continuing stable relationship, and those who achieve this relationship but do not marry.

In sum, the three traditional approaches to stress research – the social structural or family background, cumulative stressful events, and singular stressors – share a set of limitations involving conceptualizations of risk. None has provided a straightforward solution to the problem of a highly differentiated arena of stressful experiences and to the attendant problem of conceptualizing the interrelationships among variables that are associated with problems of adjustment. Assessments of risk on the one hand must be sufficiently exhaustive to make meaningful the idea of resilience, while on the other they must be studied at a level of aggregation that makes it possible to identify social psychological processes that might account both for stress effects and for subgroup variation in these pathways. In the following section we examine several conceptual models that incorporate this more complex understanding of stress, while retaining an emphasis on the psychological significance of these experiences.

Toward contextual models of stress

There seems to be considerable consensus about the benefits to understanding stressors or risks as representing complex situations. Investigators typically translate this concern into multivariate contextual models in which context becomes defined by the interplay of two or more variables. Beyond this, there have been vastly different usages of the term context. Context has been most frequently represented as a situational variable that alters the psychological significance and social demands of particular life events. For instance, in studies of child development, ongoing aspects of family functioning are seen to shape alternative responses of children to stressors such as parental divorce, or developmental transitions such as puberty.

There are subtle distinctions in these models that often hinge on

the conceptualization of the risk factor versus the contextual moderator variable. Most research on the difficulties of early adolescence
takes pubertal change or another developmental transition as the
stressor or risk, and considers other variables as the contextual modifi-
ers. However, in Elder's (1974) comparison of two age cohorts experiencing the hardships of the Great Depression, developmental status
(age) was taken as the contextual variable, shaping the impact of
family hardship. Thus, it is possible to examine the effects of nonnormative stressors (e.g., parental divorce) in developmental context
(e.g., developmental status), or examine adaptation to developmental
events (e.g., pubertal or school transition) in social context (see Gore
& Colten, 1991a).

Psychological variables that are seen to alter the meaning of environmental events may also be used as the contextual factors. For example,
in this tradition, Thoits (1991) has focused on the role of self-identity
in determining the magnitude of threat associated with acute life
stresses. Finally, background variables including gender, socioeconomic status, and race or ethnicity have been studied as contexts that
alter the relationship between stressors and measures of functioning.
For example, Simmons and associates (Simmons, Burgeson, Carlton-
Ford, & Blyth, 1987) found different relationships between transition
events and mental health in subsamples of black and white female
adolescents. Treating these sociodemographic categories as contexts
is an important alternative to controlling away this significant subgroup variation. Nettles and Pleck extend this line of thinking in their
chapter on black adolescents. Because this is a highly variable group
of youths, especially along economic and urban–rural dimensions,
they argue that research on black adolescents must examine differences among black youths in these varying contexts.

It is important to note that contextual assessments of stress have as
their goal an understanding of stress magnitude by taking into account
the personal circumstances or contexts in which stressful events or
transitions occur. This approach, as Wheaton (1990) has noted, differs from the tradition of coping and stress-buffering studies described later in this chapter, which focus on individual *responses* to
stress, with the impact of stressors being influenced by the mobilization of personal and social resources. Both approaches are contextual
and interactive in nature, but differ importantly in that a concern with

magnitude of the stressor logically precedes a consideration of resilience and stress-buffering.

There are many important theoretical underpinnings to contextual studies of stress, but the contributions of Bronfenbrenner (1979) on the ecology of human development, Pearlin and associates (Pearlin, Lieberman, Menaghan, & Mullan, 1981) on acute stressors and chronic life strains, and Brown and Harris (1989) on the cognitive meanings inherent in life events have been particularly influential in their respective fields. The major themes and some examples of these perspectives are considered here.

The work of Brown and Harris (1978, 1989) on chronic life conditions and the onset of depression among working-class women has offered an important alternative conceptualization and approach to research on stressful life events to that derived from the Holmes and Rahe (1967) tradition of life events research described earlier. Differences between Brown and Harris's conceptual framework and the life events paradigm hinge on the mechanisms through which life events become provoking agents. In contrast with the idea that overwhelming change or disruption is the vehicle through which events affect health, Brown and associates see personal meaning as the critical mechanism. Their findings in general indicate that, although the occurrence of a single significant provoking event significantly predicts episodes of depression, predictive power increases threefold when a life event is "matched" with a prior long-term life difficulty, a chronic stressor. For the women in this sample, these chronic stressors typically involved problems with children, marriage, employment, money, and housework. Thus, while preserving the importance of acute life stressors in their etiologic model, the psychological meaning of these events is seen to take on significance in the context of long-term life difficulties that establish a context for understanding the meaning of life events.

Brown and Harris (1989) give as an example a hardworking single mother who finds out her daughter is pregnant. The event – finding out about the pregnancy – triggers the onset of depression. Within the Holmes and Rahe (1967) tradition of life events research, this association would be interpreted as resulting from the cumulative nature of family changes, conflicts, and resource deficits brought about by the pregnancy event. Brown argues differently, that the dynamic driving the onset of the depressive episode is not the impact of cumulative change but the cognitive meaning of the event, which in this case is the mother's interpretation of the pregnancy as reflecting her underlying failure in raising her daughter. On the basis of these data, replicated across studies, Brown maintains that the specific cognitive-emotional quality of events defines their meaning and that these meanings are linked to disorder.

Social psychological studies similarly point to the significance of self-evaluative processes in defining the impact of environmental events and normative life transitions. Data from Brooks-Gunn's well-known studies of adolescent ballerinas (Brooks-Gunn & Warren, 1985) indicate that early timing of puberty has a negative impact only on those girls for whom the loss of thinness brings to an end the concept of self as dancer. Hammen and associates (Hammen, Ellicott, Gitlin, & Jamison, 1989; Hammen, Marks, Mayol, & deMayo, 1985) have also reported findings with college students and unipolar depressives that indicate that stressful events are more likely to be associated with symptoms of depression when they fall within domains that are personally meaningful to the subjects. For instance, their research shows that events involving interpersonal relationships were more distressing to persons who were particularly concerned with securing the approval of others.

A contextual perspective on stress has most often generated the prediction that acute stressors occurring in the context of ongoing role strains lead to exacerbated stress responses. Such findings have been documented with both children and adults. For example, Quinton and Rutter (1976) found that hospital admissions were strongly associated with emotional problems in children when they were paired with high levels of chronic family stress. However, chronic stressors may not always potentiate the effects of acute stressors. An alternative position is offered by Wheaton (1990), who calls for a consideration of those limiting cases in which acute stressors occurring in the context of chronic role difficulties produce improvements in mental health because these events offer the opportunity to alleviate or escape from the chronically disturbing situation. This perspective helps account for situations in which an event such as divorce can be a relief if the marriage is seen as bad, and a great loss only if the marriage is seen as good. To test this idea, Wheaton focused on the presence of continuing stress coupled with transition events (e.g., divorce, job loss) in a range of significant stress contexts, including marriage, relationships when unmarried, work, and parenthood. Findings confirmed the hypothesis of stress relief for most subgroups experiencing acute stressors in the context of prior problems.

Stress, development and mental health

The type of beneficial stress process noted previously suggests that research must more adequately address the processes, both positive and negative, through which context influences responses to specific stressors or developmental challenges. For example, an important theme in adolescent studies is how features of the family context shape the adolescent's social development, responses to stressors, and movement toward adulthood. Evidence indicates that some types of family stress are actually beneficial, promoting the adolescent's independence and sense of responsibility. Weiss (1979) has written how the teenage child in the single-parent family appears to "grow up faster," developing a "new salutary motivation" that comes from helping the single parent. Similarly, the research by Elder (1974) on developmental trajectories set in motion by family responses to the Great Depression indicated that for the somewhat older boys (the Oakland sample) family hardship propelled them into an earner role and early social independence, a first step in a generally successful adult mental health trajectory.

These examples highlight how certain hardships imposed on the family challenge all family members and spur the growth of adolescents on the verge of adulthood. We might assume that this salutary effect of stress reflects an "accentuation process" (Elder & Caspi, 1988) whereby the stressor emphasizes the healthy tendencies already characterizing these environments. In contrast, many stressors within the family reflect problems in these relationships, setting the stage for a very different set of adaptive processes. In a sample of adolescents drawn from three community high schools, Aseltine, Gore, and Colten (in press) found evidence that the presence of chronic family stress appears to accelerate a reorientation away from family toward friendships. Specifically, the findings were as follows: Adolescents in chronically stressed families showed a long-term trend of heightened stress and recurrent depressed mood with little social support. Although they reported higher levels of peer-related stress as well, the adolescents appeared to be orienting themselves more to the peer than family arena, as indicated by a greater reactivity both to peer stresses and supports than any of the family variables. Further analyses indicated that this shift away from the family was protective. Had those adolescents in high-stress households continued to respond to experiences in the family domain in the same way as the other adolescents, they would have become even more depressed. This pattern of findings can be interpreted to reflect a type of resilience in which the long-term effects of chronic family stress and a history of depressed mood are not "turned around" by psychologically withdrawing from a bad family environment; rather, turning to peers functions to mitigate the depressive consequences of family stress that would otherwise have been severer.

While these findings differ from those reported earlier on the positive developmental impact of family adversity, they are all consistent with the position taken by Masten, Best, and Garmezy (1990) that the older adolescent brings to stressful situations increasing control and knowledge, and the ability to seek protective relationships more actively when others fail. Although Masten and associates are here referring to the concept of protective factors, it is also the case that the maturing adolescent is more involved in shaping interests, roles, and responsibilities than is the younger child. Here we see the importance of both person and environment, with the older adolescent bringing to bear on the environment new capabilities and different goal orientations. At the same time, there are more options for the maturing adolescent. Older adolescents and young adults have an expanding social world and can find new, more gratifying roles and identities, leaving behind others (Clausen, 1991). In contrast, the well-documented stressors of childhood and early adolescence have an involuntary character and entail an element of "role captivity" (Pearlin, 1983). The early adolescent must cope with these transitions (e.g., puberty, school, and social changes) with little opportunity or capability for avoidance, denial, or autonomous withdrawal from these or other ongoing stressors, particularly those that emanate from the family.

This consideration of various family contexts provides an important set of issues for further study. Simmons and associates (Simmons et al., 1987) offer another contextual approach that casts the net wider to examine how multiple transitions and stresses across several key life domains combine to jeopardize adolescent mental health. Consistent with Coleman's "focal theory" of change (Coleman, 1974), they argue that the developing adolescent requires some "arenas of comfort" – life domains characterized by easy, habitual functioning – in order to cope successfully with other life changes. The research also draws upon Bronfenbrenner's ecological framework (1979) in its attention to the pattern and magnitude of changes across these spheres rather than to isolated events.

To test this idea, Simmons and associates identified five significant stresses or transitions occurring in key life domains (school change, pubertal change, early start of dating, neighborhood change, and family disruption). Focusing on grade point average (GPA), extracurricular participation, and self-esteem as indicators of functioning, findings indicated significant effects of cumulative change on these variables in a diverse sample of early adolescents. Importantly, for girls, the effects of multiple stressors combined multiplicatively for both GPA and self-esteem, with each additional stressor resulting in a larger deficit in functioning than would be the case if these stressors combined in a simple additive fashion. These data provided the strongest support for the "arenas of comfort" notion. For boys, in contrast, having stressors in multiple arenas was associated with increased dysfunction, but in an additive fashion.

Mediational models of stress

The research considered in the previous sections considers the multidimensional nature of stressors and offers means for understanding interrelationships among normative and nonnormative transitions and events in various social contexts. As stated in our introductory remarks, these approaches contrast with early efforts in stress and developmental research to isolate critical risk factors among a set of risk factors, many correlated with each other. Although the isolation of critical causal variables remains a goal in research on risk and resilience, contextual models considered here suggest there may be more explanatory power in considering the effects of these factors in conjunction with each other, not in isolation.

Another strategy for understanding relationships among stressors and protective factors is guided by the concept of stress mediation. The terms *stress moderation* and *stress mediation* are often used interchangeably in research on risk and resilience, reflecting the general idea that the magnitude of the stressor–mental health relationship may be attenuated if protective processes "buffer" stress effects. In fact, the terms *moderating* and *mediating* reflect very different approaches to modeling relationships among variables. In the section that follows, we will discuss the concepts of stress moderation and resilience, but here the idea of mediating process is introduced to identify a key strategy for understanding what Baron and Kenny (1986) call "the generative mechanism through which the focal independent variable is able to influence the dependent variable of interest."

The idea of a "generative mechanism" is attractive to developmentalists and stress researchers alike because it captures the idea of process, the ultimate goal of our studies, and is particularly relevant to life course themes in mental health research. For example, the research of Elder, Nguyen, and Caspi (1985), linking the family's economic hardship to child functioning, has identified parental conflict and parental socialization behavior as critical intervening or mediating processes. This body of research is compelling not only due to its longitudinal design and focus on a significant historical period, but also because it demonstrates how to cross levels of analysis in order to identify linkages among macrosocial conditions and events, family economy, marital quality and parental socialization behavior, and child development and health. In this way, Elder's use of a mediational framework exemplifies one important way to transcend more static approaches to understanding multiple risk factors in mental health research.

In studies of stress, an important treatment of this issue is found in the work of Pearlin and associates (Pearlin, 1989; Pearlin et al., 1981). Focusing on the pivotal nature of social roles in generating both chronic role strain and acute life stressors, they argue for the empirical study of the complex temporal interrelationships among social positions, chronic role strains, and acute life events. For example, stressful life events such as job loss might serve to affect adversely the ongoing social and economic conditions of life, a mechanism they observed in their study of job loss (Pearlin et al., 1981). Alternatively, the primary and secondary stressors might be reversed. For example, chronic stressors such as long-term marital or interpersonal conflict can precipitate events and transitions, a process well documented in research on divorce. In either case, stressors rarely occur singly and, instead, may be seen as forming chains of primary and secondary stressors, with new stressors "formed by problems that originated in different institutionalized roles" (Pearlin, 1989, p. 247). Thus, as in the other models we have considered, a consideration of temporal dimensions in the stress process provides further evidence of our progress in moving away from static, correlational approaches to stress and disorder (see also Monroe & Simons, 1991).

A consideration of stress-mediating processes also offers a framework for a fuller appreciation of the interrelationships among stressors and protective factors, including social supports. For some time now, researchers have observed that persons scoring high on measures of stress exposure tend to score low on measures of the quality and availability of supportive relationships. This was initially interpreted as a problem of conceptualization and measurement overlap. For example, many acute stressors assessed in life events inventories may be the opposite of a supportive resource, such as increased fights with spouse (an acute event) reflecting an absence of spouse support. This problem has suggested the need for greater methodological care, but also suggests substantive considerations in the stressor–support nexus, namely the extent to which stressors bring about disorder precisely because they alter the availability and efficacy of coping-related resources.

This idea is perhaps best illustrated in the adolescent literature in the work of Bush and Simmons (1987) on gender differences in the psychological impact of adolescent transitions. Research on the nature and significance of development during adolescence has tended to show girls as experiencing more declines than boys in self-esteem, positive emotional affect, extracurricular participation, and grade point average. Research that has collected data from adolescents at the daily level (Csikszentmihalyi & Larson, 1984; Larson & Asmussen, 1991) has also established that girls' experience of negative emotion is greater than boys, and is tied to experiences of hurt and concern about relationships. Based on a considerable body of theory regarding the salience of relationships for girls' developing identity and sense of well-being, Bush and Simmons (1987, p. 191) argue that for early adolescent girls "stressors and coping mechanisms may arise from connections with others." For example, the more disruptive nature of the transition to junior high for girls may be due to their greater dependence on the more personal social ties characteristic of the elementary school environment. While the social nature of developmental stressors is well understood, less widely recognized is the relevance of developmental change in general, and specific transitions such as school and dating, to girls' ability to develop an effective coping repertoire. Here, girls' orientation to the expectations of others becomes highly problematic because the same social changes that expose them to new challenges also make for instabilities or deficits in coping-related resources such as self-esteem, internal sense of mastery and locus of control, and instrumental or task orientation. Thus, the study of gender differences in the impact of developmental transitions offers an important opportunity for understanding the linkages between stressors and coping resources, and a window for investigating the generally held belief that interpersonal stressors and support systems are more important for girls.

Protective factors and resilience

Current models of stress and resilience routinely include protective factors that are hypothesized to reduce the likelihood of dysfunction and disorder in the presence of vulnerabilities and stressful life experiences. These protective factors are generally classified into two groups: (1) personal factors, some with a strong biological component, like physical health status and temperament; others closely linked to experiences with the social environment, such as self-esteem and mastery beliefs; and (2) environmental resources, such as family income or ties to a community of supportive social relationships. Such a classification may help to distinguish what a person brings to an encounter with the environment from the objective features of that environment. On the other hand, this dichotomy tends to obscure important forms of interrelatedness that occur between the person and the environment. As we seek to understand the roots of resilience and the role of protective factors in reducing risk, defining such interconnections becomes an important research agenda. A more refined specification of the basic stress-buffering model will require that the interconnections between protective factors become explicitly recognized and tested. Following a brief discussion of stress-buffering models, we will consider three issues. First, the degree of overlap between identified protective factors needs to be considered. Too often, individual psychological or social resources, such as self-esteem and social support, have been investigated as separate phenomena when examining stress buffering. Second, our models must allow for the possibility that protective factors may combine in nonadditive ways in producing protective effects. For example, the efficacy of social support as a stress buffer may vary as a function of the level of another potential buffer, such as self-esteem. Protective factors not only help account for individual differences in reactivity to environmental and biological risks, but there are individual differences as well in the degree of protection afforded by these factors. Third, a consideration of temporal issues highlights another way in which protective factors may be related to one another. The presence of certain protective factors determines the emergence of other protective mechanisms at some later point in time. The time span in question may be quite short, as in the case of short-term coping responses to acute stressors, or may encompass the entire life-span.

Models of stress buffering

The term *stress buffering* is used here to represent a more general class of issues related to individual differences in reactivity to a variety of psychosocial risks throughout the life course. Under this rubric we include other topics that incorporate similar notions, such as *resiliency*. Whereas investigations of resiliency are generally associated with the study of individual differences in the long-term adjustment of children at risk due to biological vulnerabilities or psychosocial adversity (e.g., Werner & Smith, 1982), research studies concerned with stress buffering have generally emerged from the adult literature on stress and coping. Both of these concepts are, in turn, specific instances of the more general topic of person–environment interactions (Rutter, 1983b, 1990).

What constitutes evidence for stress buffering? Analytically, investigators have represented stress-buffering effects in a number of ways.

The predominant approach is to test for a statistical interaction between a stressor and a protective factor. The functional form of such an interaction can vary, but the "classic" pattern is one where the risk factor or stressor has little or no effect on the outcome in the presence of high levels of the buffering factor (the regression line is flat or increases only slightly as one moves from low to high stress), but has a substantial relationship with dysfunctional outcomes when the buffer is absent. The image is one of having the buffer suppress the impact of the stressor or risk factor. In the stress and coping literature such models have been tested primarily under the following conditions: (1) the stressor is an acute event, such as illness, death, divorce, or job loss; (2) stressors are examined one at a time; (3) a single protective resource is examined; (4) the evidence for stress buffering is in the form of a two-way interaction between the stressor and the buffer.

A variant of this approach is to select a "high-risk" or "vulnerable" population (e.g., low birth weight babies; children with a schizophrenic parent; low-income, urban children) and determine variations in reactivity to environmental stressors occurring at some time in the future. This approach is characteristic of certain longitudinal studies involving children (e.g., Egeland, Breitenbucher, & Rosenberg, 1980; Garmezy, Masten, & Tellegen, 1984; Rutter & Quinton, 1984; Werner & Smith, 1982). In some of these studies, evidence for the presence of a protective factor is derived from two-group comparisons between high-risk children who are displaying elevated levels of problems and those showing low levels (i.e., resilient children). The factors found to discriminate these two groups significantly are said to be protective factors. There is an inherent ambiguity in such an approach, however, with regard to the role of protective factors. First, it doesn't tell us whether the proposed protective factors operate differently under conditions of high and low risk. Second, this approach also assumes that the two high-risk groups (with high vs. low problems) have an equivalent level of exposure to stressors, an issue we discussed earlier in reference to aggregate risk indicators. These problems may be partly resolved with the addition of a low-risk group to the study, the explicit examination of the child's response to potentially stressful experiences, and the use of longitudinal designs.

Consider an important longitudinal study of a high-risk sample of mothers and their children by Egeland and associates. In one set of analyses (Egeland & Kreutzer, 1991) children's academic performance in first and third grades was examined as a function of maternal stressful experiences at those two times as well as a protective factor termed "history of competence," which was a composite of assessments made earlier in childhood of attachment to the mother, problem-solving ability, and reactions to frustration. High-stress, high-competence children were found to do significantly better in school than high-stress, low-competence children. We cannot necessarily conclude from the analysis, however, that high levels of competency resulted in less reactivity to stress. As with other studies of resilience, attention was focused here on comparing high-risk children who do well versus those who display problems of adjustment. By not simultaneously considering a low-risk group, however, there is the potential of mistakenly assigning a risk-reducing role to the factors found to distinguish the well-functioning and poorly functioning high-risk groups. This is because competency may also improve the school performance of children under low levels of stress. A worthy goal of such research may, of course, be to identify factors that promote healthy functioning regardless of risk status, but in order to argue for the interactive, stress-buffering function of various personal and social resources, the analysis must be able to demonstrate that the resource reduces the impact of the stressor, but is less influential under low-stress conditions.

This is but one instance of the general problem of linking a hypothesized protective factor to the risk factor or stressor. This issue, however, may not always be best addressed by examining the joint effect of stressors and factors thought to buffer stress (e.g., through the estimation of interaction terms in multiple regression models). There are two additional issues that must be considered as well. First, models that represent the relationship between a stressor and a protective factor in purely additive terms may, in certain instances, constitute evidence for stress buffering. An example would be a stressful event resulting in increased supportive interactions, which, in turn, lower the likelihood of dysfunctional outcomes. In such situations we may or may not find that the resource in question has a different effect across levels of the stressor. The important point is that, given the mobilization of the resource (in this case, increased social interaction), the impact of stress is reduced. Such models have been given various names in the literature, with Wheaton (1985) calling them "stress-suppressing" models and Lin (1986), "stress-counteracting."

Second, finding evidence for a statistical interaction does not in itself tell us anything about the *process* that underlies this effect. This point has been clearly articulated by Rutter (1983b, 1990) in reference to the literature on childhood stress, but has also been addressed by stress and coping researchers focusing on adult populations (e.g., Kessler, 1983). Rutter has urged that finding a statistical interaction between a stressor and a protective factor should represent the beginning point, rather than the end point, of an attempt to understand why some persons are less vulnerable to the impact of stressors than others. The next set of questions has to do with explaining the processes responsible for these individual differences.

In the adult stress and coping literature, researchers have similarly been admonished for reifying the interaction term as an object of scientific merit, while failing to pursue the underlying processes. This has been most clearly seen in the case of the stress-buffering role of social support. Many studies have found a statistical interaction between stress and social support measures when predicting mental and physical health outcomes (cf. S. Cohen & Syme, 1985). However, relatively few have explicitly focused on the underlying social interactional processes that account for the interaction. In this instance the frequent use of measures of social support that represent an evaluation of how much the person feels supported or cared for, as opposed to measures of actual social transactions, only serves to widen the gap between finding a statistical interaction and understanding the buffering process (Coyne & Downey, 1991; Gottlieb, 1985).

It is clear, therefore, that advances to our understanding of the role of protective factors in buffering stress and reducing the risk of dysfunction are not restricted to cases where stress and a particular coping resource combine to form a statistical interaction. Other functional relationships are possible, and more complex models involving more than one protective factor must now be considered.

Relationships between two or more protective factors

Just as stressors may co-occur within a particular population or within a particular time period, protective factors are also likely to occur together to some degree. This positive correlation is most often "controlled for" through the use of multivariate analyses, and therefore not explicitly recognized and reported. This situation has been exacerbated by the common practice of examining the independent contributions of factors such as self-esteem and social support, rather than looking at their interrelationships.

Such a variable-centered approach does not provide a comprehensive view of the person under study. Topics that arise from a more holistic person-centered approach, such as the issue of the functional equivalence of certain coping resources (and hence their substitutability), are not adequately addressed when variables are considered singly. At other times, the variable-centered approach results in the construction of multivariate models where several stress or protective factors are entered together into an analysis in order to see which one will have the strongest relationship to the outcome variable. The image here is one of a horse race – independent forces racing toward the finish line. An example is seen in studies that have claimed to show that daily "hassles" have a stronger relationship to health outcomes than traditional measures of life events, and hence constitute a more important source of stress in the lives of both children and adults (i.e., win the horse race in the statistical analysis). What such interpretations overlook is the possibility that hassles may represent a mediating mechanism linking life events to outcomes, a process we described earlier when discussing primary and secondary stressors and that recent studies with adolescents and adults have confirmed (Compas, Howell, Phares, Williams, & Giunta, 1989; Eckenrode, 1984).

Similar misinterpretations are likely when two or more hypothesized protective factors are simply entered as a group into a multivariate analysis without a consideration of the relationships that may occur between them. For example, one might find that internal locus of control, when examined in isolation, is significantly related to better functioning, but when a measure of coping is added to the regression equation, the locus-of-control effect is reduced to nonsignificance. It would be a mistake to conclude from such an analysis that coping was more important than locus of control in predicting the outcome, since the true state of affairs may be that an internal locus-of-control orientation causes the adoption of more effective coping strategies, which in turn leads to better functioning. Longitudinal data are required to examine the direct and indirect effects of several variables, but even with cross-sectional data, the relationship between protective factors should routinely be considered. Likewise, alternative analytic methods, such as cluster analysis, may be useful in detecting patterns of relationships between correlated protective factors. Such an approach has been employed by Magnusson and Bergman (1990) with regard to patterns of conduct problems among adolescent boys.

To further illustrate this issue, consider the linkage between two protective factors that are routinely cited as important sources of stress buffering and resilience, namely self-esteem and social support. In the adult literature on stress and coping, social support and self-esteem, while often considered in the same study as resources for buffering stress, typically are examined separately. Both social support and a positive sense of self have been found to buffer stressful experiences in children, adolescents, and adults. However, there is an intricate relationship between intimate social ties and self-esteem that typically results in moderate correlations between these two variables. Developmentally, there is much evidence that the quality of a child's relationship with significant others, especially parents, is linked to the development of a positive sense of self (e.g., Cassidy, 1988). This represents one fundamental process by which two coping resources come to co-occur: positive social ties, particularly in the form of intimate attachments, lead to the development of a positive sense of self. Over time, this process is certainly reciprocal, with persons possessing relatively higher levels of self-esteem being more capable of maintaining existing relationships, forming new relationships, and eliciting the positive responses (social support) of others.

The second major process leading to co-occurrence between two protective factors is in the form of shared influences with some other factor or factors. For example, a child's exposure to poverty or maltreatment may result both in long-term deficits in supportive social ties and in a lowered sense of self-esteem. In both cases, co-occurrence results in these coping resources being unequally distributed throughout the population. There is a strong likelihood that persons who possess a positive self-concept are also those who have access to supportive social relationships. Likewise, individuals who show a deficit in one resource are likely to show deficits in others.

Examining large samples will undoubtedly reveal some unusual individuals who are, for example, socially isolated or otherwise lack access to supportive social ties, but who have managed to maintain a high level of self-esteem. These persons, however, must be the exception rather than the rule and become a potentially important focus for study.

What implications does the simple fact of co-occurrence between protective factors have for our understanding of stress and coping processes? We believe there are at least four.

First, it must be recognized that the clustering of protective factors within a population (versus the random distribution of these resources) results in groups of individuals at the ends of the distribution who have either many psychosocial resources or virtually no resources. The size of the correlation between the resources in question determines the size of these two groups relative to a middle group having high levels of one resource but not another. Examining resources one at a time will not uncover those individuals who have multiple strengths rather than multiple deficits in coping resources, but will focus our attention on the average effect of a given resource in buffering stress.

Second, assessing the overall pattern of resources alerts us to the possibility of one resource substituting for another in coping with stress. This is a topic about which we know very little. Can deficits in social support be made up for with high levels of self-esteem? Will stress buffering occur as long as there is at least one coping resource available, regardless of which one? It is possible that resources cannot be freely substituted for one another, since the demands of various stressors will evoke needs that may best be met through a particular resource or response. In the social support literature, for example, there has been the suggestion that optimal stress buffering occurs when the type of social support matches the type of stressor involved (S. Cohen & Wills, 1985). Likewise, there is controversy over whether friends can substitute for intimate ties in the social support functions they provide (Weiss, 1982). However, it is possible that seemingly different protective factors, such as social support and positive school experiences, may produce similar results if their impact is through common pathways, such as increases in self-esteem or mastery beliefs.

Third, explicitly recognizing co-occurrence of resources within our study populations helps prevent the misattribution of stress-buffering effects. Finding that a coping resource such as self-esteem buffers the negative effects of a stressor may provide an incomplete and potentially misleading picture if correlated resources are not also considered. For example, treating all subjects the same who score high on a single buffering variable may overlook the possibility that most of the stress-buffering effect is being carried by a smaller subgroup of persons having this resource paired with other resources.

Fourth, knowing that two or more resources are positively correlated inevitably leads to questions as to the origins of these empirical relationships. One concern is with developmental questions, especially if the correlation arose because one resource is causally related to the development of another. It is therefore no coincidence that descriptions of resilient children invariably include a mixture of personal resources, such as good temperamental qualities, a sense of mastery, social skills, and high self-esteem, together with social support resources, whether from parents, teachers, or the larger community. In addition to developmental concerns, co-occurrence of protective factors, as with co-occurrence among stressors, may also alert us to broader social structural factors that may produce such clustering. In seeking to simply "control" for the effects of such variables as socioeconomic status, gender, ethnicity, or education, researchers have often ignored the fact that protective factors operating at the individual level have links to the broader social and cultural world of the developing individual. Here again we see the importance of mediational models, in this case linking social conditions to the development of protective factors.

Nonadditive combinations of protective resources

A consideration of two or more protective factors leads to questions about the ways in which they potentially combine to buffer stressful experiences. It is possible, in many cases, that the joint effect of two or more resources is a simple additive combination of each of the individual resources. Such a function is implicitly assumed when aggregate measures of resources are created and their stress-buffering qualities assessed. This is analogous to the use of aggregate scores derived from checklists of life events to measure stress. For example, there is some evidence in the adult literature that the concept of "hardiness" as a personality trait is associated with resistance to stress. This is an aggregate personality measure composed of several underlying constructs, such as locus of control orientation and commitment (Kobasa, Maddi, & Courington, 1981). Similarly, broad measures of "competence" as a protective factor associated with resilience to stress may combine into one measure a number of constructs such as the quality of mother–child interaction, problem-solving ability, and reactions to frustration (e.g., Egeland & Kreutzer, 1991).

Theoretically, such constructs may help to provide some needed integration to the literature on protective factors, which is often characterized as lacking coherence (Garmezy & Masten, 1991). Methodologically, such aggregate constructs may also be justified by a pattern of positive correlations between the various component variables, often yielding higher-order factors with the aid of multivariate techniques such as factor analysis. The twin needs of saving precious degrees of freedom and for reducing measurement error often motivate researchers to consider such aggregate or summary variables. The increasing use of sophisticated statistical programs that incorporate measurement models into the analysis of the data, such as LISREL (Joreskog & Sorbom, 1976), have also encouraged the combination of several measured variables into one "unobserved construct."

Such advances, however, may lead to a disregard of possible nonadditive relationships between the underlying factors. An example from the stress and coping literature is provided by the study of Riley and Eckenrode (1986), who showed that the effectiveness of social support as a buffer for stressful life events among an urban sample of mothers was dependent on the presence or absence of other variables that have also been shown to moderate the impact of stress, such as socioeconomic status, education, and locus of control. Social support had little impact on buffering stress (or was even associated with an increase in negative mood) when levels of the other resources were low (e.g., for women having an external locus of control). When the accompanying resource was high (i.e., high socioeconomic status, high education, or internal locus of control), social support showed the expected interaction with stress in buffering stressful events. The processes underlying this differential effect could not be clearly delineated in this study, but these researchers speculated that social support for low-resource women carried certain costs (e.g., exposure to the supporter's problems, inability to reciprocate) not present when support was given in the context of high levels of resources. A similar result has been reported by Husaini, Neff, Newbrough, and Moore (1982), who found that social support, in the absence of a sense of personal competency, increased vulnerability to stress.

In statistical terms, these examples essentially describe a three-way interaction, with the strength or direction of stress-buffering effects being contingent on the levels of a third resource. Advances in stress-buffering research may require attention to such complex person–environment interactions, despite the demands placed on the data. Given the likely prevalence of such interactions, however, searching for complexity appears to be a better course of action than presuming simpler models, as would have been the case if, in the preceding example, the social support and personal resource measures would have been combined into a generalized coping resource measure.

The stress-buffering qualities of social relationships may also vary by sociodemographic characteristics, such as gender. There is evidence that social support may represent a more crucial stress-buffering factor for women than for men (e.g., Dean & Lin, 1977). Stressors occurring to persons in the social network outside the immediate family may also be more distressing to both adolescent and adult women than they are to men (Kessler & McLeod, 1984; Wagner & Compas, 1990), perhaps a reflection of what has been termed the "cost of caring" among women (Belle, 1982). Sex role norms result in females being more sensitive than men to feedback from their social ties in evaluating their self-worth (Douvan, 1978; Gilligan, 1982), thus making them more reactive to social losses and strains, but also more receptive of social support. This suggests that the meaning and function of "social support" varies for men and women, because of the implications for self (cf. Gore & Colten, 1991). Again, main effects models that simply control for gender when examining the stress-buffering qualities of social support or other protective resources will not uncover or may distort such complex processes.

Temporal relationships and developmental considerations

Two or more protective factors may also be related to each other temporally. Stress and coping researchers have been primarily concerned with temporal issues insofar as they represent relatively short-term processes following the onset of a stressful event. The stress-buffering processes that are set in motion following the occurrence of a stressor have generally been investigated under the domain of coping research (e.g., Lazarus & Folkman, 1984), or in terms of the mobilization of social supports (Eckenrode & Wethington, 1990). The distinction that has existed in the literature between coping "resources" and more dynamic coping "strategies" or "responses" has narrowed in recent years as empirical evidence for linkages between resources and strategies has grown. For example, Thoits (1986) attempted to show how social support may profitably be regarded as "coping assistance."

Research stemming from a more clinical tradition has often been concerned with phases of the coping process, attaching significance not only to the occurrence of a particular response (e.g., denial, anger), but also to the order in which these responses occur. There is little evidence, however, supporting the notion that particular coping responses must occur, or that they must occur in a particular temporal order, for positive adjustment to stress to take place (cf. Silver & Wortman, 1980). Although temporal issues in the short-term adjustment to stress remain an active research concern (e.g., Jacobson, 1986), some researchers have begun to suggest that the precise type or timing of a coping response may be less crucial to positive outcomes than the fact that some active attempt at coping occurs at all. Indeed, the largest differentials between persons who display negative or positive outcomes following a stressful event may be between those who do nothing as opposed to those who do anything. Similar conclusions have been put forward in the literature linking the number of intimates in a social network to health outcomes, with the greatest positive benefits of social ties observed between persons with no intimate ties and those with one (Lin, Dean, & Ensel, 1986; Miller & Ingham, 1976).

When active attempts at coping with stress take place, it is typically the case that many different strategies, both cognitive and behavioral, are employed (Folkman & Lazarus, 1980). For example, in a study using a large, representative community sample, Mattlin, Wethington, and Kessler (1990) studied six types of cognitive and behavioral coping responses following stressful life events and found that half of the sample reported using virtually all the coping strategies. Judging coping efficacy in such circumstances is difficult because of the many combinations of coping responses that may take place within the group judged to have the best (or worst) outcomes. This suggests that advances in our understanding of coping efficacy will need to go beyond a simple counting of coping responses and relating these to health outcomes. As with an assessment of the impact of stressors, contextual factors will determine the efficacy of a particular coping response or combination of responses.

There have been two main ways in which contextual factors have been considered when evaluating coping responses (cf. Folkman, 1991). First, a number of authors have proposed a set of "tasks" that are common to many stressful events or normative transitions (e.g., F. Cohen & Lazarus, 1979; Moos & Schaeffer, 1986): (1) establish the meaning and understand the personal significance of the situation; (2) confront reality and respond to the requirements of the external situation; (3) sustain relationships with family members and friends as well as other individuals who may be helpful in resolving the crisis and its aftermath; (4) maintain a reasonable emotional balance by managing upsetting feelings aroused by the situation; and (5) preserve a satisfactory self-image and maintain a sense of competence and mastery. It is interesting to note that these tasks are, in many ways, methods used to preserve valuable coping resources such as self-esteem and social support. Indeed, coping with stress in a way that preserves the individual's fund of coping resources for use in future stressful encounters may represent a more useful way to judge coping efficacy than a criterion focused solely on short-term reductions in negative mood or psychological symptoms. For example, a coping response that reduces negative affect in the short term (e.g., drug or alcohol use) cannot be judged effective if it jeopardizes the quality of the person's primary social relationships.

A second way to incorporate contextual factors into an analysis of coping relies less on tasks that are common to environmental stressors and more on personal goals, motives, and commitments that shape the cognitive appraisal of events (cf. Lazarus & Folkman, 1984) and the choice of coping strategies. In this sense coping is not disconnected with what has gone before and what is anticipated for the future. This is one way of embedding coping behavior into broader developmental and life course processes, but it does so by presuming that most coping is goal-directed. Indeed, a relevant question prior to ascertaining what is the goal of a particular coping behavior is whether the individual's coping behavior appears goal-directed at all. One is reminded of Rutter and Quinton's (1984) study of women reared in institutions as children, where "planning" was found to be a trait associated with a higher likelihood of positive life course outcomes despite the adversities these young women experienced.

Personal intentions are often bound up with personal relationships. Conspicuously absent in most research on coping is a consideration of the social context of the coping behavior, whether in terms of the influence of social relationships on the choice of coping strategies, or on the impact coping behaviors have on social relationships (cf. Eckenrode, 1991). Throughout the life course, the nature of the person's primary relationships with family and friends represents one of the crucial "proximal processes" that underlie what Bronfenbrenner calls the "engines of development" (1992). It is not surprising, therefore, that much coping behavior occurs, consciously or unconsciously, under the influence of these interpersonal processes, and that one generalized coping task involves the preservation of close relationships. Lazarus (1991) has succinctly stated this proposition as follows:

In stressful transactions between a parent and child, spouses and lovers, co-workers, and so on, I am convinced that the coping process depends, to a substantial degree, on intentions toward the other person in the relationship and toward the relationship itself. (pp. ix–xi)

A cogent example is provided by Gottlieb and Wagner's (1991) qualitative study of the coping behaviors of mothers and fathers of children diagnosed with cystic fibrosis or juvenile diabetes. Focusing on the mothers, it was clear that their own coping behaviors were influenced by their husbands' coping style, which was often marked by less emotionality. In order to preserve the quality of the spousal relationship and avoid conflict, these women often adopted "public coping" in their husband's presence that was at odds with their "private coping" strategies. In this instance, commitment to the marital relationship led to what might be called "mutual coping" strategies (Wethington & Kessler, 1991). For children, defining coping as an exclusively individual-level process is likely to be even more inaccurate since, for many stressful experiences, it will be the coping of the parents that shapes the responses of the child.

We have argued that a consideration of goals and motives is one way to link short-term responses to stressful encounters to broader developmental and life course themes. Several authors have also suggested that the impact of childhood stressors is best understood when salient developmental tasks are taken into account. Sroufe (1979) and Sroufe and Rutter (1984) have proposed that developmental issues form the context for understanding the long-term adaptation of children to stressful experiences. Other investigators have applied this perspective to understanding the developmental consequences of specific childhood stressors, such as child maltreatment (Cicchetti & Olsen, 1990; Cicchetti & Rizley, 1981). Kalter (1987) has proposed a "developmental vulnerability model" of the long-term effects of divorce on children (see also Wertlieb, 1991). In this model, the negative effects of divorce are understood by reference to three developmental tasks: managing anger and aggression, separation–individuation, and gender identity. Newcomb and Bentler (1988) also interpret continuities they observed between heavy drug use in adolescence and problematic outcomes in young adulthood within this framework. They argue that heavy drug use interferes, among other things, with the normal development of peer relationships necessary for the development of the social skills, which, in turn, form the basis of effective adult relationships.

The life course perspective extends stress and coping research beyond the immediate effects of stressful experiences. To the extent that stressful experiences compromise the achievement of central developmental tasks, we might expect to see long-term consequences. For example, Caspi, Elder, and Bem (1987) have been able to trace the negative life course consequences of a childhood history of temper tantrums, a pattern of behavior that signals an inability to effectively regulate emotional expression. A developmental or life course perspective also alerts us to the temporal connections that exist between what are often treated analytically as separate coping resources. Again in the example of temper tantrums from the research of Elder and his colleagues, there is evidence that temper tantrums exhibited early in childhood as a response to stress and frustration may compromise the development of stable sources of social support in adulthood, as shown in higher rates of marital and job instability. An example of how positive experiences are also temporally linked comes from the longitudinal study of adolescent mothers in Baltimore by Furstenberg et al. (1987). Educational achievement for these women in the form of completing high school was linked to a longer delay in the birth of a second child, which in turn had a positive impact on economic status 17 years after the birth of their first child.

The developmental perspective also blurs the sharp distinction stress and coping researchers often make between stressors, buffering factors, and outcome variables. An assessment of the outcomes of stress in childhood or adolescence should not be restricted to short-term measures of behavioral and emotional adjustment. It should also include measures assessing the impact of stress on the negotiation of age-relevant developmental tasks that represent the processes through which the particular stressor and the child's short-term responses to it are likely to influence vulnerability to future stressful experiences. With such an approach, variables such as self-esteem and social support become outcome variables as well as stress buffers.

Stress outcomes: Mental health and developmental pathways

Subgroup differences in generalized distress

Perhaps the most neglected component of the risk–resilience framework is that of *stress outcomes*, the indicators of psychological functioning and behavioral adaptation that are affected by stress processes. The variety of outcome variables selected for study certainly reflects the diverse theoretical orientations and methodological approaches that characterize the several disciplines that are represented in this field. Until very recently, research on community populations of adults and children has relied predominantly on screening instruments designed to assess numbers and severity of symptoms of generalized distress. This approach is consistent with the goals of stress research in that the effects of stress have proved to be nonspecific, that is, evidenced in a wide range of emotional and adaptive difficulties. Thus, community studies of psychosocial stress processes have frequently used dimensional symptom measures since dependent variables of this nature might be adequate proxies for the somewhat diverse outcomes likely to ensue from antecedent stressful experiences.

The decade of the 1980s has brought forth challenges to this view from both within and outside the field of stress research (e.g., Depue & Monroe, 1986). Within the field of stress studies, the considerable body of research on gender differences in vulnerability to the mental health effects of stress has raised questions about the validity of these studies, given gender differences in the prevalence of different psychiatric disorders. For example, in studies focusing on depressed mood, findings indicate that women become more depressed than men in response to some classes of stressors. However, such findings are necessarily limited because men may be more likely to experience other types of dysfunction in the face of these very same stressors (Aneshensel, Rutter, & Lachenbruch, 1991). Thus, focusing on one outcome variable may bias findings toward support of gender differentials in stress reactivity when there are none.

Problems of this nature are also evident in reviewing the child and adolescent literature on the responses of boys and girls to stressful family conditions and parental divorce. Findings from a number of major studies of familial adversity generally indicate stronger effects of conflict and disruption on boys during the childhood years. However, the research of Wallerstein and associates (Wallerstein, Corbin, & Lewis, 1988; Wallerstein & Kelly, 1980) has raised the possibility of "sleeper effects," with girls' competent functioning in the early years after divorce giving way to the later emergence of problematic sexual behavior and dysfunctions in the attachment systems during adolescence. The research of Elder and associates on gender differentials in the effects of family economic deprivation also supports the view that hardship may be more disturbing to girls when it occurs during the adolescent period (Elder et al., 1985).

In addition to the timing of assessments, methodological issues also pertain to the sources of data and nature of assessments. Most mental health research with children has relied on parental and teacher reports of conduct problems, the more socially visible manifestations of emotional disturbance. By the adolescent years, screening and diagnostic instruments that utilize self reports are appropriate, making possible a focus on the internalized affective difficulties that are more characteristic in girls. This contrast between internalizing and externalizing dimensions of adaptation and between self-report and other assessment strategies presents a major challenge for research on gender differences in mental health over the life course. Although the evidence and theory regarding gender differences are among the most sophisticated in adult and child psychiatric epidemiology, continued research on gender and vulnerability to stress is needed to clarify the timing and nature of effects and how various assessment methods influence evidence of gender differences in mental health.

Pathways to multiple mental health problems

The reliance on generalized measures of distress also proves inappropriate for investigations of processes specific to disorders and for research on comorbidity. Regarding the latter, the chapter by Compas and Hammen focuses on depression, and considers how other concurrent disorders complicate our understanding of this prevalent childhood problem. Here, we also consider the co-occurrence of multiple problems and the implications of a broad-band conceptualization of adolescent mental health for efforts to understand key etiological processes.

Again using gender as an example, the study of patterns of distress serves to highlight the unfinished business regarding the issue of gender differences in internalizing and externalizing symptoms of distress. For example, similar to other studies of adolescents, Colten, Gore, and Aseltine (1991) have reported significant gender differences on several indicators of emotional distress when these outcomes were considered separately. In this community sample, however, a focus on gender differences in *patterns* of distress yielded some unexpected findings. For boys and girls who evidenced only one mental health problem, equal proportions had some type of affective distress, data that argue against a simple conclusion regarding an excess of affective problems among girls. Boys, moreover, reported almost twice the rate of substance use problems and three times the rate of behavioral problems as girls in these single problem categories. Unexpected results were also evident in considering adolescents experiencing high rates of problems in two domains. For example, boys and girls were almost equally likely to have a combination of internalizing and externalizing problems – 27% of the boys and 32% of the girls had both, suggesting a considerable degree of cross-domain (internalizing and externalizing) problems for both sexes. These data challenge the traditional view of girls as internalizers and boys as externalizers, and suggest that a single-outcome approach has limited our understandings of gender and the expression of mental health problems.

The fact that having multiple problems can be seen as indicating more compromised development also emphasizes the need to understand within- and across-gender processes that shape these severer profiles. For example, in the study described previously, cross-sectional analyses indicated an association between the total number of stressors occurring in several role domains (family, school, peer, personal) and the probability of having multiple problem behaviors. This reinforces the importance of understanding the person–situation dynamics that account for (stress accumulation) and its association with more compromised mental health and functioning. Processes of this nature necessarily occur over significant periods of time, intervals that may incorporate changes in environment and major life transitions. Kandel and Davies (1986), for example, have noted that among adolescent girls, high levels of depressed mood predicted young adult alcohol problems, a relationship that appeared to be mediated by an early, unhappy marriage.

An important point of departure for behavioral sciences research on multiple problem behaviors and mental health problems has been the Problem Behavior Theory developed by Jessor and associates (Donovan & Jessor, 1985; Jessor & Jessor, 1977). In this framework, problems of social deviance, including drinking, drug use, and delinquency are understood to constitute a "syndrome" of problem behavior in that they co-occur commonly and appear to result from a single cause. This body of study has stimulated a number of research efforts (e.g., Osgood, Johnston, O'Malley, & Bachman, 1988) that have attempted to achieve a more unified or coherent understanding of the many facets of child and adolescent mental health.

A particularly fruitful line of research relates to our earlier discussion of the specificity between risk factors and outcomes. In a recent study of this issue, Cohen and associates (P. Cohen, Brook, Cohen, Velez, & Garcia, 1990) examined predictive associations between three classes of risk factors and several indicators of adolescent psychopathology and behavioral adaptation in a random sample of children who were first interviewed when they were ages 5 to 10. The aim of the study was to identify those factors that constituted a risk for both emotional distress and behavioral problems, in contrast to factors contributing a specific risk for only certain types of problems. The risks considered included broad indicators of environmental context (urban setting, neighborhood crime, low socioeconomic status, etc.), of parental background and family structure (parental mental health, family structure, etc.) and parent–child interaction (involvement, attention, punishment, aspirations). The broad environmental risk factors were found to influence both internalizing and externalizing problems, but these relationships disappeared when family or parent–child variables were examined. The set of parent–child interaction variables, the most proximal influences of child health, showed the most complex pattern of "uncommon" (nonshared or specific) pathways. For example, parental inattention was a risk factor for substance abuse, but not for emotional distress. Interestingly, substance use was associated with the greatest number of specific environmental influences (neighborhood crime as harmful, residential instability as protective), whereas parent–child interaction variables were influential for all syndromes, but with specific links between type of interaction and type of disorder. These findings confirm the general sense that societal-level risk factors (e.g., socioeconomic status, family structure) place a large number of children at risk for a range of disorders. At the more proximal social psychological level, which is reflected in family socialization and communication patterns, the specific interactions between person and environment become important for explanations of alternative patterns of individual response.

These considerations suggest the need to move away from menus of variables and study more complex profiles of functioning. They also argue for considering the generality or specificity of the intervening mechanisms linking risks to disorders. The next step might be to adapt Cohen and associates' work on pathways to clusters of psychological and behavioral problems, a formidable, but necessary task. In addition, because comorbidity is itself a dynamic process, and, we expect, responsive to the multiple life stresses and role transitions that are particularly characteristic of the later adolescent and early adult years, our understandings of critical pathways must be informed by an understanding of risk that goes beyond our current emphasis on the child's family environment.

Conclusions

The decade of the 1980s marked a research emphasis on the concept of resilience. This paradigmatic change from an earlier focus on risk for psychopathology has generated fresh ideas about prevention and intervention. Similar paradigmatic changes are in evidence today, with life course and life-span developmental perspectives reshaping the strategies and goals for mental health research. The theme of interrelatedness provides one perspective on the challenges that emerge from this more systemic orientation. We have considered two facets of interrelatedness: the linkages among variables that yield a holistic understanding of context, and the interplay of risk, protective factors, and mental health over time.

With respect to the major research constructs, we have characterized directions that facilitate moving from a focus on discrete indicators to uncover mechanisms that link multiple variables. For example, both social support and a positive self-concept have been found to buffer the effects of stressful experiences and most studies that include these protective factors report moderate correlations between them. This covariation in part reflects processes through which early attachment relationships shape the development of positive self-concept. Supportive attachments may also protect against environmental insults to self-concept, indicating an important mechanism through which multiple protective factors promote resiliency.

We have also considered interrelationships among the many risk variables that have been studied. Mediational models of environmental influences have been important for linking more global indicators of risk, such as socioeconomic status or single-parent household, to the more proximate social psychological influences of child functioning. Research consistently indicates, for example, that the impact of family income and structure on child and adolescent problem behaviors is transmitted via the parental control and social support processes that characterize the microsocial environment of these families. This body of research has led not only to a more fine-tuned understanding of risk, but also has provided a model for integrating sociological and psychological perspectives on problem behavior. The study of social stress similarly offers a more differentiated understanding of the experiences in high-risk environments that promote illness versus health. The early emphasis on discrete life stressors has been complemented with attention to chronic adversity and microstressors.

Each of these new developments reflects a larger process of rethinking models of risk, resilience, and development. Most important, the time has come to scrutinize the utility of frameworks that assume processes of acute stress and illness onset. It appears that such models have been best suited for investigations of the transitory problems of childhood and adolescence that for most youth are resolved without profound consequences for the life course. These approaches, however, tend to overlook illness maintenance processes involving chronic stress, chronic resource deficits, and chronic disorder, all of which contribute to a long-term burden of distress and dysfunction. A focus on acute processes is also incompatible with efforts to uncover "turnarounds" or improvements in negative mental health trajectories, a type of resilience that becomes apparent only when functioning over a long-term developmental trajectory is examined.

Finally, the issue of chronicity in stress, disorder, and health-jeopardizing behaviors also alters our understanding of person–environment transaction and offers insight into the comorbid pathways that are shaped in the adolescent and early adulthood years. As we have noted earlier, the idea of person–environment transaction is often pursued no further than the evidence of a statistical interaction between environmental risks and personal resource capabilities. Within a traditional model of risk and resiliency, it is assumed that high levels of existing protective resources significantly offset the mental health and behavioral impact of risk. Interest in the continuity of mental health problems calls for alternative conceptualizations. For example, an important question for future study is whether risk mechanisms do their harm through undermining the development of protective factors, such as support systems, self-esteem, or academic competence. This process is consistent with the view that stressors have long-term detrimental impact when they impede the achievement of critical developmental tasks. The inability to develop a set of protective resources early in life not only produces early dysfunction, but additionally provides the basis for both enhanced lifetime exposure to stress and vulnerability to dysfunction. Thus, a transactional model that focuses on chronic stress and chronic resource deficits offers one type of framework for exploring why a significant portion of youthful populations experience severer mental health problems and, failing to recover from earlier setbacks, evidence compromised functioning in a wide range of arenas by adulthood. On the positive side, to understand resilience we must ask not only about the nature of the individual's responses to stress; in addition, a developmental perspective directs attention to whether and how protective factors can develop under adversity.

In conclusion, we believe there has been considerable progress over the past 10 years in meeting the challenges put forth by editors and authors of the 1983 book *Stress, Coping, and Development in Children.*

To be sure, our task has become even more complicated as the theoretical models, research designs, and analytical approaches to these questions have become more complex, and as the sheer number of studies has increased dramatically. At the same time, there is now a sense that research on stress, coping, and resilience has moved from the sidelines of our disciplines to occupy an important place in the behavioral sciences.

References

Aneshensel, C., Rutter, C., & Lachenbruch, P. A. (1991). Social structure, stress and mental health: Competing conceptual and analytic models. *American Sociological Review, 56,* 166–178.

Aseltine, R. H., Jr., Gore, S., & Colten, M. E. (in press). Depression and the social developmental context of adolescence. *Journal of Personality and Social Psychology.*

Baron, R. M., & Kenny, D. A. (1986). The moderator–mediator variable distinction in social psychological research: Conceptual, strategic, and statistical consideration. *Journal of Personality and Social Psychology, 51,* 1173–1182.

Belle, D. (1982). The stress of caring: Women as providers of social support. In L. Goldberger & S. Bresnitz (Eds.), *Handbook of stress: Theoretical and clinical aspects* (pp. 496–505). New York: Free Press.

Bronfenbrenner, U. (1979). *The ecology of human development: Experiments by nature and design.* Cambridge, MA: Harvard University Press.

Bronfenbrenner, U. (1992). The person–process–context model in developmental research: Principles, applications, and implications. Unpublished manuscript.

Brooks-Gunn, J., & Warren, M. P. (1985). Effects of delayed menarche in different contexts: Dance and nondance students. *Journal of Youth and Adolescence, 14,* 285–300.

Brown, G. W., & Harris, T. O. (1978). *Social origins of depression: A study of psychiatric disorder in women.* New York: Free Press.

Brown, G. W., & Harris, T. O. (Eds.). (1989). *Life events and illness.* New York: Guilford.

Bush, D. M., & Simmons, R. G. (1987). Gender and coping with the entry into early adolescence. In R. C. Barnett, L. Biener, & G. Baruch (Eds.), *Gender and stress* (pp. 185–217). New York: Free Press.

Caspi, A., Elder, G., & Bem, D. (1987). Moving against the world: Life-course patterns of explosive children. *Developmental Psychology, 22,* 303–308.

Cassidy, J. (1988). Child–mother attachment and the self in six-year-olds. *Child Development, 59,* 121–134.

Cicchetti, D., & Olsen, K. (1990). The developmental psychopathology of child maltreatment. In M. Lewis & S. M. Miller (Eds.), *Handbook of developmental psychopathology* (pp. 261–279). New York: Plenum.

Cicchetti, D., & Rizley, R. (1981). Developmental perspectives on the etiology, intergenerational transmission, and sequelae of child maltreatment. *New Directions for Child Development, 11,* 31–55.

Clausen, J. S. (1991). Adolescent competence and the shaping of the life course. *American Journal of Sociology, 96,* 805–842.

Cohen, F., & Lazarus, R. S. (1979). Coping with the stresses of illness. In G. Stone, F. Cohen, & N. E. Adler (Eds.), *Health psychology* (pp. 217–254). San Francisco: Jossey Bass.

Cohen, P., Brook, J. S., Cohen, J., Velez, C. N., & Garcia, M. (1990). Common and uncommon pathways to adolescent psychopathology and problem behavior. In L. N. Robins & M. Rutter (Eds.), *Straight and devious pathways from childhood to adulthood* (pp. 242–258). Cambridge: Cambridge University Press.

Cohen, S., & Syme, S. L. (1985). Issues in the study and application of social support. In S. Cohen & S. L. Syme (Eds.), *Social support and health* (pp. 3–22). Orlando, FL: Academic Press.

Cohen, S., & Wills, T. A. (1985). Stress, social support, and the buffering hypothesis. *Psychological Bulletin, 98,* 310–357.

Coleman, J. C. (1974). *Relationships in adolescence,* Boston, MA: Routledge & Kegan Paul.

Colten, M. E., Gore, S., & Aseltine, R. H., Jr. (1991). The patterning of distress and disorder in a community sample of high school aged youth. In M. E. Colten & S. Gore (Eds.), *Adolescent stress: Causes and consequences* (pp. 157–180). New York: Aldine de Gruyter.

Compas, B., Howell, D. C., Phares, V., Williams, R. A., & Giunta, C. T. (1989). Risk factors for emotional-behavioral problems in young adolescents: A prospective analysis of adolescent and parent stress and symptoms. *Journal of Consulting and Clinical Psychology, 57,* 732–740.

Coyne, J. C., & Downey, G. (1991). Social factors and psychopathology: Stress, social support, and coping processes. *Annual Review of Psychology, 42,* 401–425.

Csikszentmihalyi, M., & Larson, R. (1984). *Being adolescent.* New York: Basic Books.

Dean, A., & Lin, N. (1977). The stress-buffering role of social support. *Journal of Nervous and Mental Diseases, 165,* 403–413.

Depue, R. A., & Monroe, S. M. (1986). Conceptualization and measurement of human disorder in life stress research: The problem of chronic disturbance. *Psychological Bulletin, 99,* 36–51.

Donovan, J., & Jessor, R. (1985). Structure of problem behavior in adolescence and young adulthood. *Journal of Consulting and Clinical Psychology, 53*(6), 890–904.

Douvan, E. (1978). Sex role learning. In J. C. Coleman (Ed.), *The school years.* London: Methuen.

Eckenrode, J. (1984). Impact of chronic and acute stressors on daily reports of mood. *Journal of Personality and Social Psychology, 46,* 907–918.

Eckenrode, J. (Ed.). (1991). *The social context of coping.* New York: Plenum.

Eckenrode, J., & Wethington, E. (1990). The process and outcome of mobilizing social support. In S. Duck (Ed.), *Personal relationships and social support* (pp. 83–103). London: Sage.

Egeland, B., Breitenbucher, M., & Rosenberg, D. (1980). Prospective study of the significance of life stress in the etiology of child abuse. *Journal of Consulting and Clinical Psychology, 48,* 195–205.

Egeland, B., & Kreutzer, T. (1991). A longitudinal study of the effects of maternal stress and protective factors on the development of high-risk children. In E. M. Cummings, A. L. Greene, & K. Karraker (Eds.), *Life-span developmental psychology: Perspectives on stress and coping* (pp. 61–83). Hillsdale, NJ: Erlbaum.

Elder, G. H., Jr. (1974). *Children of the Great Depression.* Chicago: University of Chicago Press.

Elder, G. H., Jr., & Caspi, A. (1988). Human development and social change: An emerging perspective on the life course. In N. Bolger, A. Caspi, G. Downey, & M. Moorehouse (Eds.), *Persons in context: Developmental processes* (pp. 77–113). Cambridge: Cambridge University Press.

Elder, G. H., Jr., Nguyen, T. V., & Caspi, A. (1985). Linking family hardship to children's lives. *Child Development, 56,* 361–375.

Folkman, S. (1991). Coping across the life span: Theoretical issues. In E. M. Cummings, A. L. Greene, & K. Karraker (Eds.), *Life-span developmental psychology: Perspectives on stress and coping* (pp. 3–19). Hillsdale, NJ: Erlbaum.

Folkman, S., & Lazarus, R. S. (1980). An analysis of coping in a middle-aged community sample. *Journal of Health and Social Behavior, 21,* 219–239.

Furstenberg, F. F., Jr., Brooks-Gunn, J., & Morgan, S. P. (1987). *Adolescent mothers in later life.* Cambridge: Cambridge University Press.

Garmezy, N., & Masten, A. S. (1991). The protective role of competence indicators in children at risk. In E. M. Cummings, A. L. Greene, & K. Karraker (Eds.), *Life-span developmental psychology: Perspectives on stress and coping* (pp. 151–174). Hillsdale, NJ: Erlbaum.

Garmezy, N., Masten, A. S., & Tellegen, A. (1984). The study of stress and competence in children: A building block for developmental psychopathology. *Child Development, 55,* 97–111.

Garmezy, N., & Rutter, M. (Eds.). (1983). *Stress, coping, and development in children.* New York: McGraw-Hill.

Gilligan, C. (1982). *In a different voice: Psychological theory and women's development.* Cambridge, MA: Harvard University Press.

Gore, S., & Colten, M. E. (1991). Adolescent stress, social relationships, and mental health. In M. E. Colten & S. Gore (Eds.), *Adolescent stress: Causes and consequences* (pp. 1–14). New York: Aldine de Gruyter.

Gore, S., & Colten M. E. (1991). Gender, stress, and distress: Social-relational influences. In J. Eckenrode (Ed.), *The social context of coping* (pp. 139–163). New York: Plenum.

Gottlieb, B. H. (1985). Social support and the study of personal relationships. *Journal of Social and Personal Relationships, 2,* 351–375.

Gottlieb., B. H., & Wagner, F. (1991). Stress and support processes in close relationships. In J. Eckenrode (Ed.), *The social context of coping* (pp. 165–188). New York: Plenum.

Hammen, C. Ellicott, A., Gitlin, M., & Jamison, K. R. (1989). Sociotropy/autonomy and vulnerability to specific life events in patients with unipolar and bipolar depression. *Journal of Abnormal Psychology, 98,* 154–160.

Hammen, C., Marks, T., Mayol, A., & deMayo, R. (1985). Depressive self-schemas, life stress, and vulnerability to depression. *Journal of Abnormal Psychology, 94*, 308–319.

Holmes, T. H., & Rahe, R. H. (1967). The social readjustment rating scale. *Journal of Psychosomatic Research, 11*, 213–218.

Husaini, B. A., Neff, J. A., Newbrough, J. R., & Moore, M.C. (1982). The stress-buffering role of social support and personal competence among the rural married. *Journal of Community Psychology, 10*, 409–426.

Jacobson, D. E. (1986). Types and timing of social support. *Journal of Health and Social Behavior, 27*, 250–264.

Jessor, R., & Jessor, S. (1977). *Problem behavior and psychosocial development: A longitudinal study of youth.* New York: Academic Press.

Joreskog, K. G., & Sorbom, D. (1976). *LISREL – estimation of linear structural equation systems by maximum likelihood methods.* Chicago: International Educational Services.

Kalter, N. (1987). Long-term effects of divorce on children: A developmental vulnerability model. *American Journal of Orthopsychiatry, 57*, 587–600.

Kandel D., & Davies, M. (1986). Adult sequelae of adolescent depressive symptoms. *Archives of General Psychiatry, 43*, 255–262.

Kellam, S. H., Brown, C. H., Rubin, B. R., & Ensminger, M. E. (1983). Paths leading to teenage psychiatric symptoms and substance use: Developmental epidemiological studies in Woodlawn. In S. R. Guze, F. J. Earls, & J. E. Barretts (Eds.), *Childhood psychopathology and development* (pp. 17–51). New York: Raven Press.

Kessler, R. C. (1983). Methodological issues in the study of psychosocial stress. In H. B. Kaplan (Ed.), *Psychosocial stress: Trends in theory and research* (pp. 267–341). New York: Academic Press.

Kessler, R. C., & Essex, M. (1982). Marital status and depression: The importance of coping resources. *Social Forces, 61*, 484–507.

Kessler, R. C., & McLeod, J. D. (1984). Sex differences in vulnerability to undesirable life events. *American Sociological Review, 49*, 620–631.

Kobasa, S. C., Maddi, S. R., & Courington, S. (1981). Personality and constitution in the stress–illness relationship. *Journal of Health and Social Behavior, 22*, 368–378.

Larson, R., & Asmussen, L. (1991). Anger, worry, and hurt in early adolescence: An enlarging world of negative emotions. In M. E. Colten & S. Gore (Eds.), *Adolescent stress: Causes and consequences* (pp. 21–41). New York: Aldine de Gruyter.

Lazarus, R. S. (1991). Forword. In J. Eckenrode (Ed.), *The social context of coping* (pp. ix–xi). New York: Plenum.

Lazarus, R. S., & Folkman, S. (1984). *Stress, appraisal, and coping.* New York: Springer.

Lin, N. (1986). Modeling the effects of social support. In N. Lin, A. Dean, & W. M. Ensel (Eds.), *Social support, life events, and depression* (pp. 173–209). Orlando, FL: Academic Press.

Lin, N., Dean., A., & Ensel, W. (Eds.) (1986). *Social support, life events, and depression.* Orlando, FL: Academic Press.

Magnusson, D., & Bergman, L. R. (1990). A pattern approach to the study of pathways from childhood to adulthood. In L. N. Robbins & M. Rutter (Eds.), *Straight and devious pathways from childhood to adulthood* (pp. 101–115). Cambridge: Cambridge University Press.

Masten, A. S., Best, K. M., & Garmezy, N. (1990). Resilience and development: Contributions from the study of children who overcome adversity. *Development and Psychopathology, 2,* 425–444.

Mattlin, J., Wethington, E., & Kessler, R. C. (1990). Situational determinants of coping and coping effectiveness. *Journal of Health and Social Behavior, 31,* 103–122.

Miller, P. McC., & Ingham, J. G. (1976). Friends, confidants and symptoms. *Social Psychiatry, 11,* 51–58.

Monroe, S. M., & Simons, A. D. (1991). Diathesis-stress theories in the context of life stress research: Implications for the depressive disorders. *Psychological Bulletin, 110,* 406–425.

Moos, R. H., & Schaeffer, J. A. (1986). Life transitions and crises: A conceptual overview. In R. H. Moos (Ed.), *Coping with life crises* (pp. 3–28). New York: Plenum.

Newcomb, M. D., & Bentler, P. M. (1988). Impact of adolescent drug use and social support on problems of young adults: A longitudinal study. *Journal of Abnormal Psychology, 97,* 64–75.

Nolen-Hoeksema, S. (1990). *Sex differences in depression.* Stanford, CA: Stanford University Press.

Osgood, D. W., Johnston, L., O'Malley, P., & Bachman, J. (1988). The generality of deviance in later adolescence and early adulthood. *American Sociological Review, 53,* 81–93.

Pearlin, L. I. (1983). Role strains and personal stress. In H. B. Kaplan (Ed.), *Psychosocial stress* (pp. 3–32). New York: Academic Press.

Pearlin, L. I. (1989). The sociological study of stress. *Journal of Health and Social Behavior, 30,* 241–256.

Pearlin, L. I., Lieberman, M. A., Menaghan, E. G., & Mullan, J. T. (1981). The stress process. *Journal of Health and Social Behavior, 22,* 337–356.

Quinton, D., & Rutter, M. (1976). Early hospital admissions and later disturbances of behaviour: An attempted replication of Douglas' findings.
Developmental Medicine and Child Neurology, 18, 447–459.

Richters, J., & Weintraub, S. (1990). Beyond diathesis: Toward an understanding of high risk environments. In J. Rolf, A. S. Masten, D.
Cicchetti, K. Nuechterlein, & S. Weintraub (Eds.), *Risk and protective
factors in the development of psychopathology* (pp. 67–96). Cambridge: Cambridge University Press.

Riley, D., & Eckenrode, J. (1986). Social ties: Subgroup differences in costs
and benefits. *Journal of Personality and Social Psychology, 51,* 770–778.

Rutter, M. (1983a). Stress, coping and development: Some issues and some
questions. In N. Garmezy & M. Rutter (Eds.), *Stress, coping, and development in children* (pp. 1–41). New York: McGraw-Hill.

Rutter, M. (1983b). Statistical and personal interactions: Facets and perspectives. In D. Magnusson & V. Allen (Eds.), *Human development: An interactive perspective* (pp. 295–319). New York: Academic Press.

Rutter, M. (1990). Psychosocial resilience and protective mechanisms. In J.
Rolf, A. S. Masten, D. Cicchetti, K. H. Nuechterlein, & S. Weintraub
(Eds.), *Risk and protective factors in the development of psychopathology* (pp.
181–214). Cambridge: Cambridge University Press.

Rutter, M., & Quinton, D. (1984). Long-term follow-up of women institutionalized in childhood: Factors promoting good functioning in adult
life. *British Journal of Developmental Psychology, 18,* 225–234.

Silver, R. L., & Wortman, C. B. (1980). Coping with undesirable life events.
In J. Garber & M. Seligman (Eds.), *Human helplessness: Theory and
application* (pp. 279–375). New York: Academic Press.

Simmons, R. G., Burgeson, R., Carlton-Ford, S., & Blyth, D. A. (1987).
The impact of cumulative change in early adolescence. *Child Development, 58,* 1220–1234.

Sroufe, L. A. (1979). The coherence of individual development. *American
Psychologist, 34,* 834–841.

Sroufe, L. A., & Rutter, M. (1984). The domain of developmental psychopathology. *Child Development, 55,* 17–29.

Thoits, P. A. (1986). Social support and coping assistance. *Journal of Consulting and Clinical Psychology, 54,* 416–423.

Thoits, P. A. (1991). On merging identity theory and stress research. *Social
Psychological Quarterly, 54,* 101–112.

Turner, R. J., & Noh, S. (1983). Class and psychological vulnerability among
women: The significance of social support and personal control. *Journal
of Health and Social Behavior, 24,* 2–15.

Wagner, B. M., & Compas, B. (1990). Gender instrumentality and expressivity: Moderators of the relationship between stress and psychological symptoms during adolescence. *American Journal of Community Psychology, 18*, 383–406.

Walker, E., Downey, G., & Bergman, A. (1989). The effects of parental psychopathology and maltreatment on child behavior: A test of the diathesis-stress model. *Child Development, 60*, 15–24.

Wallerstein, J. S., Corbin, S. B., & Lewis, J. M. (1988). Children of divorce: A 10-year study. In E. M. Hetherington & J. D. Arasteh (Eds.), *Impact of divorce, single parenting, and stepparenting on children* (pp. 197–214). Hillsdale, NJ: Erlbaum.

Wallerstein, J. S., & Kelly, J. B. (1980). *Surviving the breakup: How children actually cope with divorce.* New York: Basic Books.

Weiss, R. S. (1979). Growing up a little faster: The experience of growing up in a single-parent household. *Journal of Social Issues, 35*, 97–111.

Weiss, R. S. (1982). Attachment in adults. In C. M. Parkes & J. Stevenson-Hinde (Eds.), *The place of attachment in human behavior* (pp. 171–184). New York: Basic Books.

Werner, E., & Smith, R. S. (1982). *Vulnerable but invincible: A longitudinal study of resilient children and youth.* New York: McGraw-Hill.

Wertlieb, D. (1991). Children and divorce: Stress and coping in developmental perspective. In J. Eckenrode (Ed.), *The social context of coping* (pp. 31–54). New York: Plenum.

Wethington, E., & Kessler, R. C. (1991). Situations and processes of coping. In J. Eckenrode (Ed.), *The social context of coping* (pp. 13–29). New York: Plenum.

Wheaton, B. (1985). Models for the stress-buffering functions of coping resources. *Journal of Health and Social Behavior, 26*, 352–64.

Wheaton, B. (1990). Life transitions, role histories and mental health. *American Sociological Review, 55*, 209–223.

3

Parental divorce and children's well-being: A focus on resilience

Robert E. Emery and Rex Forehand

Three basic observations make a focus on resilience particularly compelling when considering the psychological health of children of divorce. First, there is little doubt that the time of divorce is surrounded by tremendous emotional distress, psychological confusion, relationship strain, and life upheaval for children and their parents. Many of these difficulties are well documented in empirical research and are readily observed in clinical work. Second, despite the substantial challenges that divorce poses, the undeniable conclusion based on a significant body of research is that most children adequately adjust to the often dramatic changes in their family life. A period of turmoil commonly is reported as children and their parents cope with a divorce. Yet, on average, children from divorced families are only slightly more troubled than children whose parents remain married as measured by various indexes of their mental health. Third, despite their successful life functioning, both children and adults frequently express disappointment, longing, and resentment about divorce when pressed to talk about their feelings in clinical interviews or intimate conversations with friends. Thus, it would seem that the experience of the children of divorce meets the criteria for Garmezy's (1991) definition of resilience: "the maintenance of competent functioning despite an interfering emotionality" (p. 466).

Consider the challenges of divorce. Feelings of hurt and pain, sadness and anger are particularly intense among children and parents shortly after the marital separation, as family members struggle to

Robert E. Emery is Professor of Psychology at the University of Virginia and Rex Forehand is Professor of Psychology at the University of Georgia.

recapture their former life, grieve their loss, or justify the choices they have made. Misunderstandings about the reasons for divorce are common, and many children hold inappropriate feelings of responsibility for their parents' continuing relationship. Other children, and more parents, externalize the blame, as they angrily attribute divorce to the failings of one parent/partner. Not surprisingly, the parents' relationship often is permeated with anger and conflict before, during, and after a divorce, a source of great and perhaps chronic distress for children. After the separation and over time, children's relationships with their nonresidential parents, most commonly their fathers, often grow distant and inconsistent. Children's relationships with their residential parents are stabler, but they also may become less supportive and more negative as parents struggle with their own burdens. Last but far from least, the adverse economic consequences of divorce are both well documented and easily observed. Financial strains can create a host of difficulties for children ranging from changes in residence, schools, and friendships to the barely adequate living standards that accompany poverty.

Now consider children's successful coping. The distress they face is considerable, yet after a period of family and individual difficulty, it is clear that the outcome of divorce for most children is *not* risk but resilience. Numerous studies have compared the adjustment of children from divorced and married families, and the clear pattern is that only small differences are found in cognitive, social, and psychological functioning. In the face of adversity, children somehow bounce back from divorce. In fact, divorce is more strongly related to parents' than to children's mental health. Apparently, many children cope with divorce more adequately than their parents do, despite the fact that at least one of the parents wanted a divorce, whereas it is rarely wanted by a child.

Finally, consider children's underlying unhappiness about their parents' divorce. Measures of children's mental health are more reliable and valid indexes of their external behavior than of their inner thoughts and feelings, making the subtler hurts of divorce more difficult to document. Still, recognition of children's successful coping must be tempered with an awareness that many children have lingering and distressing feelings about their parents' divorce. Children's distress is poignantly revealed in the sometimes overdramatized but consistently sensitive accounts of clinical investigators. In fact, children's resilience, their competent functioning despite interfering emotionality, may partially explain why clinical and empirical researchers so often come to different conclusions about the consequences of divorce for children. Empiricists use objective indexes to quantify the competent functioning, or more accurately the absence of incompetence, that is found among children of divorce as a group. In so doing, they rightly conclude that successful adaptation is the most notable outcome. Clinical investigators, in contrast, focus on the inner experience of the individual child, and often uncover hidden fears, longings, and resentments. They rightly recognize the emotionality of divorce for some children but, perhaps because of this insight, wrongly conclude that their competent functioning is a mere mask.

In this chapter, we begin by presenting selective overviews of research related to each of the three points discussed in this introductory section. Following this, a summary of research on specific risk and resilience factors in children's coping with divorce is presented. Finally, we consider the implications of these literatures for future research and clinical practice.

The challenges of divorce for children

Divorce is a common experience for children living in the United States today. Every year, approximately 2% of American children experience a divorce (Select Committee on Children, Youth, and Families [SCCYF], 1989), and demographers have estimated that 38% of white children and 75% of black children born to married parents will experience a parental divorce by the age of 16 (Bumpass, 1984). Despite the fact that divorce has become a normative experience for children, it is not a "normal" one, however.

Recent and innovative research suggests that many of the presumed "consequences of divorce," both in terms of family living circumstances and in terms of children's mental health, actually reflect family and individual difficulties that existed prior to the parental separation. This is a very important point that is emphasized throughout this chapter. Nevertheless, it is clear that some sources of strain are consequences of divorce, and others are exacerbated by it. In this section, we briefly consider the primary stressors children encounter during divorce; specifically, declining family income, loss of contact with nonresidential parents, strained relationships with residential parents, parental mental health problems, and parental conflict. The stressors are reviewed so that those factors that have been more clearly documented to be consequences of divorce are presented before those for which the documentation is less clear. It should be noted, however, that this order of factors differs considerably from their order of importance to children's mental health. For example, parental conflict is reviewed last, because fighting between parents obviously is not a mere consequence of divorce, yet parental conflict clearly is of considerable psychological significance to children.

Declining income and living standards

Increased costs and a loss of disposable income is one family change that clearly is a consequence of divorce. Although it is true that lower-income families are more likely to experience divorce, thus confounding selection and outcome (Emery, 1988), prospective, longitudinal research has documented that a family's standard of living declines as a result of divorce. This must be true simply because of economies of scale: it is less expensive to live in one household than in two.

The decline in living standards is most dramatic for women and children, 90% of whom reside primarily with their mothers following divorce (SCCYF, 1989). The average family income of women declines from $26,000 to $15,000 (in 1981 dollars) in the first year following divorce. On average, custodial mothers' postdivorce income represents 91% of predivorce family income relative to their family needs (Duncan & Hoffman, 1985). Even 5 years following divorce, single, divorced mothers have only 94% of their predivorce income relative to their current needs, while divorced mothers who remarry have 125%, and divorced fathers have 130%. In continuously married families, income relative to needs grows to 130% of its earlier level over a 5-year period (Duncan & Hoffman, 1985).

Economic distress, in turn, has been documented to necessitate other potentially difficult changes for families. A substantial percentage of women move into poverty as a result of divorce. In one national study it was found that 9.9% of white women and 33.4% of nonwhite women lived in poverty while married, but 28.7% of white women and 44.3% of nonwhite women moved into poverty following divorce (Nichols-Casebolt, 1986). Longitudinal research has demonstrated that many women move back to live with relatives (Rogers & Emery, 1992), work more hours (Duncan & Hoffman, 1985), or receive public assistance (SCCYF, 1989) in order to partially compensate for their lost incomes.

Although evidence indicates that income level or income loss explains only a small proportion of the adjustment difficulties found among children following divorce (Amato & Keith, 1991a; Rogers & Emery, 1992; Shaw & Emery, 1987), there are two reasons why these findings are not very reassuring. First, the possibility that poverty, residential changes, maternal employment, and welfare status may adversely affect children has generated enough concern that each topic constitutes an independent and active area of research in its own right. Since these factors often occur *together* as a result of divorce, continued research and social concern is easily justified. Second, even if income level or loss is only weakly related to the mental health of children, no one would disagree that it challenges children's resilience. There are numerous justifications for not wanting to rear children in poverty, even if poverty alone does not substantially increase the risk of their mental health problems following divorce.

Loss of contact with nonresidential parents

Other than income loss, perhaps the change in family life that has been most clearly documented to be a consequence, not a precursor, of divorce is children's loss of contact with their nonresidential parents. Data from a nationally representative sample of a recent cohort of divorces indicate that, on average, nonresidential parents see their children very infrequently. Seltzer (1991) used a probability sample of adults living in the United States in 1987–1988 to identify 717 families where children were living with their mothers and apart from their fathers because of divorce or separation. According to mothers' reports, she found that 18.2% of divorced fathers had not seen their children in the past year, and another 13.6% saw them only once or a few times in that year. Another 22.1% of fathers saw their children several times during the year, while 21.2% more saw them one to three times per month. Finally, only 12.4% of divorced or separated fathers saw their children weekly, while another 12.4% saw them several times per week.

This amount of contact was somewhat *higher* than that found in two other national surveys (Furstenberg, Peterson, Nord, & Zill, 1983; Seltzer & Bianchi, 1988), but the overall pattern is similar across studies. The *most* optimistic estimate indicates that following divorce approximately one-third of children see their fathers a couple of times a year or less, while only a quarter see them weekly or more.

Seltzer's (1991) data also revealed that contact between children and their fathers declines substantially as time passes after the marital separation. Decreased paternal involvement also was related to lower socioeconomic status, being nonblack rather than black, a greater distance between mothers' and fathers' residences, and the remarriage of either parent (Seltzer, 1991). Another important finding was that nonresidential fathers had considerably less contact with their children than nonresidential mothers. With the exception of inconsistent results for race, these factors also have been found to predict lower levels of contact in other national surveys (Furstenberg et al., 1983; Seltzer & Bianchi, 1988).

Changes in children's contact with their nonresidential parents are dramatic, and other evidence indicates that the quality of their relationships changes as well. In general, father–child relationships have been found to be less close and more indulgent in divorced than in married families (e.g., Hetherington, Cox, & Cox, 1976; Peterson & Zill, 1986). The importance of contact with nonresidential parents to children's mental health is a matter of empirical and political debate (Emery, 1988), but the present point is simpler. The change in children's contact with their nonresidential parents represents a clear and significant challenge that most children face as a result of divorce.

Relationships with residential parents

A substantial body of research suggests that not only are children's relationships with their nonresidential parents greatly changed by divorce, but their relationships with their residential parents also may become troubled. Evidence indicates that divorced, single parents face particular troubles with affection, parental authority, and completing household tasks. Relationships between residential parents and their children may become closer or more distant, stricter or laxer, and children may be given both more autonomy in their own lives and more responsibilities in the family (Emery, 1988).

Hetherington's (1989; Hetherington, Cox, & Cox, 1982) longitudinal study of mother custody families is the most detailed empirical investigation of single parenting after divorce. She found that divorced mothers made fewer maturity demands, communicated less well, and were less affectionate, more inconsistent, and less effective in controlling their children when compared with mothers who remained married. Mother–son relationships were especially troubled, as boys received less positive feedback and more negative sanctions than daughters. These studies also indicated that parenting difficulties increased during the first year following divorce, but 2 years after divorce, mothers were more nurturant, consistent, and in control of their children than they had been previously. Still, married mothers were found to perform more adequately in many areas of parenting. Six years after divorce, residential mothers generally were as affectionate as nondivorced mothers, but they continued to be more negative and less effective, especially in disciplining their sons. Finally, divorced mothers were found to give their children more responsibility at home, but also more independence in their own lives.

Similar findings have been reported in other investigations in which divorced, residential mothers have been found to be more negative, inconsistent, and less affectionate than married mothers (e.g., Hess & Camara, 1979; Hetherington, 1991; Wallerstein & Kelly, 1980). Caution must be raised about interpreting these findings as indicative of yet another challenge that children face as a result of divorce, however. In at least two studies in which parenting has been studied prospectively, less affectionate and more conflictual parent–child relationships were found to be present *before* the divorce (Block, Block, & Gjerde, 1988; Shaw, Emery, & Tuer, 1993). Thus, evidence on the parenting difficulties found among divorced, residential parents cannot be said to be solely a consequence of divorce.

Still, the changes over time reported by Hetherington and others strongly suggest a process of adaptation in the parenting of residential mothers. Moreover, numerous investigators have demonstrated the importance of fathers in supporting mothers' relationships with their children, especially their sons (e.g., Gjerde, 1986). Finally, the frequent reports about the strains of parenting alone that come from single mothers and single fathers should not be dismissed as unsubstantiated. Thus, we can conclude that, on average, children whose parents divorce encounter a residential parent who offers them less affection, more erratic discipline, and greater responsibility than they had previously received. Thus, children face changed and somewhat troubled relationships with both their residential and their nonresidential parents as a result of divorce, although some of these difficulties apparently predate the marital separation.

Parental mental health

Studies of adult mental health invariably find a link between marital status and psychopathology, such that married or remarried adults have fewer mental health problems than single or divorced adults. In fact, marital status has been found to be a better predictor of adult mental health than age, race, socioeconomic status, or childhood experience (e.g., Gove, Hughes, & Styles, 1983). Once again, however, the question arises as to whether the adult mental health problems are consequences of divorce, and therefore constitute a new stressor for children, or whether the parental problems predate and perhaps precipitate the divorce.

In reviewing evidence on marriage and adult mental health, Gotlib and McCabe (1990) concluded that research suggests both that preexisting psychological problems increase the risk for divorce, and that divorce increases the risk for psychological problems. They argue that evidence indicating that psychopathology causes divorce is strongest for severe emotional disorders such as schizophrenia and alcoholism, while less severe problems such as depression and anxiety appear to be at least partial consequences of divorce, especially among women. Although divorce may not be the cause of severe, prolonged mental health problems among adults, such a conclusion is consistent with the common, clinical view that divorce precipitates a period of grief among adults characterized by intense and vacillating fear, sadness, and anger (Emery, Shaw, & Jackson, 1987; Somary & Emery, 1991; Weiss, 1988).

Other evidence indicates that maternal depression explains significant variance in adolescents' psychological difficulties after divorce, even when the effects due to parenting are statistically controlled (Forehand, Thomas, Wierson, Brody, & Fauber, 1990). Although it is possible that preexisting parental psychological problems account both for divorce and for psychological difficulties among children (e.g., Lahey, Hartdagen, Frick, McBurnett, Connor, & Hynd, 1988), research and clinical observation suggest that yet another challenge that children face in divorce is increased depression, self-focus (Lee & Gotlib, 1989), and volatile moods in their parents.

Parental conflict

One source of distress that is supposed to be alleviated rather than exacerbated by divorce is the anger, tension, and conflict between parents. Some form of conflict obviously precedes divorce, but it is less clear whether a marital separation increases or decreases disputing between parents. It also is uncertain whether any change in conflict comes immediately after separation or is delayed for a period of time. Assessments of differences in conflict are difficult to make, because the topics and opportunities for fighting change once a couple separates. In one study, the *same* level of fighting in front of children was found in married families and in families where the parents had been separated for 6 months (Forehand et al., 1990). This suggests that any relief from conflict is not immediate. Moreover, evidence indicates that conflict significant enough to produce a dispute over child custody is found frequently after divorce, even if the number of actual custody hearings is small (Maccoby & Mnookin, 1992). Finally, recent evidence suggests that in the year following a custody dispute conflict escalates rather than diminishes (Emery, Mathews, & Kitzmann, in press).

Whether a divorce increases or decreases parental disputes is important, because interparental conflict is one of the most consistent correlates of the psychological health of children of divorce (Emery, 1982; Grych & Fincham, 1990). With respect to the stressors that children face as a result of divorce, two points about conflict stand out. First, parental conflict certainly does not end shortly after the marital separation, and in some cases, it continues in the form of custody disputes long after the legal divorce is final (Emery et al., in press; Kline, Johnston, & Tschann, 1991). Second, children may become an *increased* focus of their parents' conflict following a separation. This is likely because of the legal and practical issues that must be resolved, and because children are one of the few ties that give angry former spouses an opportunity for fighting (Emery, 1992).

Summary

Empirical evidence clearly supports the suggestion that the sources of distress that divorce precipitates for children are many and substantial. Family income relative to needs declines rather than grows, contact with one parent drops dramatically, relationships with the other parent become strained, parents become burdened with their own fears, sadness, and anger, and the fighting between parents continues and perhaps focuses more on the children. It is important to recognize that some of these disruptions begin before divorce, and many of them improve as time passes. Nevertheless, it is undeniable that divorce poses many challenges to children.

Children's successful coping with the challenges of divorce

The psychological consequences of divorce for children have been and continue to be debated. Some commentators suggest that children cope with divorce quite successfully, and others conclude that divorce causes severe and lasting emotional damage. As suggested earlier, this wide difference of opinion can be partially explained by the source of evidence used. Using the case study method, clinical investigators typically note more distress among children whose parents have divorced, as is discussed in the next section of this chapter. In this section, the focus is on empirical investigation and objective measurement. Empirical research clearly documents two important facts about the adjustment of children from divorced families. First, on various measures of their psychological functioning, they differ only to a small degree from children whose parents are married. Second, a substantial portion of the difficulties found among children after divorce actually begins long before a marital separation ever occurs. Thus, when combined with the evidence on the numerous stressors by divorce, the research literature attests to children's resilience.

*Psychological problems among children from married
or divorced families*

Numerous studies of varying methodological quality have compared the psychological functioning of children whose parents have divorced with that of children whose parents remain married. It is beyond the scope of this chapter to review this very large literature and the important influences of methodology on the findings that have been obtained. Qualitative reviews of this literature by the present authors have concluded that, on average, the differences between children from married and divorced families are statistically significant but small in magnitude (Atkeson, Forehand, & Rickard, 1982; Emery, 1982, 1988). In general, smaller differences are found when the methodology of the study is better, specifically when nonclinic rather than clinic samples are used, when objective measures of psychological health are employed, and when the person evaluating the children's mental health is unaware of the marital status of their parents (Emery, 1982).

These qualitative conclusions are strongly supported by a recent quantitative metaanalysis of 92 studies of divorce that involved over 13,000 children (Amato & Keith, 1991a). In this research, when all studies of children from married and divorced families were compared on all measures, an average effect size of only .14 standard deviation units was found to distinguish the two groups of children. Excluding parent–child relationship problems that are considered here to be stressors rather than outcomes (effect size = .19 for mother–child relationships, and .26 for father–child relationships), the reviewers found that the *largest* effect size for any area of psychological difficulty was .23 (for children's conduct problems). Statistically significant but consistently small effect sizes were found in comparing children from married and divorced families on all other measures of their psychological health, including indexes of their school achievement (.16), social functioning (.12), self-concept (.09), and general psychological adjustment (.08).

Based on the combination of qualitative and quantitative reviews together with some exemplary recent studies of large, nationally representative samples of children (e.g., Allison & Furstenberg, 1989), it is clear that the demonstrated differences in the average adjustment of children from married and divorced families are small in magnitude. This conclusion contains two important qualifications, however. Conclusions must be limited to demonstrated areas of measurement and to the average adjustment of children from divorced families. Greater differences might be found in areas of social or psychological health not yet measured (or not well measured) in empirical research conducted to date. Moreover, the fact that the average adjustment is similar among children from married and divorced families can obscure the likelihood that some children suffer considerably as a result of divorce. Still, other recent findings indicate that the effect sizes attributable to divorce are even smaller than indicated by existing cross-sectional studies, because many of the differences in children's psychological health were present before divorce.

Prospective studies of children and divorce

Nearly every study that has been conducted comparing children from divorced and married families has assessed children's psychological functioning after the divorce. Such research is valuable, but it is possible that the difficulties found among children after divorce actually began prior to divorce. If so, they obviously are not consequences of divorce. Rather, any difficulties found among children from divorced families may be consequences either of pathogenic family processes that began before the divorce, or of background factors that predispose young adults both to divorce and to have troubled children (Emery, 1988; Rutter, 1971).

The possibility that children's psychological difficulties begin before divorce was first addressed empirically in a small, but intensive longitudinal study of normal children and their families (Block, Block, & Gjerde, 1986). Children were studied throughout the course of their childhood in this study of normal development, but because many parents divorced after the study began, it became possible for the researchers to examine the adjustment of children both prior to and after divorce. In fact, analysis of the longitudinal data indicated that increased aggression was found among boys after divorce, but it began as many as 11 years prior to the marital separation (Block et al., 1986).

This tentative finding has been confirmed in an impressive, recent investigation of two large, nationally representative samples, one of 14,476 British children and the second of 2,279 American children (Cherlin et al., 1991). As in the Block et al. study, data were available on the behavior problems of children before and after divorce, thus allowing the investigators to compare children's adjustment following divorce with their adjustment prior to divorce. As expected, the investigators found that children whose parents were divorced had more behavior problems than children whose parents remained married. However, when various predivorce differences were statistically controlled, including demographics, family conflict, and children's preexisting behavior problems, the postdivorce differences were reduced to the point that they were no longer statistically reliable, even in these very large samples. Particularly large reductions were found for boys, who often have been found to have more problems than girls following divorce (Cherlin et al., 1991).

An independent analysis of the national sample of British children confirmed that problems found among children after divorce actually begin long before the marital separation (Elliott & Richards, 1991). In fact, *no* effects attributable to a parental divorce occurring between the ages of 7 and 16 were found on measures of children's "unhappy and worried" behavior or "disruptive" behavior. That is, statistically significant mean differences were found between the psychological adjustment of children whose parents were married and divorced at age 16, but the same differences were present at age 7 when all the children's parents were still married. Divorce was found to exacerbate predivorce differences on measures of children's reading and math achievement, however.

Thus, recent research suggests that many of the psychological troubles found among children after divorce actually begin before divorce occurs. To the extent that they do, these problems cannot be "consequences of divorce." This means that the already small effect sizes found in cross-sectional research need to be revised downward. The small differences in psychological adjustment found between children from married and divorced families are at least partially an effect either of predivorce family distress, or perhaps of genetic factors that are linked with both an increased rate of divorce and more behavior problems among children (Emery, 1988).

Summary

The literature comparing the psychological adjustment of children whose parents have divorced or remain married indicates that statistically significant differences are found between the groups, but the differences are small in magnitude. Moreover, prospective research on children's functioning before and after divorce indicates that these small differences are even smaller than they appear to be, because the differences in psychological functioning are present long before a marital separation ever occurs. These findings have many implications, but for present purposes, they lead us to a singular conclusion. Despite the many challenges that children face as a result of divorce, research on their psychological adjustment convincingly indicates that, for the most part, they cope quite successfully. Resilience, not risk, is what most clearly characterizes children whose parents divorce.

Children's underlying unhappiness despite successful coping

Clinical reports and some empirical findings suggest that children have unhappy thoughts, feelings, and memories about their parents' divorce despite their successful coping with its many challenges. Some of the most gripping suggestions that divorce has subtle, lingering, and painful effects come from the reports of clinical investigators who have interviewed children about their experiences in detail and over time. The controversial work of Judith Wallerstein is perhaps most notable in this respect (Wallerstein & Blakeslee, 1989). For example, she concluded, "Almost all children of divorce regard their childhood and adolescence as having taken place in the shadow of divorce" (p. 298).

Wallerstein's account of the consequences of divorce for children has been widely criticized as being unscientific (e.g., Forehand, 1992; Kelly & Emery, 1989), as have other clinical accounts of divorce and the method of clinical inquiry in general. Still, it is difficult to discount the poignant revelations uncovered in clinical work (including our own), portrayed in numerous films and novels, and revealed in conversations with students and friends. Empirical evidence clearly indicates that, on average, children from divorced families adapt quite successfully to their difficult circumstances, but the successful coping of many may be tinged by sadness, resentment, or longing.

In fact, a careful consideration of the empirical literature reveals some support for this assertion. For example, one study of 170 school-aged and preadolescent children, whose parents had been divorced for an average of 1.5 years, asked them to respond to a structured instrument on beliefs about divorce. Among the study's findings were 23% of children said they sometimes thought their parents would get back together; 30% said they sometimes feared both of their parents would want to live without them; and 52% said they would be upset if their friends asked a lot of questions about their parents (Kurdek & Berg, 1987). These are hardly signs of psychopathology, but they do indicate that many children feel continuing discomfort and unhappiness over their parents' divorce.

Other evidence of hidden distress comes from a study of a national sample of children. Half of all children surveyed listed their fathers as being members of their family (Furstenberg & Nord, 1985) despite the facts that (1) only 5% of their mothers did so, (2) less than 1 in 5 children saw their fathers weekly, (3) more than half of the children had not seen their fathers in a year (Furstenberg et al., 1983), and (4) the frequency of father–child contact was unrelated to indexes of the children's mental health (Furstenberg, Morgan, & Allison, 1987). As with other areas of assessment, these data suggest the importance of children's relationships with their fathers, even if they are not obvious on standardized psychological instruments.

Finally, some painful memories of parental divorce apparently continue on into adulthood. In one national survey, adults whose parents had divorced were more likely to report that childhood was the unhappiest time of their lives when compared with adults whose parents remained married (Kulka & Weingarten, 1979). More generally, research indicating a small but significant relation between psychological difficulties during adult life and parental marital status suggests that some of the children's unhappiness over their parents' divorce is carried forward in time (Amato & Keith, 1991b).

Summary

The point of this brief review is *not* to suggest that divorce creates hidden risks for children that must be uncovered. Rather, our conclusions are twofold. First, clinical concerns and some empirical evidence suggest sensitivity to the experience of individual children who are likely to find divorce painful despite their successful adaptation. Second, the emotional hurts that children apparently do overcome provide further testimony to their resilience. Most children whose parents divorce cope successfully despite the many life challenges they face and despite their own emotional upset. As noted at the beginning of this chapter, such successful coping despite interfering emotionality defines the concept of resilience (Garmezy, 1991). We turn now to consider some of the factors that predict risk or resilience among the children of divorce.

Factors predicting risk and resilience in children of divorce

The focus of most divorce research has not been on resilience, but rather on risk factors that are associated with poor functioning among children. That is, most investigators have confined their search to variables, such as intense interparental conflict, that exacerbate maladjustment following parental divorce. In contrast to this approach, resilience involves the search for protective factors that lead to successful adaptation (Masten, Best, & Garmezy, 1991).

One approach to the study of resilience is to assume that protective and risk factors represent opposite ends of the same continuum. Thus, if high parental conflict is a risk factor, then low conflict is assumed be a protective factor that promotes resilience. While this approach is common, it may not be the most accurate or helpful, because the mediating processes involved in risk and resilience may differ. For example, parental conflict may be a risk factor that creates emotional difficulties among children, whereas parental cooperation may be a protective factor that buffers children from other sources of distress in divorce. A neutral or disengaged relationship between parents thus may pose no risk, but it may simultaneously offer children no protection.

Another essential distinction is between factors that merely moderate risk (or resilience) and those that actually mediate it. Moderating variables simply are markers of an increased or decreased likelihood of psychological difficulties. Mediating variables suggest specific developmental or etiological mechanisms that explain how risk (or resilience) is translated into maladjustment (or successful coping). Although some of the factors considered here clearly are moderators (e.g., race) and others suggest mediation (e.g., parental conflict), evidence on the processes mediating the development of emotional difficulties among children from divorced families generally is weak.

Thus, despite the importance of distinguishing factors predicting risk and resilience and of separating moderators from mediators, research on children and divorce for the most part focuses on factors that moderate risk. Thus, our review of protective factors focuses primarily on the absence of risk factors with many suggestions but few conclusions about possible mediating processes.

Overview of risk and resilience factors

Although little research in the divorce literature has focused on the concept of resilience, a number of protective variables have been identified from other areas of study. These variables have been classified into three levels by Garmezy (1985, 1991): individual, familial, and extrafamilial support factors. Some of the variables identified as protective factors in these three categories are listed in Table 3.1. These variables were identified from reviews by Garmezy (1991), Gelman (1991), Luthar and Zigler (1991), Masten et al. (1991), and Rutter (1987).

In contrast to the presentation in Table 3.1, the focus in the divorce literature is well illustrated by examining Table 3.2, where factors related to a child's postdivorce functioning are delineated. As is evident, attention has been directed far more toward risk than protective factors, with the exception of the extrafamilial factors. This emphasis becomes clearer as these topics are reviewed according to Garmezy's outline in the following sections.

Individual factors

As delineated in Table 3.2, five individual factors have been associated with child or adolescent functioning following divorce. These

Table 3.1. *Three categories of protective factors identified in child resilience research*

Individual factors	Family factors	Extrafamilial support factors
Temperament (active, cuddly, good-natured)	Warm, supportive parents	Supportive network (e.g., grandparent, peers)
Gender (being female prior to adolescence & male during adolescence)	Good parent–child relations	Successful school experiences
Age (being younger)	Parental harmony	
IQ		
Self-efficacy		
Social skills		
Interpersonal awareness		
Feelings of empathy		
Internal locus of control		
Humor		
Attractiveness to others		

include children's gender, age, race, temperament, and attitudes or coping style.

Children's gender. With respect to gender, early research suggested that boys were more vulnerable to parental divorce than girls (Atkeson, Forehand, & Rickard, 1982; Emery, 1982). In particular, boys were found to have more difficulties in the area of externalizing problems. However, more recent research has begun to cast some doubt on the protective status of being a female. In a review of 27 studies of children and divorce, Zaslow (1988) found that, in 11 of the studies (40%), there were either no gender differences or girls actually fared worse than boys. In two recent metaanalyses, Amato and Keith (1991a, 1991b) found very few gender differences in the functioning of children or adults who had experienced parental divorce.

Some of the inconsistencies in research on the moderating influence

Tables 3.2. *Three categories of protective and risk factors identified in divorce research with children[a]*

Individual factors	Family factors	Extrafamilial support factors
Protective	*Protective* Supportive parent–child relation Siblings	*Protective* Contact with adult caretakers Support Group therapy
Risk Gender Age Race Temperament Attitudes/coping style	*Risk* Interparental conflict Noncustodial parent contact Parenting skills Economics	*Risk*

[a]Factors in each category are listed as protective factors or risk factors depending upon how they have been primarily examined in the literature.

of children's gender may be explained by the confound between sex of the child and sex of parent, as most children live with their mothers following divorce. Santrock and Warshak (1979) found that children living with their opposite-sex parent were less well adjusted than those living with the same-sex parent. Rather than indicating that living with the same-sex parent is a protective factor, however, this difference might reflect nonrandom selection of boys and girls into father custody (Emery, 1988). Still, it is important to consider both children's gender and the gender of the residential parent in further studies of risk and resilience.

Children's age. The role of age or developmental status of a child as a risk factor following parental divorce also has been examined; however, a clear pattern of findings does not emerge. Some research has suggested that young children adjust less well to parental divorce than older children, but other studies fail to support this conclusion (Hetherington, Stanley-Hagen, & Anderson, 1989). In fact, the recent metaanalysis by Amato and Keith (1991a) found that school-aged children fared worse than preschoolers.

Conclusions regarding age of the child as a buffer against parental divorce are difficult to reach, because children's age at divorce, the time that has passed since divorce, and children's current age are all theoretically important predictors of children's adjustment, but these three temporal variables are perfectly confounded (Emery, 1988). Based on existing research, perhaps the safest conclusion is that children of various ages do not cope better or worse with divorce, but they do cope differently because of varying cognitive abilities, developmental tasks, and access to extrafamilial support.

Children's race. Some racial differences have been noted in the adjustment of children from divorced families. Amato and Keith (1991b) concluded from their metaanalysis that, relative to adults who grew up in married families, whites from divorced families experienced divorce more often themselves and had lower educational attainment than blacks. If race does indeed moderate risk, it is likely due to sociocultural, not individual, characteristics, however. African-American communities may offer more support to single-parents through extended kinship networks, or, alternatively, their lower risk of divorce may be attributable to the multiple risks that African-Americans face from other sources. That is, divorce may pose less additive risk to blacks than to whites, because, on average, African-American children already face more stressors.

Children's temperament. In assessing children's temperament as a possible risk or protective factor in divorce, Tschann et al. (Tschann, Johnston, Kline, & Wallerstein, 1989) reported that a difficult temperament was associated with more problems in emotional adjustment following parental divorce, but it surprisingly also was associated with a better relationship with the father. These investigators suggested that fathers may try to protect temperamentally difficult children, because they view them as vulnerable. This suggests a possible mediating process wherein a child's temperament elicits different responses from the environment. It is important to note, however, that this finding should be viewed with caution as the magnitude of the relation was modest.

Hetherington (1989) reported an even more complex picture in regard to temperament and children's adjustment following divorce.

She found that temperamentally difficult children became less adaptable as stress increased, even under supportive conditions. In contrast, under supportive conditions temperamentally easy children developed more adaptive skills when exposed to moderate levels of stress (but not high or low levels). When supports were not available, both temperamentally easy and difficult children were less adaptable, although difficult children had more troubles. These findings suggest the complex situation wherein a difficult temperament is a risk factor, an easy temperament is a protective factor, but their effects interact with the level of stress and support that children encounter.

While conclusions are unclear, these initial studies of temperament suggest the importance of further study of the interaction between personality style and divorce. In further examination of temperament and divorce, researchers would do well to consider the possibility that the relation is accounted for by the third variable of parental personality. For example, antisocial parents may be more likely both to divorce and to have temperamentally difficult children (Lahey et al., 1988).

Children's coping styles. Some research suggests that children's beliefs and feelings about divorce may moderate or mediate its effect on them. Children have been found to have more difficulties when they blame themselves for their parents' divorce, or when they report having fears of abandonment (Kurdek & Berg, 1983, 1987). Of related interest, Armistead et al. (1990) found that poorer functioning among girls but not boys from divorced families was associated with the use of an avoidant coping style (i.e., they avoided dealing with divorce either cognitively or behaviorally). These potentially important findings call for more research, especially given the considerable concern among parents about how to tell children about divorce and how best to cope with their distress.

Summary. Existing evidence does not indicate that individual characteristics of children are strongly related to risk or resilience in coping with parental divorce. Children's gender appears to be less salient than originally proposed. Consistent age differences have not emerged, perhaps because of confounded temporal variables. Some racial differences have been found, but these suggest the importance of sociocultural factors rather than individual factors. Children's temperament and especially their coping style have only begun to emerge as areas of study, but clearly they deserve more attention.

In further research on individual factors, a focus on resilience would be of considerable value. For example, tentative evidence suggests that some maladaptive coping styles among children (avoidance, self-blame) may serve as risk factors. However, potentially adaptive means of coping with divorce, such as talking openly about feelings, have not been studied. Finally, research suggests that multiple factors may interact in producing risk and resilience; thus single variables cannot be fully understood in isolation.

Family factors

Considerably more attention has been devoted to family than to individual child factors that lead to risk or resilience in children's coping with divorce. This is not surprising, as various changes in family life occur as a result of marital dissolution, as reviewed earlier in this chapter. Six family factors that have been studied as predictors of children's adjustment are interparental conflict, parenting skills, contact with the nonresidential parents, a supportive relationship with at least one parent, sibling relationships, and family income.

Parental conflict. Parental conflict has been the focus of considerable research on children's postdivorce adjustment. The evidence overwhelmingly supports the contention that high levels of conflict between parents are linked with more psychological difficulties among children (Emery, 1982, 1988; Grych & Fincham, 1990; 1992; Long & Forehand, 1987). In fact, the recent metaanalysis by Amato and Keith (1991a) examined the empirical support for three theoretical perspectives used to account for the effects of divorce on children: parental loss, economic deprivation, and interparental conflict. Each perspective received some support, but the conflict hypothesis was most strongly supported. Parental conflict may even be more strongly related to children's adjustment than is divorce per se (e.g., Forehand, McCombs, Long, Brody, & Fauber, 1988).

Because of the strong evidence that conflict at least moderates risk, conceptual and empirical efforts have focused on possible mediational processes (Emery, 1982, 1988). Several mechanisms have been proposed to account for the relation between interparental conflict and postdivorce adjustment difficulties among children. Conflict has been conceptualized as a stressor that arouses negative affect in children and sensitizes them to further disputes (Cummings, 1987). Conflict has been proposed to disrupt parenting and, thereby, lead to children's behavior problems (Fauber, Forehand, Thomas, & Wierson, 1990). Parental conflict also has been suggested to lead to aggressive behavior among children by exposing them to inappropriate models of interpersonal relationships (Long & Forehand, 1987). Yet another hypothesis is that unsuccessful conflict resolution processes lead to the development of nonnormative family structures, especially a weakened parenting alliance and cross-generational alliances between children and parents (Emery, 1992). Finally, others have focused more on protection than risk, suggesting that parental cooperation is more important than conflict, as parents can protect their children if they coordinate their child-rearing efforts despite their own disagreements (Camara & Resnick, 1987, 1988).

The proposed mechanisms are not mutually exclusive, and some support has been gathered for each one. Still, evidence on mediation has not been clearly established (Grych & Fincham, 1992). What is clear, however, is the status of parental conflict as a consistent variable in moderating the risk of psychological problems among children whose parents are married or divorced.

Parenting skills. As has been noted, Hetherington's research (1989; Hetherington, Cox, & Cox, 1982) has provided convincing evidence that divorced mothers demonstrate poorer parenting skills than married mothers (e.g., fewer maturity demands, less affection, less consistency), and their children have more behavioral difficulties. This work is supported by three recent studies (Capaldi & Patterson, 1991; Fauber et al., 1990; Forehand et al., 1990) that found children in divorced homes functioned less well when poor parenting skills were manifested. The deficits examined in these studies included: (1) poor communication, problem solving, and monitoring; (2) rejection; and (3) little involvement with the child.

Not only does poor parenting appear to be a risk factor for children in divorced families, but it also may be a mediator between interparental conflict and children's behavior problems. For example,

Fauber et al. (1990) found that conflict between parents was associated with a rejecting style of parenting, which was related to both internalizing and externalizing problems in children. Thus, poor parenting does not stand alone as a risk factor for children. Rather, it is interrelated with other risk factors, and may qualify their influence.

Contact with nonresidential parents. Frequent contact between children and their nonresidential parent, typically the father, is commonly assumed to predict better adjustment following divorce. Some have found such a relation (Camara & Resnick, 1987; Hetherington et al., 1982; Wallerstein & Kelly, 1980), but somewhat surprisingly, no relation between the amount of contact with fathers and children's adjustment has been found in several studies (Furstenberg et al., 1987; Hodges, Buchsbaum, & Tierney, 1983; Thomas & Forehand, 1992). Some recent work suggests that frequent father contact is negative for boys but positive for girls in terms of behavior problems displayed (Healy, Malley, & Stewart, 1990). Other evidence suggests that contact can be beneficial or harmful depending upon other circumstances (Hetherington et al., 1982), especially the relationship between parents.

Research on the related, and still controversial, topic of joint physical custody, is relevant to the literature on father contact. Although space does not permit this growing literature to be reviewed here, it should be noted that recent evidence suggests that joint physical custody may be both the best and the worst arrangement for children following divorce. Compared with children living in other custody arrangements, joint physical custody children were found to be the best adjusted when their parents were either cooperative or disengaged (no conflict but little cooperation), whereas they were the worst adjusted when their parents continued to be in conflict (Maccoby & Mnookin, 1992).

A supportive relationship with at least one parent. A supportive relationship between children and at least one of their parents also has received considerable attention as a predictor of children's adjustment following divorce. In areas other than divorce, considerable research on resilience has found that a trusting relationship between a child and an adult, typically but not necessarily a parent, is an extremely important protective factor (Gelman, 1991). Similarly, a good parent–child relationship has been found to be an important buffering factor for children experiencing parental divorce (Camara & Resnick, 1987, 1988; Forehand, Middleton, & Long, 1987; Hess & Camara, 1979; Hetherington et al., 1982; Jenkins & Smith, 1990; Peterson & Zill, 1986; Wierson, Forehand, Fauber, & McCombs, 1989). Interestingly, a good relationship with one parent appears to buffer children from a bad relationship with the other parent, suggesting a process of resilience. Risk processes are suggested by evidence that poor relationships with both parents are linked with particularly poor child functioning (Forehand et al., 1987; Hess & Camara, 1979; Peterson & Zill, 1986).

Several hypotheses have been offered on how a warm, supportive relationship with one parent may mediate resilience. Perhaps the two major alternatives are that it helps children feel secure, and that it facilitates parents' appropriate discipline (Wierson & Forehand, 1992). At present, specific mechanisms by which a warm parent–child relationship protects children remain a matter of speculation, however.

Sibling relationships. Recent evidence from two studies suggests that the presence of siblings also may help to protect children from the stress of divorce. In a sample of 79 children from married families and 77 from divorced families, Kempton et al. (Kempton, Armistead, Wierson, & Forehand, 1991) found an interaction between marital status and number of siblings. Children from divorced families who had no siblings demonstrated more externalizing problems than children from divorced families with siblings or from married families with or without siblings. The suggestion that siblings provide support to one another as they cope with similar struggles also is supported by evidence that perceived sibling support is related to more positive attitudes and perceptions about the outcome of divorce (Cowen, Pedro-Carroll, & Alpert-Gillis, 1990). In particular, these investigators found that sibling support was related to realistic views about the children's role in the divorce and their ability to reunite their parents. Thus, although the data are limited at this time, there is some initial support suggesting that siblings may be important in promoting resilience (Jenkins & Smith, 1990).

Family economics. The economic conditions of the family have been postulated to play a role in a child's postdivorce adjustment. Several studies have found a relation between economic resources and adjustment of children following parental divorce (e.g., Shaw & Emery, 1987). However, Amato and Keith (1991a) stress that, in the studies conducted thus far, economic disadvantage appears to account for only a small amount of variance in children's functioning after divorce. In support of this conclusion, Rogers and Emery (1992) recently found only weak relations between measures of children's psychological health and predivorce or postdivorce family income relative to needs. Similarly weak associations also were found for income change from before to after divorce.

As noted earlier, income loss following divorce is not simply a matter of having fewer financial resources, but it also can lead to a number of potential changes in a child's life. These include moving, changing schools, losing contact with friends, spending more time in child care, and dealing with parents' preoccupation with financial issues. In further research, it is important to study the potential influence of such changes, as well as of total family income relative to family needs.

Summary. Relative to individual characteristics of a child, there has been substantial attention to family factors that may exacerbate or buffer a child's response to parental divorce. In particular, a substantial and convincing literature has developed around the topic of interparental conflict and, to somewhat of a lesser extent, parent–child relationships. However, as was noted with the literature regarding child characteristics, the focus has been on risk, not protective factors, with the exception of the roles of supportive parent–child and sibling relationships.

Extrafamilial factors

In contrast to factors within the family, little attention has been directed to factors outside the home that may buffer or exacerbate a child's response to parental divorce. The extrafamilial resources that have received at least some attention include grandparents, other relatives, day-care personnel and teachers, and friends. Santrock and

Warshak (1979) found that the amount of contact with adult caretakers outside the family (the noncustodial parent, babysitters, relatives, day-care personnel) was positively related to a child's functioning following parental divorce. Based on several studies, the quality of the contact would appear to be particularly important (Jenkins & Smith, 1990). In work by Hetherington et al. (1979) and Kelly and Wallerstein (1977), the attention and warmth shown by teachers was associated with positive child adjustment following divorce. More recently, Cowen et al. (1990) found that the degree of social support from adults outside the family and from childhood friends was related to a child's adjustment following divorce.

Another extrafamilial area that has received some attention is group child-centered intervention. As Grych and Fincham (1992) note, these programs, which are typically based in schools, are designed to alleviate misconceptions, negative feelings, and practical problems experienced by children after divorce. Components of such interventions include support, providing information, discussion of feelings, and social skills training. Although a number of such programs exist and are utilized in various school systems, Grych and Fincham (1992) conclude that only the Children of Divorce Intervention Project has been demonstrated to be effective. This program, developed by Pedro-Carroll and her colleagues, has been systematically compared with appropriate control groups and has demonstrated positive changes in children (e.g., Alpert-Gillis, Pedro-Carroll, & Cowen, 1989; Pedro-Carroll & Cowen, 1985). Among the demonstrated benefits are decreased anxiety, increased assertiveness, and increased positive feelings about their families, themselves, and their parents.

Research is emerging to suggest that factors outside the family may be important in promoting resilience to divorce. Few studies exist at this time, but those that have been conducted indicate that contact, support, and group therapy may serve as protective factors that promote resilience and clearly merit further research.

Summary

Research on children's functioning after a parental divorce identifies many factors associated with risk, but little research on factors related to resilience. Conclusions reached earlier suggest that this is a problematic emphasis. Divorce leads to an increase in many sources of distress for children, and these same sources of distress have been found to be risk factors that are related to increased psychological difficulties. Given these observations, one would expect children whose parents divorce to have substantial mental health problems. Research on children's adjustment following divorce indicates that this is not the case, however. Thus, we must conclude that researchers, including ourselves, have erred in overlooking moderating variables and mediational processes that lead to resilience. In the concluding section of this chapter, we examine some directions that future research might take in attempting to identify protective factors related to children's resilience.

Future research on resilience and children of divorce

Garmezy (1985) has identified three stages in the search for understanding resilience. Stage 1 is the identification of children at risk who have good coping abilities. Stage 2 involves the search for individual, familial, and extrafamilial correlates of these abilities, while stage 3 consists of the identification of the mediating processes underlying resiliency.

Clearly, the divorce literature has not followed these stages of investigation. The primary foci have been establishing the extent to which divorce is a risk factor for children and identifying additional factors associated with greater or lesser risk. Yet it can now be recognized that the majority of children successfully cope with divorce, despite the many challenges posed by their own emotions and by their life circumstances. One could argue, in fact, that the entire field is at stage 1 of Garmezy's model, and the major task for the future is to move into stages 2 and 3. With this recognition, perhaps researchers will begin to investigate the individual, familial, and extrafamilial protective factors that must characterize children whose parents divorce. This obviously will require a conceptual shift in how divorce research is conducted.

We reiterate three points raised earlier when considering future research on children's resilience in the face of a parental divorce. First, the absence of risk is not the same thing as the presence of protection. Constructs need to be carefully considered in the search for protective processes. Second, moderator variables suggest the presence of, but do not identify the nature of, mediating variables or developmental processes. Epidemiological research is valuable in identifying moderator variables, but intensive longitudinal research is needed to uncover mediation. Third, it is likely that multiple factors operate in combination to produce risk or resilience. Let us consider the examples of temperament and the coparental relationship to illustrate these three points.

The point that resilience is not necessarily the opposite of risk is not merely a matter of semantics. A difficult temperament may interact with divorce to increase the risk for psychological difficulties multiplicatively, an easy temperament may interact with divorce to protect children from any increased risk, or both temperamental styles may operate independently as risk and protective factors. Similarly, parental conflict may increase the risk for children's psychological difficulties, parental cooperation may protect children from risks posed from other sources, or both factors may operate independently.

The different models of risk and resilience suggest different approaches to measurement and statistical analysis in empirical research, as well as different approaches to clinical practice. Do temperamentally difficult children require special interventions to counteract risk, or do temperamentally easy children require little or no intervention because they are protected against risk? Is the appropriate treatment (and policy) goal to find ways to help divorced parents to cooperate with each other? Is the goal more modest, to help them to avoid fighting by encouraging little contact? Or is the appropriate goal a dual one of always discouraging conflict, but also encouraging cooperation when conflict is contained?

The second point is that moderating variables do not necessarily identify mediation. Moderator variables simply are markers of underlying processes, processes that may, in fact, be partially obscured by the nature of the moderator variable. Since understanding developmental processes is the ultimate goal, this means that it is essential to consider alternative models in the search for children's resilience. A difficult temperament may moderate the risk of psychological difficulties among children whose parents divorce, but it may not mediate risk. For example, temperamentally difficult children may have more problems after divorce, but this might reflect the mediational process wherein antisocial parents are more likely to divorce, to have children with difficult temperaments, and to exacerbate both problems with their continuing antisocial behavior. Similarly, parental conflict may not have a direct effect on children's psychological well-being, but instead it may be a marker of other mediating processes such as troubled parent–child relationships. Such suggestions imply that mediational processes will ultimately be identified only through research that is driven by theory, not just blind empiricism.

Finally, the search for protective factors and resilient development is complicated further by the likelihood that single variables do not operate in isolation. For example, an easy temperament may operate as a protective factor only when children also have adequate support, or children's contact with both of their parents may have a protective effect only when the coparental relationship is not highly conflicted. Once again, such complications suggest the importance of research that is driven by theory.

The task presented by the search for resilient processes is a huge one, but it is one that researchers who study children and divorce can no longer ignore. Empirical evidence indicates that: (1) children face numerous and potent stressors as a result of divorce; (2) many of these stressors are associated with an increased risk for psychological problems; (3) children themselves report that they feel distress, if not disturbance, as a result of their parents' divorce; and (4) yet the weight of the evidence indicates that, on average, children function competently after divorce. Risk research on children and divorce has become very sophisticated in the past decade. Indeed, the concerns with measurement, sampling, and development over time are exemplary, and serve as a model for psychosocial research on other difficult life events that children encounter. It is our hope that the next decade of research on divorce will set a similarly high standard for the study of resilience among children who face adversity.

References

Allison, P. D., & Furstenberg, F. F. (1989). How marital dissolution affects children: Variations by age and sex. *Developmental Psychology, 25,* 540–549.

Alpert-Gillis, L. J., Pedro-Carroll, J. L., & Cowen, E. L. (1989). The children of divorce intervention program: Development, implementation, and evaluation of a program for young urban children. *Journal of Consulting and Clinical Psychology, 57,* 583–589.

Amato, P. R., & Keith, B. (1991a). Parental divorce and the well-being of children: A meta-analysis. *Psychological Bulletin, 110,* 26–46.

Amato, P. R., & Keith, B. (1991b). Parental divorce and adult well-being: A meta-analysis. *Journal of Marriage and the Family, 53,* 43–58.

Armistead, L., McCombs, A., Forehand, R., Wierson, M., Long, N., & Fauber, R. (1990). Coping with divorce: A study of young adolescents. *Journal of Clinical Child Psychology, 19,* 79–84.

Atkeson, B. M., Forehand, R. L., & Rickard, K. M. (1982). The effects of divorce on children. In B. B. Lahey & A. E. Kazdin (Eds.), *Advances in clinical child psychology* (Vol. 5, pp. 255–281). New York: Plenum.

Block, J. H., Block, J., & Gjerde, P. F. (1986). The personality of children prior to divorce: A prospective study. *Child Development, 57,* 827–840.

Block, J. H., Block, J., & Gjerde, P. F. (1988). Parental functioning and the home environment in families of divorce: Prospective and concurrent analyses. *Journal of the American Academy of Child and Adolescent Psychiatry, 27,* 207–213.

Bumpass, L., (1984). Children and marital disruption: A replication and update. *Demography, 21,* 71–82.

Camara, K. A., & Resnick, G. (1987). Marital and parental subsystems in mother-custody, father-custody and two-parent households: Effects on children's social development. In J. Vincent (Ed.), *Advances in family assessment, intervention and research* (Vol. 4, pp. 165–196). Greenwich, CT: JAI.

Camara, K. A., & Resnick, G. (1988). Interparental conflict and cooperation: Factors moderating children's post-divorce adjustment. In E. M. Hetherington & J. Arasteh (Eds.), *Divorced, single-parent, and stepparent families* (pp. 169–195). Englewood Cliffs, NJ: LEA.

Capaldi, D. M., & Patterson, G. R. (1991). Relation of parental transitions to boys' adjustment problems: I. A linear hypothesis. II. Mothers at risk for transitions and unskilled parenting. *Developmental Psychology, 3,* 489–504.

Cherlin, A. J., Furstenberg, F. F., Chase-Lansdale, P. L., Kiernan, K. E., Robins, P. K., Morrison, D. R., & Teitler, J. O. (1991). Longitudinal studies of effects of divorce on children in Great Britain and the United States. *Science, 252,* 1386–1389.

Cowen, E. L., Pedro-Carroll, J. L., & Alpert-Gillis, L. J. (1990). Relationship between support and adjustment among children of divorce. *Journal of Child Psychology and Psychiatry, 31,* 727–735.

Cumming, E. M. (1987). Coping with background anger in early childhood. *Child Development, 58,* 976–984.

Duncan, G. J., & Hoffman, S. D. (1985). Economic consequences of marital instability. In M. David & T. Smeeding (Eds.), *Horizontal equity, uncertainty and well-being* (pp. 427–469). Chicago: University of Chicago Press.

Elliott, B. J., & Richards, M. P. M. (1991). Children and divorce: Educational performance and behaviour before and after parental separation. *International Journal of Law and the Family, 5,* 258–276.

Emery, R. E. (1982). Interparental conflict and the children of discord and divorce. *Psychological Bulletin, 92,* 310–330.

Emery, R. E. (1988). *Marriage, divorce, and children's adjustment.* Newbury Park, CA: Sage.

Emery, R. E. (1992). Family conflict and its developmental implications: A conceptual analysis of deep meanings and systemic processes. In C. U. Shantz & W. W. Hartup (Eds.), *Conflict in child and adolescent development* (pp. 270–298). Cambridge: Cambridge University Press.

Emery, R. E., Mathews, S. G., & Kitzmann, K. M. (in press). Child custody mediation and litigation: Parents' satisfaction and functioning a year after settlement. *Journal of Consulting and Clinical Psychology.*

Emery, R. E., Shaw, D. S., & Jackson, J. A. (1987). A clinical description of a model for the co-mediation of child custody disputes. In J. Vincent (Ed.), *Advances in family intervention, assessment, and theory* (Vol. 4, pp. 309–333). Greenwich, CT: JAI.

Fauber, R., Forehand, R., Thomas, A. M., & Wierson, M. (1990). A mediational model of the impact of marital conflict on adolescent adjustment in intact and divorced families: The role of disruptive parenting. *Child Development, 61,* 1112–1123.

Forehand, R. (1992). Parental divorce and adolescent maladjustment: Scientific inquiry versus public information. *Behavioral Research and Therapy, 30,* 319–327.

Forehand, R., McCombs, A., Long, N., Brody, G., & Fauber, R. (1988). Early adolescent adjustment to recent parental divorce: The role of interparental conflict and adolescent sex as mediating variables. *Journal of Consulting and Clinical Psychology, 56,* 624–627.

Forehand, R., Middleton, K., & Long, N. (1987). Adolescent functioning as a consequence of recent parental divorce and the parent–adolescent relationship. *Journal of Applied Developmental Psychology, 3,* 305–315.

Forehand, R., Thomas, A. M., Wierson, M., Brody, G., & Fauber, R. (1990). Role of maternal functioning and parenting skills in adolescent functioning following parental divorce. *Journal of Abnormal Psychology, 99,* 278–283.

Furstenberg, F. F., Morgan, S. P., & Allison, P. D. (1987). Paternal participation and children's well-being after marital dissolution. *American Sociological Review, 52,* 695–701.

Furstenberg, F. F., & Nord, C. W. (1985). Parenting apart: Patterns of childrearing after marital disruption. *Journal of Marriage and the Family, 47,* 893–904.

Furstenberg, F. F., Peterson, J. L., Nord, C. W., & Zill, N., (1983). The life course of children of divorce: Marital disruption and parental contact. *American Sociological Review, 48,* 656–668.

Garmezy, N. (1985). Stress-resistant children: The search for protective factors. In J. E. Stevenson (Ed.), *Recent research in developmental psychopathology. Journal of Child Psychology and Psychiatry* (Book Supplement No. 4). Oxford: Pergamon Press.

Garmezy, N. (1991). Resilience in children's adaptation to negative life events and stressed environments. *Pediatric Annals, 20,* 459–466.

Gelman, D. (1991). The miracle of resiliency. *Newsweek, 117* (26), pp. 44–47.

Gjerde, P. F. (1986). The interpersonal structure of family interaction settings: Parent-adolescent relations in dyads and triads. *Developmental Psychology, 22,* 297–304.

Gotlib, I. H., & McCabe, S. B. (1990). Marriage and psychopathology. In F. Fincham & T. Bradbury (Eds.), *The psychology of marriage* (pp. 226–257). New York: Guilford.

Gove, W. R., Hughes, M., & Styles, C. B. (1983). Does marriage have positive effects on the psychological well-being of the individual? *Journal of Health and Social Behavior, 24,* 122–132.

Grych, J. H., & Fincham, F. D. (1990). Marital conflict and children's adjustment: A cognitive-contextual framework. *Psychological Bulletin, 108,* 267–290.

Grych, J. H., & Fincham, F. D. (1992). Interventions for children of divorce: Towards greater integration of research and action. *Psychological Bulletin, 111,* 434–454.

Healy, J. M., Jr., Malley, J. E., Stewart, A. J. (1990). Children and their fathers after parental separation. *American Journal of Orthopsychiatry, 60,* 531–543.

Hess, R. D., & Camara, K. A. (1979). Post-divorce relationships as mediating factors in the consequences of divorce for children. *Journal of Social Issues, 35,* 79–96.

Hetherington, E. M. (1989). Coping with family transitions: Winners, losers, and survivors. *Child Development, 60,* 1–14.

Hetherington, E. M. (1991). Presidential address: Families, lies, and video-tapes. *Journal of Research on Adolescence, 1,* 323–348.

Hetherington, E. M., Cox, M., & Cox, R. (1976). Divorced fathers. *Family Coordinator, 25,* 417–428.

Hetherington, E. M., Cox, M., & Cox, R. (1979). Play and social interaction in children following divorce. *Journal of Social Issues, 35,* 26–49.

Hetherington, E. M., Cox, M., & Cox, R., (1982). Effects of divorce on parents and children. In M. Lamb (Ed.), *Nontraditional families* (pp. 233–288). Hillsdale, NJ: Erlbaum.

Hetherington, E. M., Stanley-Hagan, M., & Anderson, E. R. (1989). Marital transitions: A child's perspective. *American Psychologist, 44,* 303–312.

Hodges, W. F., Buchsbaum, H. K., & Tierney, C. W. (1983). Parent–child relationships and adjustment in preschool children in divorced and intact families. *Journal of Divorce, 1,* 43–58.

Jenkins, J. M., & Smith, M. A. (1990). Factors protecting children living in disharmonious homes. *Journal of the American Academy of Child and Adolescent Psychiatry, 29,* 60–69.

Kelly, J., & Emery, R. E. (1989). Review of J. S. Wallerstein & S. Blakeslee, "Second chances: Men, women, and children a decade after divorce." *Family and Conciliation Courts Review, 27,* 81–83.

Kelly, J. B., & Wallerstein, J. S. (1977). Brief interventions with children in divorcing families. *American Journal of Orthopsychiatry, 47,* 23–39.

Kempton, T., Armistead, L., Wierson, M., & Forehand, R. (1991). Presence of a sibling as a potential buffer following parent divorce: An examination of young adolescents. *Journal of Clinical Child Psychology, 20,* 434–438.

Kline, M., Johnston, J. R., & Tschann, J. M. (1991). The long shadow of marital conflict: A model of children's postdivorce adjustment. *Journal of Marriage and the Family, 53,* 297–309.

Kulka, R. A., & Weingarten, H. (1979). The long-term effects of parental divorce in childhood on adult adjustment. *Journal of Social Issues, 35,* 50–78.

Kurdek, L. A., & Berg, B. (1983). Correlates of children's adjustment to their parents' divorces. In L. A. Kurdek (Ed.), *New directions in child development: Vol. 19. Children and divorce* (pp. 47–60). San Francisco: Jossey-Bass.

Kurdek, L. A., & Berg, B. (1987). Children's beliefs about parental divorce scale: Psychometric characteristics and concurrent validity. *Journal of Consulting and Clinical Psychology, 55,* 712–718.

Lahey, B. B., Hartdagen, S. E., Frick, P. J., McBurnett, K., Connor, R., &

Hynd, G. W. (1988). Conduct disorder: Parsing the confounded relation to parental divorce and antisocial personality. *Journal of Abnormal Psychology, 97,* 334–337.

Lee, C. M., & Gotlib, I. H. (1989). Maternal depression and child adjustment: A longitudinal analysis. *Journal of Abnormal Psychology, 98,* 78–85.

Long, N., & Forehand, R. (1987). The effects of parental divorce and parental conflict on children: An overview. *Developmental and Behavioral Pediatrics, 8,* 292–296.

Luthar, S. F., & Zigler, E. (1991). Vulnerability and competence: A review of research on resilience in childhood. *American Journal of Orthopsychiatry, 61,* 6–22.

Maccoby, E. E., & Mnookin, R. H. (1992). *Dividing the child.* Cambridge, MA: Harvard University Press.

Masten, A. S., Best, K. M., & Garmezy, N. (1991). Resilience and development: Contributions from the study of children who overcome adversity. *Development and Psychopathology, 2,* 425–444.

Nichols-Casebolt, A., (1986). The economic impact of child support reform on the poverty status of custodial and noncustodial families. *Journal of Marriage and the Family, 48,* 875–880.

Pedro-Carroll, J. L., & Cowen, E. L. (1985). The children of divorce intervention program: An investigation of the efficacy of a school-based prevention program. *Journal of Consulting and Clinical Psychology, 53,* 603–611.

Peterson, J. L., & Zill, N. (1986). Marital disruption, parent–child relationships, and behavior problems in children. *Journal of Marriage and the Family, 48,* 295–307.

Rogers, K. C., & Emery, R. E. (1992). Economic consequences of divorce and children's adjustment. Unpublished manuscript, University of Virginia, Department of Psychology.

Rutter, M. (1971). Parent–child separation: Psychological effects on the children. *Journal of Child Psychology and Psychiatry, 12,* 233–260.

Rutter, M. (1987). Psychosocial resilience and protective mechanisms. *American Journal of Orthopsychiatry, 57,* 316–331.

Santrock, J. W., & Warshak, R. A. (1979). Father custody and social development in boys and girls, *Journal of Social Issues, 35,* 112–125.

Select Committee on Children, Youth, and Families (SCCYF) of the United States House of Representatives (1989). *U.S. children and their families: Current conditions and recent trends.* Washington, DC: Government Printing Office.

Seltzer, J. A. (1991). Relationships between fathers and children who live apart: The father's role after separation. *Journal of Marriage and the Family, 53,* 79–101.

Seltzer, J. A., & Bianchi, S. M. (1988). Children's contact with absent parents. *Journal of Marriage and the Family, 50,* 663–677.

Shaw, D. S., & Emery, R. E. (1987). Parental conflict and the adjustment of school age children whose parents have separated. *Journal of Abnormal Child Psychology, 15,* 269–281.

Shaw, D. S., Emery, R. E., & Tuer, M. D. (1993). Parental functioning and children's adjustment in families of divorce: A prospective study. *Journal of Abnormal Child Psychology, 21,* 119–134.

Somary, K., & Emery, R. E. (1991). Emotional anger and grief in divorce mediation. *Mediation Quarterly, 8,* 185–198.

Thomas, A. M., & Forehand, R. (1992). The role of paternal variables in divorced and married families: Prediction of teacher-report of adolescent internalizing and externalizing problems. *American Journal of Orthopsychiatry, 62.*

Tschann, J. M., Johnston, J. R., Kline, M., & Wallerstein, J. S. (1989). Family process and children's functioning during divorce. *Journal of Marriage and the Family, 51,* 431–444.

Wallerstein, J. S., & Blakeslee, S. (1989). *Second chances: Men, women, and children a decade after divorce.* New York: Ticknor & Fields.

Wallerstein, J. S., & Kelly, J. B., (1980). *Surviving the breakup: How children actually cope with divorce.* New York: Basic.

Weiss, R. S. (1988). Loss and recovery. *Journal of Social Issues, 44,* 37–52.

Wierson, M., & Forehand, R. (1992). Family stressors and deficits in adolescent functioning: A consideration of models for early versus middle adolescence. *Behavior Therapy, 23,* pp. 681–688.

Wierson, M., Forehand, R., Fauber, R., & McCombs, A. (1989). Buffering young male adolescents against negative parental divorce influences: The role of good parent–adolescent relations. *Child Study Journal, 19,* 101–116.

Zaslow, M. J. (1988). Sex differences in children's response to parental divorce: 1. Research methodology and postdivorce family forms. *American Journal of Orthopsychiatry, 58,* 355–378.

4

Mechanisms and processes of adolescent bereavement

David C. Clark, Robert S. Pynoos, M.D., and Ann E. Goebel

Bereavement and parent loss are inevitable human conditions. Small children are curious about death and frequently encounter small instances: a captured firefly or grasshopper that died in a glass jar, the death of a family pet, or the death of an uncle, aunt, or grandparent. At some point in adult life, most persons experience the death of one or both parents. So it is important to preserve the sense that bereavement following the death of loved ones is not the theoretically avoidable stressor that a parental divorce may represent, the theoretically avoidable illness state that a depressive episode may represent, or the theoretically avoidable tragedy that a natural catastrophe or war may represent. Parent loss by death should be understood as an expectable life event that occurs earlier in life (i.e., in childhood or adolescence) for some. The chief psychological and psychosocial problems that bereavement poses for adolescents have to do with the extent of their capacity to accept the tragedy of such a significant loss, their capacity to tolerate the anguish that ordinarily accompanies mourning, and their developmental need for the deceased parent in order to complete the goals of healthy maturation.

Because *parent* loss during adolescence may be the most difficult example of adolescent bereavement to consider, because prevalence rates for parent loss can be estimated more reliably than rates for other categories of adolescent bereavement, and because clinical re-

David C. Clark is Professor of Psychiatry and Psychology at Rush Medical College in Chicago; Robert S. Pynoos is Associate Professor at the Neuropsychiatric Institute of University of California at Los Angeles; and Ann E. Goebel is a graduate student at Boston University.

search has focused more intensively on the loss of a parent than of other significant others, we will focus on parent loss during adolescence as the most useful example for purposes of this paper.

What constitutes *resiliency* in the face of parental death during adolescence? In our review of the experience of parent loss in adolescence, we will anchor our conception of *resilience* in the definition provided by Masten and colleagues:

Resilience refers to the process of, capacity for, or outcome of successful adaptation despite challenging or threatening circumstances. Psychological resilience is concerned with behavioral adaptation, usually defined in terms of internal states of well-being or effective functioning in the environment or both. (Masten, Best, & Garmezy, 1990, p. 426)

Grief, mourning, and bereavement

Mental health professionals and lay people alike tend to use the terms bereavement, grief, and mourning interchangeably. The terms are used with a similar lack of consistency throughout the professional literature.

We advocate the adoption of definitions recommended by a National Academy of Science work group in a recent monograph summarizing current knowledge on the topic of bereavement (Osterweiss, Solomon, & Greene, 1984). Consensual definitions facilitate clinical discussion and research communication. *Grief* refers to the dysphoric feeling or affective response to the death of a loved one. *Mourning* describes the internal process of adaptation to death that culminates in an appropriate or maladaptive adjustment. Mourning also includes social rituals and other social expressions of grief. *Bereavement* is an umbrella term encompassing both the feelings of grief and the process of mourning – it represents the social process of coping with an emotional response to death.

Epidemiology of loss by death in childhood and adolescence

There are 65 million children younger than 18 years old in the United States. Census Bureau data show that 72% live with both biological parents, 26% live with one of their biological parents, and 2.8% live

Table 4.1. *Living arrangements of U.S. children under age 18 in 1991*

At home	Number in millions	Percent youth population
Both biological parents	46.7	71.7
Biological mother only	14.6	22.4
Biological father only	2.0	3.1
Other relatives	1.4	2.2
Nonrelatives only	0.4	0.6

Source: U.S. Bureau of the Census, Current Population Reports. (1992). *Marital status and living arrangements: March 1991* (Series P-20, No. 461). Washington, DC: U.S. Government Printing Office.

with neither biological parent in a foster care or group home, or with adoptive parents, grandparents, or other relatives (Table 4.1). One million eight hundred thousand children live with adopted parents, relatives, or in foster care (U.S. Bureau of the Census, 1992).

The proportion of children who have experienced the death of one or both parents is estimated to be 3.4%, amounting to 2,213,000 children (Table 4.2). Of children who have lost a parent by death, 73% lost a father, 25% lost a mother, and 1.2% lost both parents (U.S. Bureau of the Census, 1990).

Of children living with a widowed parent in a single-parent household, the great majority live with their mothers – 780,000 live with a widowed mother as compared with 110,000 living with a widowed father (Table 4.3). Thus 1.4% of the youth population – about 890,000 children, or 40% of all orphaned children – live with a widowed parent in a single-parent household (U.S. Bureau of the Census, 1992). Of the latter, approximately 55% are 12 to 17 years old (U.S. Bureau of the Census, 1989).

We are not aware of national prevalence data describing the sex, age, or race/ethnicity patterns for children who have lost a parent by death. Nor are we aware of reliable information about the numbers of children who have experienced the death of one or more siblings – an experience also capable of leaving a profound lifelong impact.

Because there are no reliable national data describing the age distribution of children affected by parent loss, we cannot estimate the pro-

Table 4.2. *Number of orphans in the United States including Puerto Rico and Virgin Islands in 1988 (and percent of youth population)*

Total	Father died	Mother died	Both died
2,213,000 (3.4%)	1,625,000 (2.5%)	561,000 (0.9%)	27,000 (0.04%)

Source: U.S. Bureau of the Census (1990). *Statistical abstracts of the U.S., 1990* (110th ed.). Washington, DC: U.S. Government Printing Office.

portion of child to adolescent cases. Are children aged 6, 9, 12, 15, and 18 years equally likely to experience the death of a parent in a given year?

There are indirect ways to characterize some of the qualities of parent loss in adolescence. If we assume that the parents of most teenagers fall between the ages of 35 and 54 years, national mortality data for adults in these age groups illuminate aspects of the experience (Table 4.4) (World Health Organization, 1991). More than 99% of all deaths in these adult age groups can be sorted into two general classes – the end result of a chronic illness or a sudden, relatively unanticipated event. For men and women in the age range of most parents of teenagers, 80% to 90% of all deaths are due to natural causes, and deaths attributable to chronic causes occur three times more often than deaths by sudden illness or violence. In the case of a lingering illness, the family sometimes has time to make some preparations – cognitive and emotional – for the impending death. In cases of sudden death, the family has little opportunity to prepare.

The numbers of children affected by death of a family member each year are clearly high enough to warrant greater efforts to understand children's reactions to bereavement.

The nature of bereavement in the young

The clinical problem of adolescent bereavement has been acknowledged, treated, and theorized about for many decades. Prior to the latter 1970s, most of the literature concerning adolescent bereavement consisted of metapsychological expositions or case reports of psychiatrically ill youth who were also bereaved (Arthur & Kemme, 1964; Furman, 1974; Wolfenstein, 1966). The clinical reports tended

Table 4.3. *Number of U.S. children living with divorced, separated, or widowed parent in 1991*

	With mother	With father
Divorced	5,206,000	916,000
Separated	2,946,000	405,000
Widowed	780,000	110,000

Source: U.S. Bureau of the Census, Current Population Reports. (1992). *Marital status and living arrangements: March 1991* (Series P-20, No. 461). Washington, DC: U.S. Government Printing Office.

to be unusual or "illustrative" single-case studies, begging concerns about small sample size, representativeness of samples – especially in light of the tendency for severer or more dysfunctional cases to appear for treatment – and the absence of any comparison or control samples. Metapsychological treatises, while provocative and stimulating, tended to operate within a narrow and predominantly psychoanalytic framework, inadvertently limiting the kinds of questions posed and the kinds of evidence considered meaningful.

One reason for the paucity of empirical studies is the relatively low base rate of adolescent bereavement. Most adolescents do not experience the death of a family member or loved one, so it takes time to accumulate a large sample of subjects for clinical study. A second reason was an influential and oft-repeated psychoanalytic tenet maintaining that adolescents are not developmentally capable of the kind of grief or depressive states that adults are – implying that adolescents experience a less interesting, *forme fruste* version of grief. This prevalent belief tended to discourage scientific elucidation of adolescent grief reactions (Fleming & Altschul, 1963).

A third reason is the emotional painfulness of the subject for the adolescent, family members, and the investigator, raising problems of investigator sensitivity and ethics. Historically, clinical investigators have felt the need to provide treatment for identified bereaved children and have given precedence to clinical concerns over those of research. A fourth reason is that unless the investigator has fol-

Table 4.4. *Leading causes of death for ages 35–54 years in the United States in 1988 (with rates per 100,000)*

	Men		Women	
Chronic illness deaths (TOTAL)	76,896	(602.8)	67,607	(493.3)
Cancer	52,016	(411.9)	55,778	(406.9)
Chronic heart disease	24,880	(190.9)	11,829	(86.4)
Sudden deaths (TOTAL)	37,868	(269.7)	11,577	(79.7)
Heart attack	12,698	(99.1)	3,511	(26.4)
Homicide	4,275	(28.2)	1,211	(7.7)
Suicide	6,528	(44.6)	2,209	(14.8)
Traffic accidents	6,956	(47.0)	2,812	(18.6)
Other accidents	7,411	(50.8)	1,834	(12.2)

Source: World Health Organization. (1991). *1990 World health statistics annual.* Geneva: World Health Organization Office of Publications.

lowed a large sample of adolescents longitudinally to collect new cases of adolescent bereavement as they occur, it has always been difficult to know whether individual adolescent subjects had psychological difficulties predating the key death, or whether all reactions and symptoms observed were new psychological difficulties precipitated by the death.

A 1977 monograph summarizing a National Institute of Mental Health conference on issues of childhood and adolescent depression (Schulterbrandt & Raskin, 1977) marked emerging research community consensus that childhood and adolescent depressions, as well as grief states, have their own integrity and are worthy of empirical study. In that volume, Kovacs (1977) recommended phenomenological and longitudinal studies to compare depressed and grieving children and adolescents. These comparisons, she argued, would help elucidate the differential nature of depressive and bereavement reactions. Since that landmark recommendation, empirical studies of childhood and adolescent bereavement have tended to be grounded (in terms of theory and operational definitions) in the context of depressive symptoms.

Bereavement in preadolescent children

Kranzler (cited in Weller & Weller, 1990) has reported that bereaved children as young as 3 and 4 years old manifest strong feelings of sadness, fear, and anxiety, but these feelings are not persistent – their pattern is to alternate between occasional spikes and longer-lasting "normal" states. Kranzler found that children who could put their sad (but not anxious or angry) feelings into words fared much better than those who could not.

Weller and colleagues (1988) (also reported in Sanchez, Fristad, Weller, & Weller, 1988) compared matched groups of recently bereaved, depressed, and "normal" children with respect to psychiatric symptomatology 1 month following parental death and on repeated occasions for up to 13 months. The depressed group evidenced the most depressive symptoms and the "normal" group evidenced the least. Thirty-nine percent of the bereaved children qualified for a diagnosis of major affective disorder by structured interview and DSM-III-R (American Psychiatric Association, 1987) criteria 1 month after the loss of a parent. As more time lapsed, bereaved children reported more symptoms than normal controls, but the differences were consistently nonsignificant.

Depressed children were more likely than bereaved children to report symptoms of guilt, self-depreciation, fatigue, psychic anxiety, somatic anxiety, conduct problems, enuresis, and encopresis. As one might expect, bereaved children with a prior history of psychiatric disorder or a family history of depression were more likely to evidence depressive symptoms than those with no such background.

Bereaved children showed more psychiatric symptomatology 1 month after parental death than at the 6- or 13-month follow-up assessments. Almost half of bereaved children reported experiencing dysphoria, weeping, fatigue, loss of pleasure, trouble concentrating, social withdrawal, suicidal ideation, irritability, and separation anxiety 1 month after parental death. At the 13-month follow-up, a third of bereaved children still reported experiencing sad affect, weeping, headaches, and gastrointestinal complaints.

Although there have been many theories about increased somatic problems following bereavement, particularly when the bereaved individual has failed to engage in verbal and emotional "grief work," the

Weller group observed few somatic complaints in the bereaved child sample (Sood, Weller, Weller, Fristad, & Bowes, 1987). Children who had forewarning that their parent was dying were more likely to report somatic symptoms than those who had no advance warning or preparatory anticipation. As one might expect, bereaved children with a family history of somatic complaints or a surviving parent with somatic complaints were more likely to evidence somatic symptoms.

For up to 1 year following parental death, bereaved children were less interested in school and had more behavior problems at school than "normal" controls (Fristad et al., 1988). Compared with children hospitalized for depression, however, bereaved children were more interested in school, maintained more friendships, and enjoyed their friendships more. There was evidence that bereaved children began to increase their contacts with friends as the first 6 months of bereavement passed.

In a related study, the Weller group (Weller et al., 1988) provided the first empirical evidence of the potential value for young children of attending the funeral of a loved one. They found that funeral attendance seemed to reinforce death's finality in a positive and useful way for bereaved children.

Overall the Weller studies (Weller, Weller, Fristad, & Bowes, 1991) suggest that the interval of maximum distress for bereaved children may appear at any time between 1 and 14 months after the death. Although many have hypothesized that the duration of the lag time until maximum distress, as defined by depressive symptoms, is an indicator of increased risk of ongoing stress-related pathology, there are no meaningful longitudinal studies of childhood bereavement to test this assumption.

The work by the Wellers and their colleagues (including Fristad, Sanchez, and Sood) summarized here has made particularly valuable contributions because of the use of matched control groups and systematic efforts to control for confounding influences (e.g., age and sex of child, sex of surviving parent, anticipated vs. unanticipated parental death, home environment) in virtually all their analyses. While most of these variables had little influence on the expression of psychiatric symptomatology or functioning, a better home environment and better adjustment of the surviving parent were associated with less psychiatric symptoms 1 and 6 months after loss of a parent by death. Also, the death of a father was associated with less interest in school, less enjoyment of peer friendships, and more behavior problems at school for the child than the death of a mother.

Bereavement in adolescence

Black's studies (1984) have systematically compared and contrasted the experiences of parental divorce and parental death. In the United Kingdom, she estimates, 1.6% of all children have experienced the loss by death of at least one parent. In her studies, she found that efforts to maintain psychological connection – that is, reunion fantasies – were more common among children of divorce than among bereaved children. Black argues that it is easier for bereaved children than children of divorce to digest the reality of the loss because the lost parent subsequently disappears and survives *nowhere on earth.* In most other respects, she found, orphaned children and children of divorce experienced similar emotional reactions. Under both conditions, younger children tended to exhibit regression and older children tended to exhibit sadness, depression, and anger. Like divorce, parental deaths were sometimes sudden and sometimes long, drawn-out affairs. As shown to be true for divorce in the Emery and Forehand chapter, the mental and physical health of the surviving parent was a key variable influencing the resiliency or morbidity of the affected child.

Black (1984) also initiated an intervention program for bereaved families based on studies of "sundered families." The principal aim of the intervention was to promote grieving and communication within the family unit. She reports that families participating in the intervention program functioned better as individuals and as a family at the end of 1 year as compared with families who did not participate. Among the families in treatment, good outcome was associated with families where "children cried most about the dead parent and where the parent was able to help them to do so, encouraged by [the] family therapist."

Elizur and Kaffman (1982) studied Israeli children whose fathers died violent deaths in the Yom Kippur War. Their work considers childhood grief associated with a death by violence. In the first few months after the fathers' deaths, children showed emotional responses of pain and grief – crying, moodiness, and longing for their father. Anger and protest reactions were also common. To cope, most of the children chose to believe that their fathers were near them even though no longer alive. The confusing nature of violent death was underscored by children's attempts to understand it better by asking questions and by reality testing.

In the year after the death, most children had learned to accept the reality of the loss – that is, fewer children attempted to deny the death. But as more children came to understand the death, more displayed increased anxiety. They feared being left alone, the disappearance of their mothers, the dark, receiving medical treatment, terrorists, and other external threatening stimuli. Most children coped with this anxiety by becoming more demanding of attention and clingier to and more dependent on their mothers. Some acted out with discipline problems and aggressive behavior.

Most children showed improved functioning in the third and fourth years that followed their fathers' deaths. However, one-third of the children still displayed marked emotional problems. Two interesting phenomena emerged – the adolescents of the sample exhibited general emotional restraint and exemplary behavior. They undertook new responsibilities in the family and outside, which assured adult approval and boosted their self-esteem. The two reactions seemed to display early maturation and a strong need for positive adult feedback in the children, all of whom lost a father by sudden violent death.

Silverman and Worden (1992) described the responses of a large group of children following the death of a parent as gleaned from interviews with the children and their surviving parents 4 months after the key death. These children had all lived together with both parents up until the death. Subjects were identified and recruited by the funeral directors serving their families. The sampling mechanism was not designed to identify a representative sample of the larger Boston community, however, and 49% of the families approached declined to participate.

The final sample consisted of 125 bereaved children (70 families) aged 6 to 17 years. Three-quarters of the sample had lost a father, consistent with national trends showing that children are three times more likely to lose a father than a mother. Almost 90% of the deaths were due to natural causes. In 60% of cases the illness culminating in death had been a prolonged one. The surviving parent was on average 41 years old (range 30 to 57 years), and there were an average of 2.6

children per family (range 1 to 5). Two-thirds of the families had at least 1 child under the age of 12 years. The predominantly Catholic religious affiliation of the sample (70%) was fairly representative of the larger community.

When illness allowed the family to anticipate the parental death, Silverman and Worden found that men with sick wives were likely to continue working, whereas women with sick husbands tended to stop working outside the house. Surviving fathers were more likely than surviving mothers to send their children back to school on the day following funeral services. Overall mothers coping with a dying husband seemed more in touch with the family's changing needs and more available to the children than fathers coping with a dying wife.

Twelve percent of the children were present when their parent died, and children were more likely to witness a father's rather than a mother's death. Another three-fourths of the children first learned about their parent's death from their surviving parent. On first being told about the death, the children were usually subdued, sad, or confused. On the day of death 91% broke down in tears, but girls were not more likely to shed tears than boys, and the offspring of deceased mothers were not more likely to cry than the offspring of deceased fathers. Ninety-five percent of the children attended their parent's funeral service. In the days immediately following the death, children over 12 years, especially boys, were likely to be told they "had to be more grown up now."

At the 4-month follow-up interview, Silverman and Worden found that 70% of the children were sleeping well. Seventy-four percent had been experiencing headaches, 19% were having difficulty concentrating in school, 18% were still uneasy about facing their dead parent's absence from the dinner table, 13% had symptoms of somatic anxiety, and 8% continued to cry daily – younger children were more likely to report crying. The investigators estimated that 17% of the children were in emotional distress at the 4-month follow-up in the sense that this proportion struggled with a considerable number of symptoms. The chief characteristics of those in emotional distress included doing poorly in school, experiencing more unkind remarks from peers, more intense preoccupation with thoughts of the dead parent, feeling less control over things happening to them, and more physical health problems. Sex of the child, age of the child, and sex of the deceased parent did not seem to play a role in identifying those in greater emotional distress.

In the 4 months following parental death, 4% of the children reported a serious illness. Only 35% reported no health problems. Health problems were associated with younger age, maternal loss, and more pronounced fear for the surviving parent's safety. Only 22% of children thought their school performance had changed for the worse, and 18% thought their school performance had improved. Seventy-one percent retained an ability to deal effectively with school.

With respect to efforts to maintain some kind of connection with their deceased parent, Silverman and Worden found that 57% reported speaking to their deceased parent during the first 4 months – and almost half felt they received an answer. Eighty-one percent thought their dead parent was watching them, and this frightened two-thirds who feared their dead parent's disapproval. Fifty-five percent dreamed about their dead parent, but only a small portion were frightened or saddened by the dreams. Three percent still could not believe the death was real and another 4% reported occasionally forgetting that their parent was dead.

Seventy-nine percent of the children continued to think about the dead parent at least several times a week, and 54% reminisced about things they used to do with their parent at least several times per week. Frequent thoughts about the parent were more common among those who lost a mother. Seventy-six percent of the children kept some personal belonging of the deceased parent on their person or in their room.

All the children's teachers knew about the parental death, but only half shared this information with the child's classmates. Teachers who shared the information with classmates were more likely to do this out of hearing of the subject. Only 54% of the children (more often girls) talked with friends about their dead parent; the remainder did not want to. Fourteen percent (more often young girls) felt that some children gave them a hard time because they only had one parent.

Two-thirds of the children (more often girls) reported they could talk about their parent's death and their feelings with a family member they felt close to, but 10% of the children reported not feeling close to anyone in their family. Surviving fathers reported less discussion with their children about the death than surviving mothers.

Children who lost a mother experienced more discontinuity in their daily routines than those who lost a father. Four months after parental death, 44% of the children reported an increase in required household tasks and chores – the increase was more likely in cases of mother loss. Thirty-five percent of all children reported changes in mealtime, 40% had changed bedrooms, and 27% went to bed at a different hour. Nevertheless 67% felt there was little change in the time they spent outside their homes with friends.

In their discussion of these findings, Silverman and Worden argue that the death of a parent may invariably lead to anguish, but does not necessarily lead to the development of psychiatric symptoms. They view the death of a parent as a *series* of events preceding and following the key death, rather than as a single stressful event. Along with the experience of the death itself, the associated *accumulation* of events contributes to the emergence of psychological resilience or vulnerability.

Four months after death, memories of activities shared with their dead parents and of the things the parents had done for them were an important portion of the children's thoughts. One important way the surviving parent could help the bereaved child in this phase was to give the child an opportunity to talk about the dead parent and thereby maintain a place for that parent in the child's life. However, most surviving parents did not or could not assist the child in maintaining this connection by means of conversations or reminiscing.

The impact of death pervaded most aspects of the child's life. "These children were dealing not only with the death of a person, but with the death of a way of life" (Silverman & Worden, 1992, p. 102). The death of a mother appeared to make for a greater "loss of a former way of life" than the death of a father. Children were less able to talk about their feelings and reported more changes in their daily lives after a maternal death. Surviving fathers seemed less prepared or willing to adopt some of the deceased mothers' roles than vice versa. In the same vein Harris, Brown, and Bifulco (1986) observed that it seems easier for a mother to add the bread-winning role to her repertoire than for a father to add the "mothering" role to his.

Silverman and Worden concluded that 83% of the 125 children were coping effectively with the death after 4 months had passed. "The stresses did not seem to overwhelm most of the children during this early period . . . [in the sense that] they did not express their grief in prolonged periods of crying, aggression, or withdrawal, as has been traditionally thought" (Silverman & Worden, 1992, p. 102).

Some studies have suggested that the content of efforts to maintain connection or reconnect with a deceased parent (usually referred to as "reunion fantasies") may change with development. Children of all ages have dreams in which they are reunited with the deceased. At younger ages, these dreams are sometimes interpreted literally as apparitions of ghosts. Adolescents, however, understand that these dreams are not reality. Balk (1983a) found that a third of adolescents liked dreams about their dead sibling and found them comforting. Another expression of reunion wishes is a symptom found mostly in younger children – they may be discovered carrying on a conversation with the deceased parent. When this happens, some children even insist that they have seen the parent. "While it seems that within one compartment of the child's psyche there is the overt acknowledgment of the death, in another compartment the child is behaving and acting as if the parent were still alive" (Garber, 1980, p. 14).

Other studies of adolescents demonstrate that they are not necessarily capable of a consistent intellectual, logical, and rational understanding of death (Balk, 1991). Adolescents who understand the finality and universality of death in general terms often deny this reality when the death in question touches someone close to them. Similarly, adolescents often deny the fact that they themselves are vulnerable to death.

Controlled studies of adolescent bereavement have the potential to identify symptoms and features that are common or unique to grief states, but few controlled studies have been reported to date. In one controlled study, Brent and colleagues (1992) interviewed 58 friends and acquaintances of 10 adolescent suicide victims 6 months after the death of the victims and compared incidence rates for psychiatric disorder during the 6 months since the death with those for a matched group of 58 adolescents from similar communities. Using a structured clinical interview conducted with each adolescent and parent, Brent found the incidence of major depression was higher for the group exposed to the suicide of a friend. In the exposed group, the depressive episode tended to begin in the first month after the suicide, and most who developed a depressive episode were still depressed after 6 months. Yet the friends of suicide victims did not show a higher rate of *suicide attempts* during the 6 months since the death.

In his discussion of these findings, Brent hypothesizes that exposure to the suicide of a friend precipitated a pathological bereavement reaction for many, and these pathological bereavement reactions were manifested as bona fide major depressive episodes. He bases his interpretation on observations that measures of grief and depression severity were intercorrelated, measures of grief and depression were both correlated with the closeness of the relationship to the suicide victim, the risk of developing a major depression was higher for friends with a personal or family history of major depression, and the depressive syndromes were long-lasting – often 5 or 6 months in duration at the 6-month follow-up assessment.

Alternatively, one could hypothesize that the friends of suicide victims who evidenced a variety of depressive symptoms persistently for the 6-month period following the death were simply bereaved in a severer and more prolonged fashion than might be expected, but that the quality of grief was not patently pathological and the diagnosis of major depression is not justified. The official psychiatric nomenclature (DSM-III-R) discourages the clinician from making a diagnosis of major depression in cases of acute grief unless the grief reaction is "abnormal" or accompanied by "morbid preoccupation with worthlessness, prolonged and marked functional impairment, [or] marked psychomotor retardation" (American Psychiatric Association, 1987, p. 361). Because many symptoms of acute depressive illness are also characteristic of grief states, and because "normal grief" has not yet been defined phenomenologically in any reliable fashion for any age group, it remains too easy for clinicians to label bereavement reactions as "pathological" and superimpose psychiatric diagnoses with minimal justification. This kind of confusion hinders clarification of the boundaries and overlap between grief and depressive phenomena.

Too few empirical studies have been undertaken thus far to draw any firm conclusions about the nature of the grief experience. Most studies in this area suffer from a relatively small sample size, the absence of a systematic procedure for comparing and contrasting information gleaned in a direct interview with the adolescent subject with information gleaned from parent or peer observations, uncertain reliability of their observations and ratings, focus on unique kinds of death experiences (e.g., Elizur and Kaffman's [1982] studies of children who lost fathers during a war), focus on unique cultural settings (e.g., Elizur and Kaffman's [1983] studies of the grief reactions of children living in an Israeli kibbutz), and failure to assess the phenomenology of a broad variety of bereavement reactions in terms of frequency and duration.

Follow-up studies of bereaved adolescents

One 10-year follow-up study of more than 11,000 9th-grade Minnesota public school students identified a group of 763 who lost a parent by death and another group of 715 whose parents divorced while the subjects were children or adolescents (Bendickson & Fulton, 1976; Gregory, 1965; Markusen & Fulton, 1971). The investigators found that the bereaved subjects showed more delinquent behavior in 10th grade and had committed more legal offenses in their early 20s, but the trend toward more delinquency no longer pertained in their 30s. Also, the bereaved subjects consistently showed more emotional distress and more serious medical illness at follow-up.

Brown, Harris, and Bifulco (1986) found that mother loss by death or long separation before the age of 17 years was associated with clinical depression in adult women. Two companion studies (Bifulco, Brown, & Harris, 1987; Harris et al., 1986) demonstrated that "lack of care" (i.e., neglect rather than hostile parental behavior) in the period following mother loss mediated the relationship between mother loss and adult depression, posing "lack of care" as an underlying *vulnerability*, not a provoking, factor. Breier and colleagues (1988) found that most of a sample of adults "permanently" separated from a parent between the ages of 2 and 17 years developed a major depressive disorder in adulthood. But other studies have produced evidence that does not support the idea of a link between parent loss by death in childhood and increased risk of adult psychopathology (Osterweiss et al., 1984; Van Eerdewegh, Bieri, Parrilla, & Clayton, 1982).

In a retrospective study of college-age women who had previously lost a parent by death, Silverman (1987) found that women had maintained a "vital relationship" with the deceased parent over time that was continually undergoing modification as the women grew older.

The phenomenology of adolescent grief

Some preliminary studies of the phenomenology of adolescent grief have been undertaken by the W. T. Grant Consortium on Adolescent Bereavement – including David Balk (1983a, 1983b, 1991), David Brent (1983), David Clark, Barry Garfinkel, Madelyn Gould, Emily Harris, Gerald Koocher (1986), Robert Pynoos (1992; Pynoos & Nader, 1990; Nader, Pynoos, Fairbanks & Frederick, 1990), and Elizabeth and Ronald Weller (Weller et al., 1988, Weller et al., 1990, Weller et al., 1991). The Adolescent Bereavement Consortium has proposed a number of variables thought to have influence on the quality and magnitude of adolescent bereavement reactions, conceptualized as related but *independent* variables. This list includes:

    age at death of the parent
    sex of the child
    sex of the deceased parent (and sex by sex interactions)
    cause of the parent's death (natural vs. nonnatural, violent vs.
      nonviolent)
    the foreseeability of the death and degree of individual or
      familial preparation
    the child's presence at or witnessing of the death
    the reactions of the surviving parent
    the way the surviving parent responds to the child
    the surviving parent's ability to assume a new single-parent
      household role
    the home environment
    subsequent life circumstances
    continuity or lack of continuity in the child's daily life after the
      death
    the availability of social support
    the child's prior history of psychopathology
    and family history of psychopathology

Descriptive assessment of grief symptoms

The Adolescent Bereavement Consortium has reviewed the published literature and work in progress on the adolescent grief experience to develop a structured clinical interview, the Adolescent Grief Inventory, designed for use with children ages 10 to 19 years. The original version included 142 questions, each representing one of the eight conceptual domains: reminiscences (i.e., attempts to actively remember or recapture, passive remembering, and the attendant feelings), reunion fantasies in states of wakefulness or dream, experiences of disbelief (conscious and unconscious), examples of identification with the deceased, participation in memorial activities or rituals, attempts to psychologically master the grief experience, behavioral changes not directly related to the experience of grief or sadness, and personal conception of the grief process and recovery. Responses are coded by the interviewer into a scale format.

In preliminary reliability exercises, Adolescent Grief Inventory interviews with bereaved adolescents were videotaped and circulated to eight clinicians for independent rating. The adolescent subjects had lost an immediate family member by death at various points within the most recent year. This rating exercise allowed the consortium to estimate scoring reliability among raters. Items associated with low interrater reliability were dropped from the inventory.

A subsequent principal components analysis of the expert ratings yielded a four-factor solution. Varimax rotation of the four-factor solution yielded four interpretable dimensions underlying the response scores that transected the eight conceptual domains hypothesized.

The first factor consisted of items related to actively avoiding remembering and the experience of painful, intrusive memories. The next factor contained items associated with remembering activities done together with the deceased, feeling physically close to the deceased, behavioral imitation of the deceased, and identificatory behavior. The third factor incorporated those items related to heightened perceptual vigilance, vivid affective reactions other than sadness or euthymia, and some distancing of the self from the deceased. The last factor consisted of items having to do with behavioral problems in school, experiencing reminiscences as distressing, and pessimism about one's ability to transcend the grief experience.

The finding that these four dimensions characterized individual differences cutting across our preconceived conceptual domains offers for consideration a new empirically based view of the experience of acute grief in adolescence. The first obtained factor ("painful intrusive memories/active avoidance") may describe adolescents who have been overwhelmed or traumatized by the grief experience; their responses identify painful symptoms and an acute sense of vulnerability to disturbing, invasive, and often overpowering memories. The next two factors ("physically near/behavioral imitation" and "proactive affective compensation") seem to relate to the different active coping styles associated with relief from distress and a sense of positive grief progress. The last factor ("misbehavior/distressful reminiscences/absence of grief progress") may describe an unsuccessful coping style.

Secondary consequences of adolescent loss by death: Contrasting the experience of losing a parent by death and losing a parent by divorce

The death of a parent marks the beginning of a series of recurring changes throughout the lives of the surviving family. There are strong similarities in the kinds of changes ushered in by a parental divorce and a parental death – changes in family structure, changes in financial status, and changes in the emotional well-being of the primary caretaker as discussed at length in the preceding chapter by Emery and Forehand. Researchers in the area of parent separation and divorce point out that divorce "needs to be considered a *series* of experiences involving changes in relationships between child and parents, between parents, in the physical environment, in economic conditions, and so on" (Sandler, Wolchik, Braver, & Fogas 1986, p. 67). This could just as easily be a description of the changes and stressors associated with childhood bereavement due to parental death. As in the bereavement literature, high levels of relentless change are closely associated with increased social and psychological maladjustment.

As in the case of parental divorce, one of the important secondary stresses associated with parental death relates to change in family financial status. If the parent who died was the principal breadwinner for the family, or if the family was dependent on two incomes to make ends meet, the financial pressures on the family and the attending anxiety about long-term economic survival may constitute formidable stress. This stress may take the form of difficulty putting food on the table, difficulty hiring anyone to help with child care while the surviving parent works, trouble keeping the children in clothes, or an inability for family members to do anything away from home that costs money. The quality of available child care often suffers drastically with loss of income. Children may not be able to go on to college after losing the family's main source of income.

Colin Parkes (1970) found that more than half the widows he studied were poorer after their husband's death. More than half worked outside the home following bereavement, and of these women half had never held jobs before. Because of the financial impact of a parental death, families may be required to move into smaller homes, to change neighborhoods, or to move to different regions of the country.

It is not unusual for families to move within a year of the death of a parent. The reason given for moving is most often financial need to realize the cash value of the house, though sometimes household memories of the deceased parent are too strong and too emotional to bear. There is rarely any opportunity to plan the timing of the move around consideration for the children's educational and social situation, so that the children are likely to have to adjust to a new home, a new school and teacher, a new peer social structure, a new neighborhood – and the loss of many important roles and relationships in the old neighborhood – while they adjust to mourning.

Shepherd and Barraclough (1976) studied children in the United Kingdom whose parent had committed suicide. "In 34 out of 36 cases . . . the suicide contributed to a radical and forced change in living circumstances" (Shepherd & Barraclough, 1976, p. 269). They found that after suicide 56% lived with their mother in a single-parent family (14% were already living with their single mothers before the suicide). Nineteen percent of these children had to adjust to living with stepparents. Another 19% were extracted from the family unit and placed in alternate care.

When parents divorce, parent–child relationships often change and visits with the noncustodial parent can be few and far between, but children rarely lose contact with a parent altogether. Parental death, on the other hand, involves adaptation to permanent loss of that parent. While some divorced parents suffer from major depression after the divorce, the death of a spouse often leaves the surviving parent devastated and unable to care for the children for undefined periods of time.

If the surviving parent is so grief-stricken that he or she continues to show less interest in the child over time, is less involved in the routine daily life and care for the child, or neglects the child, the child may effectively experience the loss of two parents – one living and one dead. In cases where acute bereavement impinges on the surviving parent's prior history of psychopathology or destructive behavior patterns to yield frank psychopathology (e.g., depressive illness, alcohol abuse, child neglect or abuse), the problems posed for the child are serious. The adolescent may feel the need to suppress personal feelings of depression, because he or she may not want to worry or burden further the depressed parent.

In a larger sense, the surviving parent creates a family context for the adolescent's mourning work. Some surviving parents find it impossible to talk aloud about the deceased or about their grief with their children or with anyone else, denying their offspring the opportunity to talk about their feelings, fantasies, or struggles. On interview, many adolescents admit they are reluctant to talk about the death of their parent in the presence of their surviving parent because they fear the topic is too painful for the adult to tolerate – and many of those surviving parents give the same reasons for not wanting to talk about the death in the presence of their adolescent children (Balk, 1991).

By the same token, surviving parents struggling with their own grief often report they do not have the energy, the skill, or the resources to attend to the psychological dilemma of their bereaved children. When a conscious policy of attending to the grief of their children is pursued, it often takes the form of assuming that the children are struggling with feelings and issues that are similar to those faced by the surviving parent. Under acute strain, it is not always possible for bereaved parents to take into consideration the different ages of the children in the family, the different kind of relationship they each enjoyed with the deceased parent, and differences in each child's grief responses during the first year of bereavement as they struggle to make their own adjustment as spouse and sole surviving parent.

The quality and duration of the surviving parent's grief reaction also exert a direct influence on the child's sense of safety and well-being, and models a single variant of grief response for the child to consider as a parental example. Correlations between the acute emotional distress of an adolescent and his or her parent following the death of the adolescent's sibling (Demi & Gilbert, 1987) support the hypothesis that an adolescent's ability to recognize and express emotions is influenced by parental role modeling. The main issue for the younger child is the degree to which the surviving parent's participation in the life of the child is changed and the duration of that change. The main issue for older adolescents is the degree to which the surviving parent is demoralized and rendered inoperative after the initial grief reactions.

The wealth of secondary consequences associated with adolescent loss by death suggests that large-sample prospective studies comparing adolescents who lost a parent by death and others who lost a parent by divorce would be particularly valuable for efforts to discern which aspects of adolescent bereavement are unique to the experience of grief. Within a large sample of adolescents who have a lost a parent by divorce, it would be fruitful to distinguish between subjects who maintained good contact with their noncustodial parent after the divorce and those who essentially lost all contact with their noncustodial parent after the divorce. By comparing adolescents who lost a parent by death with others who truly lost all contact with a parent after a divorce, it may be possible to discern which aspects of adolescent bereavement are unique to grief narrowly defined (i.e., loss by death as opposed to psychological loss).

Comorbidity

Depressive illness

Studies of adult bereavement have demonstrated time and time again that the degree of overlap between symptoms of normal grief and symptoms of major depression is high (Clayton, 1974; Clayton, Halikas, & Maurice, 1971; Clayton, Halikas, & Maurice, 1972). Dysphoria in the initial period after a death is common, but this decreases significantly over time. A mild depressive state is characteristic of most bereaved adolescents. Depressive symptoms may in some cases be accompanied by suicidal ideation or behavior. The most severely depressed group of adolescents seems to be adolescent boys who have lost fathers (Van Eerdewegh et al., 1982; Weller et al., 1991).

One of the most conceptually difficult questions confronting clinical investigators in grief studies is how to operationalize the task of discriminating between those who are acutely bereaved and those who develop "pathological" bereavement or a comorbid episode of major depressive illness superimposed on a normal grief state. Despite almost 75 years of theoretical formulation and debate, the problem remains far from solved. Even current-day psychiatric diagnostic criteria evade the problem. In DSM-III-R nomenclature, as mentioned earlier in this chapter, a person qualifying for a diagnosis of major depression will not ordinarily be labeled as such if the "symptoms" of grief were confined to the 1-year period following the death of a family member or close friend.

In one study of 201 relatives or intimate friends of persons who died by sudden natural or violent causes, Vargas, Loya and Hodde-Vargas (1989) found that features long associated with pathological grief (e.g., depressive symptoms, anger, difficulty relinquishing the lost object) are characteristic of many or most bereaved persons, and that the concept of "pathological" grief may have less to do with specific symptom reactions than with the frequency, intensity, and duration of these features.

One way to discriminate among normal bereavement, pathological bereavement, and depressive illness lies in the development of age-sensitive criteria for assessing grief states without resorting to depression symptom inventories. Another may emerge from longitudinal studies of preadolescents with and without a history of major affective disorder. While the lifetime risk of parent loss by death during adolescence is small (3.5%), it is still possible that large prospective studies of depressed children will yield subsamples of adolescents who unexpectedly lose a parent by death. It would be valuable to compare the phenomenology, the severity, and the duration of bereavement reactions of samples of bereaved adolescents with and without a history of affective disorder.

A critical question, then, continues to be: What is the relationship between acute bereavement and depressive illness among adolescents who have lost a parent by death? Are they independent conditions that may overlap? Are comorbid depressive illness and grief states uniquely characteristic of adolescents with a history of affective disorder predating the key death? For example, in Weller's study (Weller et al., 1991), children who had an untreated psychiatric disorder prior to the death of a parent were more likely to develop a depressive illness during the early course of their grief. On the other hand, are depressive states severer, more impairing, or more long-lasting versions of grief reactions? Or are depressive states pathological forms of grief reactions? Implicit in these questions, of course, are profoundly different viewpoints about whether distressed and symptomatic adolescents in mourning should be left to their own devices, or whether conventional protocols for treating depressive disorders should be offered them.

Is it possible that by failing to treat a severe grief reaction, we expose the adolescent to an unnecessary developmental interruption and increase the likelihood of recurring depressive episodes throughout the rest of his or her life? These kinds of questions can only be addressed in well-wrought long-term follow-up studies.

Panic and anxiety disorders

A number of studies have documented an association between parental loss in childhood and the development of panic or anxiety disorders (Faravelli, Webb, Ambonetti, Fonnesu, & Sessarego, 1985; Kendler, Neale, Kessler, Heath, & Eaves, 1992; Torgerson, 1986; Tweed, Schoenbach, Goerge, & Blazer, 1989). Debate continues over whether anxiety disorders are linked specifically to parental death, or to a broader category of loss experiences, including parental divorce, prolonged illness of a parent, other types of parent–child separation.

An Italian study of adult agoraphobic patients with panic attacks (Faravelli et al., 1985) found that not only have they experienced a greater number of traumatic life events than normal controls, but these events tended to occur during childhood. All categories of traumatic early life events were common among the agoraphobics, but events related to parental separation, especially maternal death or separation, were most dramatically overrepresented.

A study comparing adult patients with generalized anxiety disorder and others with panic disorder (Torgerson, 1986) found that the two groups were associated with equally high rates of separation from parents due to divorce or parental death prior to age 16. Interestingly, the two groups of patients could be distinguished by their level of anxiety as children. Despite the finding that both groups had experienced equivalent stressors in childhood, patients diagnosed with generalized anxiety disorder as adults were significantly less likely to have suffered from chronic anxiety as children than those patients diagnosed with panic disorder as adults.

An analysis of community-based data from the Duke Epidemiologic Catchment Area Study (Tweed et al., 1989) found that persons whose mothers died before they had reached 10 years of age were 6.9 times more likely to be diagnosed as "agoraphobic with panic attacks" than persons whose mothers were still living. Persons whose parents separated or divorced before they reached 10 years of age were also at increased risk for an anxiety disorder diagnosis – 3.4 times more likely to be diagnosed with agoraphobia with panic attacks and 4.5 times more likely to be diagnosed with panic disorder than persons whose parents did not divorce or separate.

Kendler and colleagues (1992) found that major depression and generalized anxiety disorder in women were associated with a history of parent–child separation (both maternal and paternal) but not parental death. The same investigators observed that panic disorder was associated with a history of both parental death and mother–child separation.

Posttraumatic stress reactions

The circumstances of a violent death can be more difficult for an adolescent to understand than any other form of death. Parents usually have difficulty discussing violent deaths with their surviving children – they may give misleading explanations or not discuss the death at all. This confusing situation is often compounded by the way media coverage and neighborhood accounts distort information through inaccurate reporting and rumors. Children also tend to detect when portions of details about a familial death are hidden from them. This results in the children knowing and feeling things they are not *supposed* to know or feel. The incongruence between what children are told and what they actually know may contribute to chronic confusion, an inability to identify their own feelings, and a lack of understanding of the nature of the death.

For children and adolescents, understanding the cause of death is a part of the initial work of coping with loss. Violent deaths often have a frightening aspect: homicides, suicides, and accidents may give rise to gory details. Necessary details must be explained carefully and within the child's intellectual grasp. Reassurances of safety and security are often more necessary when the death is accidental or by violent means.

Work by Pynoos (1992) provides strong evidence that children *witnessing* a violent injury or death often exhibit posttraumatic stress reactions that complicate the normal grieving process. Unlike children whose parents die of natural causes, these children are confronted with two types of reminders – reminders that the parent is indeed missing from their lives and reminders of the violent way in which the parent died. In a 1-year follow-up of children subjected to a sniper attack on the school playground, Nader and colleagues (1990) found that two distinct syndromes – one related to grief and the other to posttraumatic stress disorder – could be distinguished among children in the months that followed. Those on the playground who were exposed to gunfire and witnessed other children being injured were more likely to exhibit a posttraumatic stress disorder. Those who lost a close friend or classmate by death were more likely to develop a bereavement reaction, whether or not they had been exposed to the violence. Some children developed one of the reactions, some developed both, and some developed neither. The two reactions were associated with distinctly different symptom presentations, time courses, and outcomes.

It is common for children who witness the violent death of a loved one to develop persistent bad dreams about the violence or experience persistent intrusive images and sounds from the violent scene. For example, they will repeatedly visualize images of their parent being shot or hit by a car. These unwelcome, disturbing, and anxiety-provoking dreams and images may interfere with the adolescent's ability to reminisce about the deceased. A child who witnessed a violent death may remain in a state of hyperarousal and startle easily as a result of a traumatic reaction. Physiological reactions that keep a person preoccupied with the circumstances of the traumatic event may interfere with the ability to focus on the emotional aspect of loss.

Children who lose a parent through divorce or through death often fantasize about a possible reunion with that parent. Children who experience parental death by violence may experience revenge and intervention fantasies in addition to reunion fantasies. It is common for these children to imagine retaliating against their parent's attacker to make the attacker pay (physically or emotionally) for the crime that has been committed. Other children experience intervention fantasies in which they, the police, or an ambulance crew, for example, reach their parent in time – saving the parent from the violence or helping the parent to survive it.

Pynoos hypothesizes that in order to grieve, children with post-traumatic stress disorder need to be able to summon a physically intact mental representation of the dead individual. They must be able to reconstruct an image of the deceased as they once were– healthy and active. Psychic repair or reconstruction of the image, as achieved ideally in the course of psychotherapy, allows the bereaved child or adolescent to remember the deceased via intact and positive images and to address properly sadness at the loss.

Profound psychological numbing, emotional avoidance, and con-striction often occur after witnessing a violent death. The bereaved may attempt to avoid thoughts of the event to protect against reactions of intense horror and fear. Locations and situations that are remind-ers of the traumatic incident may also be avoided. Helping the be-reaved adolescent to address and tolerate the moments of extreme helplessness may initiate recovery from emotional constriction.

Delinquency

Raphael hypothesized that some adolescents who suppress their grief, rather than expressing their grief or "working it through," may become aggressive, hostile, uncooperative, and destructive of property, with an associated increased risk of alcohol and drug use (Raphael, 1983). When these behaviors are misunderstood as simply lawless or defiant, the child's problems are compounded by punishment (Wass, 1984).

As cited earlier in this chapter, one long-term follow-up study of more than 11,000 9th-grade Minnesota public school students found that subjects who lost a parent by death showed more delinquent behavior in 10th grade and had committed more legal offenses in their early 20s, but the trend toward more delinquency no longer pertained in their 30s (Bendickson & Fulton, 1976; Gregory, 1965; Markusen & Fulton, 1971).

Somatic symptoms

Among bereaved children who experience somatic symptoms, the most common were gastrointestinal problems, stomachaches, and headaches (Sood et al., 1987). Children may suffer digestive problems like vomiting, diarrhea, or constipation. Younger children sometimes experience a regression to loss of bladder control. Children may lose their appetite. Others suffer from a feeling of emptiness in their stomachs, tightness in their throats, and disrupted sleep (Wass, 1984).

Neurobiological indicators of grief

Recent research advances have helped clarify the relationship between immune reactions and the psychoneuroendocrine systems. During and following acutely stressful periods, many markers of the immune system (e.g., percent of helper T-cell lymphocytes) are decreased while antibody titers to infection organisms are sometimes elevated. We are not aware, however, of any large or systematic studies linking adolescent bereavement with compromised immune function.

The Wellers and colleagues (1990) examined cortisol levels in the brain as correlated with depressive symptoms of adolescents after bereavement. Using a dexamethasone suppression test (DST), they found that nonsuppressors reported more symptoms of depression than dexamethasone suppressors. Intriguingly, more bereaved adolescents were found to be nonsuppressors than normal adolescents. Children who were DST nonsuppressors were found to report more depressive symptomatology than normal controls. Increased postdexamethasone cortisol levels were found to be associated with the total number of depressive symptoms and suicidal ideation.

Models of childhood and adolescent grief

What differentiates normal feelings of grief after death from pathological grief responses? Why does the death of a parent lead to severe distress and impaired functioning in some children and not in others? Are some adolescents inherently more susceptible to severe or pathological grief reactions? Is there a particular age or developmental stage when the death of a loved one is more likely to precipitate a severe or pathological grief response?

Early thinking on the topic of childhood and adolescent bereavement tended to conceive of parental death as a single, discrete blow (the "blunt trauma model") likely to impart an emotional bruise or injury, depending on the age or immaturity of the child affected. This model assumes that the loss was a single event bounded in time, powerful in impact, and more disruptive for children than adolescents. Inherent to the model is a sense that different stressors are associated with unique results or consequences determined by the nature of the specific stressor. Some researchers working in this vein sought to establish correspondences between childhood or adolescent bereavement and adult psychiatric disorder (Breier et al., 1988; Brown et al., 1986; Engel, 1975; Hilgard, 1969).

The blunt trauma model has been criticized as linear and simplistic. For example, Berlinsky and Biller (1982) suggested that the lack of consistent results are due to a coarse oversimplification of the complexity of the life situation of the bereaved child. In the same vein, Garmezy wrote:

The effort to establish continuity between [childhood] bereavement and psychiatric disorder in adulthood has led to a variety of criticisms of such studies: the use of disputed methods in psychiatric evaluation; the failure in some studies to differentiate early separations from early death of a parent; the bias of using adult psychiatric patients in looking backward to the presence of early childhood loss; the failure to control for significant social variables; and the difficulty of ascertaining in a determinate way whether or not severe loss events in childhood play a *causal role* in adult maladaptation. (Garmezy, 1983, p. 60)

A more complex model of childhood and adolescent grief was introduced by those who proposed the death of a parent is almost invariably followed by a series of internal and external reverberations (here dubbed the "shock/aftershock wave model") (Balk, 1983a, 1983b; Parkes, 1970; Shepherd & Barraclough, 1976). The shock/aftershock wave model hypothesizes that the loss of a parent has long-lasting, changing repercussions over time in many different areas of child and adolescent functioning (e.g., psychological symptoms, physical health, interpersonal relations, academic performance, identity). The immediate impact of the death triggers a series of reactions and changes that give rise to others in ever-expanding circles, so that the remainder of the young person's life resounds with echoes of the parent's death. There may be a pattern or rhythmicity to the aftershocks, manifest as cyclical periods of renewed (e.g., "anniversary reactions") or reevoked grief. Though the emotional impact of the death may persist for extraordinarily long periods of time, the intensity of aftershock reactions nevertheless diminish with time.

Some "aftershocks" may be attributed to changes in family circumstances and alterations in the functioning of bereaved family members – e.g., loss of family income, need to sell the home months or years later for financial reasons, a chronically depressed surviving parent who can no longer participate in family activities. Other "aftershocks" may be attributed to internal changes in the experience of grief as the bereaved child matures cognitively, emotionally, and socially. Thus a child may develop a new or different awareness of the parent's death years later, and then feel very differently about the experience than was true at an earlier age.

The shock/aftershock wave model of child and adolescent grief has evolved a step further into the "life trajectory model." This model draws heavily on epigenetic principles, assuming that the course of early development has a profound but indirect impact on later life (Brent, 1983; Krupnick, 1984; Raphael, 1983). The model proposes that the influence of a parent's death on a child can be formulated as a change in the speed or direction of life course – changes in the speed of acceleration or the direction of the mapped flight arc, to remain within the physics metaphor.

The blunt trauma and shock/aftershock wave models focus the bulk of their attention on the magnitude of the initial psychological blow inherent to a parental death and the short-term aftermath. The life trajectory model, on the other hand, minimizes the significance of short-term reactions and focuses greater attention on long-term developmental consequences. A question remains, however, as to whether "life trajectories" can be traced, mapped, documented, or extrapolated in a truly empirical fashion. The "life trajectory" model implicitly claims the ability to produce empirical equations describing a child's fundamental life direction and velocity – unaffected and then affected by the key parental death.

The child's experience – and to some extent the scientist's observations – are more akin to that of a pinball in motion. Neither the child's life course nor the pinball is likely to describe a perfect geometric arc. The child's life path, like the pinball, must navigate through a forest of life events and developmental step changes (pinball bumpers), which have the capacity to slow down, accelerate, or change the direction of the child. The pattern and impact of pinball bumpers to be encountered and reencountered changes with the death of a parent, because many life events and developmental issues acquire new significance or meaning *after* a parent has died. Thus, with the death of a parent, the structure of the surrounding forest of pinball bumpers to be encountered in the future may change – sometimes imperceptibly, sometimes profoundly – with implications for grief processing far into the future.

These qualifications lead us to consider a final hybrid model: the "life trajectory/developmental cascade model" of child and adolescent grief. This model incorporates an understanding that the individual child operates in many different developmental spheres simultaneously, that the child has inherent developmental momentum that can be diverted or disrupted, that over time the child encounters and reencounters influential developmental nodal points with their own unique meaning and value, that over time the child encounters and reencounters a variety of influential life stressors with their own unique meaning and value, that the quality of encounters with developmental nodal points and life stressors alters as a function of passing time and changing child identity, and that each child has characteristic pockets of vulnerability and resiliency that buffer encounters with potentially influential developmental nodal points and life stressors (Garmezy, 1983; Krupnick, 1984).

The pinball metaphor inherent to this life trajectory/developmental cascade model helps focus the investigator's and clinician's attention on the child's experience of a never-ending series of events in the bereaved child's life that will be tinged by the experience of a parent's death, and the degree to which future encounters with watershed events (psychological and external alike) will be defined, shaped, and interpreted in light of the loss experience. The loss of a parent by death imbues all subsequent psychological and psychosocial demands with two painful qualities: a reminder of the parent and a reminder of the parent's permanent absence. In a world brimming with painful reminders, the grieving adolescent's task is twofold: to learn to tolerate the sadness and painful reminders, and to nonetheless function competently in the world.

Psychopathology in later life may result from heightened vulnerability set in motion by a parental death in childhood. Emotions associated with the death itself may be reexperienced when reminders of the death occur, and the reactivation of such emotions may lead to a renewed mourning period or vulnerability to pathology.

However, it is not only reminders of the death itself that can increase vulnerability. The secondary consequences of death (e.g., having to move to a new house at a difficult time) can also have subtle and delayed influences on a person's vulnerability later in life.

It is difficult thus to come to firm conclusions about critical stages for there are many other factors that can influence the impact of bereavement on children irrespective of age, family closeness preceding the loss, the prior relationship between the affected child and the deceased parent, whether the parent is of the same or opposite sex of the child, the religious beliefs and social class background of the family, and the suddenness as opposed to the gradual onset of the event. (Garmezy, 1983, pp. 63–64)

Thus the thesis of the life trajectory/developmental cascade model is that changes emerging in the wake of death can influence the psychological state of the bereaved person as much as the actual loss due to death – not only during the first few months following the loss but for the lifetime that follows. When evaluating a person many years after a loss by death, it is difficult to discern whether a resulting vulnerability is due to the death itself or due to a myriad of secondary consequences of the death. The hybrid model acknowledges and affirms the influence and potency of the secondary consequences and sequelae that unfold over time in addition to the expectable direct influences.

Adolescent vulnerability and resiliency in the face of grief

Coping strategies

From a developmental perspective, bereavement may be viewed as a challenge to the adaptive capacities of the person affected. Successful adaptation signifies not only the remission of dysphoric symptoms of grief, but in addition a positive achievement with consequent skill growth representing an expanded repertoire of coping skills.

It has been suggested that the idea that there are better or healthier ways of coping with a loss than others is a myth (Wortman & Silver, 1989). Five proper ways of coping with grief are commonly held by health care professionals and lay people alike. The first idea is that depression after a loss is inevitable and must be experienced before healing can start. However, the results of systematic research have failed to demonstrate truth in this theory. Another myth is that failure to experience distress after a death is a sign of psychopathology. Data show that absent or delayed grief does not always lead to mental illness. The idea that the bereaved must work through their loss is also unsubstantiated. It is expected that the person experiencing the loss will eventually recover from their feelings of grief. This too needs to be reconstructed to incorporate the few people for whom the recovery process takes a very long time. The final misconception is that the bereaved must learn to accept the loss intellectually before recovery can truly be reached. Again, there will always be people who have particular difficulty coming to terms with the death, especially if it is by violent or otherwise sudden means. According to Wortman and Silver, their coping with loss seems to be an idiosyncratic process in which what may or may not lead to psychopathology can not be readily predicted.

Risk factors

Research by Parkes (1990) on 54 psychiatric patients revealed a number of risk factors to developing psychopathology after bereavement. Experiencing multiple and sudden deaths seems to be a risk factor, because the bereaved has no preparation for the emotional aftermath.

Having had psychiatric problems after a previous bereavement can indicate the risk of developing pathological grief responses to a new loss. Low trust of the self and of others makes the bereaved unsure of their own ability to cope with the loss and reluctant to turn to others for support. Anxious parents can have children who become anxious, conflicted adults likely to develop pathological grief responses. Compulsively independent adolescents (as they often are) are likely to suffer from delayed grief when they respond to a loss of a significant other.

Krupnick (1984) and Medalie (1990) created a list of risk factors specific to adulthood bereavement. The following factors present a risk to psychopathology after the death of a parent or sibling: losses occurring before the age of 5 or during early adolescence; loss of a mother for girls younger than 11 and loss of a father for boys in adolescence; psychological problems in the youth prior to the death; having a conflicted relationship with the deceased prior to the death; a surviving parent who is overly dependent on the child; a lack of family or external support; an unstable home environment; parental remarriage; lack of a prior understanding of death; unanticipated death; and the deceased dying by suicide or homicide.

Protective factors

According to Solomon (1987), anticipation of death can be a protective factor relating to recovery from bereavement. Theoretically, anticipating death allows the bereaved to start grieving prematurely, thereby accomplishing part of their grief work before the loved one dies. People able to anticipate death are often better adjusted than those persons for whom death of a loved one comes as a shock. Having a clearly defined concept of death is also a protective factor in bereavement. Adolescents who have already experienced the death of a loved one seem to be better equipped to handle the experience again. Solomon believes that adolescents who have not experienced death have a difficult time assimilating this new experience.

Krupnick (1984) delineated multiple protective factors against the traumatic impact of the death of a father. A strong, working mother who keeps the remaining home life intact seems to strengthen her children through her own example. If the mother has her own supportive network of friends outside the home, then she is usually more able to give support to her children. It can also be protective if prior to the father's death the parental roles were well constructed, enabling early child – same sex parent identification to become firm. Parents who foster independence and have tolerance for separation can be another protective factor for their children.

A third list of protective factors can be found in the Garmezy (1983, 1991) literature. He refers to these factors as having a "steeling effect." Children who were rated by adults as friendly and well-liked by peers were often protected by the harmful effect of stressors. These children were not defensive or aggressive, and were cooperative and emotionally stable. They had positive senses of self and felt that they had power over their own lives (e.g., an internal locus of control). They were reflective as opposed to being impulsive. "Physical and psychological environment of the home was important" (Garmezy, 1983, p. 75). Parents who were concerned about the child's education and defined roles within the family seemed to be protective factors. But if no such parental figure existed, having one significant positive adult relationship, perhaps with a teacher or neighbor, proved to have an equally steeling effect. Garmezy consolidates his research into three broad protective factors: dispositional attributes within the adolescent, emotional support within the family, and the existence of an external support system.

Resiliency

Horowitz and colleagues (Horowitz, Marmar, Weiss, DeWitt, & Rosenbaum, 1984) hypothesized that a healthy grieving pattern is one in which the bereaved uses both avoidance and purposive reminiscence, whereas heavy reliance on either one to the exclusion of the other is an unhealthy pattern. Their notion is that individuals should not remain at the beck and call of all their grief experiences without relief; hence intermittent periods of avoidance are in the service of healthy bereavement. Likewise, excessive avoidance leads to a failure to develop the necessary ability to tolerate the sadness and anguish associated with the death, failure to confront the changed realities of one's life situation, and failure to reorganize one's life in acknowledgment of the loss. Where surviving parents and relatives remain psychologically able to attend to the psychological needs of bereaved adolescents, where the surviving adults recognize the need of family members to grieve in their own idiosyncratic ways and on their own idiosyncratic timetables, and where the surviving adults are willing to participate in intermittent discussions and reminiscences about the deceased parent – and evidence shows that surviving mothers are more likely to facilitate this than surviving fathers – the bereaved adolescent who is capable of a balanced repertoire of avoidance and purposive reminiscence is most likely to fare well.

Studies indicate that adolescents allowed opportunities to talk about their dead parent, thereby maintaining a place for that parent in their lives, tend to fare better. But the evidence also shows that most surviving parents have great difficulty assisting bereaved adolescents to maintain this connection by means of conversations or reminiscing. Hence, the adolescent's ability to utilize or create intimate relationships (with other relatives, with neighbors, or with peers) that permit conversations about the deceased parent, is another important quality of resilience.

In a similar vein, Black's studies (1984) suggest that adolescents who have the capacity and make the effort to maintain psychological connections with their deceased parent are more likely to make better long-term adjustments. These "psychological connections" may take the form of handling or wearing treasured possessions, informal schedules for ongoing discussions or reminiscences, or talking aloud to a ghostly presence in private moments. Clearly some adolescents spontaneously generate meaningful psychological connections and others do not. Adolescents' efforts in these directions can be actively encouraged or discouraged by parents and other adults, but the evidence is that some children persist in the activities of resilience despite discouragement and barriers.

Pynoos (1992) stresses the importance of the adolescent's ability to renegotiate the relationship with the deceased parent as he or she progresses through the normal stages of adolescent development. Although idealization of the deceased seems to be a common reaction to grief, deidealization of parents is a normal and necessary developmental task of adolescence. Pynoos has found that adolescents who are able to successfully maintain a changing mental relationship with their deceased parent – one that is not a static representation of their relationship at the time of the parent's death – are more likely to be resilient.

Intervention strategies

The most effective intervention strategies seem to be those implemented by persons familiar with the resiliency literature and those whose activities aim to promote resilience in grieving children.

Anticipatory/preparatory interventions

Anticipatory intervention can begin on the level of parents and teachers simply talking to children about death when they begin asking questions. When children do not feel at ease discussing this topic, it can become another taboo. Children who have a coherent concept of death may be better able to handle a death of a loved one based on their elaborated knowledge of what death means.

Going beyond the purely conceptual level, Koocher has reviewed studies showing the emotional benefit of being able to prepare for a loss in the case of long-term illness. When a loved one is struck with a terminal illness or long-term condition, it is normal for the people in his or her life to engage an "anticipatory mourning" – "operationally defined by such observable behaviors as discussing the possibility that a sick loved one may die, grieving in anticipation of such a loss, discussing the impending death with the patient, or making advance funeral arrangements" (Koocher, 1986, p. 3). Successful anticipatory or preparatory interventions include these behaviors as well as reconciling differences with the dying person in order to alleviate subsequent feelings of guilt or anger. The time interval between the onset of illness and the death allows family and friends gradually to detach and prepare themselves with the help of such intervention strategies.

Support groups for terminally or chronically ill people and their loved ones can be effective in facilitating adaptation to the idea of loss. Family group work is particularly important and beneficial. Groups can help support open and honest communication among family members at a time when each member's worries about the impending death can lead to a halting of the communication process.

Treatment interventions

Studies of behavioral treatment for pathological grief have focused on exposure to bereavement cues, whereby repeated, controlled exposure is thought to reduce the unwanted emotional response by means of habituation or counterconditioning.

Medalie (1990) suggests that the following goals should apply to bereavement interventions with individuals, families, or simply groups of bereaved individuals. Survivors should be aided in accepting the reality of the loss. They should be helped to deal with their overt and suppressed emotions regarding the loss – anger, guilt, sadness, abandonment. Some need help coping with new roles and new individuals entering the family system. Emotional distancing from the deceased should be encouraged, so that energy can be reinvested into new or other preexisting relationships. Particular focus should be given to times of the year which are especially difficult to the grieving process (e.g., holidays, the deceased's birthday, anniversary of the death).

Koocher and colleagues are currently conducting a study of a 12-week intervention program's effectiveness. Although the project focuses on the death of a child within the family system, its ideas about intervention strategies seem generalizable to the death of a loved one during adolescence. Family group work includes discussing the personality of the deceased (i.e., acknowledging both good and bad traits) and the events surrounding the death, better handling the discussion of the death with friends, settling unfinished conflicts with the deceased, and attempts to place the death in some perspective. Tasks such as role playing, creating a family genogram, and writing a group letter to the deceased are intended as group work tools. The intervention strategy is specifically family-focused, because it is meant to heighten family cohesiveness and support in the months following the death.

Drawing on the life trajectory/developmental cascade model discussed earlier, Pynoos (1992) is an advocate of a pulsed intervention strategy that anticipates and changes with the developmental challenges facing the bereaved adolescent. This model of intervention relies on both patient and therapist to discern what may (in the near future) be particularly developmentally challenging about his or her parent's loss, for example, starting to date, graduating from high school, planning for college. This intervention model entails initial work with the acute grief close to the time of the parental death as well as planned and unexpected interventions at specific points of difficulty in the future – requiring open communication between the patient and therapist over a long period of time. This strategy's main goal is to provide the adolescent with the support needed to maintain normal development.

Adolescents experiencing grief can be assisted at the individual, family, classroom, and community level. Individual counseling can provide the support that will lead the adolescent back to his or her original level of functioning. Adolescents need the opportunity to explore their reaction to the grief individually. At the family level, security within the home environment can be restored. The family must be a stable and supportive place where the adolescent can go for solace and support. Because each family member is affected differently by the loss, the nature of grieving must be addressed and understood. Bereaved adolescents can be helped at school by being reintegrated into the classroom by a supportive and understanding teacher. Within the community, there may be other adolescents experiencing similar losses with whom to do group work (Pynoos & Nader, 1990).

Public policy implications

In the first year following the death of a parent, the surviving family's situation often includes financial tribulations, a likelihood of moving, and altered child-care arrangements. An unknown portion of children who lose one parent by death leave the household of the surviving parent soon afterward because the surviving parent finds it financially or psychologically impossible to keep the family together. Another unknown portion of children who lose a parent by suicide find themselves under much less parental supervision as the surviving parent struggles to support the family alone. More detailed studies of the typical strains encountered might help identify resources with the potential to ease their burden and enable more children to remain with surviving parents in the supportive environment of their family.

The availability of child-care assistance for those in acute financial need might enable some households to remain intact, might provide additional parental supervision for families who cannot provide enough, and might allow the surviving parent time to access psychological services if needed. The first year following the death of a parent can be a terribly disruptive and destabilizing time for the family unit as well as for the bereaved child or adolescent, but with a little extrafamilial help many families can maintain their continuity and stability, effectively minimizing the amount of change and upset (with potential to complicate grief) the children are exposed to.

Therapeutic bereavement groups for preadolescents and adolescents have enormous potential to help children assimilate all the concurrent changes in their lives along with their grief in a social setting. Such groups should ordinarily be restricted to children with no premorbid psychopathology. Many of those with a premorbid history would benefit from individual assessment and treatment planning. For the rest, the therapeutic bereavement group setting allows children the opportunity to experience the diversity of family and grief experiences, as well as the opportunity to appreciate a variety of bereavement coping styles. The group setting is also a strategic place for the supervising professional to identify and track individual children who seem to be having more difficulty than the others, or who seem to develop pathological grief reactions.

The bereavement groups succeed best when coordinated with a concurrent psychoeducational program for surviving parents, one that provides them with a forum for: (1) thinking and talking about the ways they as parents are responding to their children's grief, (2) discussing their personal grief reactions as they choose, and (3) developing tolerance for a wide variety of grief reactions and bereavement styles. Many parents who would not otherwise tolerate a support-group process or contact with a mental health professional will do so for the explicit purpose of helping their children.

The studies reviewed show that many or most surviving parents have great difficulty assisting their children to maintain a psychological connection to the deceased parent by means of conversations or reminiscing. Children who are discouraged from talking about the dead parent, who are not provided with ways to maintain a place for that parent in their lives, ought to be detected and offered such opportunities outside the home with the informed consent of their surviving parent.

Avenues for future research

The scope of the problem of childhood and adolescent bereavement has not been described epidemiologically. What is the age distribution for children who have lost a parent by death within the past year? What causes of death are most commonly associated with childhood and adolescent bereavement? What are the family situations of these children and their families in the year following the death? How many bereaved children are separated from their surviving parent for any significant length of time in the year following the death of the other parent? Well-designed regional or national epidemiological studies have not been undertaken to study adolescent bereavement, but such studies could shed a great deal of light on the psychosocial situation of these children.

The adolescent grief experience itself has not been described and measured in comprehensive detail. In the absence of consensual empirical definitions of adolescent grief, many investigators rely on symptom scales (e.g., depressive symptom scales, anxiety scales, post-traumatic stress reaction scales) to chart the quality, intensity, and duration of grief reactions. Clearly this strategy tends to yield a skewed picture of grief phenomena.

The acute and long-term effects of bereavement need to be better documented with the aid of comparison groups. In addition to demographically matched normal controls, it would be valuable to match bereaved adolescents with adolescents who have experienced a loss that outwardly resembles loss via parental death – for instance, adolescents going through divorce, focusing on adolescents who lose virtually all contact with the noncustodial parent following the divorce. As discussed earlier, the secondary consequences of parent loss by death and parent inaccessibility following divorce have many parallels. This design strategy might allow the investigator to zero in on the experiences unique to the experience of loss by death, since so many secondary consequences are shared in common by the two groups.

While a number of treatment intervention models for bereaved adolescents have been proposed, published treatment evaluation studies using adequate comparison groups are rare. Treatment models must be applied and compared under rigorous control conditions to assess their merit and efficacy.

Finally, this review has focused attention on the plight of adolescents who have lost a parent by death, perpetuating neglect of those who lose a sibling or close friend by death, because parent loss may be the most difficult example of adolescent bereavement to consider, because prevalence rates for parent loss can be estimated more reliably than rates for other categories of adolescent bereavement, and because clinical research has focused more intensively on the loss of a parent than of other significant others. But parent loss by death may be such a complex, multidimensional stressor that the grief and bereavement experience becomes difficult to isolate and study in clear relief. Clearly studies of adolescents who have lost a sibling or close friend by death are necessary and have the potential to shed as much or more light on the central problem.

References

American Psychiatric Association. (1987). *Diagnostic and statistical manual of mental disorders* (*3rd ed., rev.*). Washington, DC: American Psychiatric Association.

Arthur, B., & Kemme, M. L. (1964). Bereavement in childhood. *Journal of Child Psychology and Psychiatry, 5,* 37–49.

Balk, D. (1983a). Adolescents' grief reactions and self-concept perceptions following sibling death: A study of 33 teenagers. *Journal of Youth and Adolescence, 12* (2), 137–161.

Balk, D. (1983b). Effects of sibling death on teenagers. *Journal of School Health, 53,* 14–18.

Balk, D. (1991). Death and adolescent bereavement: Current research and future directions. *Journal of Adolescent Research, 6* (1), 7–27.

Bendickson, R., & Fulton, R. (1976). Death and the child: An anterospective test of the childhood bereavement and later behavior disorder hypothesis. In R. Fulton, (Ed.), *Death and identity* (p. 274–287). Bowie, MD: Charles Press.

Berlinksy, E. B., & Biller, H. B. (1982). *Parental death and psychological development.* Lexington, MA: D. C. Heath.

Bifulco, A. T., Brown, G. W., & Harris, T. O. (1987). Childhood loss of parent, lack of adequate parental care and adult depression: A replication. *Journal of Affective Disorders, 12,* 115–128.

Black, D. (1984). Sundered families: The effect of loss of a parent. *Adoption and Fostering, 8,* 38–43.

Breier, A., Kelsoe, J. R., Kirwin, P. D., Beller, S. A., Wolkowitz, O. M., &

Pickar, D. (1988). Early parental loss and development of adult psychopathology. *Archives of General Psychiatry, 45,* 987–993.

Brent, D. A. (1983). A death in the family: The pediatrician's role. *Pediatrics, 72* (5), 645–651.

Brent, D. A., Perper, J., Moritz, G., Allman, C., Friend, A., Schweers, J., Roth, C., Balach, L., & Harrington, K. (1992). Psychiatric effects of exposure to suicide among the friends and acquaintances of adolescent suicide victims. *Journal of the American Academy of Child and Adolescent Psychiatry, 31,* 629–639.

Brown, G. W., Harris, T. O., & Bifulco, A. (1986). Long term effects of early loss of parent. In M. Rutter, C. E. Izard, & P. Read (Eds.), *Depression in young people: Developmental and clinical perspectives* (pp. 251–297). New York: Guilford Press.

Clayton, P. J. (1974). Mortality and morbidity in the first year of widowhood. *Archives of General Psychiatry, 30,* 747–750.

Clayton P. J., Halikas, J. A., & Maurice, W. L. (1971). The depression of widowhood. *British Journal of Psychiatry, 120,* 71–78, 1972.

Clayton P. J., Halikas, J. A., & Maurice, W. L. (1972). The bereavement of the widowed. *Diseases of the Nervous System, 32* (9), 597–604.

Demi, A. S., & Gilbert, C. M. (1987). Relationship of parental grief to sibling grief. *Archives of Psychiatric Nursing, 1* (6), 385–391.

Elizur, E., & Kaffman, M. (1982). Children's bereavement reactions following death of the father: II. *Journal of the Academy of Child Psychiatry, 21* (5), 474–480.

Elizur, E., & Kaffman, M. (1983). Factors influencing the severity of childhood bereavement reactions. *American Journal of Orthopsychiatry, 53,* 668–676.

Engel, G. L. (1975). The death of a twin: Mourning and anniversary reactions. Fragments of 10 years of self-analysis. *International Journal of Psycho-Analysis, 56* (23), 23–40.

Faravelli, C., Webb, T., Ambonetti, A., Fonnesu, F., & Sessarego, A. (1985). Prevalence of traumatic early life events in 31 agoraphobic patients with panic attacks. *American Journal of Psychiatry, 142,* 1493–1494.

Fleming, J., & Altschul, S. (1963). Activation of mourning and growth by psychoanalysis. *International Journal of Psycho-Analysis, 44,* 419–432.

Fristad, M., Galerston-Jedel, R., Weller, E. B., Weller, R., Hittner, J., & Preskorn, S. (1988, October). Peer relationships, school performance, and self-esteem in bereaved children. 35th Annual Meeting of the American Academy of Child and Adolescent Psychiatry jointly with the Canadian Academy of Child Psychiatry, Seattle, WA.

Furman, E. (1974). *A child's parent dies.* New Haven, CT: Yale University Press.

Garber, B. (1980). Mourning in children: Toward a theoretical synthesis. *Annual of Psychoanalysis, 9,* 9–19.

Garmezy, N. (1983). Stressors of childhood. In N. Garmezy & M. Rutter (Eds.), *Stress, coping, and development in children* (pp. 43–82). New York: McGraw-Hill.

Garmezy, N. (1991). Resilience in children's adaptation to negative life events and stressed environments. *Pediatric Annals, 20* (9), 459–466.

Gregory, I. (1965). Anterospective data following childhood loss of a parent. I. Delinquency and high school dropout. *Archives of General Psychiatry, 13,* 99–109.

Harris, T., Brown, G. W., & Bifulco, A. (1986). Loss of parent in childhood and adult psychiatric disorder: The role of lack of adequate parental care. *Psychological Medicine, 16,* 641–659.

Hilgard, J. R. (1969). Depressive and psychotic states as anniversaries of sibling death in childhood. *International Psychiatry Clinics, 6,* 197–211.

Horowitz, M. J., Marmar, C., Weiss, D. S., DeWitt, K., & Rosenbaum, R. (1984). Brief psychotherapy of bereavement reactions. *Archives of General Psychiatry, 41,* 438–448.

Kendler, K. S., Neale, M. C., Kessler, R. C., Heath, A. C., & Eaves, L. J. (1992). Childhood parental loss and psychopathology in women. *Archives of General Psychiatry, 49,* 109–116.

Koocher, G. P. (1986). Coping with a death from cancer. *Journal of Consulting and Clinical Psychology, 54* (5), 1–9.

Kovacs, M. (1977). Conclusions and recommendations of the subcommittee on assessment. In J. G. Schulterbrandt & A. Raskin (Eds.), *Depression in childhood: Diagnosis, treatment, and conceptual models* (pp. 155–162). New York: Raven Press.

Krupnick, J. L. (1984). Bereavement in childhood and adolescence. In M. Osterweiss, F. Solomon, & M. Green (Eds.), *Bereavement reactions, consequences, and care* (pp. 99–141). Washington, DC: National Academy Press.

Markusen, T., & Fulton, R. (1971). Childhood bereavement and behavioral disorders: A critical review. *Omega, 2,* 107–117.

Masten, A. S., Best, K. M., & Garmezy, N. (1990). Resilience and development: Contributions from the study of children who overcome adversity. *Development and Psychopathology, 2,* 425–444.

Medalie, J. H. (1990). Bereavement: Health consequences and prevention strategies. In R. B. Goldbloom & R. S. Lawrence (Eds.), *Preventing disease: Beyond the rhetoric* (pp. 168–178). New York: Springer-Verlag.

Nader, K., Pynoos, R., Fairbanks, L., & Frederick, C. (1990). Children's PTSD reactions one year after a sniper attack at their school. *American Journal of Psychiatry, 147* (11), 1526–1530.

Osterweiss, M., Solomon, F., & Greene, M. (1984). Introduction. In M. Osterweiss, F. Solomon, & M. Greene (Eds.), *Bereavement reactions, consequences, and care* (pp. 3–11). Washington, DC: National Academy Press.

Parkes, C. M. (1970). The first year of bereavement. *Psychiatry, 33,* 444–467.

Parkes, C. M. (1990). Risk factors in bereavement: Implications for the prevention and treatment of pathologic grief. *Psychiatric Annals, 20* (6), 308–313.

Pynoos, R. S. (1992, Spring). Grief and trauma in children and adolescents. *Bereavement Care, 11,* 2–10.

Pynoos, R. S., & Nader, K. (1990). Children's exposure to violence and traumatic death. *Psychiatric Annals, 20* (6), 334–344.

Raphael, B. (1983). *The anatomy of bereavement.* New York: Basic Books.

Sanchez, L., Fristad, M. A., Weller, E. B., & Weller, R. A. (1988, May). Anxiety symptoms in bereaved prepubertal children. Proceedings of the 141st Annual Meeting of the American Psychiatric Association, Montreal, Canada. Washington, DC: American Psychiatric Association.

Sandler, I. N., Wolchik, S. A., Braver, S. L., & Fogas, B. S. (1986). Significant events of children of divorce: Toward the assessment of risky situations. In S. M. Auerbach & A. Stolberg (Eds.), *Crisis intervention with children and families* (pp. 65–87). New York: Hemisphere.

Schulterbrandt, J. G., & Raskin, A. (1977). *Depression in childhood: Diagnosis, treatment, and conceptual models.* New York: Raven Press.

Shepherd, D. H., & Barraclough, B. M. (1976). The aftermath of parental suicide for children. *British Journal of Psychiatry, 129,* 267–276.

Silverman, P. R. (1987). The impact of parental death on college-age women. *Psychiatric Clinics of North America, 10,* 387–404.

Silverman, P. R., & Worden J. W. (1992). Children's reactions in the early months after the death of a parent. *American Journal of Orthopsychiatry, 62,* 93–104.

Solomon, M. L. (1987). A study of sibling survivors of suicide. Unpublished manuscript.

Sood, B., Weller, E. B., Weller, R. A., Fristad, M. A., & Bowes, J. M. (1987, October). Somatic complaints in bereaved children. Proceedings of the

Annual Meeting of the American Academy of Child and Adolescent Psychiatry, Washington, DC.

Torgerson, S. (1986). Childhood and family characteristics in panic and generalized anxiety disorders. *American Journal of Psychiatry, 143,* 630–632.

Tweed, J. L., Schoenbach, V. J., George, L. K., & Blazer, D. G. (1989). The effects of childhood parental death and divorce on six-month history of anxiety disorders. *British Journal of Psychiatry, 154,* 823–828.

U.S. Bureau of the Census, Current Population Reports. (1989). *Marital status and living arrangements: March 1989* (Series P-20, No. 445). Washington, DC: U.S. Government Printing Office.

U.S. Bureau of the Census. (1990). *Statistical abstracts of the U.S., 1990* (110th ed.). Washington, DC: U.S. Government Printing Office.

U.S. Bureau of the Census, Current Population Reports. (1992). *Marital status and living arrangements: March 1991* (Series P-20, No. 461). Washington, DC: U.S. Government Printing Office.

Van Eerdewegh, M. M., Bieri, M. D., Parrilla, R. H., & Clayton, P. J. (1982). The bereaved child. *British Journal of Psychiatry, 140,* 23–29.

Vargas, L. A., Loya, F., & Hodde-Vargas, J. (1989). Exploring the multidimensional aspects of grief reactions. *American Journal of Psychiatry, 146,* 1484–1489.

Wass, H. (1984). Parents, teachers, and health professionals as helpers. In H. Wass & C. A. Corr (Eds.), *Helping children cope with death: Guidelines and resources* (pp. 75–130). New York: Hemisphere.

Weller, E. B., & Weller, R. A. (1990). Grief in children and adolescents. In B. Garfinkel, G. Carlson, & E. B. Weller (Eds.), *Psychiatric disorder in children and adolescents* (pp. 37–47). Philadelphia: Saunders.

Weller, E. B., Weller, R. A., Fristad, M. A., & Bowes, J. M. (1988, May). Depressive symptoms in acutely bereaved children. Proceedings of the 141st Annual Meeting of the American Psychiatric Association, Montreal, Canada. Washington, DC: American Psychiatric Association.

Weller, E. B., Weller, R. A., Fristad, M. A., & Bowes, J. M. (1990). Dexamethasone suppression test and depressive symptoms in bereaved children: A preliminary report. *Journal of Neuropsychiatry, 2* (4), 418–421.

Weller, E. B., Weller, R. A., Fristad, M. A., & Bowes, J. M. (1991). Depression in recently bereaved prepubertal children. *American Journal of Psychiatry, 148* (11), 1536–1540.

Weller, E. B., Weller, R. A., Fristad, M. A., Cain, S. E., & Bowes, J. M. (1988). Should children attend their parent's funeral? *Journal of the American Academy of Child and Adolescent Psychiatry, 27* (5), 559–562.

Wolfenstein, M. (1966). How is mourning possible? *Psychoanalytic Study of the Child, 21*, 93–123. New York: International Universities Press.

World Health Organization. (1991). *1990 World health statistics annual.* Geneva.

Wortman, C. B., & Silver, R. C. (1989). The myths of coping with loss. *Journal of Consulting and Clinical Psychology, 57* (3), 349–357.

5

Risk, resilience, and development: The multiple ecologies of black adolescents in the United States

Saundra Murray Nettles and Joseph H. Pleck

After decades of reliance on pathology, social class, or cultural deviance theories, research on black* adolescents is now turning to an exploration of the mechanisms that underlie competent and healthy functioning (Consortium for Research on Black Adolescence, 1990; Jones, 1989; McKenry, Everett, Ramseur, & Carter, 1989; Spencer, Brookins, & Allen, 1985). One motivation for the shift is the search for solutions to the problems of African-American youths. Another reason is the desire to broaden knowledge about this population across biological, psychosocial, and ecological domains (Bell-Scott & Taylor, 1989; Slaughter-Defoe, Nakagawa, Takanishi, & Johnson, 1990).

This essay examines protective factors and the process of "resilience" (Garmezy, 1985; Masten, Best, & Garmezy, 1990; Rutter, 1987; Werner, 1990) as it applies to black adolescents. In addition to the optimism implied by these concepts, researchers are exploring these factors because they suggest possibilities for designing interventions that have cost-effective and lasting effects (Nettles, 1991;

Saundra Murray Nettles is Principal Research Scientist at the Johns Hopkins University Center for Research on Effective Schooling for Disadvantaged Students, and Joseph H. Pleck is Senior Research Associate at the Wellesley College Center for Research on Women.
* In this chapter we use the terms black and African-American interchangeably as group names (see Tiedt & Tiedt, 1990, for a discussion of the use of "group names") that emphasize the sub-Saharan (African) origins of a population. Such names (e.g., Hispanics and Native Americans) reflect changes in how groups prefer to be identified, although in the literature the same labels often connote (at times, imprecisely) ethnicity or race. Where researchers have used labels that connote aspects of ethnicity (e.g., country of origin, language), we so note.

Winfield, 1991). Nevertheless, some have expressed concern about the "politics" of the concept of resilience (Garmezy, 1987). That is, focusing on the small proportion of youths who surmount adverse circumstances leads many in society to conclude that individual fortitude rather than social conditions determines success. This belief can undermine support needed for social interventions.

To put our discussion of resilience into perspective, we begin with an overview of the incidence of health- and life-compromising outcomes among black youths. We discuss resilience, risk, and protection against risk at the individual and ecological levels and review research on these concepts as they pertain to black adolescent populations.

Many of the studies we report use the race-comparative paradigm, which has been criticized in several sources (see, e.g., McLoyd, 1990). Unfortunately, there are few data available that permit systematic description of within-group variations in risk factors and outcomes in black youths. Statistics drawn from studies of inner-city populations reflect in large measure the experience of poor black youths, who constitute 45% of all blacks under the age of 18. However, these data are often uncritically assumed to hold true for all black youths, although the majority (55%) of African-American youths are not poor. Data from nationally representative samples are often reported without differentiating social class, locale or region, country of origin, recency of immigration, language, and other characteristics. Treating black adolescents as a monolith obscures important distinctions (McKenry et al., 1989; Spencer & Dornbusch, 1990).

The inattention to diversity within populations of black adolescents is one issue in the research. Another equally serious problem is the confounding of race and social class (Spencer & Dornbusch, 1990). In studies that compare blacks and whites, the interaction of race and socioeconomic status is often unreported. Interpretations of results can therefore be problematical. Reviews by McKenry et al. (1989) and Slaughter-Defoe et al. (1990) discuss this and other examples of bias in research on black populations.

Incidence of health- and life-compromising outcomes

In this section, we briefly review research on the incidence of risk outcomes for black youths in seven areas: health, school completion

and related issues, employability, police involvement, risky sexual behavior, alcohol and drug use, and psychological symptoms and suicide.
We note particular research on conceptual issues that have arisen in
each area as they pertain to black adolescents and discuss the role of
problem behaviors as risk outcomes for further adverse outcomes.

The point we made at the outset about the need to distinguish
low-income from other black adolescents is particularly relevant to
reviewing rates of negative health outcomes. Statistics drawn from
studies in inner-city schools and programs disproportionately reflect
the experience of poor black youths. Statistics from national representative samples reporting data for blacks as an undifferentiated
group obscure the important distinction between poor and nonpoor
blacks. The statistics presented here are generally of the latter type.
Readers should realize that the levels of these indicators are worse
for poor black youths than these statistics would suggest, but better
than these figures denote for black youths living above poverty. It
should also be noted that because of special concern for African-
American adolescent males, more data on most of the areas reviewed
here exist for males than females. More research attention to
African-American adolescent females is needed.

Health

The elevated rate of poverty among black children leads to increased
rates of a variety of health risk outcomes in childhood and adolescence such as malnutrition, anemia, lead poisoning, lack of immunization, and lack of dental care. These and other health risks produce
higher rates of child and adolescent mortality (Jaynes & Williams,
1989, pp. 406–410).

Young African-American males report acute medical conditions at
the same rate as young Hispanic males, both higher than among white
males (National Center for Health Statistics, 1984). Black youths
account for 36% of all AIDS cases reported among 13- to 19-year-
olds, although black youths are 15% of this population (Miller, Turner, & Moses, 1990). African-American males die from AIDS in
disproportionate numbers (U.S. Bureau of the Census, 1990).

Young African-American males die from homicide at a rate almost
eight times that of young white males. Rates are half as high for

Latinos but still much greater than that for whites (Committee on Ways and Means, 1990; National Center for Health Statistics, 1991).

School completion and school-related problems

Education is one area where African-American males do significantly better than Latino males, although they still lag behind white males: The percentages of each group who are high school graduates are 64%, 52%, and 78% (U.S. Bureau of the Census, 1990). These data reflect in part that in recent years there was a significant reduction in the dropout rate among young black men. Their estimated cumulative proportion of those dropping out was reduced from 32% in 1973 to 20% in 1983 (Wetzel, 1989). The same pattern exists for the proportions of those who are two or more grades behind in school, among 15-year-olds: 10%, 12%, and 6% (Duany & Pittman, 1990).

Employability

Young African-American males have higher youth unemployment rates and lower labor force participation rates than young Latino males, although they do less well than white males. In 1988, 32% of black youths were unemployed, compared to 13% for white youths and 22% for Hispanic youths (Wetzel, 1989). This disparity appears incongruent with the finding, just noted, that African-American males do better than Latino males on indicators of school completion and being in grade. It is also noteworthy that African-American male dropouts are much less likely to find employment than Latino male dropouts (Duany & Pittman, 1990). As another indicator of employability, young African-Americans are also less likely to marry than Latino males (Duany & Pittman, 1990; U.S. Bureau of the Census, 1990).

Police involvement

Arrest rates are much higher for black male youths than for any other group. While black youths make up 15% of the juvenile population, 23% of juveniles arrested in 1986 were black, and 52% of males under 18 arrested for violent crimes committed by those under 18 were black (Dryfoos, 1990). A recent report from the Sentencing Project found that 23% of young African-American males and 10% of young Latino males (compared to 6% of similar whites) are either in prison, jail, on probation, or on parole on any given day (Mauer, 1990). Black-white differences are not as striking in self-reported delinquent behavior as they are for arrest rates. For example, in 1976 data from the National Youth Survey, behaviors classifiable as index offenses were reported by 29% of black youths aged 10–17 during the past year, but by 19% of white youths (Dryfoos, 1990). Two major recent surveys found that black youths self-report delinquent behavior at a lower frequency than white youths (Bachman, Johnston, & O'Malley, 1988; Pleck, Sonenstein, & Ku, in press). One interpretation is that delinquent behavior leads to police involvement for black youths. However, it is also possible that black youths underreport delinquent activity.

Risky sexual behavior

Because of the complexity and multiple implications of adolescent sexual behavior, we provide more detail here than for the areas already considered. Surveys conducted in 1988 provide the most recent national data on rates of sexual activity and contraceptive use in African-American adolescents. Black males show higher rates of sexual activity than other males between ages 15 and 19: 68% of black males were sexually active at age 15, 90% at age 17, and 96% at age 19. Comparison with data from a 1979 national survey (limited to 17- to 19-year-olds in metropolitan areas) indicated substantial increases in rates of sexual activity for black males aged 17–19, for example, from 60% in 1979 to 90% in 1988 among urban 17-year-olds (Sonenstein, Pleck, & Ku, 1989). Among black adolescent females in the 1988 National Survey of Family Growth (NSFG), 51% of 15- to 17-year-olds and 78% of 18- to 19-year-olds were sexually active in 1988. The proportion of sexually active black adolescent females rose relatively little in recent years. Among 15- to 17-year-olds, the 1988 rate of 51% compared with a 1982 rate of 44%, and among 17- to 19-year-olds, rates in the 2 years were almost identical (Forrest & Singh, 1990). Rates of sexual activity are higher for black adolescents than for other groups; the sources cited provide detailed comparisons.

Sonenstein, Pleck, and Ku (1991) analyzed in greater depth other indicators of sexual activity among black and other males. At every age, black adolescent males report more lifetime sexual partners, and more sexual partners in the last 12 months and in the last 4 weeks, than do white and Hispanic males. (These and other race differences cited in the paper concerning sexual behavior and substance use are significant at p < .05 or better, unless otherwise stated.) However, when the number of years since first intercourse is controlled, differences on these indicators of activity between black and white males disappear. That is, the greater frequency of recent sexual partners among black males is a function of their starting sexual activity earlier.

Regarding contraceptive use, in data from black males in 1988, 66% reported using a condom, either alone or with another method, at last intercourse, a higher proportion than among white males (54%) (Sonenstein et al., 1989). Black adolescent males' higher rate of condom use at last intercourse was also evident in multivariate analyses of consistency of condom use (Pleck, Sonenstein, & Ku, 1991) and in analyses of earlier 1979 national data (Pleck, 1989). Further, 80% of black males in the 1988 data reported that some effective method of contraception had been used at last intercourse (Sonenstein et al., 1989). In data from the 17- to 19-year-old urban subgroup that could be compared with 1979 data, rates of condom use and effective contraception use rose markedly since that earlier survey; in 1979, 50% reported use of an effective method, rising to 81% in 1988. Data on contraceptive use for black adolescent females in the 1988 National Survey of Family Growth (NSFG) have not yet been reported (Forrest & Singh, 1990; Mosher, 1990).

Black teens have substantially higher birth rates than white teens. In 1985 data for women aged 15–19, the nonwhite rate was 89.7 per 1,000, about double the white rate. The rate among nonwhites declined about 10% between 1977 and 1985 (Henshaw & Van Vort, 1989) but has risen somewhat since then (*Facts at a Glance*, 1991). The likelihood of pregnancy over the course of the teen years among black females has been estimated as 41% before age 18, and 63% before age 20 (Hofferth & Hayes, 1987, p. A-68). Most research concludes that becoming a mother significantly reduces teen females' life chances (Hofferth & Hayes, 1987; Scott-Jones & Turner, 1990). However, there are some indications that the negative consequences of teen motherhood may be less severe for black and white females

(Rudd, McKenry, & Nah, 1990). The Rudd et al. analysis also demonstrated racial differences in the pathways by which early parenthood influenced outcomes.

Recent research on adolescent sexuality is focusing increasingly on behavior that puts the individual at risk for AIDS. Studies have documented high rates of risky sexual behavior in samples including high proportions of low-income black youths (Cargill, 1991). Mays and Cochran (1990) trenchantly analyze a variety of methodological issues in the assessment and prediction of AIDS risk-related behaviors in African-Americans.

Alcohol and drug use

African-American youths register marginally lower levels of self-reported substance use than white youths. Surveys consistently indicate that African-American youths use alcohol and "soft" drugs less often than white youths, although some of the differences are small and significance testing is not reported (Jaynes & Williams, 1989; McKenry, 1990a; National Institute on Drug Abuse, 1991). For example, in the 1990 National Household Survey on Drug Use, 10.8% of 12- to 17-year-old black males used marijuana in the last year, compared with 12.2% of white males; among black and white females, the figures were 7.8 and 11.8. Among black males aged 12–17, 16.1% used alcohol in the past month, compared with 28.7% among whites, for females, the rates were 14.6% and 27.3%.

There is some evidence that black youths may underreport drug use more often than whites. Mensh and Kandel (1988) observed that black youths are significantly more likely than white youths to say they have "never" used marijuana in a later interview in a longitudinal survey when they reported such use earlier. A more recent and systematic analysis of inconsistencies in reports of drug use in the National Household Survey of Drug Abuse, however, found such inconsistent reporting to be only slightly more frequent among black respondents (Cox, Witt, Traccarella, & Perez-Michael, 1992). Nonetheless, the possibility that black youths' marginally lower self-reported rate of substance use reflects only underreporting cannot be ruled out.

A further important trend in survey data on alcohol and soft drug use is that although African-Americans show marginally lower use than whites during adolescence, in adulthood African-Americans' rates of use equal or exceed whites (National Institute on Drug Abuse, 1991). This "crossover" in black–white rates of alcohol and drug use suggests that the transition from adolescence to adulthood is a period of special risk for African-American youths. African-American youths experience severer negative consequences from substance use than do other youths. For example, Gibbs (1988) notes that a higher proportion of black than white males are diagnosed with alcohol-related disorders. Another illustration is that black youths use the hardest drugs more, and suffer disproportionately from the consequences of serious drug use. Young African-American males are as likely as young white males to experience a cocaine-related emergency room episode, although there are 80% fewer young African-American males (National Center for Health Statistics, 1991). Young Latino males had significantly fewer episodes (National Institute on Drug Abuse, 1987).

Psychological symptoms and suicide

Although some studies find that black youths report more symptoms of depression than white youths (Langner, Gersten, & Eisenberg, 1974; Schoenbach, Kaplan, Wagner, Grimson, & Udry, 1980), more studies do not (Comstock & Helsing, 1978; Roberts, Stevenson, & Breslow, 1981; McKenry, Browne, Kotch, & Symons, 1990). The McKenry et al. study is particularly valuable in investigating levels of both depressive symptoms and clinical diagnosis of depression in a sample at high risk: adolescent mothers at the time of birth, and 1 year postpartum. Its results mirror the relatively weak differences found in other studies. With levels of stressors and resources controlled, black teen mothers were higher on depression only on one measure at one time period. Dornbusch et al.'s (Dornbusch, Mont-Reynaud, Ritter, Chen, & Steinberg, 1991) investigation in a general adolescent sample examined a broader range of psychological symptoms, finding that both black males and females registered lower symptomatology than whites, and that this differential persisted even when the level of stressful life events was controlled.

As reviewed by McKenry (1990b), in past years, suicide was relatively rare in the black community. However, the rate of completed and attempted suicides among black adolescents has increased markedly in the last three decades, especially for males. Blacks' rate of suicide is still lower than whites' among adolescents, though in the 20–34 age group for males it approaches that of whites. It is also noteworthy that the black suicide rate peaks in young adulthood, whereas the white rate peaks after age 65 (Freedberg, 1986). It is possible that rates of black youths' suicidal behaviors would be higher if more accurate reporting procedures and treatment facilities were available in the black community. The dynamics of suicidal behavior have been studied far less in black female than male adolescents.

McKenry (1990b) observes that one major explanation for the increase in the black adolescent suicide rate is that it signifies an overall decrease in well-being, and greater sense of estrangement from society and anomie in black youths. As McKenry (1990b) notes, "much of the research has supported a frustration–aggression hypothesis and concluded that suicidal behaviors among black youths are related to an increasing sense of diappointment and despair at continuing discrimination as blacks progress closer to mainstream society" (p. 58).

Risk behaviors as risk factors

The health- and life-compromising outcomes discussed earlier may themselves function as risk factors for further negative outcomes. Empirically, problem behaviors are generally intercorrelated (Ketterlinus & Lamb, in press). In addition, problem behavior theory (Gore & Eckenrode, this volume; Jessor & Jessor, 1977) considers the presence of one problem behavior in an individual, viewed as a factor in the personality system, to potentiate the occurrence of other problem behaviors. Thus, those problem behaviors occurring at high rates among black youths may be conceptualized as risk factors for development in other areas.

One important analysis suggests that problem behaviors of different types appear to be less closely linked among blacks than whites. In Mott and Haurin's (1988) analyses using the National Longitudinal Survey of Youth, minority youths at any given age were more likely than white youths to have engaged only in sex or only in substance abuse, but not both. Other analyses showed that these problem behaviors were more independent in their age of onset among black youths than among either white or Hispanic youths. Only 11% of black male youths initiated sex and use of alcohol and marijuana within one year of each other, while 26% of white male youths did so. Among black and white females, the parallel percentages were 26% and 13%. (Significance testing was not reported for this analysis, based on a sample of 12,200 respondents.)

There may be a variety of reasons why problem behaviors might be empirically correlated to a greater or lesser degree among different groups. One possibility is that different problem behaviors less often reflect underlying personality or social control processes among black adolescents than among whites, and are more subject to opportunity factors. Alternately, the social contexts in which minority youths engage in problem behaviors may less often function as "gateways" to other adverse outcomes than is the case for majority adolescents. Since observed covariance among problem behaviors has been a starting point for much contemporary work on adolescent health-compromising behavior, the extent and possible sources of lower covariance among minority youths deserves further study.

Summary

Past research suggests two conclusions about the incidence of health- and life-compromising risk outcomes in black adolescents: (1) black youths register higher rates than whites of many risk outcomes in health, education, and sexual behavior; (2) at the same time, black adolescents show a prevalence of alcohol use, drug use, and depression equal to or marginally lower than white youths. There is some evidence, however, that in the early adult years, these risk outcomes become relatively more frequent among blacks, especially males, suggesting that the transition from adolescence to young adulthood is a period of special vulnerability for African-American youths.

Risk, protective factors, and resilient outcomes

We now turn from the consideration of adverse outcomes to issues concerning resilient outcomes and the related notions of risk and protection. The discussion focuses on three of the ecologies of black adolescents: family, school, and community. In each account, we consider three questions:

What are the important risk factors associated with each
setting?
What factors at the individual level are associated with resilient outcomes?
What mechanisms at the social ecological level promote resilience in individuals?

To frame the issues, the following briefly discusses the concepts used.

Resilience and protective factors are conceptualized in various
ways. Masten, Best, and Garmezy (1990) defined three kinds of resilience. The first, "overcoming the odds," captures the popular notion
of resilience as a quality of particular personal strength within an
individual. Risk factors are defined as correlates of negative or poor
outcomes. The second concept of resilience is coping, or sustained,
competent functioning in the presence of chronic or acute major life
stressors (such as divorce). The third refers to recovery from trauma.

Regardless of the way in which resilience is understood, formal
research generally operationalizes resilience as the result of specific
protective factors, which may be external to the individual (e.g., in the
family or wider community) or internalized qualities (such as sense of
personal efficacy) that can be influenced by external conditions. One
conception of protective factors (illustrated, e.g., in Dubow and
Luster's [1990] work on the adjustment of children born to teen
mothers) views them as simply the opposite ends of the dimension
defining risk factors.

Rutter (1987) formulated an alternative conception, which defines
factors or processes as protective if they exert a moderating (or interactive) effect on the influence of a risk factor. Empirical studies suggest
four types of processes: (1) reduction of risk impact, including processes that alter the risk or the person's exposure to the risk; (2)
reduction of negative chain reactions that follow exposure to the
threatening effect and contribute to long-term effects of exposure; (3)
self-esteem and self-efficacy, developed through personal relationships, new experiences, and task accomplishment; and (4) opening up
of opportunity, processes that permit the individual to gain access to
resources or to complete important life transitions.

Studies of resilience are more numerous in populations of young
children than adolescents (Werner, 1990), and studies of black adoles-

cents are rare. Nevertheless, some attempts have been made to identify protective factors retrospectively and, in a small number of studies, through longitudinal designs. As in research with other populations, studies of black adolescents indicate that protective factors fall into three categories identified in Garmezy's (1991) work: individual factors, family factors, and supportive persons in the environment. However, focusing on diverse ecologies, as we do in the following sections, permits us to examine additional protective factors (such as social composition, norms, and type of school) at the ecological level.

The family ecology

Risk factors. High rates of two family characteristics are considered particularly important risk factors for black youths: poverty, and being raised in a single-parent family headed by a teenage female. Recent statistics confirm the high rate of poverty among black children and adolescents. In 1990 data, 44.8% of all blacks under age 18 lived in poverty, compared with 38.4% among Latino children and 15.9% among white children. Altogether, there were 4.5 million poor black children (*CDF Reports*, 1991). The poverty rate for black families has risen in the past two decades, from 20% in 1969 to 30% in 1987 (Hill, 1990).

It is well documented that a substantial minority of black children and adolescents live in families headed by single-parents. More than half lived with only one parent in 1989, compared with less than a third of Hispanic children and about a fifth of white children (Lewin, 1990). The extent to which being raised in a single-parent family per se is a risk factor in child and adolescent development, and the mechanisms by which this risk operates, are controversial (Furstenberg, 1991). There is consensus, however, that the poverty often associated with being raised in a single-parent family poses hazards to development. Children of single mothers are more likely to be poor if they are black. In 1987 data, 81% of households headed by young black single mothers were impoverished (Wetzel, 1989). In a somewhat different comparison in older data, 66% of black children in single-parent families are in poverty, compared with 42% of white children (Kamerman & Hayes, 1982).

There is also general agreement that being raised in a single-parent family resulting from a teen birth creates a risk of adverse developmental consequences for the child. Recent national data on the proportion of black children in this specific circumstance have not been located. In Hofferth and Hayes's (1987) review, the age of the mother at childbearing has an effect on her child's intelligence and achievement test scores, and on other indicators of school performance. This effect holds true for blacks as well as whites, but the size of the effect is small. However, Hofferth and Hayes note that the mother's birth age has important indirect effects, through its consequences for family structure, maternal education, and family size.

An important recent analysis of data from the National Survey of Children found that children of teen births (43% of whom were black) score one standard deviation below the population mean on measures of intellectual functioning, and one standard deviation above the mean on total behavior problems and on antisocial behavior. They performed within the average range across academic achievement tests, however. Further analyses indicated that within this group, poverty status, urban residence, and mother's low self-esteem acted as risk factors for academic and behavioral adjustment. Child intelligence and self-esteem and quality of home environment functioned as protective factors (Dubow & Luster, 1990). Thus, various conditions and circumstances influence the outcomes shown by children of teen parents. However, research has not investigated similarities and differences in the risk and protective factors most influential in different racial or ethnic groups.

Resilience and adolescent parenthood. Bearing a child in adolescence is a stressful event because it triggers many changes in the physical, emotional, and social life of the teenager. Among the well-documented consequences are leaving school, caring for a child who may have serious health and development problems, poverty, and depression (Dryfoos, 1990; McKenry et al., 1990; but see Geronimus, 1991). Many of the consequences have a negative impact on the teenager as well as the child. Hence, researchers and program developers have sought to understand the factors that serve to protect against delayed sexual activity and childbearing and the factors that promote resilient outcomes among teenagers who do bear children.

Educational opportunity is a critical protective mechanism; hence staying in school despite pregnancy or childbirth is important. For example, Scott-Jones and Turner (1990) found that educational attainment mediated the impact of teenage pregnancy on income. In Polit and Kahn's (1987) study, extremely poor teenaged mothers who were enrolled in school when baseline data were collected had completed or were enrolled in an educational program 2 years later. In contrast, only 28% of girls who had dropped out at baseline were in an educational program.

Among the individual factors that serve as a critical mechanism are high educational expectations. Scott-Jones and White (1990) found that young black teenaged girls (ages 13 and 14) who had such expectations were less likely to become sexually active than girls who had low expectations. According to Danziger and Farber (1990), black teenaged girls who stayed in school, compared with their counterparts who were out of school, had a strong sense of personal motivation.

Family support for achievement and support from caring adults in the community were protective mechanisms identified in Danziger and Farber's study. In Polit and Kahn's (1987) study, girls who had received educational counseling during the second year of data collection were more likely than other girls to have completed or be enrolled in an educational program. Social support also serves to facilitate adjustment to teenage parenthood. In McKenry and associates' (1990) study of 157 adolescent mothers (73% of whom were black), social support of the teenager's mother predicted depression at the birth of the adolescent's child, but not 1 year later. General social support (as defined by contacts with friends and relatives, religious activities, group memberships, and telephone contacts), however, mediated depression at birth and 1 year postpartum.

The family environment and school success. R. Clark's (1983) study of black adolescent school achievement highlights the importance of protective factors in the family environment. In this study, Clark used extensive interview, participant observation, and questionnaire data to identify patterns of home experience among 10 high- and low-achieving high school seniors. All families lived in low-income neighborhoods and had total family incomes below the government-defined poverty level.

High-achieving students in these families had qualities associated with individual resilience (see Werner, 1990, for a review), notably (1) a positive sense of self, which was reflected in positive self-talk, a sense of academic competence, and appropriate attribution of failure, and (2) a sense of responsibility and the determination to overcome obstacles. These students also had a positive racial identity and could recall at least one teacher who provided time, attention, and nurturing during the elementary or intermediate grades.

In contrast to parents of low achievers, parents of high achievers were nurturing and supportive, and they established clear role boundaries, monitored their children's activities inside the home and in the community, consistently enforced rules, and frequently engaged children in learning activities (including home maintenance, informational, and recreational activities). The parents of high achievers described their upbringing in home environments that were organized to support social and academic learning.

A different perspective on the family environment comes from a survey of 15,000 students (Steinberg, Dornbusch, & Brown, 1992). These investigators found in questionnaire responses that parental authoritativeness (defined as behavioral control, warmth, and psychological autonomy granting) was unrelated to school performance of Asian-American and African-American students. Hispanic and white students whose parents were authoritative performed better in school than students whose parents were nonauthoritative. However, across groups, parental authoritativeness was related to psychological adjustment.

The school ecology

Risk factors. Poor performance in school at an early age is a risk factor that signals the probability of problems in all major areas of development. Much attention to risk factors for school failure has focused on individual characteristics and behavior in the elementary years, such as lack of engagement in instructional activities, poor performance on tests and other classroom tasks, low self-esteem, and poor attendance.

Several reviews and edited works address the role of school policies and practices as sources of risk for ethnic minorities, girls and women, and low-income students (e.g., American Association of University Women, 1992; Boyd, 1991; Council of Chief State School Officers,

1988; Natriello, McDill, & Pallas, 1990). For example, a sizable body of evidence shows that, within secondary schools, disproportionate numbers of black and Hispanic students occupy the general and vocational tracks, in contrast to whites, who are overrepresented in college preparatory tracks (Braddock, 1990; Oakes, 1985). Fine (1988) identifies three elements that contribute to inequitable outcomes in secondary schooling: (1) educational policies and structures (such as tracking); (2) silencing and discrediting those who raise issues regarding educational inequity; and (3) pedagogical and curricular practices that transform students' strengths into pathologies.

Having black or poor classmates is assumed to put students at risk of adverse academic and psychosocial outcomes. Due to methodological problems, however, it has been difficult to determine the extent to which risk is attributable to the presence of poor or minority classmates or neighbors (i.e., social composition) or to family characteristics that are not influenced by where the family lives. Jencks and Mayer (1990) addressed this issue, which has important implications for policies regarding economic segregation in schools and neighborhoods, in a comprehensive review of studies that clearly separated ecological from family effects.

They found that, for students in general, the chances of dropping out of high school increase as school socioeconomic status (SES) falls and minority enrollment increases. However, the school's mean SES affects black and white students' chances of dropping out differently. The chances of dropping out increase for both white and black students as mean SES decreases, but the difference in the increase is smaller for black than white students. Attending school with low SES and minority classmates increases the probability of black, white, and Hispanic girls of any SES having a child before graduating.

However, a high school's mean SES has an effect on black students' cognitive growth but little effect on that of whites. Attending a high-SES school may have positive effects on black high school students' aspirations to college, while both mean SES and test scores affect college attendance positively. In contrast, for white students, the effects of mean SES are negligible. Similarly, a school's racial mix does not affect white students' college attendance, but attending integrated schools affects northern black high school students' college entrance and persistence. However, desegregation affects southern black students' college attendance negatively.

Self-esteem, locus of control, and social identity. Low self-esteem is often cited as the ultimate source of poor academic achievement and self-destructive behavior among adolescents. Thus one might argue that a positive self-concept must be an especially important protective mechanism for African-American youths for whom "membership in a disfavored group typically exacerbates puberty-linked insecurities" (Spencer, Swanson, & Cunningham, 1991, p. 368).

In the extensive literature on self-evaluation and the self-concept, many constructs and measures have been developed. In addition to the core concept of self-esteem, researchers have proposed alternate constructs focusing, for example, on self-perceptions of efficacy and competence (Bandura, 1997; Elias, 1991; Elias & Weissberg, this volume; Harter, 1983). Connell (1990) has developed a model that defines self-system processes in relation to fundamental psychological needs for competence, autonomy, and relatedness. However, the empirical studies comparing black and other adolescents overwhelmingly employ measures of self-esteem.

Most empirical studies find that blacks have self-esteem comparable with whites at all ages (see reviews in Blascovich & Tomaka, 1991; Ramseur, 1989, 1990; Taylor, 1976). Taylor (1976) and Gibbs (1985) found that the attitude of significant others (parents, peers, and teachers) toward the child was a source of black children's self-esteem, and that the primary focus of social comparison among blacks is within the black social context. Other key findings in Ramseur's (1989) review of this literature are that the black family and community can act as protectors from racist and other negative images by providing a "system-blame" explanation of failure to cushion blows to self-esteem.

Thus, the evidence does not suggest that low self-esteem is a risk factor of particular importance for African-American youths, in the sense of occurring more frequently among them than among other groups. Research has not investigated, however, whether low self-esteem might have severer consequences in black adolescents than in other groups. It is possible that variations in self-esteem might have less impact on risk outcomes among blacks than other groups, because other factors are of relatively greater importance (Emery & Forehand, this volume). For example, Spencer (1987) asserts that race pride may lead to use of positive coping strategies. Thus, the role of low self-esteem as a risk factor for African-American adolescents needs further study.

Locus of control has also been central in research comparing blacks and whites on personality characteristics, and has been viewed as a particularly important determinant of blacks' school achievement. The concept has been formulated and operationalized in a variety of ways, beyond the scope of this chapter to review. Graham's (1989) review, giving particular attention to studies with children and adolescents, concludes that although some earlier studies found blacks to have a less internal locus of control, "much of the more recent comparative research suggests that Blacks are no less internal than Whites." Graham notes that since internal locus of control and academic achievement are usually found to be correlated, this result is inconsistent with blacks' generally poorer school performance.

As reviewed by Slaughter-Defoe et al. (1990), theoretical perspectives on achievement-related behavior among black youths have shifted substantially over the decades. Recent research has focused on the role of social identity and social relations. M. Clark (1991) reviewed research on friendship patterns, social identity, and school support to identify protective factors in academic achievement. Individual factors that fostered resilience were bicultural or raceless social identity and perceptions of school as supportive. Close friendships, particularly with friends who valued education, and active parental support for achievement were also important factors. In contrast, an oppositional social identity, which is characterized by angry and rebellious responses to racism, is hypothesized as a source of vulnerability in school settings.

However, in reviewing the research on social identity, Clark noted that African-American adolescents who are resilient in school settings may be at risk of poor social development: "Alienation from same-race peers may be problematic, especially for African-American adolescents who live in black communities and attend majority-black schools. Their peer support system is lacking at a stage when peers should play an important role in their development" (p. 43).

This view is consistent with Fordham and Ogbu's (1986) findings regarding some black adolescents' conflict between achievement pursuits ("acting white") and being popular with peers, and with Steinberg et al.'s (1992) finding that among African-American students, low peer support for achievement undermines parental authoritativeness. However, among African-American males in eighth grade, athletes are more likely to have high standing among peers and to plan to enroll in academic or college preparatory curricula (Braddock, Royster, Winfield, & Hawkins, 1991). These effects were obtained after controlling for age, family structure, achievement test scores, school size, poverty concentration, urbanicity, and ability-group placement.

The social context of the school. Natriello and associates (1990) argue that the social context of the school is the major source of disadvantage or advantage regarding educational outcomes. Research has begun to examine Catholic schooling and its positive effects on the performance of black adolescents. Using samples drawn from High School and Beyond, Hoffer, Greely, and Coleman (1985) found that Catholic schooling had a positive impact on growth in mathematics and verbal achievement, that the size of the effect was greater among black, Hispanic, and lower-income students, and that the effects were due to course requirements. In a recent analysis of data from the National Assessment of Educational Progress, Lee, Winfield, and Wilson (1991) found that eighth-grade African-American students in Catholic schools used their time more positively (i.e., reading, doing homework, not watching television) than their counterparts in public schools.

One important study is *Fifteen Thousand Hours* (Rutter, Maughan, Mortimore, & Ouston, 1979), a study of 12 secondary schools in one section of inner London. With students' presecondary home backgrounds and personal characteristics controlled, these investigators found striking differences in student achievement, attendance, persistence in school, and delinquency among schools that varied in "ethos" or climate, defined as the attitudes, values, and behaviors that characterize the school. Although this and Mortimore and associates' (Mortimore, Sammons, Stoll, Lewis, & Ecob, 1988) study are cited as evidence of the "effective school" movement in the United States, the U.S. research on how schools can reduce risk among urban students is fraught with methodological problems (Boyd, 1991).

The community ecology

Risk factors. We now consider the social and physical characteristics of communities that serve as risk and protective factors for black adolescents. We define communities broadly, referring to both locales or places, such as neighborhoods and schools, and to social interactions that can occur within a locale or transcend locale and boundaries of place. Our discussion focuses on compositional characteristics (such as socioeconomic status and racial composition). The physical characteristics of communites (such as the layout and decoration of interior spaces, crowding, and noise levels) can affect children's development (Austin, 1968; Moos, 1979; Scott-Jones, 1984; Wohlwill & vanVliet, 1985); research on environmental risks among black student populations has focused on young and elementary age children rather than adolescents.

We do not discuss the risk status of black youths who live in suburban and rural locales. There is scant research on these adolescents, although they make up a substantial minority of the total black adolescent population: 30% of nonpoor black adolescents and 18% of poor black adolescents live in the suburbs, whereas in rural areas the percentages are 16% and 25% for nonpoor and poor adolescents respectively; 57% of poor black adolescents and 54% of nonpoor black adolescents live in neighborhoods in central cities (Dryfoos, 1990).

It has been well documented that adolescents who live in minority or poor neighborhoods are more likely to commit or be victims of crimes, have children out of wedlock, be victims of racial discrimination, have problems with substance abuse, and have lower educational attainment and earnings than adolescents who live in affluent or white neighborhoods (Byrne & Sampson, 1986; G. Gottfredson, 1987). According to popular assumptions, having black or poor neighbors puts youthful residents at risk of being victimized or engaging in self-destructive or illegal behaviors.

According to the review by Jencks and Mayer (1990), growing up in a poor neighborhood reduced educational attainment of males, regardless of race, but neighborhood racial composition had different effects on black and white males. White males attained more education if they had black neighbors, and black males got more schooling if they had white neighbors.

Only two studies in the review addressed neighborhood effects on delinquency: One had a white sample and the other pooled the data for black and white subjects. The studies produced contradictory findings on how living in a low-SES neighborhood affected delinquency among low-income teenagers. In one, low neighborhood SES lowered delinquency among low-income youths, whereas in the other study, low neighborhood SES increased delinquency.

Fewer than a handful of studies examined neighborhood characteristics that put teenage girls at risk of getting pregnant, but these studies suggested that growing up in poor neighborhoods exerts a large effect on sexual behavior. For example, Hogan and Kitagawa (1985) found that the risk of pregnancy was a third higher for teenagers living in low-status Chicago neighborhoods. Neighborhood quality was defined by a measure composed of poverty rates, median family income, and juvenile delinquency among boys, among other indexes.

Individual-level factors and resilience. Although available studies have focused on protective factors that promote resilience in academic settings, some theoretical and empirical work has considered mechanisms that are important in different community environments. For example, Ogbu's (1985) cultural-ecological model of inner-city child rearing and development specifies competencies that African-Americans in the inner-city expect children to acquire and the cultural factors that shape the type and content of such competencies.

One such competency is mutual exchange, which is based on the well-documented norm of reciprocity that exists in poor, urban neighborhoods. Other competencies that Ogbu defined include conventional employment, clientship, hustling, pimping, entertainment, and collective struggle. Ogbu asserts that all of these competencies are necessary for survival in neighborhoods whose economy embraces conventional and "street" or "underground" forces. Thus a given individual may be employed in a conventional job and yet occasionally engage in hustling. Protection against the risks associated with the street culture may hinge on the range of competencies at the individual's command and the skill with which they are applied. However, success in school hinges on the use of alternative strategies that protect the student against adverse community or peer influences. Such strategies include, for example, gender-specific camouflage (e.g., for males, participating in sport), participating in interventions, and attending private schools (Ogbu, 1991).

In rural communities, black adolescents face many of the risks associated with poverty (see Lee, 1989; and Okwumabua, Okwumabua, Winston, & Walker, 1989). Successful development in this context is facilitated by strong family support and social networks of peers and respected elders (Lee, 1984, 1989). Indeed, a form of protection for urban youths may be "time out" in a rural setting. In this regard, Lee comments: "It is interesting to note that often when family situations in urban centers become chaotic, black parents will send their children for a period of time to live with extended family members in the rural South. It is anticipated that in a southern rural family environment, young people will experience order, stability and a sense of tradition" (Lee, 1989, p. 85).

Participation in a church community and belief in a higher power were particularly important in the lives of rural youths, although religion has been identified as a protective factor for African-American youths in diverse settings. Reviewing the function of religion as a protective factor, Brown and Gary (1991) and Masten, Best, and Garmezy (1990) report that religion is associated with competence and educational attainment. Anderson (1991), however, speculates that, among very poor girls, fundamentalist religious beliefs about the power of fate may render them indifferent to the possibilities of pregnancy.

Qualitative studies of neighborhoods provide another perspective on the complexity of risk and protective mechanisms that operate within communities. For example, Anderson (1991), drawing on two decades of work in black neighborhoods in Chicago and Philadelphia, describes the street culture in very poor, inner-city neighborhoods as a contributor to negative outcomes. He comments that "the relative prominence of this culture in the poorest inner-city neighborhoods brings about not only the prevalence of much antisocial behavior but the high incidence of teenage parenthood as well" (Anderson, 1991, p. 376). However, Anderson also notes that factors such as clear options for the future may serve to protect the adolescent from adversity. Having educational plans predicted enrollment in postsecondary education and training among black males (Wilson-Sadberry, Winfield, & Royster, 1991) and was important in delaying risky sexual behavior in girls (Scott-Jones & Turner, 1990).

Social processes. The following considers the role of processes and mechanisms presumed either to mediate the effects of compositional characteristics or to contribute directly to developmental outcomes. There are many theories about the mechanisms through which neighborhoods affect adolescent behavior. Jencks and Mayer (1990) classify the theories into four types: (1) contagion theories, which specify that social problems are spread through peer influence; (2) institutional theories, ones that emphasize the influence of formal organizations within the community; (3) collective socialization theories, which emphasize the roles of adults in neighborhoods as agents of social control and models of behavior; and (4) social competition theories, which focus on such influences as competition and deprivation.

Few quantitative studies rigorously test the implictions of these theories. One reason for the paucity of data is that the measurement of neighborhood effects requires data both on individual behaviors and neighborhood characteristics. However, two recent studies provide evidence about the role of mechanisms through which the social mix influences the behavior of adolescents. The first (Crane, 1991) tested one of the assumptions underlying the epidemic theory of ghettos, a variation of the contagion theory. According to the epidemic theory, if the incidence of a social problem reaches a critical level in a neighborhood, the neighborhood will experience an explosive increase in the incidence of the problem. Crane tested the specific implication that in large, inner-city neighborhoods that are near the top of the distribution of neighborhood quality, individuals will be less likely to have adverse outcomes.

Crane used the 1970 Public Use Microdata Sample, indexing neighborhood quality by the percentage of workers who held managerial or professional jobs. Among black females, aged 16 to 19, the chances of having a child were lowest in the neighborhoods with the highest proportion of high-status workers: at 31.2%, the probability was .08; at 5.6%, .12; and at 3.5%, the probability was .16. Crane found similar patterns for white females, but for girls in the worst neighborhoods, the chance of having a baby was .10.

Dramatic effects were also found at the lowest-status levels for dropping out among black and white males and females. The effects were particularly large for black males. Outside of urban ghettos, neighborhood effects on both dropping out and childbearing were smaller and the nonlinear increases were not significant.

The second study (D. Gottfredson, McNeill, & Gottfredson, 1991) is a multilevel analysis that examined the effects of neighborhood SES on delinquency and the role of social bonding and peer influence as theoretical intervening variables. The sample included 3,729 adolescents (71% black and 2% Hispanic) in 10 high-crime middle and junior high schools in four cities. Area, or neighborhood, measures (disorganization, defined by indicators such as high male unemployment, and affluence, defined by dimensions indicative of high SES) were computed for each census block in which an individual in the sample lived, and the measures were merged with individual records from surveys conducted in the schools. The surveys measured individual background variables, including parental SES, race, age, and elements of social bonding (e.g., school attachment) and peer influence.

The results formed a complex and often counterintuitive pattern. For example, living in a less affluent neighborhood was protective for males: Males who lived in such neighborhoods reported *less* criminal behavior than males who lived in high SES areas. Males in disorganized areas also reported *less* involvement in drugs regardless of race, age, or social class. However, community disorganization had no effect on male theft, vandalism, and interpersonal aggression.

In contrast, neither area affluence nor disorganization affected female delinquency, with one exception: Females in disorganized neighborhoods engaged in interpersonal aggression more often than their counterparts in less disorganized areas. However, in disorganized neighborhoods, females and males alike reported that they were negatively influenced by peers and less attached and committed to school. According to the analytical model, these mechanisms increase delinquency.

As in quantitative studies reviewed by Jencks and Mayer (1990), the magnitude of neighborhood effects was small. Ethnographic research, such as Sullivan's (1989) comparative study of delinquent careers among young men in three Brooklyn neighborhoods, indicates that variations in the social ecology of neighborhoods, more than individual differences, account for differences among groups in crime and other outcomes. Yet another perspective, suggested by S. Gottfredson and Taylor's (1986) work on the prediction of recidivism in Baltimore neighborhoods, provides support for person–environment interactions. Exploring these varied possibilities is a major direction for future research.

Conclusion

Using the concepts of risk, resilience, and protection, we explored selected developmental outcomes among black adolescents. Clearly the conceptualization is a useful one for understanding why some youths, despite impediments associated with social and economic disadvantage, prevail and sometimes flourish against the odds. Studies indicate that individual, familial, and community resources contribute to the resilience of black youths, and that social identity and type of community may determine which factors are important for different subgroups of black youths.

However, applying this perspective to black youths in one common and apparently plausible way – to predict levels of risk outcomes at the aggregate level among black youths, solely from knowing aggregate levels of risk factors among black youths – is not useful. Although black youths have higher rates of poverty than white youths, black adolescents register levels of self-esteem equivalent to those in whites, and also report lower rates of certain risk outcomes: alcohol use, soft drug use, and depression.

Poor black youths are disproportionately represented in the ranks of adolescents at risk for educational failure, police involvement, and problems associated with sexual behavior; hence black adolescents have been participants in many of the major social and health-oriented programs that have been implemented during the past 25 years. Overall, findings from well-designed program evaluations, though sparse, indicate that programs can be effective in preventing or delaying high-risk behavior or alleviating the short-term impact of exposure to risk (see Dryfoos, 1990; Nettles, 1993; Pless & Stein, this volume; Schorr, 1988; and W. T. Grant Foundation, 1988, for reviews).

From longitudinal studies, however, we have learned that effects vanish when the intervention ends (Dryfoos, 1990). The limited effectiveness of interventions raises the question, What adjustments are needed to sustain favorable outcomes?

Our essay suggests three possibilities:

First, progam designs can incorporate needs assessments that not only evaluate risk, but identify existing sources of protection (such as a relationship with a caring adult, or participation in enriching activities) in the adolescent's life. Such environmental or personal resources can be used in selecting or adjusting the type, timing, and intensity of programmatic "treatments" for a given individual or group. Moreover, efforts can be directed at either strengthening naturally occuring sources of protection or designing protective structures that will continue in the adolescent's life after the intervention or participation in the intervention ends. Such adjustments could be formally assessed in terms of their effectiveness in sustaining program inputs over the long run.

Second, interventions need to be designed with knowledge of African-American culture if they are to be effective with African-American youths. As an example, Mays and Cochran (1990) point out that many risk-reduction messages for the practice of safe sex promote these activities in the context of "fun," such as posters saying "Play It Safe" or "Plan Safe." Mays and Cochran argue that the view of sex as play or leisure activity implicit in this message conflicts with fundamental religious teachings about sex that are prevalent in black communities. Further, this message "paints a vacation-like framework for viewing sexual activity," presuming individuals have the time and privacy to enjoy fully their sexuality.

Third, program designs must incorporate developmental processes. As presumed in Levitt, Selman, & Richmond's (1991) developmental conceptual model of risk-taking behavior, resilience is fostered through the synchronous development of three psychosocial components: knowledge, management skills, and personal meaning. According to the investigators, "The questions of prevention shift, then, from how do we promote specific risk-resistent behavior (e.g., smoking cessation) to how do we promote higher levels of knowledge, management skills, and personal meaning?" (p. 371). Issues raised by this model might have a particular application in programs for black adolescents. For example, variation in the types and development of social identity, as noted in the preceding section, may be important considerations in designing contexts that have personal meaning for individuals in this population.

Several directions for future study are evident. There remains the need for analyses of risk factors and outcomes that distinguish groups by gender, socioeconomic status, community residence, and other factors of known and hypothesized importance. Research directions suggested by the limited data on successful adaptation in diverse ecologies include investigations into the development in out-of-school contexts of behaviors that make future goals more attainable and the effects of peer support and social identity on persistence and success in academic settings.

In exploring the contribution of community factors as stressors and sources of protection, attention must be given to how social properties are conceptualized and measured, to the inclusion of psychosocial factors as dependent variables, and to the role of person–environment interactions. Factors affecting parents' abilities to provide guidance and surveillance, and how such factors exert direct and indirect effects on development, are also important to study.

Another pressing need is for studies of black adolescent females, who have been overlooked in recent discourse about the problems of poverty and discrimination. Finally, intervention research can make important contributions to our understanding of resilience and protective mechanisms. The design of interventions that address critical transitional periods is a priority, as is the continued search for ways to enhance and sustain the effects of programs to foster favorable outcomes.

References

American Association of University Women Educational Foundation and National Education Association. (1992). *How schools shortchange girls.* Washington, DC.

Anderson, E. (1991). Neighborhood effects on teenage pregnancy. In C. Jencks & P. E. Peterson (Eds.), *The urban underclass* (pp. 375–398). Washington, DC: Brookings Institution.

Astin, A. W. (1968). *The college environment.* Washington, DC: American Council on Education.

Bachman, J., Johnston, L. D., & O'Malley, P. (1988). *Monitoring the future: Questionnaire responses from the nation's high school seniors.* Ann Arbor, MI: Institute for Social Research.

Bandura, A. (1977). Self-efficacy: Toward a unifying theory of behavioral change. *Psychological Review, 84,* 191–215.

Bell-Scott, P., & Taylor, R. (Eds.). (1989). Black adolescents. *Journal of Adolescent Research, 4*(2), Special issue.

Blascovich, J., & Tomaka, J. (1991). Measures of self-esteem. In J. P. Robinson, P. R. Shaver, & L. S. Wrightsman (Eds.), *Measures of personality and social-psychological attitudes* (pp. 115–160). New York: Academic Press.

Boyd, W. L. (1991). What makes ghetto schools work or not work? In P. W. Thurston & P. P. Zodhiates (Eds.), *Advances in Educational Administration* (pp. 83–129), Greenwich CT: JAI.

Braddock, J. H. (1990). *Tracking: Implications for student race-ethnic subgroups, Report No. 1.* Baltimore: Johns Hopkins University Center for Research on Effective Schooling for Disadvantaged Students.

Braddock, J. H., Royster, D. A., Winfield, L. F., & Hawkins, R. (1991, November). Bouncing back: Sports and academic resilience among African-American students. *Education and Urban Society, 24*(1), 113–131.

Brown, D. R., & Gary, L. E. (1991). Religious socialization and educational attainment among African Americans: An empirical assessment. *Journal of Negro Education, 60,* 411–426.

Byrne, J. M., & Sampson, R. J. (Eds.). (1986). *The social ecology of crime.* London: Springer-Verlag.

Cargill, V. (1991). *AIDS-related sexual behaviors, knowledge and attitudes in teens: Cause for more than concern.* Abstract submitted to the Society of General Internal Medicine.

CDF Reports. (1991, November). Child poverty worsens in 1990. pp. 1, 5.

Clark, M. L. (1991). Social identity, peer relations and academic competence of African-American adolescents. *Education and Urban Society, 24,* 41–52.

Clark, R. (1983). *Family life and school achievement: Why poor Black children succeed or fail.* Chicago: University of Chicago Press.

Committee on Ways and Means, U.S. House of Representatives. (1990). *Overview of entitlement programs: 1990 Green Book.* Washington, DC: U.S. Government Printing Office.

Comstock, G. W., & Helsing, R. (1978). Symptoms of depression in two communities. *Psychological Medicine, 6,* 551–563.

Connell, J. P. (1990). Context, self, and action: A motivational analysis of self-system processes across the lifespan. In D. Cicchetti & M. Beeghly (Eds.), *The self in transition: Infancy to childhood* (pp. 61–97). Chicago: University of Chicago Press.

Consortium for Research on Black Adolescence. (1990). *Black adolescence: Current issues and annotated bibliography.* Boston: G. K. Hall.

Council of Chief State School Officers. (1988). *School success for students at risk.* Orlando, FL: Harcourt Brace Jovanovich.

Cox, B. G., Witt, M. B., Traccarella, M. A., & Perez-Michael, A. M. (1992). Inconsistent reporting of drug use in 1988. In C. F. Turner, J. T. Lessler, & J. C. Gfroerer, (Eds.), *Survey measurement of drug use: Methodological studies* (pp. 109–154). Rockville, MD: National Institute on Drug Abuse.

Crane, J. (1991). The epidemic theory of ghetto and neighborhood effects on dropping out and teenage childbearing. *Journal of Sociology, 96,* 26–59.

Danziger, S. K., & Farber, N. B. (1990). Keeping inner-city youths in school: Critical experience of young black women. *Social Work Research and Abstracts, 26,* 32–39.

Dornbusch, S. M., Mont-Reynaud, R., Ritter, P. R., Chen, Z., & Steinberg, L. (1991). Stressful events and their correlates among adolescents of diverse backgrounds. In M. E. Colten & S. Gore (Eds.), *Adolescent stress: Causes and consequences* (pp. 111–130). New York: Aldine de Gruyter.

Dryfoos, J. G. (1990). *Adolescents at risk: Prevalence and prevention.* New York: Oxford University Press.

Duany, L., & Pittman, K. (1990). *Latino youths at a crossroads.* Washington, DC: Children's Defense Fund.

Dubow, E. F., & Luster, T. (1990). Adjustment of children born to teen mothers: The contribution of risk and protective factors. *Journal of Marriage and the Family, 52,* 393–404.

Elias, M. (1991). The integral role of self-esteem and children's confidence and competence on quality education. *Focus on Education, Fall,* 1–11.

Facts at a glance. (1991). Washington, DC: Child Trends.

Fine, M. (1988). De-institutionalizing educational inequity: Contexts that constrict and construct the lives and minds of public-school adolescents. In Council of Chief State School Officers, *School success for students at-risk* (pp. 89–119). Orlando, FL: Harcourt Brace Jovanovich.

Fordham, S., & Ogbu, J. U. (1986). Black students' school success: Coping with the burden of "acting white." *Urban Review, 18*(3), 176–206.

Forrest, J. D., & Singh, S. (1990). The sexual and reproductive behavior of American women, 1982–1988. *Family Planning Perspectives, 22,* 206–214.

Freedberg, L. (1986, January–February). For black males suicide rates peak at prime of life. *Youth Law News, 7,* 13.

Furstenberg, F. F. (1991). As the pendulum swings: Teenage childbearing and social concern. *Family Relations, 40,* 127–138.

Garmezy, N. (1985). Stress-resistant children: The search for protective factors. In J. E. Stevenson (Ed.), *Recent research in developmental psychopathology* (pp. 213–233). *Journal of Child Psychology and Psychiatry* (Book Supplement No. 4). Oxford: Pergamon Press.

Garmezy, N. (1987). Stress, competence, and development: Continuities in the study of schizophrenic adults, children vulnerable to psychopathology, and the search for stress-resistant children. *American Journal of Orthopsychiatry, 57*(2), 159–174.

Garmezy, N. G. (1991). Resilience in children's adaptation to negative life events and stressed environments. *Pediatric Annals, 20*(9), 459–466.

Geronimus, A. T. (1991). Teenage childbearing and social and reproductive disadvantage: The evolution of complex questions and the demise of simple answers. *Family Relations, 40,* 463–471.

Gibbs, J. T. (1985). City girls: Psychosocial adjustment of urban Black adolescent females. *Sage, 2*(2), 28–36.

Gibbs, J. T. (1988). The new morbidity: Homocide, suicide, accidents, and life-threatening behaviors. In J. T. Gibbs (Ed.), *Young, black, and male in America: An endangered species* (pp. 258–293). New York: Auburn House.

Gottfredson, D., McNeill, R. J., & Gottfredson, G. D. (1991). Social area influences on delinquency: A multilevel analysis. *Journal of Research in Crime and Delinquency, 28,* 197–226.

Gottfredson, G. D. (1987). American education: American delinquency. *Today's Delinquent, 6,* 5–71.

Gottfredson, S. D., & Taylor, R. B. (1986). Person–environment interactions in the prediction of recidivism. In J. M. Byrne & R. J. Sampson (Eds.), *The social ecology of crime* (pp. 133–155). New York: Springer-Verlag.

Graham, S. G. (1989). Motivation in Afro-Americans. In G. Benny & S. Asamen (Eds.), *Black students: Psychological issues and academic achievement* (pp. 40–68). Newbury Park, CA: Sage.

Harter, S. (1983). Competence as a dimension of self-evaluation: Toward a comprehensive model of self-worth. In R. Leehy (Ed.), *The development of the self.* New York: Academic Press.

Henshaw, S. G., & Van Vort, J. (1989). Teenage abortion, birth and pregnancy statistics: An update. *Family Planning Perspectives, 21,* 85–88.

Hill, R. B. (1990). Critical issues for black families by the year 2000. In *The state of black America 1989* (pp. 41–62). New York: National Urban League.

Hoffer, T. Greeley, A. M., & Coleman, J. S. (1985). Achievement growth in public and Catholic schools. *Sociology of Education, 58,* 74–97.

Hofferth, S. L., & Hayes, C. D. (1987). *Risking the future: Adolescent sexuality, pregnancy, and childbearing* (Vol. 2). Washington, DC: National Academy Press.

Hogan, D. P., & Kitagawa, F. M. (1985). The impact of social status, family structure, and neighborhood on the fertility of black adolescents. *American Journal of Sociology, 90,* 825–855.

Jaynes, G. D., & Williams, R. M., Jr. (1989). *A common destiny: Blacks and American society*. Washington, DC: National Academy Press.

Jencks, C., & Mayer, S. E. (1990). The social consequences of growing up in a poor neighborhood. In the National Research Council, *Inner-city poverty in the United States* (pp. 111–186). Washington, DC: National Academy Press.

Jessor, R., & Jessor, S. L. (1977). *Problem behavior and psychological development: A longitudinal study of youth*. New York: Academic Press.

Jones, R. (Ed.). (1989). *Black adolescents*. Berkeley, CA: Cobb & Henry.

Kamerman, S. B., & Hayes, C. D. (1982). The dimensions of change: Trends and issues. In S. B. Kamerman & C. D. Hayes (Eds.), *Families that work: Children in a changing world* (pp. 12–36). Washington, DC: National Academy Press.

Ketterlinus, R. D., & Lamb, M. E., (in press). *Adolescent problem behaviors*. Hillsdale, NJ: Erlbaum.

Langner, T. S., Gersten, J. C., & Eisenberg, J. G. (1974). Approaches to measurement and definition in the epidemiology of behavior disorders: Ethnic background and child behavior. *International Journal of Health Services, 4*, 483–501.

Lee, C. C. (1984). An investigation of psychosocial variables related to academic success for rural Black adolescents. *Journal of Negro Education, 53*(4), 424–434.

Lee, C. C. (1989). Rural black adolescents: Psychosocial development in a changing environment. In R. Jones (Ed.), *Black Adolescents* (pp. 79–95). Berkeley, CA: Cobb & Henry.

Lee, V. E., Winfield, L. F., & Wilson, T. C. (1991). Academic behaviors among high-achieving African-American students. In L. F. Winfield (Ed.), *Education and Urban Society, 24*(1), 65–86.

Levitt, M. Z., Selman, R. L., & Richmond, J. B. (1991). The psychosocial foundations of early adolescents' high-risk behavior: Implications for research and practice. *Journal of Research on Adolescence, 1*, 349–378.

Lewin, T. (1990, July 11). Rise in single-parent families found continuing. *New York Times*, p. 17.

Masten, A. S., Best, K. M., & Garmezy, N. (1990). Resilience and development: Contributions from the study of children who overcame adversity. *Development and Psychopathology, 2*, 425–444.

Mauer, M. (1990). *Young black men in the criminal justice system*. Washington, DC: Sentencing Project.

Mays, V. M., & Cochran, S. D. (1990). Methodological issues in the assessment and prediction of AIDS risk-related sexual behaviors among Black Americans. In B. Voeller, J. M. Reinsch, & M. Gottlieb (Eds.),

AIDS and sex: An integrated and biobehavioral approach (pp. 97–120). New York: Oxford University Press.

McKenry, P. C. (1990a). Drug abuse. In Consortium for Research on Black Adolescence (Ed.), *Black adolescence: Current issues and annotated bibliography* (pp. 45–56). Boston: G. K. Hall.

McKenry, P. C. (1990b). Suicide. In Consortium for Research on Black Adolescence (Ed.), *Black adolescence: Current issues and annotated bibliography* (pp. 57–68). Boston: G. K. Hall.

McKenry, P. C., Browne, D. H., Kotch, J. B., & Symons, M. J. (1990). Mediators of depression among low-income, adolescent mothers of infants: A longitudinal perspective. *Journal of Youth and Adolesence, 19,* 327–347.

McKenry, P., Everett, J., Ramseur, H., & Carter, C. (1989). Research on black adolescents: A legacy of cultural bias. *Journal of Adolescent Research, 4*(2), 254–264.

McLoyd, V. C. (1990). Minority children: Introduction to the special issue. *Child Development 61*(2), 263–266.

Mensh, B. S., & Kandel, D. B. (1988). Underreporting of substance use in a national longitudinal youth cohort. *Public Opinion Quarterly, 52,* 101–124.

Miller, H. G., Turner, C. F., & Moses, L. E. (1990). *AIDS: The second decade.* Washington, DC: National Academy Press.

Moos, R. H. (1979). *Evaluating educational environments.* San Francisco: Jossey-Bass.

Mortimore, P., Sammons, P., Stoll, L., Lewis, D., & Ecob, R. (1988). *School matters.* Berkeley: University of California Press.

Mosher, W. D. (1990). Contraceptive practice in the United States, 1982–1988. *Family Planning Perspectives, 20,* 198–205.

Mott, F. L., & Haurin, R. J. (1988). Linkages between sexual activity and alcohol and drug use among American adolescents. *Family Planning Perspectives, 20,* 128–136.

National Center for Health Statistics (1984). *Health indicators for Hispanic, Black, and White Americans.* Vital and Health Statistics Series 10, no. 148, Washington, DC: U.S. Government Printing Office.

National Center for Health Statistics. (1991). *Health, United States, 1990.* Hyattsville, MD: Public Health Service.

National Institute on Drug Abuse. (1987). *Use of selected drugs among Hispanics: Mexican Americans, Puerto Ricans, Cuban Americans.* Rockville, MD: U.S. Department of Health and Human Services.

National Institute on Drug Abuse. (1991). *National household survey on drug abuse: Main findings.* Rockville, MD.

Natriello, G., McDill, E. L., & Pallas, A. M. (1990). *Schooling disadvantaged children: Racing against catastrophe.* New York: Teachers College Press.

Nettles, S. M. (1991a). Community contributions to school outcomes of African-American students. *Education and Urban Society, 24*(1), 132–147.

Nettles, S. M. (1991b). Community involvement and disadvantaged students: A review. (1991a). *Review of Educational Research, 61,* 379–406.

Oakes, J. (1985). *Keeping track: How schools structure inequality.* New Haven, CT: Yale University Press.

Ogbu, J. U. (1985). A cultural ecology of competence among inner-city blacks. In M. E. Spencer, G. K. Brookins, & W. R. Allen (Eds.), *Beginnings: The social and affective development of black children* (pp. 45–66). Hillsdale, NJ: Erlbaum.

Ogbu, J. U. (1991). Minority coping responses and school experience. *Journal of Psychohistory, 18*(4), 433–456.

Okwumabua, J. O., Okwumabua, T. M., Winston, B. L., & Walker, H. (1989). Onset of drug use among rural black youth. *Journal of Adolescent Research, 4,* 238–246.

Pleck, J. H. (1989). Correlates of black adolescent males' condom use. *Journal of Adolescent Research, 4,* 247–253.

Pleck, J. H., Sonenstein, F. L., & Ku, L. C. (1991). Adolescent males' condom use: Relationships between perceived cost-benefits and consistency. *Journal of Marriage and the Family, 53*(4), 733–746.

Pleck, J. H., Sonenstein, F. L., & Ku, L. C. (in press). Problem behaviors and masculinity ideology in adolescent males. In R. D. Ketterlinus & M. E. Lamb (Eds.). *Adolescent problem behaviors.* Hillsdale, NJ: Erlbaum.

Polit, D. F., & Kahn, J. R. (1987). Teenage pregnancy and the role of the schools. *Urban Education, 22,* 131–153.

Ramseur, H. P. (1989). Psychologically healthy black adults: A review of research and theory. In R. Jones (Ed.), *Black adult development and aging* (pp. 215–241). Berkeley, CA: Cobbs & Henry.

Ramseur, H. P. (1990). Psychological health. In Consortium for Research on Black Adolescence (Ed.), *Black adolescence: Current issues and annotated bibliography* (pp. 17–26). Boston: G. K. Hall.

Roberts, R. E., Stevenson, J. M., & Breslow, L. (1981). Symptoms of depression among blacks and whites in an urban community. *Journal of Nervous and Mental Diseases, 169,* 774–779.

Rudd, N. M., McKenry, P. C., & Nah, M. (1990). Welfare receipt among black and white adolescent mothers. *Journal of Family Issues, 11,* 334–351.

Rutter, M. (1987). Psychosocial resilience and protective mechanisms. *American Journal of Orthopsychiatry, 57,* 316–331.

Rutter, M., Maughan, B., Mortimore, P., & Ouston, J. (1979). *Fifteen thousand hours: Secondary schools and their effects on children.* Cambridge, MA: Harvard University Press.

Schoenbach, V. J., Kaplan, B. H., Wagner, E. H., Grimson, R. C., & Udry, J. R. (1980). Depression symptoms in young adolescents. *American Journal of Epidemiology, 42,* 440.

Schorr, L. B. (1988). *Within our reach: Breaking the cycle of disadvantage.* New York: Doubleday.

Scott-Jones, D. (1984). Family influences on cognitive development and school achievement. *Review of Research in Education, 11,* 259–304.

Scott-Jones, D., & Turner, S. L. (1990). The impact of adolescent childbearing on educational attainment and income of Black females. *Youth and Society, 22,* 35–53.

Scott-Jones, D., & White, A. B. (1990). Correlates of sexual activity in early adolescence. *Journal of Early Adolescence, 10,* 221–238.

Slaughter-Defoe, D. T., Nakagawa, K., Takanishi, R., & Johnson, D. J. (1990). Toward cultural/ecological perspectives on schooling and achievement in African- and Asian-American children. *Child Development, 61,* 363–383.

Sonenstein, F. L., Pleck, J. H., & Ku, L. C. (1989). Sexual activity, condom use, and AIDS awareness among adolescent males. *Family Planning Perspectives, 21,* 152–158.

Sonenstein, F. L., Pleck, J. H., & Ku, L. C. (1991). Levels of sexual activity among adolescent males. *Family Planning Perspectives, 23*(4), 162–167.

Spencer, M. (1987). Black children's ethnic identity formation: Risk and resilience of castelike minorities. In J. Phinney & M. J. Rotheram (Eds.), *Children's ethnic socialization* (pp. 103–116). Newbury Park, CA: Sage.

Spencer, M., Brookins, G., & Allen, W. (Eds.). (1985). *Beginnings: The social and affective development of black children.* Hillsdale, NJ: Erlbaum.

Spencer, M., & Dornbusch, S. (1990). Challenges in studying minority youth. In S. Feldman & G. Elliott (Eds.), *At the threshold: The developing adolescent* (pp. 123–146). Cambridge, MA: Harvard University Press.

Spencer, M., Swanson, D., & Cunningham, M. (1991). Ethnicity, ethnic identity, and competence formation: Adolescent transition and cultural transformation. *Journal of Negro Education, 60*(3), 366–387.

Steinberg, L., Dornbusch, S. M., & Brown, B. B. (1992, June). Ethnic differences in adolescent achievement: An ethnological perspective. *American Psychologist, 47*(6), 723–729.

Sullivan, M. L. (1989). *Getting paid: Youth crime and work in the inner city.* Ithaca, NY: Cornell University Press.

Taylor, R. (1976). Psychosocial development among black children and youth. *American Journal of Orthopsychiatry, 46,* 4–19.

Tiedt, P., & Tiedt, I. (1990). *Multicultural teaching: A handbook of activities, information, and resources.* Boston: Allyn and Bacon.

U.S. Bureau of the Census. (1990). *Statistical abstract of the United States, 1990.* Washington, DC: U.S. Government Printing Office.

W. T. Grant Foundation Commission on Work, Family and Citizenship. (1988). *The forgotten half: Pathways to success for America's youth and young families.* Final Report. Washington, DC.

Werner, E. E. (1990). Protective factors and individual resilience. In S. Meisel & J. Shonkoff (Eds.), *Handbook of early childhood intervention.* Cambridge: Cambridge University Press.

Wetzel, J. R. (1989). *American youth: A statistical snapshot.* New York: W. T. Grant Foundation.

Wilson-Sadberry, K., Winfield, L. F., & Royster, D. A. (1991, November). Resilience and resistance of African-American males in postsecondary enrollment. *Education and Urban Society, 24*(1), 87–102.

Winfield, L. F. (1991). Resilience, schooling, and development in African-American youth: A conceptual framework. *Education and Urban Society, 24,* 5–14.

Wohlwill, J. J., & vanVliet, W. (Eds.). (1985). *Habitats for children: The impact of density.* Hillsdale, NJ: Erlbaum.

6

The stress–illness association in children: A perspective from the biobehavioral interface

Ronald G. Barr, W. Thomas Boyce, and Lonnie K. Zeltzer

Psychobiologic research in the latter half of the 20th century has produced dramatic changes in the conceptualization and study of disease etiology. Beginning with early observations on the temporal linkage between major life events and occurrences of illness, investigators from a diversity of fields have produced strong evidence for a robust and arguably causal relationship between emotional stressors and susceptibility to human disease. These pioneering studies have introduced new and fundamentally different categories of pathogenic "agents" into the lexicon of medicine and human biology. Taking their place alongside traditional agents of disease – microbiologic organisms, physical toxins, and genetic anomalies – psychosocial factors have become increasingly recognized as "predisposing" agents in the events leading to the development of physical and mental disorders.

In support of the causal status of associations between psychosocial experience and disease, a remarkable evolution has occurred in psychobiology over the past 20 years. Pathways and mechanisms have been traced from symbolically meaningful events to physiologic, pathogenic processes. In part this has been a function of the development of a plethora of biochemical assays and physiologic measures,

Ronald G. Barr, M.D.C.M., F.R.C.P., is Associate Professor of Pediatrics, McGill University, Montreal Children's Hospital, Montreal, Quebec; W. Thomas Boyce, M.D., is Associate Professor of Pediatrics, University of California, San Francisco; and Lonnie K. Zeltzer, M.D., is Professor of Pediatrics, Director, Pediatric Pain Program, School of Medicine, University of California, Los Angeles.
The authors appreciate the contributions of Christopher Coe, Candace Feiring, Megan Gunnar, Michael Lewis, Stephen Porges, and Carol Worthman.

significantly enhanced by the power and availability of "on line" computerization. As a result, stress research is approaching a crossroads in the history of psychobiologic investigation. These changes in technology are permitting theoretical postulates to be tested empirically, concepts to be redefined, and current paradigms to be challenged.

One of the more obvious results has been a significant enhancement in the plausibility of the association between stress and illness. Nevertheless, while these stress–illness relationships have repeatedly been shown to be statistically significant, the association has remained modest in strength. It has also become clear that, in contrast to many traditional investigations of causality in clinical medicine, stress is neither a necessary nor a sufficient condition for any specific illness, or for illness in general. As a result, investigations of the stress-illness association have been increasingly interested in elucidating individual differences that might help "explain" vulnerability (or invulnerability) to stress, and in identifying these differences at both behavioral and biological levels of description. The relatively rapid pace of developmental change in children contributes an additional challenge to these tasks, which has only begun to be appreciated. Nevertheless, the identification of individual behavioral and biological differences may contribute substantially to our understanding of stress-related clinical phenomena.

In this chapter, we consider examples of these research strategies with regard to two areas of interest: stress and patterns of illness, and pain experience in children. We take as a starting point the recognized association between stress and illness, consider a sampling of psychobiological measures being applied to these questions, and illustrate how they are being considered both as mediator and moderator variables to better define the nature of the association. These approaches are also illustrated with regard to an experience of particular clinical relevance, namely, pain perception in children. Although the examples concern "physical" illness that (except for acute pain) is primarily chronic, the arguments related to biological plausibility and individual differences apply in similar ways to other stress–illness associations. Finally, some implications of the successful pursuit of both mediator and moderator roles for psychobiological variables are considered.

The stress–illness association in children

Recent epidemiologic research has directed increasing attention to the role of behavioral and psychosocial factors in the causation of human disease. Beginning with the seminal work of Hinkle and Wolff (1957) and Selye (1950), investigators from a variety of disciplinary perspectives have examined the relationships between emotional stressors and morbidity experience within defined populations followed over time. The work of Holmes and Rahe (1967) elucidated significant, prospective associations between short-term accumulations of major life changes and the incidence of acute and chronic alterations in health status. Brown and colleagues (Brown & Harris, 1989) and others (Antonovsky, 1987; Boyce, Schaefer, & Uitti, 1985) focused on the importance of *meaning* in the health-altering effects of stressful events, and Lazarus (1981) noted the salience of cognitive appraisal and coping processes in determining the actual pathogenicity of a given stressor. Cassel (1974, 1976) introduced the concept of bidirectional effects of social experience and studied the role of social supports in buffering or blunting the potentially deleterious influences of emotional stress. All of this early work was conducted in samples of adult subjects and addressed health end points – such as hypertension or mortality – of principal relevance to middle and late adult life.

The pioneering studies of Haggerty and colleagues (Haggerty, 1980; Haggerty, Roghmann, & Pless, 1975; Meyer & Haggerty, 1962) in the 1960s expanded the territory of stress research into investigations of pediatric illness outcomes and addressed developmental issues of primary concern for *childhood* health and well-being. Meyer and Haggerty (1962) found a significant, prospective association between chronic family stressors and the incidence of streptococcal disease in children and adults followed over a 1-year period. Boyce et al. (1977) studied respiratory illnesses occurring in a preschool sample and found that both the duration and severity of illnesses increased with higher levels of parent-reported stressful events in the child's immediate past. Over the past three decades, epidemiologic work in childhood samples has documented significant associations between psychosocial adversity and a broad variety of pediatric health end points, including the incidence of infectious illnesses (Boyce et al., 1977; Graham, Douglas, & Ryan, 1986; Miller, 1960), minor and severe injuries (Boyce, Sobolewski, & Schaefer, 1989; Horwitz, Morgenstern, DiPietro, & Morrison, 1988; Padilla, Rohsenow, & Bergman, 1976; Plionis, 1977), and psychiatric disorders (Rutter, 1983; Rutter, 1989; Werner, Bierman, & French, 1971; Werner & Smith, 1983).

Taken together, these and other studies have provided support for the following general conclusions:

1. Although sometimes of modest magnitude, significant, prospective associations can be demonstrated between measures of psychosocial adversity and child health status.
2. The proposed stress–illness association appears to hold for a variety of childhood morbidities, ranging from respiratory illnesses and injuries to psychiatric disorders and depression. Both the character of acute illness episodes and the long-term course or trajectory of chronic diseases have been shown to be related to children's previous or concurrent experiences with psychosocial stress.
3. The meaning of individual stressors is an important dimension that appears to be capable of altering their inherent pathogenicity. Undesirable events are, in general, more closely associated with measures of morbidity than are equally disruptive but desirable events.

Despite the accumulation of evidence for a robust and replicable association between stress and childhood illness, important difficulties and dilemmas remain. In particular, two central problems have consistently emerged from the evolving discourse on the stress–illness relationship. First, until recently the relationship's biological plausibility has remained a serious obstacle to inferences regarding causality. According to both historical (Koch, 1882; Topley & Wilson, 1936) and contemporary (Evans, 1976) rules of evidence, the causal credibility of an association depends in part on the elucidation of mediating biological mechanisms. Thus, an essential step in evaluating putative causality is an examination of the potential biologic "connectors" between experiences of psychosocial stress and the development of disease. There is a central and important need to explain how environmental and psychological stressors, in effect, "get into the body."

Second, and even more problematic for the utility and importance of stress research, documented associations between stress and illness have remained tenaciously modest in magnitude, despite continuing advances in the design of studies and in the psychometric measurement of stressful experience. As reviewed by Rabkin and Struening (1976) and others (Boyce & Jemerin, 1990; Jemerin & Boyce, 1990), bivariate correlations between stressors and morbidity have seldom exceeded 0.30. The modest magnitude of such associations indicates that stressors account, in isolation, for no more than 10% of the variance in illness end points.

Why have associations between stress and illness been found to be persistently significant statistically, but universally weak in regard to explanatory power? One possible explanation is that the models on which such investigations have been based have been inadequate. In these circumstances, low bivariate correlations can be due to "suppression effects" of variables that only become apparent when these other factors are brought into the model. Another possible explanation is that psychometric approaches to measuring stressors have failed to attain the validity required to locate subjects accurately along a continuum of low- to high-stress reactivity. Such misclassification is rendered less plausible, however, by the intensive work over the past 20 years on the development of instruments to enumerate life events (Coddington, 1972; Dohrenwend & Dohrenwend, 1974; Holmes & Rahe, 1967), to weigh the undesirability of individual events (Dohrenwend & Dohrewend, 1981; Dohrenwend, Krasnoff, Askenasy, & Dohrenwend, 1978; Kanner, Coyne, Schaefer, & Lazarus, 1981), to measure chronic stress processes (Dohrenwend & Dohrenwend, 1981; Dohrenwend, Kransnoff, Askenasy, & Dohrenwend, 1978; Kanner, Coyne, Schaefer, & Lazarus, 1981), and to assess daily, low-intensity stressors, or "hassles" (DeLongis, Coyne, Dakof, Folkman, & Lazarus, 1982; Kanner, Felman, Weinberger, & Ford, 1987). None of these strategies has resulted in dramatic increments in explanatory power.

A plausible third possibility for the modest magnitude of the observed stress–illness associations is that important individual differences exist in subjects' behavioral, emotional, or biological responses to stressors. In all previous studies addressing the health consequences of stress, anomalous individuals have been identified who sustained either more or less illness than would have been expected on the basis of their observed or reported stress experiences. This variability in illness experience following major life stressors has led to the proposal that *individual differences in psychobiologic stress reactivity* may be responsible for the observed heterogeneity in consequent morbidity and may account for the modest magnitude of stress–illness associations (Boyce, Barr, & Zeltzer, 1992; Boyce & Jemerin, 1990; Jemerin & Boyce, 1990).

In the sections that follow, these two fundamental problems in childhood stress research – biological plausibility and the modest magnitude of the primary stress–illness association – are explored. It is argued that recent developments in the psychobiology of stress render a linkage between psychosocial stressors and illnesss eminently plausible from the perspective of biological mediation. Further, a hypothesis is developed and supported that the magnitude of past association between stress and illness has been systematically undermined by a failure to measure and address individual differences in psychobiologic stress responses. It is argued that such individual differences in biobehavioral reactivity to stress constitute *moderator* variables that alter the illness consequences of stress exposure.

Biological plausibility: Psychobiologic factors as mediators of the stress–illness association

Basic knowledge of the biological substrates for psychological stress has grown exponentially in recent years. Founded on the early physiological studies of Walter Cannon (1929) and Hans Selye (1950), recent investigations have provided an increasingly detailed picture of the biological changes that accompany and contribute to the experience of emotional stress (Asterita, 1985; Boyce & Jemerin, 1990; Jemerin & Boyce, 1990). Cannon's description of the "fight or flight" reaction to threat or challenge has been characterized by activation of the *sympathetic-adrenomedullary axis* and by the target organ effects of the catecholamines epinephrine, norepinephrine, and dopamine. Two phases of sympathetic-adrenomedullary activation are apparent. In the first, more immediate phase, cortical and limbic structures in the brain project information via the amygdala to hypothalamic centers, which activate the sympathetic arm of the autonomic nervous system. In the second, slower, and more sustained phase, sympathetic stimulation of the adrenal medulla results in catecholamine secretion into the circulation, ultimately augmenting the peripheral effects of neural activation such as heart rate acceleration, increased cardiac contractility, bronchial dilatation, increased blood glucose, mental vigilance, and an augmentation in basal metabolism. Epinephrine and norepinephrine exert different profiles of effects on target organs, and appear to be preferentially secreted in different emotional states. Work by Frankenhaeuser (1975) and others (Dimsdale & Moss, 1980; Mason, 1968), for example, suggests that epinephrine is predominantly secreted in contexts involving emotional arousal or distress; whereas norepinephrine is more likely to predominate in settings characterized by effort or vigilance alone. The catecholamines also interact at both the peripheral and central nervous system (CNS) levels with other neurotransmitters and neuroendocrine systems, providing an integrated and highly complex orchestration of biological stress responses (Ciaranello, 1983).

A second physiologic pathway intimately involved in the biological response to stressful experience is the hypothalamic-pituitary-adrenocortical axis. Selye's classic description of the general adaptation syndrome defined a set of systemic changes that were observed reliably to accompany prolonged exposure to noxious stimuli in the rat – namely, involution of the thymus, adrenal hyperplasia, and gastric ulcers. These changes have now been associated with glucocorticoid secretion by the adrenal medulla and are the end points of a sequence of events set in motion by the release of corticotropin-releasing hormone (CRH) from the median eminence of the hypothalamus. CRH is conveyed to the anterior lobe of the pituitary by the hypophyseal portal circulation, where it stimulates the release of adrenocorticotropic hormone (ACTH). We now know that vasopressin, released from the posterior pituitary, operates synergistically to potentiate the effects of CRH in the anterior pituitary. ACTH, in turn, is transported by the circulation to the adrenal cortex and activates the cellular mechanisms responsible for cortisol secretion. Cortisol has a broad range of metabolic effects on a variety of target organs. For example, blood glucose is augmented by hepatic gluco-neogenesis, inhibition of insulin secretion, and increased glucagon production. Protein catabolism increases in most tissues, and a number of anti-inflammatory and immune suppressive changes occur.

These most well-known biological effects of cortisol – its anti-inflammatory and immunosuppressive effects – take place via a broad variety of mechanisms. Normal inflammatory changes are curtailed through a direct stabilizing effect on lysosomal membranes, and indirectly through inhibition of intercellular mediators such as bradykinin and the prostaglandins. Cortisol also causes a decline in lymphocyte proliferation and a redistribution of circulating T cells to the bone marrow, which together produce a general inhibitory effect on immune surveillance. Downregulation of immunologic intercellular messengers – the lymphokines – is one likely mechanism through which cortisol exerts its immunosuppressive influences.

The actual role of glucocorticoids in the organism's coordinated biological response to stress is an issue that remains unclear. From Selye's early formulation, the function of cortisol was seen as aiding bodily defenses by promoting protective influences against the source of stress. It is difficult to reconcile this formulation, however, with many of the known physiologic effects of cortisol. Most recently, Munck, Guyre, and Holbrook (1984) have proposed that the general role of glucocorticoids in the stress response is to limit or modulate the activity of normal body defenses, as a means of protecting against the potentially deleterious effects of an overvigorous defensive response. As summarized by Gunnar (Gunnar, 1987, 1992; Gunnar, Mangelsdorf, Larson, & Hertsgaard, 1989), the hypothalamic-pituitary-adrenocortical system appears to play at least three roles in stress resistance: (1) it increases the energy available for action by way of its gluconeogenic activities, (2) it modulates the activity of other stress-responsive physiologic systems, and (3) it affects emotions and learning via feedback influences on CNS structures. A parsimonious explanation for the seeming discrepancies may be that the adaptive versus maladaptive aspects of the adrenocortical response depend on both the magnitude and duration of the response.

A third and more recently recognized physiologic system that appears closely involved in the psychobiology of human stress response is the *endogenous opioid system*. Following from the recognition of

opioid receptors on cell surfaces, the existence of endogenous mor-
phinelike substances in the brain first became apparent in 1975 (Cooper, Bloom, & Roth, 1986). Endogenous opioids were found not only
in the central nervous system, but in the peripheral nervous system,
blood, and gastrointestinal tract as well. Beta-endorphin – one of several classes of opioid species found in humans – is a polypeptide
fragment that is cosecreted with ACTH by the anterior pituitary, as a
derivative of the pro-opiomelanocortin (POMC) precursor protein.
Opioid peptides have been discovered to have broad, complex influences on a number of physiologic systems, most notably the nociceptive systems involved in pain perception and response (Anand & Carr,
1989). Postoperative levels of beta-endorphin, for example, have been
shown to be inversely related to the amount of morphine required to
control pain (M. Cohen, Pickar, & Dubois, 1983), and naloxone – an
opioid antagonist – blocks normal stress-induced analgesia (Willer,
Dehen, & Cambier, 1981).

In addition to their effects on pain experience, endogenous opioids
also appear to have important roles in the regulation of cardiovascular
function, in immune modulation, and in behavior, learning, and emotion. Recent evidence suggests, for example, that opioid peptides exert
regulatory influences on blood pressure, peripheral vascular resistance, and cardiac contractility, and the magnitude of blood pressure
responses to laboratory stressors can be ablated among highly reactive
individuals by administration of naloxone (McCubbin, Surwit, & Williams, 1988). Further, opiate receptors have been identified on the cell
surfaces of T lymphocytes, and the administration of exogenous opiates and opiate antagonists has been associated with measurable alterations in immune functions (Hall & Goldstein, 1981). The complex
effects of opioid peptides on behavior and learning are still being elucidated. Finally, there is evidence that emotional experience – such as
anxiety during lumbar puncture (M. Cohen et al., 1983) – may be
related to blood and cerebrospinal fluid levels of endogenous opioids.

As summarized earlier, these three stress-responsive systems – the
sympathetic-adrenomedullary axis, the hypothalamic-pituitary-adrenocortical axis, and the endogenous opioids – exert complex and integrated effects on a variety of organ systems. Furthermore, cortisol and
endorphins are but two of the responsive hormones within the
neuroendocrine axis. These systemic effects, in turn, may profoundly

alter resistance and influence the host's susceptibility to the pathogenic agents of disease, such as toxins, physical agents, and microor-
ganisms. Depression of immune function related to cortisol or opioid
secretion could, for example, contribute to the development of infectious illnesses or even certain types of cancer, and persistent eleva-
tions of circulating catecholamines may play a significant role in the
onset of cardiovascular disease, such as hypertension.

Increasingly, these initially speculative links between psychobiologic reactions to stress and the occurrence of disease are being empirically documented in laboratory and clinical research. As reviewed
by Schleifer et al. (Schleifer, Scott, Stein, & Keller, 1986) and
Borysenko and Borysenko (1982), animal studies with both rodents
and primates have demonstrated stress-induced alterations in hu-
moral and cellular immune responses. In Friedman's (S. Friedman,
Ader, & Glasgow, 1965) early work with Coxsackie virus in laboratory
mice, clinical manifestations of the infection were only apparent when
introduced to the organism concurrently with unpredictable shock;
neither factor alone was capable of inducing clinical disease. More
recent research by Coe and colleagues (Coe, Lubach, Ershler, &
Klopp, 1989; Coe, Lubach, Schneider, Dierschke, & Ershler, 1992;
Coe, Rosenberg, Fischer, & Levine, 1987) has documented alterations in a range of immune parameters – including mitogen-induced
lymphocyte proliferation, antibody response to antigenic challenge,
and complement activity – following maternal separations in infant
primates.

Clinical research in human populations has produced remarkably
concordant results. In epidemiologic work with a sample of pregnant
Navajo women, Boyce et al. (1989) reached conclusions parallel to
the laboratory findings of Friedman and co-workers. The risk of
perinatal infectious complications was significantly related to the
combined effects of genital tract colonization with *Mycoplasma
hominis* and acculturative stress. Neither factor in isolation was associated with an elevated rate of puerperal infection. The link between
psychological state and alterations in immune responses and competence has now been found in a variety of situations. Schleifer et al.
(1983) found decreased mitogen responses in B and T lymphocytes
during the first 2 months following bereavement, with some subjects
showing immune suppression at 1 year. S. Cohen, Tyrrell, and

Smith (1991) have recently shown that the incidence of clinically apparent respiratory tract infection among virus-inoculated adult volunteers was significantly related to the magnitude of stressful experience in the weeks preceding inoculation. Glaser et al. (1987) showed that, in medical students, academic examination periods were associated with both a decline in laboratory measures of immune function and a concomitant increase in the incidence of self-reported infectious illnesses.

Thus, the widespread influences of stress-responsive neuroendocrine systems appear to have direct or indirect consequences in the alterations of rate or character of clinical disease processes. These disease consequences are demonstrable in both animal and human subjects and, at least in some studies, can be clearly linked to both the inciting stressful experience and its neuroendocrine and immune sequelae. The epidemiologically documented association between stress and human morbidity has become increasingly plausible from a biological perspective, allowing new attention to be directed toward the association's other and perhaps more challenging dilemma: the striking individual differences in psychobiologic stress response.

The mediator–moderator distinction

Medical inquiries regarding the stress–illness association have tended to address the mechanisms that may account for, or mediate, the relationship. Consideration of psychobiological variables as markers of individual differences that moderate the relationship may, however, prove equally valuable. The distinction between mediators and moderators is an important one, and has received increasing attention, especially in the psychological literature (see, e.g., Baron & Kenny, 1986). This distinction is heuristically helpful (and perhaps strategically important) as a framework for indicating that both mediator and moderator models are being used to understand the role of psychobiological factors in stress-related childhood illness.

In general terms, psychobiological variables function as mediators if they transform or transduce the stimulus in a way that leads to the outcome. They function as moderators if the direction and/or the strength of the relationship between the stimulus and outcome is changed, but the stimulus itself is not transformed. To paraphrase Baron and Kenny's (1986) description, mediators describe *how* or *why* two variables are related; moderator variables specify *when* or *in whom* the relationship between two variables will hold.

In the association between stress and illness, a psychobiological variable is of interest as a mediator if it accounts for the relationship between stress and illness. As a mediator, it must have the properties of being correlated both to stressor and consequent (the illness). In this case, variation in the stressor accounts for variation in the psychobiological mediator variable, and variation in the psychobiological mediator variable accounts for variability in illness. When variation in the psychobiological mediator variable is controlled, the relation between stress and illness disappears if the psychobiological factor is the only mediating influence, or is significantly reduced when the relationship has multiple determinants. As discussed in the previous section, a psychobiological variable shown to be a mediator would most likely be one of many determinants in the case of the stress–illness association.

A psychobiological variable is manifest as a moderator if the relationship between stress and illness is different in direction, or stronger, as a function of the interaction of the psychobiological variable with the stressor. It is the interaction that is strengthened by a moderator variable. Variation in the psychobiological variable may or may not itself vary with illness, but would not correlate with variation in the level of the stressor. To be useful as a moderator, the *interaction* between the stressor and the psychobiological variable would be more strongly related to the illness than the stressor alone.

Generally speaking, mediator strategies tend to be employed when the relationship between independent and dependent variables is strong, and variables are selected for study when theoretical considerations suggest that they will provide a mechanism for the relationship. Moderator strategies tend to be pursued when the relationship is weak or inconsistent, and there is greater interest in the variable as a predictor of when or with whom the relationship will hold (Baron & Kenny, 1986). As discussed previously, the stress–illness association more closely approximates the latter than the former. Although interest in psychobiological variables is often driven by mediator considerations, the role of psychobiological variables as moderators may prove equally helpful in "explaining" the association.

Exemplar I: Psychobiological factors as mediators and moderators in patterns of morbidity

In Rutter's 1983 review of issues and questions involved in investigations of childhood stress and coping, individual differences between children in physiologic responses to stress are particularly noted as a promising area for future work. Rutter cites the studies of Rose (1980) on air traffic controllers as an example of data showing marked individual differences in biological responses to potentially stressful events. In the same volume, Ciaranello (1983) notes intersubject differences in catecholamine-related responses, and reviews work from his laboratory documenting genetic control of catecholamine biosynthetic enzymes, catechol receptors, and the density of neurons in dopaminergic regions of the brain. These and more recent reviews (Boyce & Jemerin, 1990; Jemerin & Boyce, 1990; Zeltzer, Barr, Mcgrath, & Schechter, 1992;) have focused attention on the potential importance of individual differences in biological reactivity to stress and the possible genetic basis for such differences.

In the years since the reviews appeared in the volume by Garmezy and Rutter (1983), an expanding body of behavioral medicine and psychobiologic research has provided evidence for extensive differences in biological reactivity, within several physiologic domains. Included in this have been a number of studies by investigators attending principally to psychobiological reactivity in children. The work of Kagan and colleagues (Kagan, Reznick, Clarke, Snidman, & Garcia-Coll, 1984; Kagan, Reznick, & Snidman, 1987; Kagan, Reznick, & Snidman, 1988; Reznick et al., 1986), for example, has centered on a subset of shy or "behaviorally inhibited" preschool children, who consistently withdraw and show signs of autonomic arousal under conditions of environmental challenge. Strikingly similar findings have emerged from Suomi's laboratory (Suomi, 1988, 1991) in studies with infant primates. In his work, a subgroup of rhesus monkey infants has been identified that, like Kagan's inhibited children, show withdrawal from challenge, elevated heart rates, and hormonal evidence of neuroendocrine arousal.

Paralleling the work of Manuck (Manuck, Kasprowicz, Monroe, Larkin, & Kaplan, 1989; Manuck, Kasprowicz, & Muldoon, 1990) and others (Chesney & Rosenman, 1985; Friedman & Rosenman,

1974) in adult subjects, developmental psychologists have documented a second biobehavioral pattern in childhood involving the constellation of findings surrounding Type A behavior. Type A behavior pattern is characterized by aggressiveness, easily aroused hostility, time urgency, and competitive striving elicited by environmental challenge. In children, such characteristics appear as efforts to control, suppression of fatigue, impatience, anger, and evidence of autonomic reactivity (Lundberg, 1986; Visintainer & Matthews, 1987). Type A behaviors in children appear to show moderate stability from childhood to adolescence and from adolescence to adult life. This is truer for males than for females, but the stability is somewhat less than that seen for adults over comparable numbers of years (Keltikangas-Jarvinen, 1989; Matthews & Woodall, 1988; Visintainer & Matthews, 1987). The studies of Matthews et al. (Matthews & Haynes, 1986; Matthews & Woodall, 1988), Lundberg et al. (Lundberg, 1985; Lundberg, Westermalk & Rasch, 1987), and others (Siegal, 1982; Weidner, Sexton, & Matarazzo, 1988) have extensively described the childhood characteristics of Type A behavior, developed evidence for partial heritability, and documented a variety of physiologic correlates.

In agreement with adult findings, recent studies have shown that competitive, aggressive children display greater heart rate and blood pressure reactivity during challenging or mildly stressful laboratory procedures (Lundberg et al., 1987; Matthews & Woodall, 1988). Most recently, Manuck et al. (Manuck, Cohen, Rabin, Muldoon, & Bachen, 1991) and Stone et al. (Stone, Valdimarsdottir, Katkin, Burns, & Cox, 1992) have shown that individuals with hyperdynamic cardiovascular responses to laboratory challenges also demonstrate greater immunologic reactivity, as reflected in suppression of lympocyte mitogenesis during a mental arithmetic task. Thus concordance between cardiovascular and immunologic measures of stress response in all likelihood represents separate physiologic events, both driven by an underlying commonality in exaggerated neuroendocrine reactivity.

In most past work, psychobiologic markers of stress response – such as blood pressure reactivity or cortisol secretion – have been viewed as *mediator* variables, which answer questions about how or why stressors affect health. Research on the relationship of Type A behavior or hostility to cardiovascular disease serves as an instructive example of this approach. An impressive body of previous research led to the confirmation of a significant, prospective association between Type A behavior pattern and the incidence of coronary heart disease (CHD) (Rosenman, Brand, Sholtz, & Friedman, 1976). An accumulation of more recent negative and contradictory evidence has resulted in the identification of specific subcomponents of Type A behavior, such as aggression or hostility, that have even stronger relationships to CHD. There is strong suspicion that hostility and aggression may be the "toxic" components of Type A behavior, and that recent work showing no relationship between Type A and long-term CHD mortality may be attributable to insufficient focus on hostility, as opposed to the broader behavior pattern (Chesney, 1988).

The credibility of these associations has been augmented by a series of compelling psychobiologic studies showing heightened blood pressure reactivity in Type A subjects and more extensive coronary disease in reactive individuals. As reviewed by Manuck (Manuck, Kaplan, & Matthews, 1986) and Krantz and Manuck (1984), a considerable body of evidence suggests that cardiovascular reactivity to stressors may constitute an important risk factor for the development of both hypertension and CHD. Parker and associates (Parker et al., 1987), for example, found a relationship between childhood reactivity and resting blood pressures 4 years later, and Keys et al. (Keys, Taylor, Blackburn, Brozek, Anderson, & Somonson, 1971) reported a significantly higher CHD incidence among individuals with excessive blood pressure reactivity in a 23-year cohort study. The primate studies of Krantz, Manuck, and their co-workers (Krantz & Manuck, 1984; Manuck, Kaplan, Adams, & Clarkson, 1988) further supported these findings by providing experimental evidence that reactivity can accelerate atherogenesis in monkeys fed high-cholesterol diets. Work on the physiologic mediators of the Type A–CHD association has focused on cardiovascular reactivity, rather than hypertension per se. Some investigators in the adult CHD field feel that reactivity may be a precursor for hypertension. Nevertheless, the evidence is that Type A is associated with reactivity, not hypertension. The solidity of this relationship is in males, not in females (Contrada & Krantz, 1988).

The work reviewed above thus stands as a prototypic case exemplifying the utility of psychobiologic factors in their role as mediators of primary associations. In this specific example, the relationship between Type A behavior and heart disease was supported by work delineating the possible components of biological mediation. In the language used by Baron and Kenny (1986), the cardiovascular reactivity found in hostile, Type A individuals "explains" how external stressors take on internal, pathogenic significance.

A second and more recent utility in the study of psychobiologic factors is their possible role as *moderator* variables that provide fresh insights into the replicable, but modest, associations between stressors and illness. Two studies under way in the clinical research laboratory of Boyce and colleagues serve as examples of this second approach. In the first, preschool children attending four child-care centers were followed for 1 year, prospectively ascertaining child-care–related stressors and teacher-reported injuries meeting standardized criteria. In addition, laboratory sessions at the onset of the study year provided independent measures of cardiovascular reactivity to challenging tasks presented by a previously unknown examiner. Results showed a significant interaction between child-care stressors and cardiovascular reactivity in the prediction of injury incidence (Figure 6.1). Children displaying exaggerated reactivity in the laboratory setting had injury rates comparable with their minimally reactive peers under low-stress conditions. In high-stress conditions, however, significantly greater injury rates were found, but only among highly reactive children (Boyce, Chesney, Kaiser, Alkon-Leonard, & Tschann, 1992). Cardiovascular reactivity thus functioned as a moderator variable, altering the effect size associated with environmental stress.

In the second study, 5-year-old children were assessed twice – 1 week prior to and 1 week following primary school entry – in order to examine changes in immune competence occurring at kindergarten entry. At both points in time, static and dynamic immunologic parameters were assayed, using blood obtained from venipunctures. Immune measures included an enumeration of helper and suppressor T lymphocytes, proliferative response to pokeweed mitogen, and antibody responses to a polyantigenic pneumococcal vaccine. Following completion of the immunologic assays, children were prospectively followed for a 12-week period, ascertaining the incidence and severity of respiratory tract infections. During the first year of this study, the 1989 San Francisco Bay Area Loma Prieta earthquake occurred at the midpoint of the respiratory illness surveillance period, thus creating a natural experiment with predisaster measures of immunologic competence.

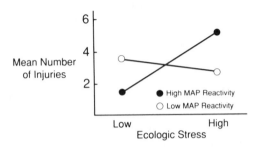

Figure 6.1.   Child care stressors, cardiovascular reactivity, and the prediction of injury incidence

Comparison of immune measures from the pre- to postkindergarten entry time points showed broad variability in the magnitude and direction of change, with subgroups of children showing minimal change, downregulation, and upregulation. Following the earthquake, the level of disaster-related parental distress was assessed with a validated self-reported questionnaire, and the incidence of respiratory illnesses was compared for pre- versus postearthquake periods. Immune reactivity reflecting upregulation of helper–suppressor cell ratios and mitogenic response was strongly and significantly predictive of increased post-earthquake illness incidence (Boyce et al., 1991). Children who had shown upregulation of immune function measures following kindergarten entry sustained higher rates of respiratory illnesses in the weeks following the earthquake event. In addition, an interaction was noted (but not statistically tested due to the small sample size) similar to that found in the prior study (Figure 6.2). Under conditions of low disaster-related parental stress, both reactive and nonreactive children showed minimal changes in illness incidence. By contrast, the children of parents reporting high levels of stress showed widely divergent illness rates: Immune reactive children had strikingly higher postearthquake rates, whereas nonreactive children had substantially lower rates. These results suggest that individual differences in immune response to a minor, normative stressor may be related to the rate of infection following a major stressful event.

Both studies employed measures of psychobiologic reactivity – a cardiovascular measure in the former case, an immunologic measure in the latter – and both approached the psychobiologic measures as

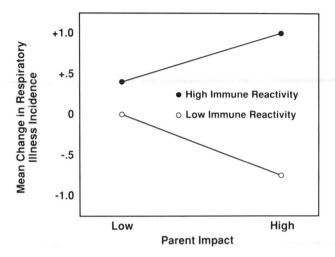

Figure 6.2. Disaster-related parental stressors, cardiovascular reactivity, and the prediction of illness incidence

putative moderator variables. That is, both studies set out to explore whether measurable individual differences in stress reactivity might alter the direction or the strength of an association between stressors and morbidity. In both cases and in separate study samples, a significant moderator effect was confirmed.

Exemplar II: Psychobiological responses as mediators and moderators of pain experience in children

A remarkably similar set of problems associated with the psychobiology of stress surrounds our understanding of pain experience in children and infants. Pain phenomena are of special interest in the context of stress research for at least two reasons. First, they represent a particular subset of the individual's experience with stress. As such, they provide a specific case in which the relation between a stress stimulus and a behavioral or illness outcome can be assessed. Since many of the stimuli (at least those associated with procedures) tend to be similar from individual to individual, response to pain stimuli may provide a useful marker of an individual's vulnerability and/or resilience to stressor stimuli in general. Second, understanding of psychobiological reactivity as a mediator and/or a moderator should have direct consequences for pain treatment. The importance of this is highlighted by the now well-documented undertreatment of pain in children relative to adults (Beyer, DeGood, Ashley, & Russell, 1983; Eland & Anderson, 1977; Schechter, 1989).

Conceptual and measurement problems in pain research in children and infants

Despite its importance, our understanding of pain experience in children is remarkably scant. An important contributor to this state of affairs is the difficulty attendant on operationalizing the concept of pain in children, and the implications of this for pain measurement. Pain experience, as Melzack (1973) and others have pointed out, is an essential, virtually universal, and private experience. To understand whether adults experience pain, one has access to a rich and sophisticated verbal vocabulary. The fact that, within bounds, and subject to some cultural variability, adults use words in the same way permits some confidence that we "know" what adults mean when they describe their pain experience (Barr, in press).

Knowing what constitutes a pain experience is particularly problematic in the case of children and infants. In children, it is not so clear that they have the same vocabulary, use it in the same way, or are "as articulate" in describing their pain experiences. In infants who are preverbal or seriously compromised children who are nonverbal, even that channel is closed. As a result, clinical evaluation has often depended on parents' descriptions of their children's "pain," sometimes to the exclusion of the children's description (Barr, 1989a). Perhaps more important, it is often not clear whether children, and especially preverbal infants, are describing or experiencing pain or generalized distress. Put another way, it is often not clear whether the verbal, behavioral, and psychological reaction indicates the particular experience of pain (analogous to cold, sweetness, etc.) or the more general experience of a nonspecific stress reaction.

To some extent, this reflects a dilemma determined by the rules of our language. In ordinary discourse, the term *pain* is a quintessentially *subjective* phenomenon. There is no "objective" marker by which one can say that pain is (or is not) experienced, even in adults. In the

Wittgensteinian sense, the rules of the language game for the term pain do not include a marker independent of the solipsistic world of the experiencer. However, it is at least meaningful to ask adults whether they experience, for example, pain or pressure when undergoing a lumbar puncture. With preverbal infants and to varying extents with children, such access to pain experience is denied a priori. Consequently, in the primary sense in which the word pain is used in our language, the question applied to infants is unanswerable. Infants cannot, so to speak, answer "I don't just feel pressure, I feel pain" to our question (Barr, in press).

One can, however, describe whether infants and children manifest *nociceptive responses*, that is, responses to stimuli or tissue injury or such insults as are "known" to be painful in adults. Indeed, the terms pain and nociceptive activity are often used interchangeably. This permits the description of responses to noxious stimuli in infants at a variety of levels (except the verbal subjective level) very much as is done in adults. What is measured, however, is not the pain experience, but the behavioral and physiologic response to the stressful, and *presumably* painful, stimulus. This means that the evidence concerning the pain experience is of necessity indirect and inferential. Because of this ambiguity, the term *pain stress* will be used to refer to the presumed pain experience that accompanies the general stress of noxious stimuli or tissue injury.

It has by now been well documented that all infants and children are capable of mounting a behavioral and physiological response to pain stress that includes manifestations of many of the psychobiological response systems previously described. Even in preverbal infants, the pain stress response has been demonstrated to include a typical constellation of crying, facial patterning, and motoric activity (Franck, 1986; Grunau & Craig, 1987; Izard et al., 1980, 1983, 1987; Johnston & Strada, 1986; Owens & Todt, 1984) and physiological changes including adrenocortical, heart rate, vagal tone, transcutaneous oxygen saturation, respiratory rate, and palmar water loss (Anders, Sachar, Kream, Roffward, & Hellman, 1972; Gunnar, Fisch, & Malone, 1984; Harpin & Rutter, 1982; Lewis & Thomas, 1990; Owens & Todt, 1984; Porter, 1989; Rawlings, Miller, & Engel, 1980; Talbert, Kraybill, & Potter, 1976). However, the evidence that a particular behavior, physiologic response, or concatenation of behavioral–physiological responses is *specific* to pain sensation alone is not compelling (e.g. McGrath, 1987). Consequently, it is meaningful to measure and describe behavioral and biological components of the pain stress response in infants and children of all ages, as long as the claim that it relates specifically to pain experience is understood to be an inference.

Parallel dilemmas in stress and pain research in children

Acknowledging this conceptual distinction, some of the dilemmas in research on pain in children are remarkably parallel to those concerning the stress–illness association. Specifically with regard to infants, evidence supporting the *biological plausibility* that infants have the neurological substrate for experiencing noxious stimuli or tissue injury as pain was missing. However, our understanding of the anatomy, physiology, neurochemistry, and behavior of preterms and newborns increasingly supports the concept that the neurological elements that constitute the known components to the adult nociceptive system are both present and functional well before term in normally growing fetuses and infants. The evidence for this has been systematically and articulately reviewed by Anand and Hickey (1987) and Anand and Carr (1989; see also Newburger & Sallan, 1981) and includes the following findings:

1. Cutaneous nociceptive nerve endings are present in all cutaneous and mucous surfaces by the 20th week of gestation; furthermore, the density of these nerve endings may equal or exceed that found in adult skin.
2. Myelination to the thalamus is complete by 30 weeks.
3. Dendritic arborization of cortical neurons, and synaptogenesis between thalamic afferents and cortical neurons begin to be established between 20 and 24 weeks of gestation.
4. Myelination of the thalamocortical fibers is complete by 37 weeks.

Evidence for the functional maturity of these pathways includes:

1. The ability to detect cortical components of visual, auditory, and somatosensory evoked potentials by 30 weeks gestation;

2. EEG patterns and behavioral evidence of well-defined periods of sleep and wakefulness; and

3. *In vivo* measures of maximal rates of cerebral glucose utilization over the essential sensory areas of the neonatal brain.

What is thought to develop later are the important *descending* pathways that inhibit and modulate the afferent signal. What remains unknown is when the connections between these brainstem, thalamic, and cortical centers and the limbic system, hypothalamus, and associative areas of the cerbral cortex are formed.

As a result, it is decreasingly likely that the behavioral and physiological responses generated by a noxious stimulus or tissue injury represent simply a generalized stress response unmodified by the specific perception of pain. Furthermore, it is reasonable to infer that the previously described psychobiological stress response systems may be useful as markers of pain stress. This has important consequences for both mediator and moderator strategies in pain research with children and infants. To the extent that these response systems are implicated in illness, pain experience itself may be not simply a consequence of noxious stimuli, but also a contributor to illness outcome. To the extent that these response systems reflect individual differences in reaction to noxious stimuli, they may be useful in detecting "pain vulnerability" or "pain resilience" that could moderate children's illness experience. Finally, once the biological plausibility of pain perception in infants is acknowledged, important and tantalizing questions concerning other aspects of the pain experience (e.g., memory of pain) and the ethics of pain nontreatment become manifest.

Second, as with stress and illness, associations between pain and illness in children have been weak or, more often, assumed to be nonexistent. There are at least two identifiable sources for this neglect. The first follows from the previous lack of evidence for the biological plausibility of pain perception in infants and young children. If pain is not perceived, it is unlikely to be a factor in subsequent illness. The second follows from the weak correlation between noxious stimuli and the more proximal outcome of pain response. As with stress and illness, the associations between noxious stimuli and behavioral and physiological responses have been robust, but the magnitudes of these associations have been consistently weak. In practical terms, noxious stimuli have not been highly predictive of pain response; consequently, if considered at all, they are unlikely to be predictive of illness outcome.

This consistently present but weak correlation has been a classic dilemma in pain research in both adults and children. Evidence that the response to tissue injury or noxious stimuli varies widely from individual to individual has always been strikingly apparent clinically. In an early seminal study in adults, Beecher (1956) reported that only 25% of men with leg wounds obtained in battle requested narcotics for pain relief, whereas 80% of civilians with similar surgical wounds produced under anaesthesia wanted medical relief. Similarly, clinicians have often noticed how different the behavioral reaction to a venipuncture is for children with hemophilia compared with children with leukemia. For the former, the venipuncture is associated with imminent relief from pain, whereas for the latter the venipuncture is usually associated with disease exacerbation and additional discomfort from chemotherapy. Gonzales et al. showed that children receiving injections displayed more "distress behaviors" when mothers were present in the treatment room than when they were excluded (Gonzales et al., 1989; Shaw & Routh, 1982). Such observations have usually been interpreted as evidence of contextual influences on individual response.

More formal pediatric studies assessing the value of interventions to reduce pain have also provided indirect evidence of response variability. While the primary aim of these studies has been to demonstrate safer ways to administer opioid analgesics and the efficacy of a variety of behavioral interventions, they have also provided evidence of large within-group response differences. For example, doses of morphine sulfate have ranged from 1 to 100 mg/hour across patients of the same weight to achieve the same level of analgesia (Dahlstrom et al., 1979; Lynn & Slattery, 1987; Miser et al., 1983; Miser, Miser, & Clark, 1980). Similarly, although hypnosis has been found to be an effective psychological pain control strategy, there is large within-group variability in children's pain response with hypnosis (Zeltzer, Jay, & Fisher, 1989; Zeltzer & LeBaron, 1982).

Such findings dramatically illustrate that the degree of tissue damage is not sufficient to account for the pain stress observed, and that factors other than the noxious stimulus determine the pain response. This has long been apparent clinically, but seldom documented formally in children (Schechter, Bernstein, Beck, Hart, & Scherzer, 1991). As with other stress research, problems of validity and reliability of measures have been the subject of intense investigation (McGrath, 1990). Consequently, it has become increasingly clear that the between-subject variation in response to the same noxious stimulus persists despite residual problems in measurement. Such response differences have usually focused attention on the extent to which contextual factors, the meaning of the stimulus for the subject, and characteristics such as the predictability of the stimulus vary with the pain response.

However, response variability to noxious stressors has highlighted the additional possibility that *individual differences in psychobiologic reactivity to pain stress* may be responsible for the observed heterogeneity in pain response. Such individual differences might include cognitive differences (such as memory of previous painful experiences or the ability to take contextual factors into account) and/or physiological differences reflecting constitutional variability in the structure and function of the peripheral and central nociceptive system. If so, the pain stress response may have utility not only in the investigation of pain as a mediator of the relationship between stress and illness, but also as a moderator variable in predicting pain vulnerability in particular, and perhaps stress vulnerability in general.

Psychobiologic responses to pain stress as mediators of illness

The most recent and clinically important example of the study of pain stress mediating illness has been a series of studies by Anand and his colleagues describing differences in outcome among different analgesic regimes in preterm and term infants undergoing major surgery (1985a, 1985b, 1987b, 1988a, 1988b, 1990, 1992). In a randomized controlled trial in preterms undergoing ligation of a patent ductus arteriosus (Anand, Sippell, & Aynsley-Green, 1987b), the group receiving the opioid fentanyl in addition to the standard curare and nitrous oxide provided to the control group manifested significantly reduced hormonal responses during surgery, and fewer subsequent metabolic and circulatory complications. Some of these changes (particularly protein breakdown) persisted until the third postoperative day. The clinical complications included hypotension, poor peripheral circulation, metabolic acidosis, and intraventricular hemorrhage. In studies of animals and adults, the stress response to surgery has been shown to be mediated by neural impulses in the nociceptive system and abolished by opioid anaesthesia. Consequently, they reasonably inferred that an important contribution to the improved stress response was the more effective dampening of pain perception through the addition of fentanyl to the anaesthetic regimen. This is of particular relevance since anesthetic regimens in preterm and newborn infants have been based on the assumption that responses to pain and surgical stress are not clinically important and that the addition of narcotic analgesics may predispose to respiratory or circulatory complications (Anand & Hickey, 1992). The inappropriateness of this assumption was further challenged by their most recent study, in which newborn infants undergoing surgery for complex congenital heart defects were randomly assigned to receive "deep" intraoperative anaesthesia (high dose sufentanil) and postoperative opiate infusion or "light" anaesthesia (halothane plus morphine) and postoperative intermittent morphine and diazepam (Anand & Hickey, 1992). In addition to significantly reduced endogenous opioid, catecholamine, and adrenocortical responses, the deep anaesthesia group had a decreased incidence of sepsis, metabolic acidosis, disseminated intravascular coagulation, and fewer postoperative deaths.

The exact mechanisms by which the pain stress was associated with medical complications occurring in these studies remain to be determined. However, changes in the hormonal stress responses, with their possible relationship to immune function, seem likely to be important. This is consistent with the finding that the surviving infants in the halothane group had milder hormonal and metabolic responses than those who died postoperatively (Anand, Hansen, & Hickey, 1990). Although there has been no work in humans in the area of immunologic compromise due specifically to pain, recent findings in an animal model of postoperative pain (Page, Ben-Eliyahu, Yirmiya, & Liebeskind, in press) have shown that pain stress can be associated with a reduction in levels of natural killer (NK) cell levels. In an NK sensitive tumor model, there is a significant increase in postoperative pulmonary metastases associated with a decrease in NK cells, neither of which occurs when morphine analgesia is administered. In this study, the preoperative implantation of the NK sensitive tumor was designed to test the biological significance of the previous finding of reduced NK cell levels associated with pain.

Psychobiological reactivity as a moderator of pain response

A second strategy is the study of psychobiological factors as *moderator* variables to identify "pain-vulnerable" and "pain-resilient" infants and children. In these studies, the variability that is being studied is limited to the more proximal outcome of physiological and behavioral reactivity to the pain stress. Potentially, however, individual differences in pain response might predict illness outcome from pain stress.

As indicated previously, evidence for individual differences is difficult in the clinical setting because of the lack of standardization of context, of clinical condition, and of the multitude of influences that are likely to contribute to behavioral and physiological pain responses. Furthermore, studies in which these factors can be controlled are understandably few in light of the ethical constraints on inducing pain when no benefit accrues to the child. However, standardized clinical settings in which noxious stimuli are experienced by *normal* children reduce variability due to contextual and experiential factors. For example, Schechter et al. (1991) exploited the opportunity of examining the range of self-report and behavioral "pain" responses of normal 5-year-old children to diphtheria-pertussis-tetanus (DPT) immunization. On both measures, a considerable range of response was reported, despite the absence of illness and standardization of setting and procedure (Schechter et al., 1991). Similarly, Worobey and Lewis (1989) took advantage of the routine newborn heelstick procedure to screen for phenylketonuria (PKU) and the 2-month DPT inoculation to examine stability of behavioral reaction over time. Despite differences in the two procedures, significant stability (r ranging from .32 to .37) was reported for two of the three behavioral measures.

Because of the constraints of clinical settings, laboratory pain analogue paradigms provide a particularly important strategy for defining individual differences in psychobiological reactivity in relatively standard and context neutral settings. Zeltzer and her colleagues (LeBaron, Zeltzer, & Fanurik, 1989; Zeltzer, Fanurik, & LeBaron, 1989)

have documented the feasibility and safety of the cold pressor procedure for children. They found individual differences in children's
pain ratings and behavioral tolerance to cold pressor pain stress and in
response to a standard hypnotic intervention. There is increasing
evidence that stability of response across time and/or stimuli is demonstrable. Fanurik, Mizell and Zeltzer (1991) found significant consistency in children's cold pressor pain ratings and tolerance over a 2-
week period and pain tolerance over a 2-year period (Mizell, Fanurik,
& Zeltzer, 1992a). Lacey and Lacey (1962) reported stability of cardiovascular responses to the cold pressor test in children 6 to 17 years old
who were tested during two laboratory sessions 4 years apart. The
stability of children's cardiovascular responses across paradigms (e.g.,
serial subtraction, isometric handgrip, video games, and others) has
been demonstrated by Matthews et al. (Matthews, Manuck, & Saab,
1986; Matthews, Rakazsky, Stoney, & Manuck, 1987).

In summary, systematic clinical studies and analogue laboratory
procedures converge in suggesting that consistent individual differences in reactivity to pain stress may contribute to the variable association between noxious stimuli and pain response, and that these gener-
alizations hold for self-report, behavioral, and physiological measures.
It is therefore of considerable interest that current concepts of the
structure and function of the neural nociceptive system provide bio-
logically plausible mechanisms by which individual differences in reactivity may be mediated

Of these features, probably the most important in terms of individual differences in nociception is the complex descending pain inhibitory system and activity in particularly dense areas of nociceptive
modulation (e.g., periaquaductal gray area, limbic system). Ascending
nociceptive transmittal neurons are interwoven with descending excita-
tory and inhibitory projections resulting in variability in enhancement
and filtering of potentially painful afferent stimuli. However, the development of a large aspect of the "hard wiring" of this complex system
takes place during infancy and early childhood in the form of dendritic branching and molding/shaping of the interconnections within
it. Thus, the developmental refinement of these sensory interconnections may be genetically driven and/or be shaped by infancy and early
childhood nociceptive experiences. Acting singly or in combination,
biologic predisposition and early pain experiences could bequeath to

the older child, adolescent, and adult a nociceptive neural architecture that renders the individual "pain vulnerable" or "pain resilient."

Recent evidence from preclinical studies suggests that early pain stress experiences may have longer-lasting effects by influencing brain growth. For example, Fitzgerald (1991) demonstrated that early pain perturbations disrupted the normal patterning of C and A-delta fibers in the developing rat nervous system. Significant early nociceptive stimuli led to increased branching of these fibers resulting in a generalized lowered threshold for nociception and significant overlap of sensory dermatomes. As these rats developed, they continued to manifest increased sensitivity to subsequent noxious stimuli. Second, opioid peptides, both endogenous and exogenous agonists, can regulate neural growth, and this process is mediated by specific opioid receptors. In a study of the effects of morphine in primary cultures of murine glial cells, this opioid agonist was found to inhibit proliferation and induce morphologic differentiation in developing astrocytes. This process was reversed by the addition of the opioid antagonist naloxone (Stiene-Martin, Gurwell, & Hauser, 1991). In primary mixed glial cultures of mouse cerebra, both delta and nondelta (mu, kappa) opioid receptors were found to mediate the effects of endogenous opioids on the growth of astrocytes and astrocyte progenitor cells (Stiene-Martin & Hauser, 1991). Zagon and McLaughlin (1991) found that a subgroup of opioid peptides derived from proenkephalin A were endogenous inhibitory factors regulating the proliferation of cells destined to be neurons and glia in the developing nervous system (cerebellar cortex) of 6-day-old rats. Concomitant exposure to naloxone blocked the inhibition of DNA synthesis by these opioid peptides.

Similar considerations are reflected in Melzack's theory to explain phantom limb pain (1992), in which it is postulated that the "memory" of significant pain experiences may set into play a sustained "representation" of that pain experience in the cortex as well as continued activation of an internuncial pool of neurons, both of which become independent of peripheral nociceptive stimulation. If confirmed, such postulations of how early pain experiences may alter the reactivity of anatomical pathways of nociception may have important implications for understanding individual differences in pain vulnerability.

Under a moderator strategy, individual differences in psychobiological reactivity would be of interest if the relationship between a noxious stimulus and the response to it were different in direction, or stronger, as a function of an interaction between the psychobiological variable and the stressor. To be useful as a moderator, the *interaction* between the stressor and the psychobiological variable would be more strongly related to the response than the noxious stimulus alone.

An example from Zeltzer's laboratory illustrates the potential value of moderator approaches to understanding pain stress response. In this case, the psychobiological variable of interest is the coping style of the subject (Fanurik et al., 1991). They have been able to classify children into attenders (those who primarily direct their focus of attention toward the cold pressor-induced sensations in an effort to tolerate the water) or distractors (those who divert their attention away from the cold pressor experience). Over a 2-week period, high within-child stability has been demonstrated in choice of coping style. In a study using pain tolerance measures as an outcome, distractors were also shown to have the highest pain tolerance (Fanurik, Zeltzer, Roberts, & Blount, 1993).

The potential importance of this behavioral dimension was highlighted when children were taught interventions to modify their pain response that were either "matched" or "mismatched" to their preferred coping style (Fanurik et al., 1993). Thus, for example, some of the children who were distractors were taught to use imagery (a distraction technique *matched* to distraction coping preference) and some were taught to focus on the sensations of the cold pressor task (a sensory monitoring attention technique *mismatched* to distraction coping preference). Overall, children were randomly assigned to three groups (control, matched, or mismatched interventions) with each group balanced for coping style (attenders, distractors). A significant interaction was found between coping style and intervention with the greatest *increase* in pain tolerance found for the distractors who were taught imagery (the matched intervention) and greatest *decrease* in tolerance (and *increase* in pain ratings) found for the distractors provided with sensory monitoring (the mismatched intervention). The attenders did not significantly change their pain responsivity with either intervention strategy.

Together, these results suggest that the ability to identify individual differences in coping style might be useful as a marker of pain response, which, in addition, is correlated with systematic differences in physiological response. Furthermore, there is at least preliminary evidence that measures of pain severity and pain tolerance in the cold pressor procedure correlate with response to painful clinical procedures in ill children and with a variety of health-related outcomes in normal children (Mizell, Fanurik, & Zeltzer, 1992). In eight children with cancer who have undergone cold pressor testing and lumbar puncture, the children tended to use the same coping strategy for both laboratory and clinical pain (attending or distracting). Compared with distractors, attenders demonstrated lower tolerance for the cold pressor task, endorsed more sensory descriptors of pain during both laboratory and clinical pain events, reported more anxiety prior to their lumbar punctures, reported more somatic symptoms and higher symptom intensity on a Child Somatic Checklist, and displayed greater variability in both heart rate and systolic blood pressure changes in the laboratory. Given other evidence for stability of individual differences in response to cold pressor stress (Matthews et al., 1986; Matthews et al., 1987), it seems likely that the investigation of psychobiological differences might well contribute to the identification of pain-vulnerable and pain-resilient children.

Preliminary evidence from Zeltzer and Fanurik's cold pressor studies also suggests that response to the cold pressor stimulus may predict stress response in everyday settings outside of the laboratory (Shin, Fanurik, Ifekwunigwe, LeGagnoux, & Zeltzer, 1992). In a school-based study of cold pressor responses in normal children, high laboratory pain ratings were associated with more somatic complaints (vague pains, stomachaches, headaches, feeling "unwell" or other vague symptoms), higher symptom intensity, more school nurse visits for acute illnesses (upper respiratory symptoms or other observable signs of illness), and more school absences. High laboratory pain tolerance was associated with more school nurse visits for injuries. These findings suggest that individual characteristics that lead to "pain vulnerability" may be the same or similar characteristics that render a child "stress vulnerable" as well.

Summary and implications

In summary, two areas of new research have been highlighted in which individual differences in children's responses to environmental events are invoked as a means of accounting for the modest and highly variable relationship between stressors and health. First, preliminary studies were reviewed suggesting that the modest association between stressful events and child morbidity may be moderated by individual differences in psychobiologic reactivity, indexed by cardiovascular or immune measures of stress response. Second, a series of parallel studies were examined in which between-child differences in pain "susceptibility" were used to explain variability both in the response to pain in individual children and the effects of pain on the trajectory of illness. Common to both sets of observations is an approach in which psychobiological factors can be usefully viewed as either mediator variables that elucidate *how* or *why* an effect occurs or moderator variables that explain *in whom* or *under what conditions* an effect can be anticipated.

There are implications of these approaches both for the design of future investigations of the stress–illness association in children and for the eventual development of intervention strategies. The design of future research should increasingly take into account the potential role of psychobiologic factors not only as mediator variables, but also as moderator variables. Whereas psychobiologic factors treated as mediators may inform the search for mechanisms in the stress response, the same factors studied as moderators may fundamentally alter our understanding of the conditions and settings in which psychological stress becomes relevant to health and disease. The enterprise of stress research may ultimately be even better served by the discovery of important environment–organismic interactions than by the mechanistic plausibility that psychobiologic factors have thus far provided.

The discussion of individual differences in psychobiologic reactivity serves to highlight a number of as yet unanswered questions. As one example, most studies have concentrated on measures of individual reactivity within, rather than across, particular developmental stages. An important question concerns whether we should expect that individual differences in one developmental stage will be constant throughout the life-span. The evolving work with the concept of temperament represents the most detailed inquiry to date of the importance of individual differences across developmental stages, even as the concept itself undergoes challenge and redefinition (Goldsmith et al., 1987; Kagan, 1992; Lewis, 1989; Prior, 1992). As a second example, the emphasis on how individual differences are manifest in interaction with environmental stressors has increased the appreciation of context as a determinant of outcome. This has inevitably raised challenges to our prior understanding of what contexts and responses should be taken as "normative" – a challenge with important implications for both normal and clinical studies (e.g., Barr, 1989b; Wolff, 1989). Third, the examples discussed have related primarily to physical disease as exemplars of illness outcomes. However, the logic of the characteristics of the relationship between stress and physical illness is similar in the case of "mental" illness, and similar roles for psychobiologic reactivity might be expected in understanding depression, anxiety, and other behavioral syndromes. Fourth, much remains to be determined as to whether individual differences are important as moderators across the whole range of stress experiences, or only for mild to moderate stress. In the face of severe, catastrophic, and/or prolonged stress witnessed, for example, in relation to famine in children, the characteristics and generalizability of such stress–illness relationships may be significantly altered. Finally, of course, individual difference characteristics need not be described only at the level of, for example, cardiovascular or immune system reactivity of individual organisms. Investigations measuring variables as apparently disparate as cultural differences and regulator genes continue to inform the discourse on individual differences, mechanisms, and processes.

The strategic implications of moderator effects in the design and elaboration of future *intervention* studies may be of substantial, or even critical, importance. Future research may confirm what is now only dimly suggested by the preliminary findings reviewed here: that most psychological and emotional stressors are relevant illness risk factors for only a subset of children, perhaps even a small subset. Further, membership in that subset may vary by the type of stressor or the context in which it is experienced. If such findings were confirmed, intensive, cost-effective interventions could be created and targeted for the small proportion of children most affected by adversity and perturbations in the social environment.

References

Anand, K. J. S., Brown, R. C., Bloom, & M. J., Aynsley-Green, A. (1985a). Studies on the hormonal regulation of fuel metabolism in the human newborn infant undergoing anaesthesia and surgery. *Hormone Research, 22,* 115–128.

Anand, K. J. S., Brown, R. C., Causon, R., Christofides, S. R., Bloom, S. R., & Aynsely-Green, A. (1985b). Can the human neonate mount an endocrine and metabolic response to surgery? *Journal of Pediatric Surgery, 20,* 41–48.

Anand, K. J. S., & Carr, D. B. (1989). The neuroanatomy, neurophysiology, and neurochemistry of pain, stress, and analgesia in newborns and children. *Pediatric Clinics of North America, 36,* 795–822.

Anand, K. J. S., Hansen, D. D., & Hickey, P. R. (1990). Hormonal-metabolic stress responses in neonates undergoing cardiac surgery. *Anesthesiology, 73,* 661–670.

Anand, K. J. S., & Hickey, P. R. (1987a). Pain and its effects in the human neonate and fetus. *New England Journal of Medicine, 317,* 1321–1347.

Anand, K. J. S., & Hickey, P. R. (1992) Halothane-morphine compared with high-dose sufentanil for anesthesia and postoperative analgesia in neonatal cardiac surgery. *New England Journal of Medicine, 326,* 1–9.

Anand, K. J. S., Sippell, W. G., & Aynsley-Green, A. (1987b). A randomized trial of fentanyl anesthesia undergoing surgery: Effect on the stress response. *Lancet, 1,* 243–248.

Anand, K. J. S., Sippell, W. G., Schofield, N. M., & Aynsley-Green, A. (1988a). Does halothane anesthesia decrease the stress response of newborn infants undergoing operation? *British Medical Journal, 296,* 668.

Anand, K. J. S., & Ward-Platt, M. P. (1988b). Neonatal and pediatric stress responses to anesthesia and operation. *International Anesthesiology Clinics, 26,* 218.

Anders, T. F., Sachar, E. J., Kream, J., Roffward, H., & Hellman, L. (1972). Behavioral state and plasma cortisol response in the human newborn. *Pediatrics, 49,* 250–259.

Antonovsky, A. (1987). *Unraveling the mystery of health: How people manage stress and stay well.* San Francisco: Jossey-Bass.

Asterita, F. (1985). *The physiology of stress.* New York: Human Sciences Press.

Baron, R., & Kenny, D. (1986). The moderator–mediator variable distinction in social psychological research: Conceptual, strategic, and statistical considerations. *Journal of Personality and Social Psychology, 51*(6), 1173–1182.

Barr, R. G. (1989a). Pain in Children. In P. D. Wall & R. Melzack (Eds.),

Textbook of Pain (2nd ed., Ch. 40, pp. 568–588). London: Churchill Livingstone.

Barr, R. G. (1989b). Recasting a clinical enigma: The case of infant crying. In P. R. Zelazo & R. G. Barr (eds.), *Challenges to developmental paradigms: Implications for theory, assessment and therapy*, (Ch. 4, pp. 43–64). Hillsdale, NJ: Erlbaum.

Barr, R. G. (in press). "Is this infant in pain?": Caveats from the clinical setting. *Journal of the American Pain Society*.

Beecher, H. K. (1956). Relationship of significance of wound to pain experienced. *Journal of the American Medical Association, 161*, 1609.

Beyer, J., DeGood, D., Ashely, L., & Russell, G. (1983). Patterns of postoperative analgesic use with adults and children following cardiac surgery. *Pain, 17*, 71–81.

Borysenko, M., & Borysenko, J. (1982). Stress, behavior and immunity: Animal models and mediating mechanisms. *General Hospital Psychiatry, 4*, 59–67.

Boyce, W. T., Barr, R. G., & Zeltzer, L. K. (1992). Temperament and the psychology of childhood stress. *Pediatrics, 90* (suppl.), 483–486.

Boyce, W. T., Chesney, M., Kaiser, P., Alkon-Leonard, A., & Tschann, J. (1992). Childcare stressors, cardiovascular reactivity, and injury incidence in preschool children (abstract). *Pediatric Research, 31*, 9A.

Boyce, W. T., Chesterman, E. A., Wara, D., Cohen, F., Folkman, S., & Martin, N. (1991). Immunologic changes occurring at kindergarten entry predict respiratory illnesses following the Loma Prieta earthquake. *Pediatric Research, 29*(4), 8A.

Boyce, W. T., & Jemerin, J. J. (1990). Psychobiological differences in childhood stress response: I. Patterns of illness and susceptibility. *Journal of Developmental and Behavioral Pediatrics, 11*, 86–94.

Boyce, W. T., Jensen, E. W., Cassel, J. C., Collier, A. M., Smith, A. H., & Ramey, C. T. (1977). Influence of life events and family routines on childhood respiratory tract illness. *Pediatrics, 60*, 609–615.

Boyce, W. T., Schaefer, C., Harrison, H. R., Haffner, W. H. J., Lewis, M., & Wright, A. L. (1989). Sociocultural factors in puerperal infection among Navajo women. *American Journal of Epidemiology, 129*(3), 604–615.

Boyce, W. T., Schaefer, C., & Uitti, C. (1985). Permanence and change: Psychosocial factors in the outcomes of adolescent pregnancy. *Social Science and Medicine, 21*, 1279–1287.

Boyce, W. T., Sobolewski, S., & Schaefer, C. (1989). Recurrent injuries in school-age children. *AJDC, 143*, 338–342.

Brown, G. W., & Harris, T. O. (1989). *Life events and illness*. New York: Guilford Press.

Cannon, W. B. (1929). *Bodily changes in pain, hunger, fear and rage.* New York: Appleton.

Cassel, J. (1974). Psychosocial processes and "stress": Theoretical formulation. *International Journal of Health Services, 4,* 471–482.

Cassel, J. (1976). The contribution of the social environment to host resistance. *American Journal of Epidemiology, 104,* 107–123.

Chesney, M. A. (1988) The evolution of coronary-prone behavior. *Annals of Behavioral Medicine, 10*(2), 43–45.

Chesney, M. A., & Rosenman, R. H. (Eds.). (1985). *Anger and hostility in cardiovascular and behavioral disorders.* Washington, DC: Hemisphere Publishing.

Ciaranello, R. D. (1983). Neurochemical aspects of stress. In N. Garmezy & M. Rutter (Eds.), *Stress, coping, and development in children* (pp. 85–105). New York: McGraw-Hill.

Coddington, R. D. (1972). The significance of life events as etiologic factors in the diseases of children: I – A survey of professional workers. *Journal of Psychosomatic Research, 16,* 7–18.

Coe, C. L., Lubach, G. R., Ershler, W. B., & Klopp, R. G. (1989). Influence of early rearing on lymphocyte proliferation responses in juvenile rhesus monkeys. *Brain, Behavior, and Immunity, 3,* 47–60.

Coe, C. L., Lubach, G. R., Schneider, M. L., Dierschke, D. J., & Ershler, W. B. (1992). Early rearing conditions alter immune responses in the developing infant primate. *Pediatrics, 90* (supp.), 505–509.

Coe, C. L., Rosenberg, L. T., Fischer, M., Levine, S. (1987). Psychological factors capable of preventing the inhibition of antibody responses in separated infant monkeys. *Child Development, 58,* 1420–1430.

Cohen, M. R., Pickar, D., & Dubois, M. (1983). The role of the endogenous opioid system in the human stress response. *Psychiatric Clinics of North America, 6,* 457–471.

Cohen, S., Tyrrell, D. A. J., & Smith, A. P. (1991). Psychological stress and susceptibility to the common cold. *New England Journal of Medicine, 325,* 606–612.

Contrada, R. J., Krantz, D. S. (1988). Stress, reactivity, and type A behavior: Current status and future directions. *Annals of Behavioral Medicine 10*(2), 64–70.

Cooper, J. R., Bloom, F. E., & Roth, R. H. (1986). *The biochemical basis of neuropharmacology.* New York: Oxford University Press.

Dahlstrom, B., Bolme, P., Feychting, H., et al. (1979). Morphine kinetics in children. *Clinical Pharmacological Therapy, 26,* 354–365.

DeLongis, A., Coyne, J. C., Dakof, G., Folkman, S., & Lazarus, R. S. (1982). Relationship of daily hassles, uplifts, and major life events to health status. *Health Psychology, 1*(2), 119–136.

Dimsdale, E., & Moss, J. (1980). Plasma catecholamines in stress and exercise. *Journal of the American Medical Association, 243*, 340–342.

Dohrenwend, B. S., & Dohrenwend, B. P. (1974). *Stressful life events: Their nature and effects.* New York: Wiley.

Dohrenwend, B. S., & Dohrenwend, B. P. (1981). *Stressful life events and their contexts.* New Brunswick, NJ: Rutgers University Press.

Dohrenwend, B. S., Krasnoff, L., Askenasy, A. R., & Dohrenwend, B. P. (1978). Exemplification of a method for scoring life events: The PERI life events scale. *Journal of Health and Social Behavior, 19*, 205–229.

Eland, J. M., & Anderson, J. E. (1977). The experience of pain in children. In A. Jacox (Ed.), *Pain: A source book for nurses and other health professionals* (pp. 453–473). Boston: Little Brown.

Evans, A. S. (1976). Causation and disease: The Henle-Koch postulates revisited. *Yale Journal of Biology and Medicine, 49*, 175–195.

Fanurik, D., Mizell, T., Zeltzer, L. (1991). Individual differences in children's responses to cold pressor pain. (abstract). *Journal of Pain and Symptom Management,* 180.

Fanurik, D., Zeltzer, L., Roberts, M. C., & Blount, R. L. (1993). The relationship between children's coping styles and psychological interventions for cold pressor pain. *Pain, 53*, 213–222.

Fitzgerald, M. (1991, May). The impact of nociception on neural development. Presented at the First International Symposium on Pediatric Pain, Montreal, Canada.

Franck, L. S. (1986). A new method to quantitatively describe pain behavior in infants. *Nursing Research, 35*, 28–31.

Frankenhaeuser, M. (1975). Experimental approach to the study of catecholamines and emotion. In L. Levi (Ed.), *Emotions: Their parameters and measurement.* New York: Raven Press.

Friedman, S. B., Ader, R., & Glasgow, L. A. (1965). Effects of psychological stress in adult mice inoculated with Coxsackie B viruses. *Psychosomatic Medicine, 27*(4), 361–368.

Friedman, M., & Rosenman, R. (1974). *Type A behavior and your heart.* New York: Knopf.

Garmezy, N., & Rutter, M. (Eds.). (1983). *Stress, coping, and development in children.* New York: McGraw-Hill.

Glaser, R., Rice, J., Sheridan, J., Fertel, R., Stout, J., Speicher, C., Pinsky, D., Kotur, M., Post, A., Beck, M., & Kiecolt-Glaser, J. (1987). Stress-related immune suppression: Health implications. *Brain, Behavior, and Immunology, 1,* 7–20.

Goldsmith, H. H., Buss, A. H., Plomin, R., Rothbart, M. K., Thomas, A., Chess, S., Hinde, R. A., & McCall, R. B. (1987). Roundtable: What is temperament? Four approaches. *Child Development, 58,* 505–529.

Gonzales, J. C., Routh, D. K., Saab, P. G., Armstrong, F. D., Shifman, L., Guerra, E. & Fawcett, N. (1989). Effects of parent presence on children's reaction to injections: Behavioral, physiological and subjective aspects. *Journal of Pediatric Psychology, 14,* 449–462.

Graham, N., Douglas, R. M., & Ryan, P. (1986). Stress and acute respiratory infection. *American Journal of Epidemiology, 124,* 389–401.

Grunau, R., Craig, K. (1987). Pain expressions in neonates: Facial action and cry. *Pain, 28,* 395–410.

Gunnar, M. R. (1987). Psychobiological studies of stress and coping: An introduction. *Child Development, 58,* 1403–1407.

Gunnar, M. R. (1992). Reactivity of the hypothalamic-pituitary-adrenocortical system to stressors in normal infants and children. *Pediatrics, 90* (supp.), 491–497.

Gunnar, M. R., Fisch, R. O., & Malone, S. (1984). The effects of a pacifying stimulus on behavioral and adrenocortical responses to circumcision. *Journal of the American Academy of Child Psychiatry, 23,* 34–38.

Gunnar, M. R., Mangelsdorf, S., Larson, M., & Hertsgaard, L. (1989). Attachment, temperament, and adrenocortical activity in infancy: A study of psychoendocrine regulation. *Developmental Psychology, 25,* 355–363.

Haggerty, R. J. (1980). Life stress, illness and social supports. *Developmental Medicine and Child Neurology, 22,* 391–400.

Haggerty, R. J., Roghmann, K. J., & Pless, I. B. (1975). *Child Health and the Community: Health, medicine, and society.* New York: Wiley.

Hall, N. R., & Goldstein, A. L. (1981). Neurotransmitters and the immune system. In R. Ader (Eds.), *Psychoneuroimmunology* (pp. 521–544). New York: Academic.

Harpin, V. A., & Rutter, N. (1982). Making heel pricks less painful. *Arch Dis Child, 71,* 226–228.

Hinkle, L. E., & Wolff, H. G. (1957). The nature of man's adaptation to his total environment and the relation of this to illness. *Archives of Internal Medicine, 99,* 442–460.

Holmes, T. H., & Rahe, R. H. (1967). The social readjustment rating scale. *Journal of Psychosomatic Research, 11,* 213–218.

Horwitz, S. M., Morgenstern, H., DiPietro, L., & Morrison, C. L. (1988).

Determinants of pediatric injuries. *American Journal of Diseases and Children, 142*, 605–611.

Izard, C. E., Hembree, E. A., Doughtery, L. M., Spizzirri, C. C. (1983). Changes in facial expressions of 2–19 month old infants following acute pain. *Developmental Psychology, 19*(3), 418–426.

Izard, C. E., Hembree, E. A., Hembree, R. R. (1987). Infants' emotional expressions to acute pain: Developmental changes and stability of individual differences. *Developmental Psychology, 23*(1), 105–113.

Izard, C. E., Juebner, R. R., Risser, D., McGinnes, G. C., & Dougherty, L. M. (1980). The young infant's ability to produce discrete emotion expressions. *Developmental Psychology, 16*, 132–140.

Jemerin, J. J., & Boyce, W. T. (1990). Psychobiological differences in childhood stress response: II. Cardiovascular markers of vulnerability. *Journal of Developmental and Behavioral Pediatrics, 11*(3), 140–150.

Johnston, C. C., & Strada, M. E. (1986). Acute pain response in infants: A multidimensional description. *Pain, 24*, 373–382.

Kagan, J. (1992). Behavior, biology, and the meanings of temperamental constructs. *Pediatrics, 90* (supp.), 510–513.

Kagan, J., Reznick, J. S., Clarke, C., Snidman, N., & Garcia-Coll, C. (1984). Behavioral inhibition to the unfamiliar. *Child Development, 55*, 2212–2225.

Kagan, J., Reznick, J. S., & Snidman, N. (1987). The physiology and psychology of behavioral inhibition in young children. *Child Development, 58*, 1459–1473.

Kagan, J., Reznick, J. S., & Snidman, N. (1988). Biological bases of childhood shyness. *Science, 240*, 167–171.

Kanner, A. D., Coyne, J. C., Schaefer, C., & Lazarus, R. S. (1981). Comparison of two modes of stress measurement: Daily hassles and uplifts versus major life events. *Journal of Behavioral Medicine, 4*, 1–39.

Kanner, A. D., Feldman, S. S., Weinberger, D. A., & Ford, M. E. (1987). Uplifts, hassles, and adaptational outcomes in preadolescents. *Journal of Early Adolescence, 7*(4), 371–394.

Keltikangas-Jarvinen, L. (1989). Stability of type A behavior during adolescence, young adulthood, and adulthood. *Journal of Behavioral Medicine, 12*(4), 387–396.

Keys, A., Taylor, H. L., Blackburn, H., Brozek, J., Anderson, J. T., & Somonson, E. (1971). Mortality and coronary heart disease among men studied for 23 years. *Archives of Internal Medicine, 128*, 201–214.

Koch, R. (1882). The aetiology of tuberculosis. *Berlin Klin Wschr, 19*, 221.

Krantz, D. S., & Manuck, S. B. (1984). Acute psychophysiological reactivity and risk of cardiovascular disease: A review and methodologic critique. *Psychological Bulletin, 96,* 435–464.

Lacey, J. I., & Lacey, B. C. (1962). The law of initial value in the longitudinal study of automatic constitution: Reproducibility of autonomic responses and response patterns over a four-year interval. *Annals of the New York Academy of Science, 98,* 1257–1289.

Lazarus, R. S. (1981). The stress and coping paradigm. In C. Eisdorfer, D. Cohen, & A. Kleinman (Eds.), *Model for clinical psychopathology* (pp. 177–214). New York: Spectrum.

LeBaron, S., Zeltzer, L., & Fanurik, D. (1989). An investigation of cold pressor pain in children: Part I. *Pain, 37,* 161–171.

Lewis, M. (1989). Culture and biology: The role of temperament. In P. R. Zelazo & R. G. Barr (Eds.), *Challenges to developmental paradigms: Implications for theory, assessment and treatment.* (Ch. 11, pp. 203–226). Hillsdale, NJ: Erlbaum.

Lewis, M., & Thomas, D. (1990). Cortisol release in response to inoculation. *Child Development, 61,* 50–59.

Lundberg, U. (1985). Psychobiological stress responses and behavior patterns in preschool children. In J. Sanchez-Sosa (Ed.), *Health and clinical psychology* (pp. 77–91). North-Holland: Elsevier Science Publishers.

Lundberg, U. (1986). Stress and Type A behavior in children. *Journal of the American Academy of Child Psychiatry, 25,* 771–778.

Lundberg, U., Westermalk, O., & Rasch, B. (1987). *Type A behavior and physiological stress responses in preschool children: Sex differences at the ages of 3 and 4* (Report number 664). University of Stockholm, Department of Psychology.

Lynn, A. M., & Slattery, G. T. (1987). Morphine pharmacokinetics in early infancy. *Anesthesiology, 66,* 136–139.

Manuck, S. B., Cohen, S., Rabin, B. S., Muldoon, M. F., & Bachen, E. A. (1991). Individual differences in cellular immune response to stress. *Psychological Science, 2*(2), 111–115.

Manuck, S. B., Kaplan, J. R., Adams, M. R., & Clarkson, T. B. (1988). Studies of psychosocial influences on coronary artery atherogenesis in cynomolgus monkeys. *Health Psychology, 7*(2), 113–124.

Manuck, S. B., Kaplan, J. R., & Matthews, K. A. (1986). Behavioral antecedents of coronary heart disease and atherosclerosis. *Arteriosclerosis, 6,* 2–14.

Manuck, S. B., Kasprowicz, A., Monroe, S. B., Larkin, K. T., & J. R. Kaplan, R. (1989). Psychophysiologic reactivity as a dimension of individual differences. In N. Schneiderman, S. M. Weiss, & P. Kaufmann

(Eds.), *Handbook of methods and measurements in cardiovascular behavioral medicine* (pp. 365–382). New York: Plenum.

Manuck, S. B., Kasprowicz, A. L., & Muldoon, M. F. (1990). Behaviorally-evoked cardiovascular reactivity and hypertension: Conceptual issues and potential associations. *Annals of Behavioral Medicine, 12*(1), 17–29.

Mason, J. W. (1968). A review of psychoendocrine research on the sympathetic-adrenal medullary system. *Psychosomatic Medicine, 30,* 631–653.

Matthews, K., & Haynes, S. (1986). Type A behavior pattern and coronary disease risk: Update and critical evaluation. *American Journal of Epidemiology, 123,* 923–960.

Matthews, K. A., Manuck, S. B., & Saab, P. G. (1986). Cardiovascular responses of adolescents during a naturally occurring stressor and their behavioral and psychophysiological predictors. *Psychophysiology, 23,* 198–209.

Matthews, K. A., Rakazsky, C. J., Stoney, C. M., & Manuck, S. B. (1987). Are cardiovascular responses to behavioral stressors a stable individual difference variable in childhood? *Psychophysiology, 24,* 464–473.

Matthews, K. A., & Woodall, K. L. (1988). Childhood origins of overt Type A behaviors and cardiovascular reactivity to behavioral stressors. *Annals of Behavioral Medicine, 10*(2), 71–77.

McCubbin, J. A., Surwit, R. S., & Williams, R. B. (1988). Opioid dysfunction and risk for hypertension: Naloxone and blood pressure responses during different types of stress. *Psychosomatic Medicine, 50,* 8–14.

McGrath, P. A. (1987). An assessment of children's pain: A review of behavioral, physiological, and direct scaling techniques. *Pain 31,* 147–176.

McGrath, P. A. (1990). *Pain in children: Nature, assessment & treatment.* London: Guilford Press.

Melzack, R. (1973). *The puzzle of pain.* New York: Basic Books.

Melzack, R. (1992, April). Phantom limbs. *Scientific American,* pp. 120–126.

Meyer, R. J., & Haggerty, R. J. (1962). Streptococcal infections in families: Factors altering individual susceptibility. *Pediatrics, 29,* 539–549.

Miller, F. J. W. (1960). *Growing up in Newcastle-upon-Tyne.* London: Oxford University Press.

Miser, A. W., Davis, D. M., Hughes, C. S., Mulne, A. F., & Miser, J. S. (1983). Continuous subcutaneous infusion of morphine in children with cancer. *American Journal of Diseases of Children, 137,* 383–385.

Miser, A. W., Miser, J. S., & Clark, B. S. (1980). Continuous intravenous infusion of morphine sulfate for control of severe pain in children with terminal malignancy. *Journal of Pediatrics, 96,* 930–932.

Mizell, T., Fanurik, D., Zeltzer, L. K. (1992a). Stability of children's responses to cold pressor pain: A two-year follow-up. *Clinical Research, 40*(1), 117a.

Mizell, T., Fanurik, D., & Zeltzer, L. (1992b). Development of a laboratory model to predict pain in children with cancer. *Clinical Research, 40,* 117A.

Munck, A., Guyre, P. M., & Holbrook, N. J. (1984). Physiological functions of glucocorticoids in stress and their relation to pharmacological actions. *Endocrinology Review, 5*(1), 25–43.

Newberger, R. F., & Sallan, S. E. (1981). Chronic pain: Principles of management. *Journal of Pediatrics, 98,* 180–189.

Owens, M. E., & Todt, E. H. (1984). Pain in infancy: Neonatal reaction to heel lance. *Pain, 20,* 77–86.

Padilla, E. R., Rohsenow, D. J., & Bergman, A. B. (1976). Predicting accident frequency in children. *Pediatrics, 58,* 223–226.

Page, G. G., Ben-Eliyahu, S., Yirmiya, R., & Liebeskind, J. C. (in press). Surgical stress promotes the metastatic growth and suppresses killer cell function in rats. *Journal of Pain Symptom Management.*

Parker, F. C., Croft, J. B., Cresenta, J., Freedman, D. S., Burke, G. L., Webber, L. S., & Berenson, G. S. (1987). The association between cardiovascular response tasks and future blood pressure levels in children: Bogalusa heart study. *American Heart Journal, 113,* 1174.

Plionis, E. M. (1977). Family functioning and childhood accident occurrence. *American Journal of Orthopsychiatry, 47,* 250–263.

Porter, F. (1989). Pain in the newborn. *Clinical Perinatolology, 16,* 549–564.

Prior, M. (1992). Childhood temperament. *J Child Psychol Psychiat, 33,* 249–279.

Rabkin, J. G., & Struening, E. L. (1976). Life events, stress and illness. *Science, 194,* 1013–1020.

Rawlings, D. J., Miller, P. A., & Engel R. R. (1980). The effect of circumcision on transcutaneous pO2 in term infants. *American Journal of Diseases and Children, 134,* 676–678.

Reznick, J. S., Kagan, J., Snidman, N., Gersten, M., Baak, K., & Rosenberg, A. (1986). Inhibited and uninhibited children: A follow-up study. *Child Development, 57,* 660–680.

Rose, R. M. (1980). Endocrine responses to stressful psychological events. *Psychiatric Clinics of North America, 2,* pp. 53–81.

Rosenman, R. H., Brand, R. J., Sholtz, R. I., & Friedman, M. (1976). Multivariate prediction of coronary heart disease during 8.5 year follow-up in the Western Collaborative Group Study. *American Journal of Cardiology, 37,* 903–910.

Rutter, M. (1983). Stress, coping, and development: Some issues and some questions. In N. Garmezy & M. Rutter (Eds.), *Stress, coping, and development in children* (pp. 1–41). New York: McGraw-Hill.

Rutter, M. (1989). Pathways from childhood to adult life. *Journal of Child Psychology and Psychiatry, 30*(1), 23–51.

Schechter, N. L. (1989). The undertreatment of pain in children. *Pediatric Clinics of North America, 36,* 781–795.

Schechter, N. L., Bernstein, B. A., Beck, A., Hart, L., & Scherzer, L. (1991). Individual differences in children's response to pain: Role of temperament and parental characteristics. *Pediatrics, 87,* 171–177.

Schleifer, S. J., Keller, S. E., Camerino, M., Thornton, J. C., & Stein, M. (1983). Suppression of lymphocyte stimulation following bereavement. *Journal of the American Medical Association, 250,* 374–377.

Schleifer, S. J., Scott, B., Stein, M., & Keller, S. E. (1986). Behavioral and developmental aspects of immunity. *Journal of the American Academy of Child Psychiatry, 26,* 751–763.

Selye, H. (1950). *Stress: The physiology and pathology of exposure to stress.* Montreal, Quebec: Acta Medical Publishers.

Shaw, E. G., & Routh, D. K. (1982). Effect of mother presence on children's reaction to aversive procedures. *Journal of Pediatric Psychology, 7,* 33–42.

Shin, D., Fanurik, D., Ifekwunigwe, M., LeGagnoux, J., & Zeltzer, L. (1992). The relationship between children's laboratory pain responses and their health behaviors. *Clinical Research, 40*(1), 117A.

Siegal, J. (1982). Type A behavior and self-reports of cardiovascular arousal in adolescents. *Journal of Human Stress, 24–30.*

Stiene-Martin, A., Gurwell, J. A., & Hauser, K. F. (1991). Morphine alters astrocyte growth in primary cultures of mouse glial cells: Evidence for a direct effect of opiates on neural maturation. *Developmental Brain Research, 60,* 1–7.

Stiene-Martin, A., & Hauser, K. F. (1991). Glial growth is regulated by agonists selective for multiple opioid receptor types in vitro. *Journal of Neuroscience Research, 29,* 538–548.

Stone, A. A., Valdimarsdottir, H. B., Katkin, E. S., Burns, J., & Cox, D. S. (1992). Mitogen-induced lymphocyte responses are reduced following mental stressors in the laboratory.

Suomi, S. J. (1988). Genetic and maternal contributions to individual differences in Rhesus monkey biobehavioral development. In N. Krasnagor (Ed.), *Psychobiological aspects of behavioral development.* New York: Academic Press.

Suomi, S. J. (1991). Early stress and adult emotional reactivity in rhesus monkeys. In G. R. Bock & J. Whelan (Eds.), *The childhood environment and adult disease* (pp. 171–188). Chichester: Wiley.

Talbert, L. M., Kraybill, E. N., Potter, H. D. (1976). Adrenal cortical response to circumcision in the neonate. *Obstetrics and Gynecology, 48,* 208–210.

Topley, W. W. C., & Wilson, G. S. (1936). *The principles of bacteriology and immunity* (2nd ed.). Baltimore: Wood.

Visintainer, P. F., & Matthews, K. A. (1987). Stability of overt type A behaviors in children: Results from a two- and five-year longitudinal study. *Child Development, 58,* 1586–1591.

Weidner, G., Sexton, G., & Matarazzo, J. (1988). Type A behavior in children, adolescents, and their parents. *Developmental Psychology, 24,* 118–121.

Werner, E. E., Bierman, J. M., & French, F. F. (1971). *Children of Kauai: A longitudinal study from the prenatal period to age ten.* Honolulu: University of Hawaii Press.

Werner, E. E., & Smith, R. S. (1983). *Vulnerable but invincible: A study of resilient children.* New York: McGraw-Hill.

Willer, J. C., Dehen, H., & Cambier, J. (1981). Stress-induced analgesia in humans: Endogenous opioids and naloxone-reversible depression of pain reflexes. *Science, 212,* 689–691.

Wolff, P. H. (1989). The concept of development: How does it constrain assessment and therapy? In P. R. Zelazo & R. G. Barr (Eds.), *Challenges to developmental paradigms: Implications for theory, assessment and treatment,* (Ch. 2, pp. 13–28). Hillsdale, NJ: Erlbaum.

Worobey, J., Lewis, M. (1989). Individual differences in the reactivity of young infants. *Developmental Psychology, 25,* 663–667.

Zagon, I. S., & McLaughlin, P. J. (1991). Identification of opioid peptides regulating proliferation of neurons and glia in the developing nervous system. *Brain Research, 542,* 318–323.

Zeltzer, L. K., Barr, R. G., McGrath, P. A., Schechter, N. L. (1992). Pediatric pain: Interacting behavioral and physical factors. *Pediatrics, 90,* 816–821.

Zeltzer, L., Fanurik, D., & LeBaron, S. (1989). The cold pressor pain paradigm in children: Feasibility of an intervention model. Part II. *Pain, 37,* 305–313.

Zeltzer, L. K., Jay, S. M., & Fisher, D. M. (1989). The management of pain associated with pediatric procedures. *Pediatric Clinc of North America, 36,* pp. 1–24.

Zeltzer, L., & LeBaron, S. (1982). Hypnosis and nonhypnotic techniques for reduction of pain and anxiety during painful procedures in children and adolescents with cancer. *Journal of Pediatrics, 101,* 1032–1035.

7

Child and adolescent depression: Covariation and comorbidity in development

Bruce E. Compas and Constance L. Hammen

Raymond is a 16-year-old adolescent boy who lives alone with his single mother. At the time that Raymond is referred to a psychology clinic for mental health services, both he and his mother report that he is experiencing a variety of emotional and behavioral problems. For the past few months he has been persistently sad and unhappy, overcome with feelings of personal worthlessness. He is socially withdrawn from others, spending most of his time alone at home or avoiding contact with his peers on those days when he manages to attend school. He is constantly tired but still finds it difficult to sleep, lying awake at night and then struggling to drag himself from bed in the morning. Both he and his mother are concerned about his weight, which has increased substantially due to his inability to control his appetite for chips, candy, and soda. Even if he makes it to school, he finds he is unable to concentrate on his work.

Raymond's listlessness and withdrawal are countered, however, by his frequent outbursts of anger and aggression. He frequently lashes out in rage at his mother, recently punching his fist through a wall and a door at home. He has also been involved in several fights with other students at school as a result of being teased by his peers. He rarely

Bruce E. Compas is Professor of Psychology at the University of Vermont and Constance L. Hammen is Professor of Psychology at the University of California at Los Angeles. This chapter reflects ideas generated during meetings of the W. T. Grant Foundation Consortium on Child and Adolescent Depression. In addition to the authors the members include Anne Petersen (who initiated the consortium), William Beardslee, Jeanne Brooks-Gunn, Norman Garmezy, Nadine Kaslow, Helen Orvaschel, Arnold Sameroff, and Stephen Suomi. The authors are grateful to these colleagues for their valuable input.

complies with rules and limits either at home or at school, resulting in frequent conflicts with his mother and with school authorities. Finally, the event that precipitated the current referral was Raymond's arrest for shoplifting at a local store.

Raymond personifies several important issues that face the field of developmental psychopathology. First, the central features of what is considered a depressive disorder appear to be recognizable in this adolescent boy. However, Raymond's symptoms raise the question of whether a depressive disorder in adolescence or childhood takes the same form as depression when it occurs in adulthood. Second, symptoms such as Raymond's sadness, concentration problems, and overeating exist on a continuum, ranging from mild to severe. Do Raymond's symptoms differ from more normative behavior only in degree or is there a qualitative difference between his behavior and that of others whose problems are less severe? Finally, Raymond's depressive symptoms are not the only difficulties that he is currently experiencing. To what extent is depression accompanied by symptoms associated with other disorders, such as conduct disorder and delinquency?

These three issues together challenge some of our current notions of childhood and adolescent depression as a distinct experience that is similar in youth and adulthood. A striking feature of depressive phenomena in young people is the degree to which these experiences are associated with other maladaptive behaviors, emotions, syndromes, and disorders. Evidence now indicates that depressive moods, syndromes, and disorders are more likely to occur along with other symptoms and disorders than they are to occur alone. Although substantial research has documented these patterns of co-occurrence and comorbidity, the implications of these patterns of interrelatedness of depressive phenomena and other problems remain to be explored.

The issue of comorbidity or covariation of childhood and adolescent depression with other psychologically or behaviorally dysfunctional conditions goes to the heart of several major issues. For instance, questions such as what is childhood depression, is it continuous with depression in later life, and what are factors specific to depression that are related to risk and resilience, developmental course and treatment, are all matters that will only be resolved when more is understood about the meaning and consequences of comorbidity and covariation. Even the questions of what are the appropriate methods, samples, and research designs for approaching such issues depend on fully understanding the nature and implications of comorbidity and covariation.

Our purpose in the present chapter is to explore some of these issues and their implications, and to propose some suggestions for further research. We will first review central definitional issues. This will be followed by a brief review of what we know about the patterns of covariation and comorbidity and the nature and course of depressive phenomena during childhood and adolescence. Then, we present implications – ending with some suggestions for further research.

Defining key concepts

In acknowledgment of confusion that may arise in depression research, it is essential to distinguish among three levels of depressive phenomena: depressed mood, depressive syndromes, and depressive disorders. Further, when considering how problems may co-occur, it is important to distinguish among the concepts of covariation, comorbidity, and interrelatedness.

Depressive phenomena

The term *depression* has been used to describe a wide range of emotions, symptoms, syndromes, and disorders that vary in their severity, duration, and scope. Three levels of analysis have been identified in research on depressive phenomena in children and adolescents: depressed mood, depressive syndromes, and depressive disorders (e.g., Angold, 1988; Cantwell & Baker, 1991; Compas, Ey, & Grant, 1993; Kovacs, 1989; Petersen, Compas, Brooks-Gunn, Stemmler, Ey, & Grant, 1993). Although these three concepts are closely related, they each reflect different underlying assumptions about the assessment and taxonomy of depressive phenomena.

The first approach to depressive phenomena does not involve a full taxonomic or assessment paradigm but is concerned with *depressed mood* and affect, as represented by the work of Petersen (e.g., Petersen, Kennedy, & Sullivan, 1991) and of Kandel (e.g., Kandel & Davies, 1982). This approach is concerned with depression as a symptom, and refers to the presence of sad mood, unhappiness, or blue feelings for an unspecified period of time. This approach has emerged from developmental research in which depressive emotions are studied along with other features of adolescent development. The second approach concerns *depressive syndromes*, referring to a set of emotions and behaviors that have been found statistically to occur together in an identifiable pattern at a rate that exceeds chance, without implying any particular model for the nature or causes of these associated symptoms. Depressive syndromes are identified empirically through the reports of children, adolescents, and other important informants on their behavior (e.g., parents, teachers). This strategy involves the use of multivariate empirical methods in the assessment and taxonomy of child and adolescent psychopathology, represented by the multiaxial taxonomy of Achenbach (1985, 1991). The third approach is the *categorical diagnostic* approach, based on assumptions of a disease model of psychopathology, and is currently reflected in the categorical diagnostic system of the Diagnostic and Statistical Manual, Third Edition–Revised (DSM-III-R) of the American Psychiatric Association (1987) and the International Classification of Diseases and Health Related Problems (ICD-10) of the World Health Organization (1990). This approach not only includes the presence of an identifiable syndrome of associated symptoms, but it also assumes that these symptoms are present for a certain minimal duration and involve a significant level of functional impairment. Differences between individuals are considered in terms of quantitative and qualitative differences in the pattern, severity, and duration of symptoms.

Continuity. The existence of three levels of depressive phenomena also reflects the struggle to understand whether psychopathology is continuous or discontinuous with normative behavioral processes, and whether elevated depression symptoms are continuous with categorically diagnosed depression. In all three approaches, depressive symptoms can be measured on a continuum, ranging from mild to severe. For example, all individuals experience sadness at various points in their lives, with some individuals encountering severer or more prolonged periods of sadness than others. All three approaches have also conceptualized depression as a qualitative deviation from normal functioning as well. Cutoffs or criteria are established in each approach to distinguish severe or clinical cases of depressions from milder forms of the problem. When cutoffs are used, it is implied that individuals who exceed these criteria differ from those who do not. Individuals above the cutoff are considered different, not only in the amount of depressive symptoms that they have, but also in other aspects of their degree of impairment and current life functioning. However, the validity of generalizing from mildly symptomatic to clinical samples remains to be established. Studies have indicated convergent validity between self-report scales and diagnostic categories. Although the convergence has been adequate to establish psychometric soundness of certain depression scales, agreement has been far less than perfect, so that the continuity issue is unresolved.

Elsewhere Hammen has argued that in adults, high scorers on symptom inventories should not be assumed, without evidence, to be on a continuum with the clinically depressed – in view of likely differences in symptom duration, impairment, and recurrence that render the symptom experiences quite different (e.g., Gotlib & Hammen, 1992). However, with children there is increasing evidence that those with elevated symptom scores in the absence of clinical diagnoses display worrisome impairment in social, academic, and family functioning (reviewed in Gotlib & Hammen, 1992). Thus, the continuity issue is an important empirical question, and the eventual conclusions to be reached may differ for child and adult populations.

Covariation, comorbidity, and interrelatedness

The tendency for several emotional and behavioral problems to cluster or co-occur in the same individuals is widely recognized in the behavioral sciences and mental health. Distinct terminology has emerged in different fields, however, each connoting a specific meaning. Three terms most frequently used are covariation, interrelatedness, and comorbidity.

Covariation. Statistical covariation has been examined in research on depressed mood and depressive syndromes of child and adolescent psychopathology. Quantitative analyses of checklist responses by parents, teachers, and adolescents have been used to identify syndromes of multiple behaviors, scored on continua (Achenbach, 1991). Correlations among the different syndromes are then examined to determine the degree of covariation. Achenbach and colleagues have identified substantial covariation among core syndromes that exist across age, sex, and source of information (Achenbach, 1991). In contrast to continuous scores defining covariation, comparison of discrete categories or behaviors forms the basis for examining comorbidity and interrelatedness.

Interrelatedness. The observation that a variety of deviant behaviors are interrelated is central to problem behavior theory (e.g., Donovan & Jessor, 1985; Donovan, Jessor, & Costa, 1988; Gilmore et al., 1991; Jessor & Jessor, 1977). Research has indicated that deviant behaviors including substance abuse, school problems, delinquency, and early sexual activity are strongly interrelated in adolescence and early adulthood. This interpretation is based on the observed statistical relations among these behaviors as determined through factor analytic methods. Thus, in this research interrelatedness is used to refer to the statistical association of the occurrence of specific behaviors.

Depressed mood has been examined most extensively in relation to problem behaviors in a large epidemiological study of adolescents by Kandel and Davies (1982). Patterns were somewhat different for boys and girls in a sample of 8,206 public high school students in New York State. For boys, depressed mood was related only to more minor delinquency and more days absent from school. For girls, depressed mood was associated with higher frequency of delinquent acts, days absent from school, lower school grades, alcohol and cigarette use, and use of other illicit drugs.

Comorbidity. Comorbidity refers to the co-occurence of two or more diagnostic categories, although sometimes the term is used when symptoms but not the full syndrome of an independent disorder occur. Due to differences in the underlying assumptions of dimensional and categorical approaches (Caron & Rutter, 1991), we "expect" covariation of syndromes described dimensionally, but do not necessarily expect to see comorbidity of supposedly independent categories. From the categorical perspective the question arises whether two distinct disorders actually coexist, or whether the appearance of comorbidity is a result of measurement or conceptual artifact.

Maser and Cloninger (1990) distinguish among diagnostic, pathogenic, and prognostic comorbidity. With regard to diagnostic comorbidity, Klein and Riso (1992) have pointed out various ways in which the nosological system itself might contribute to comorbidity: overlapping diagnostic criteria; larger numbers of diagnostic categories (narrowness and specificity of categories leading to multiple diagnoses); lower thresholds for diagnosing, leading to greater prevalence, which in turn increases likelihood of co-occurence by chance; and other features. Additionally, there are very few signs and symptoms that are specific to a particular disorder. No single feature is a necessary and sufficient indicator of a disorder (Maser & Cloninger, 1990). The severer an individual's psychiatric difficulties, the more likely numerous symptoms might be apparent. For instance, agitation, irritability, poor concentration, and negative thoughts about the self and the world are likely to occur in many disorders besides depression, possibly leading to artifactually high rates of comorbid diagnoses. Finally, we note that invalidity of the diagnostic criteria might also contribute to high rates of comorbidity. As an example, the frequent coexistence of depression and anger (sometimes leading to separate diagnoses of depression and conduct disorder) might reflect the actual way in which depression is experienced in young adolescents, as suggested by recent research on normal youth by Renouf and Harter (1990). That is, developmental considerations may not be adequately represented in current diagnostic criteria for depression in youngsters, leading to apparent comorbidity of conditions. Thus, there are numerous conceptual and measurement matters that might contribute artifactually to comorbidity.

Pathogenic comorbidity arises when a particular disorder leads to certain other symptoms or disorders, which are therefore considered to be etiologically related. Maser and Cloninger (1990) note, for example, that diabetes is related to renal and cardiovascular problems. Depressive disorders in youngsters might cause other conditions, or might be a consequence of the other conditions – for example, depression causing substance abuse, or consequences of conduct disorder causing depression. Comorbidity findings, therefore, might have important etiological implications.

Prognostic comorbidity occurs when one disorder represents an earlier manifestation of another (see also Caron & Rutter, 1991). It has been hypothesized, for example, that anxiety disorders in children may be an early version of depressive disorders (e.g., Kovacs,

Gatsonis, Paulauskas, & Richards, 1989). Critical issues about the progression of depressive (and other) disorders in children might be embedded in the comorbidity findings.

In addition to the conceptual and definitional matters that affect how we should interpret the coexistence of various symptoms of depression and other conditions, measurement matters further confuse the picture. A review of various symptom, mood, and syndrome scales, interviews, and inventories is beyond the scope of the present work. However, it is apparent that not only do the diverse methods have somewhat different aims, but also there is surprisingly limited information on whether dimensional and categorical methods yield similar findings. As noted earlier, studies aimed at establishing validity of self-report measures of depression have generally found some, but imperfect, agreement between scores and diagnoses. Significant questions of measurement remain unresolved, such as the extent of overlap between different types of instruments purporting to measure the same construct or different constructs, and the extent of valid sampling of symptoms and experiences. Also, to a great extent our instruments for understanding depressive experiences in children and adolescents have relied extensively on what the child can report. Additional measures of functioning in the social, cognitive, family, and academic areas are needed to help characterize the core aspects of depressive experiences. Research on measurement matters would contribute to our understanding of the true nature and structure of depressive experiences in youngsters.

Covariation/comorbidity of depressive disorders in children

Up to now we have set the stage by defining terms; in this section we confront the striking evidence for covariation and comorbidity. What can data on covariation and comorbidity tell us about the nature of depressive phenomena in young people?

Covariation of depressed mood

A number of studies have shown that although children and adolescents clearly experience depressed mood, it may not be a distinct emotional state. First, monomethod studies (i.e., studies relying on a single method, such as adolescents' self-reports) have failed to distinguish depressed mood (and other symptoms of depression) from other negative emotions including anxiety, anger, and hostility (e.g., Saylor, Finch, Spirito, & Bennett, 1984). Further, multitrait-multimethod validity studies examining reports from different informants (e.g., children, teachers, parents) of various negative emotions (depression, anxiety, anger) have failed to establish the discriminant validity of measures of depressed mood (e.g., Finch, Lipovsky, & Casat, 1989; Wolfe et al., 1987). Finch et al. (1989) suggest that anxiety and depression are not separable in children and adolescents and that the distinction between these two forms of negative affect should be put to rest.

These findings can be understood by considering them within the broader framework of theories of emotion (e.g., Watson & Tellegen, 1985). Extensive evidence from studies of the structure of emotions in children, adolescents, college students, and adults indicates that self-rated mood is dominated by two broad factors: *negative affect,* which comprises negative emotions and distress, and *positive affect,* which is made up of positive emotions (e.g., Watson, 1988; Watson & Tellegen, 1985). Depressed mood is one component of the broader construct of *negative affectivity,* whereas positive emotions are important in distinguishing among subtypes of negative emotion (Watson & Clark, 1984).

Numerous studies have shown that a constellation of negative emotions including sadness, fear, guilt, anger, contempt, and disgust are moderately to strongly intercorrelated in self-reports (Watson & Kendall, 1989). It appears that depressed affect is most often experienced in combination with these other negative emotions. Similarly, factor analytic studies of multivariate measures of child and adolescent emotional and behavioral problems have consistently identified a broadband factor that has been labeled "internalizing" or "overcontrolled" problems (Achenbach & Edelbrock, 1978). This syndrome includes problems related to depression, anxiety, social withdrawal, and somatic difficulties.

Depressed mood or negative affectivity has also been shown to covary with symptoms other than negative affect. For example, Cole and Carpentieri (1990) found that in a nonclinical community sample of children, depressed mood and symptoms of conduct disorder co-occurred. The correlation between depressive and conduct disorder symptom scores as reported by children, parents, and peers was .73, after controlling for sources of shared method variance. The authors speculate that children who are high on both depressed mood and conduct disorder symptoms appear to be at especially high risk for future academic, emotional, and behavioral problems. Similarly, Garber and colleagues found that reports of symptoms of depression and aggression from children, parents, teachers and peers were significantly correlated after controlling for method variance (Quiggle, Garber, Panak, & Dodge, 1992).

Syndrome covariation

The most direct evidence of the covariation of depressive symptoms with other types of problems is evidenced by the failure of a "pure" depressive syndrome to emerge from the principal components analyses of the reports of parents, teachers, and adolescents (Achenbach, 1991). Depressive symptoms correlated with other symptoms to form a syndrome that included both anxious and depressed symptoms, including nervousness, fearfulness, worries, loneliness, crying, needing to be perfect, feeling worthless, feeling guilty, and sadness. This strong interrelationship among depressed and anxious symptoms is similar to the findings regarding the association between depressed mood and the broader construct of negative affectivity. Thus, from the outset, research on depressive syndromes reflects covariance between depression and anxiety.

Examination of the intercorrelation of the anxious/depressed core syndrome with the other core syndromes also indicates substantial levels of covariance (overall mean $r = .48$). These correlations have been reported separately for the Child Behavior Checklist (CBCL), Teacher Report Form (TRF), and Youth Self-Report (YSR) for clinically referred and nonreferred adolescent boys and girls (Achenbach, 1991). Further, the anxious/depressed syndrome correlated highly with both internalizing syndromes (withdrawn, somatic complaints) and externalizing syndromes (aggressive, attention problems) (see also Edelbrock & Costello, 1988). Covariation of the anxious/depressed syndrome with other syndromes is consistent with an overall pattern of high covariation among all of the core syndromes identified by Achenbach (1991).

Diagnostic comorbidity

Child and adolescent psychopathology is marked by coexistence of disorders – in general, and not just for depression. For example, the large New Zealand community survey of 11-year-olds determined that 55% of those who had a diagnosable condition had two or more disorders (Anderson, Williams, McGee, & Silva, 1987). It has been determined from community surveys that the rates of coexisting disorders and symptom patterns significantly exceed that which would be expected to occur by chance alone (Caron & Rutter, 1991).

With respect to depression specifically, it is safe to say that comorbidity is the rule rather than the exception. Fleming and Offord (1990), in a review of community epidemiological studies of child and adolescent depression, reported that estimates of comorbidity of depressive disorders with any other disorder ranged from 33% to 100%. In the following sections, we briefly review the findings on the comorbidity of depression with other disorders, chiefly anxiety and conduct problems.

On a methodological note, since many of the studies are based on clinical samples, they should not be interpreted to reflect true base rates of comorbidity, since clinic populations probably reflect the "worst cases," which may include large proportions of patients displaying comorbidity (Caron & Rutter, 1991). Despite limited generalizability, therefore, such studies nevertheless serve to remind us that the meaning of depressive disorders that co-occur with other disorders may be very different from those occurring as distinct disorders. However, it is important to consider data from clinical and community samples separately to see if similar patterns exist.

Depression with anxiety disorders. One of the most frequent types of coexisting diagnoses in depressed children and adolescents is an anxiety disorder, commonly separation anxiety, overanxious disorder, severe phobia, or obsessive-compulsive disorder – although the specific subcategory is not always indicated. In an extensive review of existing studies, Kovacs (1990) concluded that among clinically depressed children, up to 70% had significant anxiety symptoms, and 30–75% had diagnosable anxiety disorders. Similar figures were noted by Fleming and Offord (1990), who noted that variability in rates across studies was due to different informants and methods.

As examples, two studies of community samples provide contrasting rates of the comorbidity of depression and anxiety disorders. Kashani et al.'s (1987) study of a small community sample of adolescents found that 75% of those diagnosed with a depressive disorder had anxiety disorders. Rohde, Lewinsohn, and Seeley (1991) found a lifetime comorbidity rate of 21% of depression and anxiety disorders in a community sample of 1,710 adolescents, as compared with a 5.6% lifetime prevalence rate for anxiety disorders among nondepressed adolescents (prevalence odds ratio of 4.45). These studies differed on a variety of parameters, including sample size, severity level of the disorders reported by the samples, and measures (Rohde et al., 1991).

Several studies have reported on additional aspects of comorbidity in clinical samples. Kovacs et al. (1989) found that 41% of her child sample had anxiety disorders during their index episode of depression. Notably, the investigators determined that most of the anxiety disorders had an onset between 9 and 11 years of age, and in two-thirds of the cases of major depression, the anxiety developed before the depression (the reverse was true for dysthymic disorder). Those who had comorbid anxiety disorders had an earlier age of onset of depression than those who did not; anxiety that antedated the major depressive episodes typically persisted beyond the episode of major depression.

Kovacs (1990) also reviewed the few studies of children with anxiety disorders who were also assessed for depression, and indicated that high rates of coexisting or lifetime major depressive disorder have been documented in those groups as well. The effect is particularly striking for clinically referred anxious children, whereas for coexistence of symptoms only, a somewhat different pattern occurs: Depressed children tend to be anxious, but anxious children do not tend to be depressed. Kovacs notes that differences in sample sizes, ages, and types of anxiety disorders might account for the somewhat different findings across samples.

Kovacs and colleagues speculate that depression and anxiety in children are sometimes a single disorder with anxiety temporally preceding, or that they are distinct – with the combination marking a particularly greater vulnerability and negative prognosis. Kovacs (1990) suggests that high rates of coexisting (or sequential) separation anxiety and depression might mark a particular outcome due to disruptive parent–child relationships as suggested by Bowlby (1973, 1980). Longitudinal studies of the course and outcomes of coexisting depressive disorders are greatly needed.

Comorbidity of depression and conduct disorder. Many externalizing disorders in children appear to "mask" the depression in the sense that the behavioral disturbances are usually the ones that come to parental attention and result in treatment referral. One such disruptive coexisting diagnosis is conduct disorder, frequently found in community and clinical samples.

In their review of community studies of child and adolescent depression, Fleming and Offord (1990) reported covariance with conduct disorder ranging from 17–79%, 0–50% with oppositional-defiant disorder, 0–57% with attention deficit disorder, and 23–25% with alcohol or drug abuse. Kashani et al. (1987) reported that 33% of their small depressed sample also received a diagnosis of conduct disorder, and 50% received a diagnosis of oppositional-defiant disorder. Rohde et al. (1991) combined conduct disorder and oppositional-defiant disorder diagnoses into a single category labeled disruptive behavior and found a current comorbidity rate of 8.0% in the large depressed sample (compared with 1.6% in the nondepressed group) and a lifetime comorbidity rate of 12.1% in the depressed group (compared with 6.1% in the nondepressed group). As with anxiety disorders, the comorbidity of depression and disruptive behavior disorders exceeded the level that would be expected from the base rates of the disorders in their samples.

Clinical samples of children and adolescents have also found substantial rates of comorbidity. Puig-Antich (1982) reported that one-third of a sample of depressed children also had a conduct disorder. In a somewhat overlapping sample of both children and adolescents, Ryan et al. (1987) reported that at least mild conduct disorder symptoms were present in 38% of the children and in 25% of the adolescents, with severer levels in 16% of the children and 11% of the adolescents. In their longitudinal study of 104 depressed children, Kovacs et al. (Kovacs, Paulauskas, Gatsonis, & Richards, 1988) reported a rate of 16% concurrent conduct disorder and a lifetime probability of 36% comorbidity with conduct disorder in this sample. Mitchell et al. (Mitchell, McCauley, Burke, & Moss, 1990) reported rates of comorbidity of conduct disorder and depression of 16% in a sample of 45 depressed children and 14% in a sample of 50 depressed adolescents. They further analyzed these data by gender and found that 26% of the preadolescent depressed boys had a comorbid conduct disorder whereas none of the preadolescent girls received this diagnosis. Among the depressed adolescents, 10% of the males and 17% of the females were identified with a conduct disorder. Relatedly, depressed adolescents have been found to have higher rates of illicit drug use and alcohol use or abuse than do depressed children (Kashani et al., 1987; Keller et al., 1988).

Based on their longitudinal follow-up of the sample, Keller et al. (1988) concluded that youngsters with nonaffective disorders concurrent with depression had a much more chronic course of depression. It should be noted that in most cases, the nonaffective disorder predated the onset of depression. These observations are also consistent with the community sample of Rohde et al. (1991). These investigators found a rate of 42% comorbidity in their depressed youngsters, and typically the depression followed rather than preceded onset of the other disorder. Also, comorbidity was associated with greater frequency of suicidal behaviors and treatment seeking, but did not affect the duration or severity of depression. In addition to studies of coexisting diagnoses in depressed children and adolescents, it is also apparent in studies of high-risk children of depressed parents that comorbidity of depression and additional diagnoses is common (e.g., see reviews in Hammen, 1991; Weissman, 1988).

Characteristics of child and adolescent depression

In this section we briefly review the current status of empirical data on child and adolescent depression. In defining what we do know, we also attempt to highlight the gaps and deficiencies in our knowledge. Many of the unanswered questions concerning childhood depression are directly related to the issues raised by comorbidity or covariation of depression.

Features of depression

Until fairly recently there were several prevailing myths about child-hood depression: It is rare if it exists at all; it is transitory; it is a developmentally normal stage; if it exists it is "masked" as "depression equivalents" such as behavior and conduct disorders, somatic complaints, school problems, or "adolescent turmoil" instead of directly expressed. Thus, from the very outset of the history of studies of childhood and adolescent depression, our understanding has been clouded by unresolved issues of the covariation of depression syndromes with other conditions and developmentally salient expressions of dysfunction.

Countering these earlier assumptions, however, clinical observations increasingly made it clear that children exhibited the essential features of the adult depression disorder, and that depressive conditions could be diagnosed using adult criteria with age-specific modifications. Researchers established that even when a behavior disorder might be the more obvious presenting problem, the clinical syndrome of depression is frequently detectable if the adult criteria are specifically applied (e.g., Carlson & Cantwell, 1980; Cytryn, McKnew, & Bunney, 1980; Kashani et al., 1981). Thus, there is ample evidence that diagnosable depressive disorders, as well as depressive mood and syndromes, exist in children and adolescents. Nevertheless, successful application of diagnostic criteria does not resolve theoretical and practical issues concerning the meaning of depression.

Developmental issues in symptom expression

At the level of depressed mood, older children are much more likely to express dysphoria and unhappiness than are younger children. Indeed, by early adolescence significant proportions of youngsters report depressed mood (Kandel & Davies, 1982; Petersen, Kennedy, & Sullivan, 1991; Roberts, Lewisohn, & Seeley, 1991; Rutter, 1986) – in rates ranging from 18% to 59%, depending on the assessment instrument, age, and gender. Significant gender effects appear to emerge in the expression of depressed mood in adolescence, with girls reporting higher rates than do boys from early adolescence (e.g., Allgood-

Merten, Lewinsohn, & Hops, 1990; Kandel & Davies, 1982; Petersen, Sarigiani, & Kennedy, 1991).

With respect to *diagnoses* of depression, although adult criteria may be applied to children and adolescents, aspects of the presentation of depression differ according to the youngster's developmental level. Preschoolers, for instance, are cognitively unequipped to report subjective experiences of depression, but might instead complain of somatic symptoms. As Kashani and Carlson (1987) note, physically unjustified or exaggerated complaints may develop against a background of misery and distress that are not directly reported (and of which parents may be unaware). Kashani, Holcomb, and Orvaschel (1986) studied children in nursery schools, and found that the depressed children showed high levels of irritability and anger – not depressed mood – and were apathetic and uncooperative.

For older children, there have been only a few studies that compared the phenomenology of depression at different ages. Kashani, Rosenberg, and Reid (1989) found a few age-related symptoms in a community cohort of 8-, 12-, and 17-year-olds. Carlson and Kashani (1988) presented a type of metaanalysis of depressive symptoms in clinic-referred populations based on four different samples of different ages (preschool, preadolescent, adolescent, and adult). Kashani and colleagues concluded that although there are somewhat specific developmental modifications, in general severe depression presents the same picture regardless of age.

Ryan et al. (1987) also found relatively few significant differences in the depressive experiences of clinic-referred children and adolescents. However, children showed greater depressed appearance, somatic complaints, psychomotor agitation, and separation anxiety, while the adolescents had greater anhedonia, hopelessness, hypersomnia, weight change, and drug/alcohol use. The investigators concluded that the similarities outweighed the differences across this age range, but nevertheless suggested several minor modifications of DSM III-R criteria: irritability/anger might be considered equivalent to sad/depressive mood, and low self-esteem might be equivalent to excessive guilt. Also, somatic complaints, social withdrawal, and hopelessness are common in children and adolescents with major depressive disorder, and Ryan et al. (1987) recommended their inclusion in the diagnostic criteria.

A depression-related feature that has occurred with some frequency in adolescent girls warrants mention. Allgood-Merten et al. (1990) hypothesized that body image, an important part of self-esteem, may be a source of particular vulnerability for young women and an important aspect of adolescent female depression. They found significant sex differences in body image, and determined that negative body image is a particularly salient aspect of self-esteem for girls, in turn associated with depression (se also Petersen, Sarigiani, & Kennedy, 1991).

Finally, comparisons of adolescent and adult diagnosed depressed patients suggest few differences in symptom presentation (Carlson & Strober, 1983; Friedman, Hurt, Clarkin, Corn, & Aronoff, 1983).

Developmental patterns of covariance and comorbidity

Overall, the relatively few systematic studies comparing presentation of depressive symptoms in different age groups have found more similiarities than differences. Nevertheless, it is important to be sensitive to developmental differences in symptom expression. It is also important to bear in mind that many of the studies examining age-related expressions of symptoms have not controlled for the possible coexistence of other psychological conditions.

As we noted at the outset of this chapter, child and adolescent psychopathology must be framed in the context of developmental processes associated with both continuity and change. The key question to consider here is the degree to which patterns of covariation and comorbidity of depression remain stable or change with development. More specifically, in what instances is depression experienced alone over the course of development? In what instances does depression precede the manifestation of other disorders? In what instances does depression follow the onset of other disorders? What are the individual differences (both psychological and biological) and social factors that distinguish cases when depression occurs alone versus in the presence of other disorders?

Data on the developmental course of covariation and comorbidity of depressive phenomena are sparse. This is not surprising in light of the relative recency of attention given to this issue. However, there are data to suggest that anxiety is a companion of depression throughout development, whereas other problems change in their association with depression from childhood to adolescence and adulthood. Anxiety symptoms, syndromes, and disorders are associated with depressive phenomena in children, adolescents, and adults (Maser & Cloninger, 1990). Further, several studies have found that anxiety disorders are significantly more likely to precede depressive disorders than to follow depression (e.g., Kovacs et al., 1989).

Other problems show more varied patterns of association with depression. For example, attention deficit–hyperactivity disorder and conduct disorders are more likely to co-occur with depressive disorders in childhood than in adolescence or adulthood. Eating disorders are more likely to accompany depression and depressive symptoms in adolescence than in childhood. In adulthood, in addition to the high rates of comorbidity of anxiety disorders, the highest rates of comorbidity are found for alcohol abuse and depression (e.g., Helzer, 1987). These changing patterns of comorbidity may be an artifact, however, of the fundamental changes in the base rates of these disorders with development. Eating disorders and alcohol abuse are rare in childhood, decreasing the possibility of co-occurrence with depression during this developmental period. On the other hand, the changing base rates of these disorders with development may reflect important processes about the expression of psychological distress at different points in the life-span. It is necessary to determine whether the rates of comorbidity of depression with these disorders exceeds the rate expected by chance in the general population at any given point in development (Caron & Rutter, 1991). Epidemiological data to examine this question are not yet available. Moreover, the extent to which co-existing diagnostic states alter the developmental aspects of depression is an important and unresolved issue.

Incidence and course of depression in children and adolescents

Depressive phenomena, both as symptoms and as diagnostic entities, appear to increase with age. Depression in preschool-age children is rare, estimated to occur in less than 1% of the population of children beginning as young as 2 or 3, based on limited samples of community children and surveys of child guidance populations (e.g., Kashani et al., 1986; Kashani & Carlson, 1987). In community samples of school-age children approximately 6 to 12 years of age, the rate appears to be less than 2% including both major depressive episodes and dysthymia (Anderson et al., 1987; Costello et al., 1988; Kashani & Simonds, 1979). *Treatment* samples indicate that about 15% of school-age children referred to clinics meet diagnostic criteria for depressive disorders (Kashani, Cantwell, Shekim, & Reid, 1982; Kazdin, French, Unis, Esveldt-Dawson, & Sherick, 1983).

In contrast to the relatively low rates of clinical depression in children, rates of depression in adolescents are high – approximately the same as adult rates. Several relatively small-scale studies indicate about a four-fold increase in adolescent depression compared with the rate in childhood depression (Kashani et al., 1987; Kashani et al., 1989; Rutter, 1986). A sample of over 3,500 clinic-referred children and adolescents also showed a sharp increase in depression in adolescence – particularly for girls (Angold & Rutter, 1992). Similar results emerge in large community surveys (Lewinsohn, Hops, Roberts, & Seeley, 1988; Whitaker et al., 1990). Increases in rates of depression in adolescence also raise the intriguing possibility of increased depression in recent birth cohorts (reviewed in Klerman & Weissman, 1989). The teenage years are additionally noteworthy for the emergence of the marked sex differences in depression that characterize adult patterns as well, with markedly higher rates for females.

In light of high rates of depression comorbidity and covariation, numerous unresolved issues come to light. For instance, the relatively low rate of depressive disorders in children, high rates in adolescents, and emergence of sex differences in adolescence may all be related to depression covariation. There may be developmental progressions in symptom expression, with earlier rates of nonspecific distress giving rise to more specific diagnosable syndromes later on. Sex role socialization and differing roles of males and females may shape the expression of distress and the age-related focus on particular symptoms. Earlier adjustment difficulties that affect social and academic functioning may give rise to depression and demoralization because of dysfunction and its negative impact on self-esteem. These are but a few of the unresolved issues related to incidence and prevalence of depression – and that also affect the course of disorder, to which we now turn.

Course of disorder in childhood and adolescent depression. Relatively few studies have charted the course of depression in youngsters, and the paucity of longitudinal studies is a striking gap in the field. In general, however, the same principle holds with children as with adults who are depressed: Past depression predicts future depression. While there is considerable temporal fluctuation in youngsters' mood level, the past-predicts-future pattern generally holds both for studies of the stability of depressed mood (e.g., Billings & Moos, 1985; Garrison, Jackson, Marsteller, McKeown, & Addy, 1990), and for diagnosable conditions (Hammen, Burge, Adrian, & Burney, 1990; Lee & Gotlib, 1989). The likelihood of relapse or recurrence of clinical episodes, for example, is relatively high, ranging from 40% within 2 years to 72% within 5 years (Asarnow et al., in press; Hammen et al., 1990; Kovacs, Feinberg, Crouse-Novak, Paulauskas, & Finkelstein, 1984a; Kovacs et al., 1984b). There is also some evidence that youngsters whose depression co-occurs with other clinical conditions have a longer time to recovery or a severer course (e.g., Keller et al., 1988; Kovacs et al., 1984a; Kovacs et al., 1984b; Rohde et al., 1991). Thus, comorbidity likely alters the course of depressive disorders in children and adolescents, suggesting several possibilities for further consideration: There is a temporal progression; dual conditions have a severer course; a third variable (e.g., deficits in expected functioning) intervenes between an initial condition and subsequent depression.

A crucial question in the course of childhood depression is whether childhood onset predicts a depression that recurs in adulthood, and whether childhood-onset depression occurring in adults has similar features to adult-onset depression. There is some reason to expect that childhood-onset depression predicts a worse course of disorder (e.g., Hammen, 1991; Kovacs et al., 1984a; Kovacs et al., 1984b). However, there is only limited information available on the continuity between childhood and adult depression. That which is available, however, suggests that those with childhood or adolescent onset are indeed more likely to have symptoms and diagnoses of depressive disorders as adults (Harrington, Fudge, Rutter, Pickles, & Hill, 1990; Kandel & Davies, 1986).

This brief survey of incidence, symptom expression, and course of disorder has noted many gaps in the empirical understanding of depression. These gaps are undoubtedly compounded by the general failure of much of the research to take into account either the presence or the implications of coexisting conditions. Perhaps we would even say that what we know about childhood depression is really about mixed conditions, and that we have largely ignored the meaning and contribution of the "mix" to the understanding of depressive phenomena.

Implications of covariation and comorbidity

The evidence just summarized clearly indicates that depressed mood syndromes and disorders are strongly related to other symptoms and disorders during childhood and adolescence. The implications of the high degree of covariation and comorbidity of depressive phenomena are far-reaching, as they touch on several of the core aspects of child and adolescent depression. We have noted that comorbidity raises key questions about the characterization and diagnosis of depression in youngsters, and confounds what we think we know about its course and correlates.

In addition, the extent and meaning of coexisting patterns of symptoms in depression raise significant questions about etiological and treatment matters. Sources of risk and protection for depression, the developmental course of depression, and interventions for the prevention and treatment of depression all must be considered carefully in light of the co-occurrence of other problems. This important perspective has received little empirical attention, however. Therefore, our comments here are mostly speculative and form the basis for directions for future research.

Risk and resilience

If depressive phenomena are related to a variety of other symptoms and disorders, what does this tell us about the nature of risk factors associated with depression? Are there risk factors specific to depression? Are there risk factors that distinguish individuals who develop "pure" depressive symptoms and disorders from those who display a more heterogenous pattern of problems? Further, what do patterns of covariation and comorbidity say about sources of resilience or protection from these risk factors? In considering these questions it is helpful to consider biological, psychological and social sources of risk and resilience, and the extent to which sources of risk and resilience may themselves be interrelated.

The study of risk processes is concerned with the identification of those characteristics of individuals and their social environments, as well as ongoing transactions between individuals and environments, that increase the probability of developing specific symptoms, syndromes, or disorders. For example, researchers have actively searched to identify the risk factors associated with depression in adults (Monroe & Simons, 1991). However, the high rates of covariation and comorbidity of depressive phenomena with other symptoms and disorders during childhood and adolescence challenge traditional notions of risk. It is misleading to examine those factors that are associated with increased levels of depressive phenomena alone, as these same factors may be concurrently related to a wider range of other manifestations of distress and disorder. Further, a risk factor may contribute to the development of one disorder, which in turn leads to depression.

The challenge facing researchers is to distinguish between those factors that predispose individuals to general distress and psychopathology as opposed to those that are related specifically to depression. The problems in determining specificity in risk for psychopathology, however, are formidable (Garber & Hollon, 1991). Research on risk for child and adolescent depression is at a very early stage and research designs necessary to determine specificity have rarely been employed. Therefore, we will comment briefly on the state of current knowledge and offer several possible avenues for future research to clarify sources of risk for depression in young people. We will broadly distinguish among risk processes that reflect biological, psychological, and social factors, followed by suggestions of ways to integrate these lines of research.

Biological processes. Relatively little biological research on depression has addressed or contended with the comorbidity issue. Biological factors associated with risk for depressive phenomena fall into two general categories, genetic factors and neuroendocrine functioning. Genetic risk studies have focused on patterns of co-occurrence of depression and other disorders – especially anxiety disorders – primarily in the offspring of depressed probands. Offspring studies can help to focus on the specificity of risk for particular disorders rather than general psychopathology (Weissman, 1990). Similarly, twin studies can be used to establish the rates of comorbidity of single as opposed to multiple disorders in siblings who vary in their degree of genetic similarity.

Family studies indicate that children of depressed parents are at high risk for both depression and anxiety disorders, as are children of parents with anxiety disorders (Weissman, 1990). Moreover, rates of child depression and anxiety disorders are approximately equal in six studies of children of depressed parents and in two studies of children of parents with anxiety disorders (see Weissman, 1990). Parents of children with depression or anxiety disorders also have been found to have high rates of both disorders.

Studies of biological risk factors associated with the comorbidity and covariation of disorders and symptoms other than anxiety are rare. Several studies of children of depressed parents have found substantial rates of externalizing disorders, including attention deficit hyperactivity disorder (Orvaschel, Walsh-Allis, & Ye, 1988) and disruptive behavior disorders (Billings & Moos, 1983; Hammen et al., 1987). Moreover, there is considerable evidence that risk for depressive symptoms and disorders is high in children of alcoholic parents (Phares & Compas, 1992; West & Prinz, 1987). Just as parental depression appears to be a nonspecific risk factor for both depression and anxiety in offspring, parental alcoholism appears to function as a nonspecific risk for both internalizing symptoms, including depression, as well as externalizing symptoms including conduct disorder, aggression, delinquency, and substance abuse.

Research on genetic risk factors for depression and comorbid conditions has been limited in several ways. First, the use of true behavior genetic designs in which the variance attributable to genes and environment can be partitioned has been rare. For example, inferences about the role of genetic processes underlying parent–child similarities are open to the alternative explanation that these similarities are due to environmental rather than genetic processes.

Second, the status of both parents is rarely examined; that is, one parent, typically the mother, is identified as depressed but the psychiatric status of the spouse (father) is rarely reported. Evidence for patterns of assortative mating by depressed women (Hammen, 1991; Merikangas & Spiker, 1984; Rutter & Quinton, 1984), the possibility that both spouses may develop disorders in response to shared familial and extramfamilial stress, and the importance of considering the psychiatric status of both mothers and fathers (Phares & Compas, 1992) all suggest the importance of considering both parents. This is especially important if a child is raised in a home with a depressed mother and an alcoholic father. Patterns of comorbid disorders in offspring may reflect the separate contributions of both parents.

Third, the status of all children within the family is also rarely examined. This has overlooked possible similarities and differences between siblings as a result of genes, shared environmental factors, and nonshared environmental factors (Plomin & Daniels, 1987). These factors may function differently in normal as opposed to clinical samples of children. For example, Rende (1991) found that shared environmental influences were greater for siblings who scored extremely high or low on the Children's Depression Inventory than for children in the midrange on this scale. Rende (1991) hypothesized that these findings suggest that extreme depressive symptoms reflect a greater etiological contribution of shared environmental processes than is true for most children and adolescents.

Finally, studies of neuroendocrine functioning have focused on dysregulation of the limbic system. The limbic system, involved in the regulation of drive, instinct, and emotions, has been studied through two key pathways: the hypothalamic-pituitary-adrenal axis (HPA) and the hypothalamic-pituitary-thyroid axis (HPT); readers are referred to Shelton et al. (1991) and Butler and Nemeroff (1990) for discussions of neuroendocrine processes. Although we know of no studies specifically exploring this topic with respect to comorbidity, we note that Gold, Goodwin, and Chrousos (1988) hypothesize depression vulnerability to be a consequence of dysregulation of HPA-related biological responses to stress – processes that would seem to entail experiences of anxiety as well, or possibly implicate a temporal sequence or causal link involving different emotional reactions.

Psychological processes. Dysfunctional cognitive styles, including maladaptive causal attributions, self-schema, and cognitive errors, have received the most attention as psychological markers of risk for child and adolescent depressive symptoms and disorders. At issue is whether different expressions of child and adolescent psychopathology are associated with cognitive deficits, distortions, or both (Kendall, Stark, & Adam, 1990). Kendall et al. (1990) suggested, for example, that impulsive children show deficits in cognitive processes that govern self-control, whereas depressed and anxious children show distortions in processing self-relevant information. Theories concerning adult depression have specifically focused on depression related to cognitions concerning diminished self-worth, with anxiety associated with expectations of future threat or danger; presumably the co-occurrence of anxiety and depression would involve a mixture of related cognitions (e.g., Beck, Brown, Steer, Eidelson, & Riskind, 1987; see also Alloy, Kelly, Mineka, & Clements, 1990, for a similar position concerning helplessness and hopelessness cognitions). Beck (e.g., 1976) has also speculated that beliefs in others' intention to cause harm leads to the experience of anger. Despite theoretical formulations that encompass comorbidity of disorders due to multiple cognitive risk factors, there has been little exploration of the issue in adult studies, and also little among child and adolescent populations.

A few studies have compared cognitive processes in young people who display high levels of depressive symptoms, aggressive symptoms, or both types of symptoms. Garber and colleagues (Quiggle et al., 1992) found that children high in depressed, aggressive, and aggressive-depressed symptoms all displayed a tendency to perceive hostile intent in the behavior of others, even in benign or positive situations. However, only depressed and depressed-aggressive symptomatic children displayed a dysfunctional attributional style characterized by self-blame for negative events. Thus, children with depressive and/or aggressive symptoms were characterized by a hostile attributional bias, whereas only children with high depressive symptoms displayed a helpless attributional style. These findings suggest that depressive symptoms are uniquely related to a helpless attributional style but that aggression is not uniquely associated with a hostile attributional bias. A tendency to perceive hostile intent in the behavior of others may be a cognitive factor contributing to the covariation of depressive and aggressive symptoms.

Self-perceptions of competence have also been found to be related to both internalizing problems, of which depressive symptoms are a subtype, and externalizing problems, which include symptoms of conduct disorder and aggression. For example, Compas, Phares, Banez, and Howell (1991) found that adolescents in the clinical range on internalizing, externalizing, and both internalizing and externalizing symptoms reported lower levels of global self-worth and lower self-perceptions of behavioral conduct and physical appearance than adolescents in the normal range on these problems. Adolescents high on both types of problems (i.e., those who showed a high level of covariation of these syndromes) did not differ from those youths who were experiencing either internalizing or externalizing problems alone on perceptions of competence or attributional style. In fact, those with mixed internalizing and externalizing problems were distinguished only by high levels of psychological symptoms reported by their fathers (Compas, Phares, Banez, & Howell, 1991).

Findings from these and other studies suggest that low perceived competence and a hostile attributional style are shared features of the cognitive styles of youth high in both depressive and aggressive symptoms. However, the ways in which these cognitions contribute to the expression of depressed and aggressive emotions and behaviors have not been delineated (Quiggle et al., 1992).

Social processes. Research investigating two aspects of the social environment, psychosocial stress and family processes, has produced rich and interesting information on risk factors associated with child and adolescent depressive phenomena. Much of this research has proceeded, however, without attention to patterns of covariation and comorbidity.

Stressful life events and chronic stresses and strains have been found to be associated with depressed mood, syndromes, and disorders in children and adolescents in over 40 recent studies (Compas, Grant, & Ey, in press). However, in every study in which symptoms of other disorders were measured, stressful events were related to these other symptoms as well as to depressive symptoms. The clearest interpretation of these data is that stressful events and processes operate as nonspecific risk factors for a variety of symptoms and disorders, including depression. This is at least in part the result of the failure to distinguish among subtypes of stressful events and processes in most studies. That is, the most frequent research design is to examine the association between the accumulation of a wide range of major and daily stressors and a variety of different symptoms, including depression, anxiety, aggression, and substance abuse. This type of design will not be able to detect patterns of specificity in stress–symptom relations.

The most informative data on child and adolescent stress and depressive symptoms have come from studies of interpersonal loss events and subsequent depression. Childhood loss of a parent through death or divorce has been found to be associated with depressive disorders in adulthood and childhood (e.g., Brown & Harris, 1978; McLeod, 1991). A strength of these studies has been the focus on a specific stressor that most theorists agree has implications in the etiology of depressive phenomena. Studies of childhood loss have been limited in their ability to inform us about patterns of covariation and comorbidity, however, in that they have typically focused only on depressive outcomes (e.g., McLeod, 1991) and have not addressed the association between loss and other symptoms and disorders.

A second important context for understanding social processes related to child and adolescent depression has been family processes and interactions (Hammen, 1991). The general design of these studies is similar to that described for investigations of genetic links between parental and child depression. A crucial difference is that investigations of family processes have also included measures of characteristics of the transactions within the family that may be important mechanisms for the transmission of parental disorder to offspring. Several recent reviews have implicated the emotional unavailability of parents (e.g., Lee & Gotlib, 1991), dysfunctional parent–child interactions (e.g., Burge & Hammen, 1991), and marital conflict (e.g., Cummings & Davies, 1993; Downey & Coyne, 1990) as important sources of risk for children in families of depressed parents.

Children of depressed parents are exposed to a variety of dysfunctional family interactions and processes that may contribute to the range of symptoms and disorders that they manifest. One puzzle for researchers has been to determine whether there are unique family patterns that contribute to depressive as opposed to other outcomes in these children. Downey and Coyne (1990) reviewed several alternative models of risk within these families and tentatively suggested that depressive symptoms in children may be a unique outcome of parental depression, whereas externalizing problems may be the consequence of marital discord and conflict in these families. This model suggests that covariation and comorbidity of problems in children of depressed parents may be the consequence of unique rather than shared risk factors.

Summary. Research on genetic, cognitive, and social sources of risk for depression and related disorders have developed separately. As a result, the way in which these various sources of risk may be interrelated has received little attention. It is provocative to consider, however, that the high rates of covariation and comorbidity of depressive phenomena are the result of the exposure of high-risk children to multiple sources of risk that contribute independently to negative outcomes. Thus, children who develop symptoms of multiple syndromes or disorders may be exposed to multiple risk factors, including genetic vulnerabilities, dysfunctional styles of thinking, and multiple sources of stress and family dysfunction. We must also consider that having one disorder increases the risk for another disorder, so that identifying a risk factor for a particular disorder might be spurious – if it is only a risk factor for a disorder that caused that disorder (Robins, Locke, & Regier, 1992).

Intervention

One of the most important implications of the covariation and comorbidity of depressive phenomena concerns the prevention and treatment of these problems. The key question is whether prevention and treatment programs exert their effects specifically on depressive symptoms and disorders as opposed to a wider range of problems. Not surprisingly, the evidence indicates that covariation and comorbidity are important to consider when examining the efficacy of interventions for depression.

Pharmacotherapy. Building on research with adults, several varieties of psychoactive medications have been evaluated as treatments for adolescent depression. These have included tricycle antidepressants (TCAs, including amitriptyline, desipramine, imipramine, mianserin, nortriptyline), monamine oxidase inhibitors (MAOIs, including tranylcypromine and phenelzine), and lithium. The results of several studies have generally not supported the efficacy of pharmacotherapy for child or adolescent depression (e.g., Boulos et al., 1991; Geller, Cooper, Graham, Marsteller, & Bryant, 1990; Ryan et al., 1986; Ryan et al., 1988; Strober, Freeman, & Rigali, 1990).

In light of the importance of considering the comorbidity of adolescent depression with other disorders, it is noteworthy that the high rates of comorbid disorders in these samples have received little attention in evaluations of the effects of pharmacological treatment. Since an initial study by Ryan et al. (1986) reported that adolescents with associated separation anxiety showed a significantly poorer response to treatment of their depressive symptoms than did those with major depression alone, subsequent studies have failed to investigate possible differences in medication response as a function of comorbid conditions. Further, all dependent variables that have been reported in pharmacologic studies pertain to depressive symptoms and diagnoses. Thus, any beneficial or adverse effects of these medications as a function of comorbid conditions have not been examined. Boulus et al. (1991) make reference to this concern when they note that desipramine, because of its stimulating qualities, may not be an appropriate medication for individuals who display comorbid depressive and anxious features. Unfortunately, no data were reported on posttreatment levels of anxiety symptoms in this sample. Clearly, further investigation of the role of comorbid disorders in adolescent pharmacotherapy is needed.

Psychosocial and psychotherapeutic treatments. A variety of psychosocial and psychotherapeutic interventions have been applied to the treatment of adolescent depression. Four studies have evaluated the effectiveness of various forms of psychotherapeutic and psychosocial interventions as compared with other interventions and/or wait-list controls. The preliminary evidence from these studies is encouraging. The three studies that included no-treatment control groups all provide some confirmation that depression or depressive symptoms can be significantly reduced through treatment (Kahn, Kehle, Jenson, & Clark, 1990; Lewinsohn, Clarke, Hops, & Andrews, 1990; Reynolds & Coats, 1986).

These studies also suggest that treatment effects are not limited to depressive symptoms. This evidence comes from two sources. First, two studies measured anxiety as well as depression, and in both cases significant reductions were found in anxiety symptoms as well as in depressive symptoms (Lewinsohn et al., 1990; Reynolds & Coats, 1986). This indicates that the treatments may have affected other symptoms related to depression. Second, relaxation training, which is designed to reduce anxiety, tension, and nervousness, has been effective in reducing symptoms of depression (Kahn et al., 1990; Reynolds & Coats, 1986). It is a reasonable hypothesis that relaxation training lowered levels of both anxious and depressed emotions.

The strongest interpretation of these studies can be framed in terms of their impact on the construct of negative affectivity. Reductions in self-reports of both depressive and anxiety symptoms indicate that the programs may have had their impact on general negative affect or, more specifically, on individuals who would fit a profile for "mixed anxiety-depression" (Clark & Watson, 1991). The effect of the interventions on "purer" diagnosable depressive disorders is more difficult to determine from the available data. Only Lewinsohn et al. (1990) used structured clinical interviews to diagnosis major depression and dysthymic disorder. Although they found significant reductions in diagnosable cases as a function of treatment, over half of the treated groups continued to meet diagnostic criteria for MDD or DD after the intervention. No data were reported on the characteristics that might distinguish responders from nonresponders. It will be important to determine if differences in response to interventions for depression vary as a function of the presence of mixed anxiety and depression as opposed to only depressive symptoms – and what the mechanisms of specific and general change might be.

Summary and directions for future research

The extent and patterns of comorbidity and covariation of symptoms of depression and other problems in children and adolescents raise critical issues for our field. The fact that comorbidity appears to be the rule, rather than the exception, calls into question our very conceptualization of depression, as well as our understanding of its causes and consequences.

The recognition that depression can be diagnosed in children and adolescents using the same criteria as applied to adults has sparked a great deal of research with important theoretical and practical implications. Nevertheless, it may have contributed to the illusion that we thereby understand depressive phenomena in youngsters, although what we know is largely based on samples of mixed disorders. We conclude by offering an agenda for future research in this area involving six steps.

Depressed mood, depressive syndromes, and depressive disorders

The first order of business involves further clarification of the relations among depressed mood, depressive syndromes, and depressive disorders. Although several cross-sectional studies have established that there is substantial but imperfect overlap among measures of these three levels of depression (e.g., Edelbrock & Costello, 1988), longitudinal data on these concepts have been rare. Cross-sectional data indicate that they reflect increasingly severer manifestations of depressive phenomena. However, longitudinal data are needed to determine if they are sequentially related (Compas et al., 1993). Specifically, are children and adolescents who report high levels of depressed mood at risk for subsequent high scores on depressive syndromes and for higher rates of depressive disorders? Similarly, are young people who score high on depressive syndrome measures at risk for episodes of depressive disorders at a later time? Once these issues are clarified, it can then be determined if the presence of other symptoms or disorders increases the likelihood that depressed mood or a depressive syndrome will develop into a depressive disorder.

Artifactual and real covariation and comorbidity

To what extent are the observed covariation of symptoms and syndromes and the comorbidity of disorders real? To what extent are they artifacts of methodological, referral, and nosological problems? These issues are complex and can only be addressed through continued examination of the contribution of different measures and different taxonomic systems to covariation and comorbidity (Achenbach, 1990/1991; Caron & Rutter, 1991; Maser & Cloniger, 1990). Studies in which measures of depressed mood, behavioral checklists, and diagnostic interviews are used with community and clinical samples – in longitudinal designs – are necessary to disentangle the contributions of these factors. We encourage study of both symptom overlap and conceptual overlap in our understanding and measurement of different conditions. Also, exploration of naturally occurring symptom clusters, observed over time, would be necessary, along with experimentation with different diagnostic criteria based on different phenomenology and diagnostic thresholds. Also, it would be useful to explore similarities between levels of assessment. For example, are the levels of covariation of other syndromes with a depressive syndrome similar to the rates of comorbidity of other disorders with depression when measures of these two phenomena are administered to the same sample? Are rates of covariation and comorbidity similar when different informants (e.g., parents, children) are used to assess depressive syndromes or disorders? Is the level of covariation of symptoms on continuous scales similar to the degree of comorbidity of discrete diagnostic categories? Do the rates of covariation and comorbidity differ in predictable ways when compared across demographically matched samples of clinically referred and nonreferred children and adolescents? Determining the contributions of measurement and sampling biases to covariation and comorbidity will enable researchers to turn their attention to true manifestations of co-occurrence of depression with other problems.

Sequences of covariation and comorbidity involving depressive phenomena

Although some researchers have attempted to determine *if* depression precedes or follows other disorders, this is probably the wrong question. Rather, the issue is *when* depressive phenomena precede other symptoms and disorders and *when* they follow other problems. Does depression follow anxiety disorders and conduct disorders, but precede eating disorders and substance abuse? Are these sequences different depending on the developmental point at which the initial depressive symptoms or disorder emerges? These issues point to the need to study not only the apparent sequencing of symptoms, but also their functional relationships. Recently, in noting the extent of co-occurence of disorders in adults, Robins et al.

(1992) speculated that having one disorder puts the person at risk for developing another disorder. We suspect this is commonly true for childhood and adolescent depression, and urge study of the possible mechanisms of such a process. Only longitudinal studies with large samples of children and adolescents will allow for the determination of patterns and causal mechanisms of co-occurrence among syndromes and disorders.

Longitudinal consequences of covariation and comorbidity

If it can be determined that depressive phenomena co-occur with other problems in specific developmental sequences, researchers can then turn attention to long-term consequences of covariation and comorbidity. Are the consequences different when depressive phenomena co-occur with other internalizing problems (e.g., anxiety) as opposed to externalizing problems (e.g., conduct disorder)? Are the consequences of covariation and comorbidity simply the result of greater overall levels of distress and impairment in young people with multiple problems, or are there unique consequences that result from the association of certain problems with depression? And do the consequences of comorbidity vary depending on the sequence of occurrence of the disorders involved? That is, are the consequences different if depression precedes or follows another disorder?

Risk factors for depressive phenomena and other problems

What are the factors that predispose children and adolescents to depressive symptoms alone as opposed to multiple symptoms and disorders? It has been suggested that there are distinct risk factors associated with depression (e.g., parental depression) as opposed to disruptive behavior problems (e.g., parental marital discord), but that these risk factors tend to co-occur in families (Downey & Coyne, 1990; Walker, Downey, & Nightingale, 1989). On the other hand, depressive and anxious symptoms and disorders may share the same underlying risk factor that contributes to both of these problems. Identification of unique, shared, and overlapping risk factors will be important for understanding the etiology and ultimately the prevention of depression and other related disorders.

Effects of covariation and comorbidity on prevention and treatment

Data on covariation and comorbidity provide a warning to intervention researchers that their outcome measures need to be broad rather than narrow if they are to assess fully the impact of their intervention programs. Some interventions may have effects that reach beyond depressive syndromes and disorders and contribute to the prevention or remediation of other problems. On the other hand, the effectiveness of some interventions may be compromised by the co-occurrence of other problems. In either case, it is clear that the implications of covariation and comorbidity for the effective management of depression are far-reaching.

References

Achenbach, T. M. (1985). *Assessment and taxonomy of child and adolescent psychopathology.* Newbury Park, CA: Sage.

Achenbach, T. M. (1990/1991). "Comorbidity" in child and adolescent psychiatry: Categorical and quantitative perspectives. *Journal of Child and Adolescent Psychopharmacology, 1,* 271–278.

Achenbach, T. M. (1991). *Integrative guide for the 1991 CBCL/4–18, YSR, and TRF Profiles.* Burlington: University of Vermont, Department of Psychiatry.

Achenbach, T. M., & Edelbrock, C. (1978). The classification of child psychopathology: A review and analysis of empirical efforts. *Psychological Bulletin, 85,* 1275–1302.

Allgood-Merten, B., Lewinsohn, P. M., & Hops, H. (1990). Sex differences and adolescent depression. *Journal of Abnormal Psychology, 99,* 55–63.

Alloy, L. B., Kelly, K. A., Mineka, S., & Clements, C. M. (1990). Comorbidity of anxiety and depressive disorders: A helplessness/ hopelessness perspective. In J. D. Maser & C. R. Cloninger (Eds.), *Comorbidity of anxiety and mood disorders.* Washington, DC: American Psychiatric Press.

American Psychiatric Association (1987). *Diagnostic and statistical manual of mental disorders* (3rd ed. rev.). Washington, DC.

Anderson, J. C., Williams, S., McGee, R., & Silva, P. A. (1987). DSM-III disorders in preadolescent children. *Archives of General Psychiatry, 44,* 69–76.

Angold, A. (1988). Childhood and adolescent depression I. Epidemiological and aetiological aspects. *British Journal of Psychiatry, 152,* 601–607.

Angold, A., & Rutter, M. (1992). Effects of age and pubertal status on depression in a large clinical sample. *Development and Psychopathology, 4,* 5–28.

Asarnow, J. R., Goldstein, M. J., Carlson, G. A., Perdue, S., Bates, S., & Keller, J. (in press). Childhood-onset depressive disorders: A follow-up study of rates of rehospitalization and out-of-home placement among child psychiatric inpatients. *Journal of Affective Disorders.*

Beck, A. T. (1976). *Cognitive therapy and the emotional disorders.* New York: International Universities Press.

Beck, A. T., Brown, G., Steer, R. A., Eidelson, J. I., & Riskind, J. H. (1987). Differentiating anxiety and depression: A test of the cognitive content-specificity hypothesis. *Journal of Abnormal Psychology, 96,* 179–183.

Billings, A. G., & Moos, R. H. (1983). Comparisons of children of depressed and nondepressed parents: A social-environmental perspective. *Journal of Abnormal Child Psychology, 11,* 463–486.

Billings, A. G., & Moos, R. H. (1985). Children of parents with unipolar depression: A 1-year follow-up. *Journal of Abnormal Child Psychology, 14,* 149–166.

Boulos, C., Kutcher, S., Marton, P., Simeon, J., Ferguson, B., & Roberts, N. (1991). Response to desipramine treatment in adolescent major depression. *Psychopharmacology Bulletin, 27,* 59–65.

Bowlby, J. (1973) *Separation: Anxiety and anger: Vol. 2. Attachment and loss.* New York: Basic Books.

Bowlby, J. (1980). *Loss: Sadness and depression.* New York: Basic Books.

Brown, G. W., & Harris, T. O. (1989). Depression. In G. W. Brown & T. O. Harris (Eds.), *Life events and illness* (pp. 49–93). New York: Guilford.

Burge, D., & Hammen, C. (1991). Maternal communication: Predictors of outcome at follow-up in a sample of children at high and low risk for depression. *Journal of Abnormal Psychology, 100,* 174–180.

Butler, P. D., & Nemeroff, C. B. (1990). Corticotropin-releasing factor as a possible cause of comorbidity in anxiety and depressive disorders. In J. D. Maser & C. R. Cloninger (Eds.), *Comorbidity of mood and anxiety disorders* (pp. 413–435). Washington, DC: American Psychiatric Press.

Cantwell, D. P., & Baker, L. (1991). Manifestations of depressive affect in adolescence. *Journal of Youth and Adolescence, 20,* 121–133.

Carlson, G. A., & Cantwell, D. P. (1980). Unmasking depression in children and adolescents. *American Journal of Psychiatry, 137,* 445–449.

Carlson, G. A., & Kashani, J. H. (1988). Phenomenology of major depression from childhood through adulthood: Analysis of three studies. *American Journal of Psychiatry, 145,* 1222–1225.

Carlson, G. A., & Strober, M. (1983). Affective disorders in adolescence. In D. P. Cantwell & G. A. Carlson (Eds.), *Affective disorders in childhood and adolescence: An update* (pp. 85–96). New York: Spectrum.

Caron, C., & Rutter, M. (1991). Comorbidity in child psychopathology: Concepts, issues and research strategies. *Journal of Child Psychology and Psychiatry, 32,* 1063–1080.

Clark, L. A., & Watson, D. (1991). Tripartite model of anxiety and depression: Psychometric evidence and taxonomic implications. *Journal of Abnormal Psychology, 100,* 316–336.

Cole, D. A., & Carpentieri, S. (1990). Social status and the comorbidity of child depression and conduct disorder. *Journal of Consulting and Clinical Psychology, 58,* 748–757.

Compas, B. E., Ey, S., & Grant, K. E. (1993). Taxonomy, assessment, and diagnosis of depression during adolescence. *Psychological Bulletin, 114,* 323–344.

Compas, B. E., Grant, K. E., & Ey, S. (in press). Psychological stress and child/adolescent depression: Can we be more specific? In W. M. Reynolds & H. F. Johnston (Eds.), *Handbook of depression in children and adolescents.* New York: Plenum.

Compas, B. E., Phares, V., Banez, G. A., & Howell, D. C. (1991). Correlates of internalizing and externalizing behavior problems: Perceived competence, causal attributions, and parental symptoms. *Journal of Abnormal Child Psychology, 19,* 197–218.

Costello, E. J., Costello, A. J., Edelbrock, C., Burns, B. J., Dulcan, M. K., Brent, D., & Janiszewski, S. (1988). Psychiatric disorders in pediatric primary care. *Archives of General Psychiatry, 45,* 1107–1116.

Cummings, E. M., & Davies, P. T. (1993). Parental depression, family functioning, and child adjustment: Risk factors, processes, and pathways. In D. Cicchetti & S. Toth (Eds.), *Rochester Symposium on Developmental Psychopathology: Vol 4. A developmental approach to affective disorders.* Rochester, NY: University of Rochester Press.

Cytryn, L., McKnew, D. H., & Bunney, W. E. (1988). Diagnosing depression in children: A reassessment. *American Journal of Psychiatry, 137,* 22–25.

Donovan, J. E., & Jessor, R. (1985). Structure of problem behavior in adolescence and young adulthood. *Journal of Consulting and Clinical Psychology, 53,* 890–904.

Donovan, J. E., Jessor, R., & Costa, F. M. (1988). Syndrome of problem behavior in adolescence: A replication. *Journal of Consulting and Clinical Psychology, 56,* 762–765.

Downey, G., & Coyne, J. C. (1990). Children of depressed parents: An integrative review. *Psychological Bulletin, 108,* 50–76.

Edelbrock, C., & Costello, A. J. (1988). Convergence between statistically derived behavior problem syndromes and child psychiatric diagnoses. *Journal of Abnormal Child Psychology, 16,* 219–231.

Finch, A. J., Lipovsky, J. A., & Casat, C. D. (1989). Anxiety and depression in children and adolescents: Negative affectivity or separate constructs? In P. C. Kendall & D. Watson (Eds.), *Anxiety and depression: Distinctive and overlapping features.* (pp. 171–197). New York: Academic Press.

Fleming, J. E., & Offord, D. R. (1990). Epidemiology of childhood depressive disorders: A critical review. *Journal of the American Academy of Child and Adolescent Psychiatry, 29,* 571–580.

Friedman, R. C., Hurt, S. W., Clarkin, J. F., Corn, R., & Aronoff, M. S. (1983). Symptoms of depression among adolescents and young adults. *Journal of Affective Disorders, 5,* 37–43.

Garber, J., & Hollon, S. D. (1991). What can specificity designs say about causality in psychopathology research? *Psychological Bulletin, 110,* 129–136.

Garrison, C. Z., Jackson, K. L., Marsteller, F., McKeown, R., & Addy, C. (1990). A longitudinal study of the depressive symptomatology in young adolescents. *Journal of the American Academy of Child and Adolescent Psychiatry, 29,* 581–585.

Geller, B., Cooper, T. B., Graham, D. L., Marsteller, F. A., & Bryant, D. M. (1990). Double-blind placebo-controlled study of nortriptyline in depressed adolescents using a "fixed plasma level" design. *Psychopharmacology Bulletin, 26,* 85–90.

Gilmore, M. R., Hawkins, J. D., Catalano, R. F., Day, L. E., Moore, M., & Abbott, R. (1991). Structure of problem behaviors in preadolescence. *Journal of Consulting and Clinical Psychology, 59,* 499–506.

Gold, P. W., Goodwin, F. K., & Chrousos, G. P. (1988). Clinical and biochemical manifestations of depression: Relation to the neurobiology of stress, Part II. *New England Journal of Medicine, 319,* 413–420.

Gotlib, I., & Hammen, C. (1992). *Psychological aspects of depression: Toward a cognitive-interpersonal integration.* Chichester: Wiley.

Hammen, C. (1991). *Depression runs in families.* New York: Springer-Verlag.

Hammen, C., Burge, D., Burney, E., & Adrian, C. (1990). Longitudinal study of diagnoses in children of women with unipolar and bipolar affective disorder. *Archives of General Psychiatry, 47,* 1112–1117.

Hammen, C., Gordon, D., Burge, D., Adrian, C., Jaenicke, C., & Hiroto, D. (1987). Maternal affective disorders, illness, and stress: Risk for children's psychopathology. *American Journal of Psychiatry, 144,* 736–741.

Harrington, R., Fudge, H., Rutter, M., Pickles, A., & Hill, J. (1990). Adult outcomes of childhood and adolescent depression: Psychiatric status. *Archives of General Psychiatry, 47,* 465–473.

Helzer, J. (1987). Epidemiology of alcoholism. *Journal of Consulting and Clinical Psychology, 55,* 284–292.

Jessor, R., & Jessor, S. L. (1977). *Problem behavior and psychosocial development: A longitudinal study of youth.* New York: Academic Press.

Kahn, J. S., Kehle, T. J., Jenson, W. R., & Clark, E. (1990). Comparison of cognitive-behavioral, relaxation, and self-modeling interventions for depression among middle-school students. *School Psychology Review, 19,* 196–211.

Kandel, D. B., & Davies, M. (1982) Epidemiology of depressive mood in adolescents. *Archives of General Psychiatry, 39,* 1205–1212.

Kandel, D. B., & Davies, M. (1986). Adult sequelae of adolescent depressive symptoms. *Archives of General Psychiatry, 43,* 255–262.

Kashani, J. H., Cantwell, D. P., Shekim, W. O., & Reid, J. C. (1982). Major depressive disorder in children admitted to an inpatient community mental health center. *American Journal of Psychiatry, 139,* 671–672.

Kashani, J. H., & Carlson, G. A. (1987). Seriously depressed preschoolers. *American Journal of Psychiatry, 144,* 348–350.

Kashani, J. H., Carlson, G. A., Beck, N. C., Hoeper, E. W., Corcoran, C. M., McAllister, J. A., Fallahi, C., Rosenberg, T. K., & Reid, J. C. (1987). Depression, depressive symptoms, and depressed mood among a community sample of adolescents. *American Journal of Psychiatry, 144,* 931–934.

Kashani, J. H., Holcomb, W. R., & Orvaschel, H. (1986). Depression and depressive symptoms in preschool children from the general population. *American Journal of Psychiatry, 143,* 1138–1143.

Kashani, J. H., Husain, A., Shekim, W. O., Hodges, K. K., Cytryn, L., & McKnew, D. H. (1981). Current perspectives on childhood depression: An overview. *American Journal of Psychiatry, 138,* 143–153.

Kashani, J. H., Rosenberg, T. K., & Reid, J. C. (1989). Developmental perspectives in child and adolescent depressive symptoms in a community sample. *American Journal of Psychiatry, 146,* 871–875.

Kashani, J., & Simonds, J. F. (1979). The incidence of depression in children. *American Journal of Psychiatry, 136,* 1203–1205.

Kazdin, A. E., French, N. H., Unis, A. S., Esveldt-Dawson, K., & Sherick, R. B. (1983). Hopelessness, depression, and suicidal intent among psychiatrically disturbed inpatient children. *Journal of Consulting and Clinical Psychology, 51*, 504–510.

Keller, M. B., Beardslee, W., Lavori, P. W., Wunder, J., Dils, D. L., & Samuelson, H. (1988). Course of major depression in non-referred adolescents: A restrospective study. *Journal of Affective Disorders, 15*, 235–243.

Kendall, P. C., Stark, K. D., & Adam, T. (1990). Cognitive deficit or cognitive distortion in childhood depression. *Journal of Abnormal Child Psychology, 18*, 225–270.

Klein, D., & Riso, L. (1992). Psychiatric disorders: Problems of boundaries and comorbidity. In C. G. Costello (Ed.), *Basic issues in psychopathology*. New York: Guilford Press.

Klerman, G. L., & Weissman, M. M. (1989). Increasing rates of depression. *Journal of the American Medical Association, 261*, 2229–2235.

Kovacs, M. (1989). Affective disorders in children and adolescents. *American Psychologist, 44*, 209–215.

Kovacs, M. (1990). Comorbid anxiety disorders in childhood-onset depressions. In J. D. Maser & C. R. Cloninger (Eds.), *Comorbidity of mood and anxiety disorders* (pp. 272–281). Washington, DC: American Psychiatric Press.

Kovacs, M., Feinberg, T. L., Crouse-Novak, M. A., Paulauskas, S. L., & Finkelstein, R. (1984a). Depressive disorders in childhood: I. A longitudinal prospective study of characteristics and recovery. *Archives of General Psychiatry, 41*, 229–237.

Kovacs, M., Feinberg, T. L., Crouse-Novak, M. A., Paulausakas, S., Pollack, M., & Finkelstein, R. (1984b). Depressive disorders in childhood: II. a longitudinal study of the risk for a subsequent major depression. *Archives of General Psychiatry, 41*, 643–649.

Kovacs, M., Gatsonis, C., Paulauskas, S. L., & Richards, C. (1989). Depressive disorders in childhood: IV. A longitudinal study of comorbidity with and risk for anxiety disorders. *Archives of General Psychiatry, 46*, 776–782.

Kovacs, M., Paulausakas, S., Gatsonis, C., & Richards, C. (1988). Depressive disorders in childhood: III. A longitudinal study of comorbidity with and risk for conduct disorders. *Journal of Affective Disorders, 15*, 205–217.

Lee, C. M., & Gotlib, I. H. (1989). Maternal depression and child adjustment: A longitudinal analysis. *Journal of Abnormal Psychology, 98*, 78–85.

Lee, C. M., & Gotlib, I. H. (1991). Family disruption, parental availability and child adjustment. In R. Prinz (Ed.), *Advances in behavioral assessment of children and families* (Vol. 5, pp. 173–202). New York: Kingsley.

Lewinsohn, P. M., Clarke, G. N., Hops, H., & Andrews, J. (1990). Cognitive-behavioral treatment for depressed adolescents. *Behavioral Therapy, 21,* 385–401.

Lewinsohn, P. M., Hops, H., Roberts, R. E., & Seeley, J. R.. (1988, November). The prevalence of affective and other disorders among older adolescents. Paper presented at the annual meeting of the American Public Health Association, Boston.

Maser, J. D., & Cloninger, C. R. (1990). Comorbidity of anxiety and mood disorders: Introduction and overview. In J. D. Maser & C. R. Cloninger (Eds.), *Comorbidity of mood and anxiety disorders* (pp. 3–12). Washington, DC: American Psychiatric Press.

McLeod, J. D. (1991). Childhood parental loss and adult depression. *Journal of Health and Social Behavior, 32,* 205–220.

Merikangas, K., & Spiker, D. G. (1984). Assortative mating among inpatients with primary affective disorder. *Psychological Medicine, 12,* 753–764.

Mitchell, J., McCauley, E., Burke, P. M., & Moss, S. J. (1990). Phenomenology of depression in children and adolescents. *Journal of the American Academy of Child and Adolescent Psychiatry, 27,* 12–20.

Monroe, S. M., & Simons, A. D. (1991). Diathesis-stress theories in the context of life stress research: Implications for depressive disorders. *Psychological Bulletin, 110,* 406–425.

Orvaschel, H., Walsh-Allis, G., & Ye, W. (1988). Psychopathology in children of parents with recurrent depression. *Journal of Abnormal Child Psychology, 16,* 17–28.

Petersen, A. C., Compas, B. E., & Brooks-Gunn, J. (1991). *Depression in adolescence: Current knowledge, research directions, and implications for programs and policy.* Washington, DC: Carnegie Council on Adolescent Development.

Petersen, A. C., Compas, B. E., Brooks-Gunn, J., Stemmler, M., Ey, S., & Grant, K. E. (1993). Depression in adolescence. *American Psychologist, 48,* 155–168.

Petersen, A. C., Kennedy, R. E., & Sullivan, P. (1991). Coping with adolescence. In M. E. Colton & S. Gore (Eds.), *Adolescent stress: Causes and consequences* (pp. 93–110). New York: Aldine de Gruyter.

Petersen, A. C., Sarigiani, P. A., & Kennedy, R. E. (1991). Adolescent depression: Why more girls? *Journal of Youth and Adolescence, 20,* 247–271.

Phares, V., & Compas, B. E. (1992). The role of fathers in child and adolescent psychopathology: Make room for daddy. *Psychological Bulletin, 111,* 387–412.

Plomin, R., & Daniels, D. (1987). Why are children in the same family so different from one another? *Behavioral and Brain Sciences, 10,* 1–60.

Puig-Antich, J. (1982). Major depression and conduct disorder in prepuberty. *Journal of the American Academy of Child and Adolescent Psychiatry, 21,* 118–128.

Quiggle, N. L., Garber, J., Panak, W. F., & Dodge, K. (1992). Social-information processing in aggressive and depressed children. *Child Development, 63,* 1305–1320.

Rende, R. (1991). *Depressive symptomatology in adolescence: Etiology of individual differences and extreme scores.* Unpublished doctoral dissertation, Pennsylvania State University.

Renouf, A., & Harter, S. (1990). Low self-worth and anger as components of the depressive experience in young adolescents. *Development and Psychopathology, 2,* 293–310.

Reynolds, W. M., & Coats, K. I. (1986). A comparison of cognitive-behavioral therapy and relaxation training for the treatment of depression in adolescents. *Journal of Consulting and Clinical Psychology, 54,* 653–660.

Roberts, R. E., Lewinsohn, P. M., & Seeley, J. R. (1991). Screening for adolescent depression: A comparison of depression scales. *Journal of the American Academy of Child and Adolescent Psychiatry, 30,* 58–66.

Robins, L., Locke, B., & Regier, D. (1992). An overview of psychiatric disorders in America. In L. Robbins & D. Regier (Eds.), *Psychiatric disorders in America: the Epidemiological Catchment Area Study* (pp. 328–366). New York: Free Press.

Rohde, P., Lewinsohn, P. M., & Seeley, J. R. (1991). Comorbidity of unipolar depression: II. Comorbidity with other mental disorders in adolescents and adults. *Journal of Abnormal Psychology, 54,* 653–660.

Rutter, M. (1986). The developmental psychopathology of depression: Issues and perspectives. In M. Rutter, C. E. Izard, & P. B. Read (Eds.), *Depression in young people: Clinical and developmental perspectives* (pp. 3–30). New York: Guilford.

Rutter, M., & Quinton, P. (1984). Parental psychiatric disorder: Effects on children. *Psychological Medicine, 14,* 853–880.

Ryan, N. D., Puig-Antich, J., Ambrosini, P., Rabinovich, H., Robinson, D., Nelson, B., Iyengar, S., & Twomey, J. (1987). The clinical picture of major depression in children and adolescents. *Archives of General Psychiatry, 44,* 854–861.

Ryan, N. D., Puig-Antich, J., Cooper, T., Rabinovich, H., Ambrosini, P., Davies, M., King, J., Torres, D., & Fried, J. (1986). Imipramine in adolescent major depression: Plasma level and clinical response. *Acta Psychiatrica Scandinavica, 73,* 275–288.

Ryan, N. D., Puig-Antich, J., Rabinovich, H., Fried, J., Ambrosini, P., Meyer, V., Torres, D., Dachille, S., & Mazzie, D. (1988). MAOIs in adolescent major depression unresponsive to tricyclic antidepressants. *Journal of the American Academy of Child and Adolescent Psychiatry, 27,* 755–758.

Saylor, C. F., Finch, A. J., Spirito, A., & Bennett, B. (1984). The Children's Depression Inventory: A systematic evaluation of psychometric properties. *Journal of Consulting and Clinical Psychology, 52,* 955–967.

Shelton, R. C., Hollon, S. D., Purdon, S. E. & Loofen, P. T. (1991). Biological and psychological aspects of depression. *Behavioral Therapy, 22,* pp. 201–228.

Strober, M., Freeman, R., & Rigali, J. (1990). The pharmacotherapy of depressive illness in adolescence: I. An open label trial of imipramine. *Psychopharmacology Bulletin, 26,* 80–84.

Walker, E., Downey, G., & Nightingale, N. (1989). The nonorthogonal nature of risk factors: Implications for research on the causes of maladjustment. *Journal of Primary Prevention, 9,* 143–163.

Watson, D. (1988). Intraindividual and interindividual analyses of positive and negative affect: Their relation to health complaints, perceived stress, and daily activities. *Journal of Personality and Social Psychology, 54,* 1020–1030.

Watson, D., & Clark, L. (1984). Negative affectivity: The disposition of experience aversive emotional states. *Psychological Bulletin, 96,* 465–490.

Watson, D., & Kendall, P. C. (1989). Common and differentiating features of anxiety and depression: Current findings and future directions. In P. C. Kendall & D. Watson (Eds.), *Anxiety and depression: Distinctive and overlapping features* (pp. 493–508). New York: Academic Press.

Watson, D., & Tellegen, A. (1985). Toward a consensual structure of mood. *Psychological Bulletin, 98,* 219–235.

Weissman, M. M. (1988). Psychopathology in the children of depressed parents: Direct interview studies. In D. L. Dunner & E. S. Gershon (Eds.), *Relatives at risk for mental disorders,* pp. 143–159. New York: Raven Press.

Weissman, M. M. (1990). Evidence for comorbidity of anxiety and depression: Family and genetic studies of children. In J. D. Maser & C. R.

Cloninger (Eds.), *Comorbidity of mood and anxiety disorders* (pp. 349–365). Washington, DC: American Psychiatric Press.

West, M. O., & Prinz, R. J. (1987). Parental alcoholism and childhood psychopathology. *Psychological Bulletin, 102,* 204–218.

Whitaker, A., Johnson, J., Shaffer, D., Rapoport, J. L., Kalikow, K., Walsh, B. T., Davies, M., Braiman, S., & Dolinsky, A. (1990). Uncommon troubles in young people: Prevalence estimates of selected psychiatric disorders in a nonreferred adolescent population. *Archives of General Psychiatry, 47,* 487–496.

Wolfe, V. V., Finch, A. J., Saylor, C. F., Blount, R. L., Pallmeyer, T. P., & Carek, D. J. (1987). Negative affectivity in children: A multitrait-multimethod investigation. *Journal of Consulting and Clinical Psychology, 55,* 245–250.

World Health Organization (1990). *International classification of diseases, injuries, and causes of death* (10th ed.). Geneva.

8

The school-based promotion of social competence: Theory, research, practice, and policy

The Consortium on the School-based Promotion of Social Competence

Over the past 10 years, significant changes have occurred in the conceptualization and implementation of school-based interventions to promote social competence. These changes have been fueled in part by grim statistics suggesting the serious plight of youth in America today. However, advances in research about risk and protective factors and increasingly sophisticated conceptualizations of the skills needed for competent behavioral performance and of the conditions needed to facilitate the development and expression of those skills may be heralding an important turning point in efforts to improve the well-being of children in America.

This chapter begins with a summary of data concerning the present health status of American youth. A risk and protective factors perspective on the prevention of behavioral dysfunction and promotion of healthy functioning is outlined, followed by an examination of the construct of social competence. Next, the chapter addresses several issues about social competence promotion, including: (1) presentation of a case for schools serving as the hub of community-based social competence promotion efforts; (2) a review of evidence concerning the effects of interventions; (3) a discussion of the mechanisms and processes believed to make social competence promotion and preventive interventions effective and the way that these are operationalized

The consortium members are: Maurice J. Elias, Roger P. Weissberg, J. David Hawkins, Cheryl L. Perry, Joseph E. Zins, Kenneth A. Dodge, Philip C. Kendall, Denise C. Gottfredson, Mary Jane Rotheram-Borus, Leonard A. Jason, and Renée Wilson-Brewer. The Consortium expresses its sincere gratitude to the William T. Grant Foundation for its confidence, inspiration, and support.

in the intervention procedures and their implementation methods, as reflected in what appear to be the most empirically well supported "best practices" for school-based interventions; and (4) the importance of taking an organizational and systems perspective on classroom and school-based interventions. Multicomponent, multi-year, theoretically guided risk-reduction and protection-enhancing models incorporating both skills training and environmental change are described as promising forms for future research in the field, and several examples of operating programs are presented. The chapter concludes with an articulation of the major challenges facing social competence promotion researchers and others in the field over the course of the next decade.

Health status of American children and youth

Prevalence of problem behaviors

A growing segment of America's young people experience or are at risk for social, behavioral, and health problems that interfere with both their successful school performance, psychological health, and their potential to become productive contributing citizens and workers (Dryfoos, 1990; Gans, Blyth, Elster, & Gaveras, 1990). Recent epidemiological data indicate that 15% to 22% of children and adolescents have mental health problems severe enough to warrant treatment (Costello, 1990; National Advisory Mental Health Council, 1990; Tuma, 1989; Zill & Schoenborn, 1990). However, fewer than 20% of these youngsters with mental health problems currently receive appropriate services (Tuma, 1989).

In addition to the high prevalence of young people with mental disorders, there are also large numbers of youth who engage in behavior that put them at high risk for negative psychosocial health and behavior outcomes such as drug abuse, teen pregnancy, AIDS, delinquency, and dropping out of school (e.g., Dryfoos, 1990; Gans et al., 1990). Recent estimates suggest that 25% of Americans between 10 and 17 years old are extremely vulnerable, and an additional 25% are moderately vulnerable, to the negative consequences of engaging in multiple high-risk social and health behaviors (Dryfoos, 1990; Report of the Task Force on Education of Young Adolescents, 1989). The remaining 50%, who currently are at low risk for engaging in such behaviors, may nonetheless require strong, ongoing support to avoid such involvement.

Recently, the National Commission on the Role of the School and the Community in Improving Adolescent Health (1990) expressed grave concern about the current unprecedented health crisis in our nation. The Commission indicated that the country's state of adolescent health constitutes a national emergency that has serious economic and social ramifications. For the first time, young people are less healthy and less prepared to assume responsible places in our society than were their parents. This situation is especially worrisome inasmuch as society is more complex and competitive than ever before.

The exacerbation and increase in health and behavior problems are due to significant family, school, and neighborhood changes that have occurred during the past few decades. Major social and economic changes include increased poverty rates among children; the breakdown of traditional neighborhoods and extended families; reduced amounts of meaningful and supportive personal contact between young people and positive adult role models; inadequate housing and unsafe neighborhood environments; changing demographics so that large numbers of young people are entering school in a state of economic and educational disadvantage; the proliferation of health-damaging media messages; and societal attitudes and behaviors that hurt ethnic minorities (Cherlin, 1988; National Commission on the Role of the School and the Community in Improving Adolescent Health, 1990). Given such difficult societal conditions, we are faced with critical questions concerning the most realistic, cost-effective ways to meet the psychological, social, and health needs of our young people.

Prevention through risk reduction

The goal of prevention is the reduction or elimination of behavior or health problems by intervening before such problems occur. Risk-focused prevention has emerged as a model for achieving this goal. The premise of risk-focused prevention is this: To prevent a disorder, it is necessary to reduce, eliminate, or mitigate the effects of factors that put people at risk for the disorder. These risk factors have been identified for a number of different disorders by epidemiological and etiological studies. The results of this research serve as a foundation for prevention science.

Risk factors from several domains have been shown to predict adolescent health and behavioral problems. For example, risk factors for drug abuse, delinquency, dropping out of school, and teen pregnancy have been identified within individuals, in family environments and interactions, in school experiences, in peer and other social interactions, and in community contexts (Dryfoos, 1990; Hawkins, Catalano, & Miller, 1992; Simcha-Fagan, Gersten, & Langner, 1986). Among the constellation of interrelated variables that have been most reliably identified as risk factors for adolescent drug abuse and other forms of antisocial behavior are the following:

1. *Individual level:* physiological factors, early and persistent conduct problems, alienation and rebelliousness, attitudes favorable to drug use or crime, and early onset of drug use or crime;
2. *Family environment and interactions:* poor and inconsistent family management practices, family discord and conflict, drug behaviors and substance abuse–supportive attitudes of family members, parental criminality, and low bonding to family;
3. *Peer and social interactions:* peer rejection in the elementary grades and association with drug using or delinquent peers;
4. *School experiences:* academic failure; low degree of commitment to school, and low expectations for performance by school staff; and
5. *Community contexts:* laws and norms favorable toward problem behaviors, availability of substances, extreme neighborhood deprivation, and neighborhood disorganization.

Research indicates that these risk factors are common antecedents of diverse disorders (Dryfoos, 1990; Elliott, Huizinga, & Menard, 1989). Furthermore, exposure to multiple risk factors results in an increasing likelihood of disorder (Newcomb, Maddahian & Bentler, 1986; Rutter, 1980). Garmezy (1987), for example, reported that risk factors operate with a multiplicative effect, such that having 0 or even 1 risk factor does not denote a high level of risk, but having 2 risk factors increases the likelihood of psychopathology by 4 times, and having 4 increases the risk by 10 times. This evidence has stimulated a variety of successful interventions that have proved effective in reducing risk factors for problems as divergent as heart and lung disease (Bush et al., 1989; Vartianen, Pallonen, McAlister, & Puska, 1990), drug abuse (Hawkins, Catalano, Morrison, et al., 1992; Pentz et al., 1989), and school failure (Berrueta-Clement, Schweinhart, Barnett, Epstein, & Weikart, 1984).

Risk reduction by enhancing protective factors

Research also has been directed toward finding protective factors, or processes, that mitigate the effects of exposure to risk (Cowen & Work, 1988; Garmezy, 1985; Rutter, 1980; Werner, 1989). To date, evidence supporting three categories of protective factors has been generated (Garmezy, 1985; Lerner & Vicary, 1984; Rutter, 1980, 1985; Werner, 1989):

1. *Attributes of the individual,* including resilient temperament, positive social orientation and activity level, accurate processing of interpersonal cues, good means–ends problem solving skills, an ability to evaluate alternative actions from both instrumental and affective perspectives, the capacity to enact behaviors that accomplish desired outcomes in interpersonal or social situations, and a sense of self-efficacy;
2. *A supportive family environment,* including bonding with adults in the family, low family conflict, and supportive relationships; and
3. *Environmental supports,* including those which reinforce and support coping efforts and recognize and reward competence.

Among individuals, resilience has been identified as a protective characteristic. Masten, Best, and Garmezy (1990) define resilience as the process of, capacity for, or outcome of successful adaptation despite challenging or threatening circumstances. There are three types of well-documented resilience phenomena: good outcomes in high-risk children, sustained competence in children under stress, and recovery from trauma. Avoidance of significant negative outcomes appears to be associated with the presence of protective factors such as positive relationships with competent adults, good learning and problem-solving skills, good social approach and social engagement skills, and areas of perceived competence and value to self and society. This conceptualization also includes the idea that there are critical periods, often interacting with development capabilities, at which the effect of various stressors may be particularly deleterious and resilience is most strongly tapped. In general, the evidence suggests that as children get older, they increase their capacity to use their own personal coping and problem solving resources to buffer the impact of stressful events (Masten et al., 1990).

However, the current circumstances of increasing child poverty, deepening social intolerance of differences, expanding diversity, and growing competition for scarce resources conspire to disrupt relationships between adults and children. This limits access to instruction, models, and reinforcement for learning interpersonal skills, thoughtful problem solving, positive and patient social approach and engagement skills, and a sense of value to society. It is all too easy to be lured into antisocial subcultures when these provide reinforcement for a sense of personal worth and convey value for the display of certain (antisocial) competencies. Also associated with increasing poverty and scarce social resources is the declining state of health of children, which certainly conspires to sap their strengths and to make them less able to show resilience, especially under sustained or acute adversity.

Garmezy (1987) has devoted needed attention to those factors which test resilience most among families. In his view, engagement and disruptiveness are two potent familial socialization processes. Parental engagement appears to set into motion a series of occurrences likely to impart to children a positive sense of self, physical health, access to positive models, and trust in others as resources. Disruptions in these processes, such as those resulting from child abuse or neglect, or parents' severe illness, divorce, or death, interfere with positive development and increase the likelihood that the child will become disengaged from adults, school, or familial or social values. Following from this is greater frequency of noncompliant behavior, which leads to further degeneration of interactions with others.

The concept of protective factors or protective processes suggests that the goals of risk-focused prevention may be accomplished both through direct efforts at risk reduction and through the enhancement of protective factors that moderate or mediate the effects of exposure to risk. This is consistent with Rutter's (1987) seminal discussions about trajectory-changing processes as carrying significance for both risk and protection. Rutter urges a particular focus on the way in which experiences, events, and relationships can interrupt and sometimes reverse a downward negative spiral of maladaptive behavior. Processes that have been identified as protective mechanisms are those that foster diminished impact of stressful situations, reduction of negative chain reactions that characterize pathogenic family and school situations, development and maintenance of self-efficacy, and opportunities for positive educational, vocational, or personal growth. The operation of these processes is heightened at certain points in people's lives. Such points can be conceptualized as consisting largely of events of trajectory-changing potential, and include such stressors as starting day care, birth of a sibling, transition to middle school, or parental loss.

The extent to which protective mechanisms are engaged and risk factors are buffered influences the life trajectory that is followed as events unfold. Essential in the course that is followed, however, are the skills that the individual brings to these events, to the choice points faced, and to the many subsequent decisions that an individual faces. These skills comprise the basis of the construct of social competence and must be addressed by efforts to promote social competence. In the following section, the meaning of these terms is explored.

Defining "social competence" in children and adolescents

Attempts to define social competence have a rich and controversial history, and diverse descriptions of the construct have been presented (Zigler & Berman, 1983). During the late 1960s and early 1970s, a "panel of experts" – convened by the federal Office of Child Development, the Rand Corporation, and the Educational Testing Service – described it in terms of 29 component areas, including motor dexterity, general knowledge, quantitative concepts, and self-regulation (White, 1988). Others have urged a more narrow focus on social competence as referring to key processes relating to social interaction and their development over time and under different environmental conditions (Waters & Sroufe, 1983).

The present authors have come to believe that social competence involves the capacity to integrate cognition, affect, and behaviors to achieve specified social tasks and positive developmental outcomes. It comprises a set of core skills, attitudes, abilities, and feelings given functional meaning by the contexts of culture, neighborhood, and situation. Thus, social competence can be viewed in terms of "life skills for adaptation to diverse ecologies and settings." This perspective incorporates the possibility that in certain cultures, neighborhoods, and situations, so-called undesirable behaviors (e.g., aggressive, selfish, or passive behavior) may be required if one is to be perceived as "well adjusted" or to avoid being subject to harm. Also, it implies that behaviors that may appear to reflect a lack of competence may instead be adaptations to idiosyncratic or harmful ecological circumstances.

Defining social competence has become further complicated to the extent to which some view social competence as including an indication of the extent to which an individual's actions are judged to be prosocial and appropriate for a particular situation (Dodge, Pettit, McClaskey, & Brown, 1986). This can lead to social competence being used to define both skills and outcomes. The distinction between social competence as a set of judgments and social competence as a set of skills must be kept clear to avoid tautologies in research (Felner, Lease, & Phillips, 1990).

If one accepts this distinction, one then is confronted with the reality that an understanding of the links of the skills of social competence to judgments of adjustment cannot occur without a detailed understanding of the social contexts surrounding individuals and the meanings they attach to their life, roles, relationships, and future. Expressions of competence may take unpopular forms, an issue that must continue to draw the attention of researchers who focus on peer relationships and social competence. For example, a child with competencies in studying and academic work will, in some environments, be perceived as less well adjusted by peers than someone with skills in interpersonal aggression. Is social competence related to aggression or to popularity? Or is social competence related to factors in the peer, parental, school, or neighborhood environments?

Ultimately, a perspective on social competence must reflect the ever increasing complexity of our society. The application of skills occurs across a variety of life tasks, social contexts, and what we have come to view as sociocultural/linguistic contexts. This implies, for example, that one should be prepared to examine differences within American subgroups as one would consider differences between nations; from this perspective, we are less likely to overestimate the parameters of generalization of knowledge, attitudes, and skills to these subgroups than is currently the case. Illustratively, for a classroom teacher in Texas, it would be unwise to assume that there is a strong "American" consensus between a Mexican American child in Texas and a Puerto Rican American child in his or her class; rather, this is a nontrivial empirical question.

Although social contexts must be considered when one attempts to understand social competence, there nevertheless appears to be an array of skills that are required to display effective social behaviors across diverse situations and settings. Researchers have identified several cognitive and affective factors that seem to play a determining role in social behavior (e.g., Dodge, 1986; Dodge & Feldman, 1990; Elias, 1990; Kendall, 1991; Jason et al., 1992; McFall, 1983; Weissberg, Caplan, & Sivo, 1989). These factors include the encoding of relevant social cues (as in attending to others' facial expressions and to the norms of a social context); the accurate interpretation of the encoded social cues (as in perspective taking, reading intentions, and empathy); the generation of effective solutions to interpersonal problems; the realistic anticipation of consequences of, and potential obstacles to, one's actions (as in delaying immediate gratification for long-term reward and in understanding that some behaviors might have negative consequences for oneself or others); the translation of social decision into effective behavior (as in being able to approach and converse with peers and adults, showing appropriate eye contact, using an appropriate tone of voice, displaying proper posture, and using appropriate language); and the expression of a positive sense of self-efficacy (as seen in a general optimism about outcomes of one's personally initiated actions).

These skills appear to satisfy White's (1988) criteria for providing a workable perspective concerning social competence. They represent aspects of functioning that are reasonably distinct but clearly interrelated; are presented in practical terms that lend themselves to observation and lay discussion; can be translated into areas for intervention and training at both personal and environmental levels (i.e., efforts can be directed toward creating environments that will encourage the development, nurturance, and continuing of broad expression of the skills across various role contexts); are interrelated with other competencies not explicitly identified (which means that efforts to build the competencies identified earlier will have a radiating effect without having to attempt to impact on each skill separately); and are likely to be associated with positive "adjustment."

The social competence construct has additional heuristic value in that there is a clear link of skills related to social competence and the concept of risk and protective factors. Rutter (1987) reviewed socialization factors that seem to assist children and adolescents in overcoming adaptation difficulties. He identified specific "mechanisms" that serve a protective function to individuals even when they are in circumstances that most would find to be harmful. These mechanisms are based in certain key skills, such as planning, anticipating consequences, and reacting to obstacles, that overlap with the cognitive and affective skills noted earlier as undergirding social interaction. Similarly, "risk" may be conceptualized not only in terms of deficiencies in skills, but also in the preparation necessary to apply those skills across roles and across environments.

In conclusion, there is evidence from a variety of sources that a high level of agreement exists concerning domains that reflect social competence. Further, there is a fundamental view that the existing data warrant teaching children and adolescents cognitive, affective, and behavioral skills as a means toward promoting positive social, psychological, personal, and health outcomes (Consortium on the School-Based Promotion of Social Competence, 1991; DeFreise, Crossland, MacPhail-Wilcox, & Sowers, 1990; Hamburg, 1990; National Mental Health Association, 1986; Perry & Jessor, 1985; U.S. Department of Education, 1990; Weissberg, Caplan, & Harwood, 1991; Zins & Forman, 1988). Moreover, there is broad consensus about the characteristics that constitute the end points of successful socialization and intervention processes: establishing and maintaining positive social relationships; refraining from harming others; serving as constructive, contributing members of one's peer group, family, school, workplace, and community; engaging in health-enhancing and health-protective behaviors; and avoiding engaging in behavior that may lead to negative consequences such as substance abuse, unwanted teen pregnancy, AIDS, social isolation, serious physical injury, dropping out of school, depression, suicide, unemployment, or criminal prosecution (Consortium on the School-Based Promotion of Social Competence, 1991; Freedman, Rosenthal, Donahoe, Schlundt, & McFall, 1978; National Mental Health Association, 1986; Westchester County Social Competence in the Schools Task Force, 1990). This agreement provides unity to efforts at the prevention of mental, emotional, and behavioral disabilities and the promotion of social competence. It is this common denominator, rather than agreement on the precise definitions of constructs, that unites the work to be reported herein.

Social competence promotion efforts

Using the school as a base

"We can no longer take for granted the life skills training and social support systems that were built into human experience over millions of years. Now, increasing attention is being given to formal education to provide or at least supplement the life skills training (including social skills) that historically were built into the formal processes of family and kin relations" (Hamburg, 1990, p. iv).

Schools are widely acknowledged as the major setting in which activities should be undertaken to promote students' competence and prevent the development of unhealthy behaviors. In contrast to other potential sites for intervention, schools provide access to all children on a regular and consistent basis over the majority of their formative years of personality development (Elias & Clabby, 1992; Rutter, 1980; Weissberg et al., 1989). Most parents and guardians are also reasonably accessible through the schools.

Society has entrusted and mandated that these institutions prepare children to become responsible citizens. In addition, there are federal, state, and local requirements to provide systematic kindergarten through 12th grade instruction regarding drug and alcohol abuse. There is a recognition that proper school readiness beginning in the preschool years is an essential pathway to avoiding school failure and other psychosocial difficulties. Finally, the issue of violence in the schools has come to the fore in the beginning of the 1990s, and it is recognized as a mirror of similar trends outside the schoolyard. All of these issues, as well as traditional areas of academic achievement, are part of the new agenda of American education formalized in their promulgation as national education goals (The White House, 1990).

Consequently, schools as organizations enjoy unequaled influence – both informal and formalized – in children's lives with respect to social, moral, intellectual, academic, and behavioral development. With respect to social adjustment, schools are particularly well suited as sites to promote children's development. They provide numerous daily opportunities – within classrooms, on the playground, during travel to and from school – for children to learn, to practice, to discuss, and to modify their social interaction skills and understanding in naturalistic situations. Further, the highly skilled, professional staffs and the organizational frameworks found in schools make them well adapted to engage in prevention and competence promotion programs. Most also offer a variety of extracurricular activities that likewise are important in the development of social competence. Thus, generalization and maintenance of developing and newly acquired skills can more readily be facilitated than it can be through traditional person-centered interventions or through other community organizations (Weissberg & Allen, 1986).

Finally, there are both economic and social-demographic realities that make it virtually essential that social initiatives be linked to schools. The largest proportion of spending for children and youth in all states is tied to schools (Hawkins, Catalano, & Associates, 1992). Reported spending figures for two states and the federal government serve to illustrate this fact. In South Carolina, 85% of the funds for at-risk children were spent in the public schools in 1989, while nearly 98% of the 1991–1993 biennial budget was allocated for k-12 education in the state of Washington. Similarly, at the federal level, almost 42% of the dollars spent on children (excluding entitlement funds) went to education (Hawkins, Catalano, & Associates, 1992). Thus, to access these resources, schools must be enlisted as active participants in social competence promotion efforts.

Ours can no longer be an education system that revolves around the Caucasian middle-class majority because it, like the nuclear family, is undergoing serious sociodemographic erosion. Whether the schools will function as a melting pot, mosaic, Mulligan's stew, or paella, they nevertheless will house a culturally diverse array of students in a system now beset by gaps and cracks that appear to disproportionately attract African-American, Hispanic, and Native American students, as well as those with physical, intellectual, or emotional handicaps (National Commission on Children, 1991). There is an imperative to make a commitment to the dignity of all children, and it is clear that the schools must be at the center of all such efforts (Cohen & Naimark, 1991; Melton, 1991).

Thus, a convergence of the educational reform movement and other social forces is likely to affect the ecological landscape of schools, making it impossible to disconnect school-based social competence promotion from the larger issues of the mission, philosophy, and structure of schools as they emerge from this period of change. Schools consequently are recognized as playing a pivotal role in preparing students for future citizenship. Hence, the concept of *school-based programming* has been advanced to suggest that schools serve as the hub of activities that attempt to incorporate parents, employers, neighborhood residents, social agencies, and the health care system. The resulting efforts would perhaps be most properly labeled as "Comprehensive Health and Social Competence and Problem Prevention Programming" (Weissberg et al., 1991).

Empirical warrant for school-based efforts

Among the most widely used and recommended types of programs are those focusing on teaching children personal and social competencies such as problem solving, decision making, social approach and engagement, stress-management, and communication skills. These types of social competence promotion programs have been the focus of considerable study for approximately 2 decades. Unfortunately, most programs are of short duration (i.e., less than 1 year) and/or have not been subject to rigorous empirical research (Rogers, Howard-Pitney, & Bruce, 1989). Concerns about gaps in the findings, modest effect sizes, inadequate data concerning how to maximize the role of the most efficacious aspects of programs, and the precise impact of programs on teachers, parents, school, peer, and community norms raise significant questions about the state of intervention practice in schools and communities. The follow-up designs used to date assess students' progress from a point of completion of the intervention, which has meant that interventions were not subject to systematic reinforcement and follow-through. Clearly, for reasons to be discussed shortly, this is not an optimal intervention design. The net result of these circumstances is that findings tend to erode over the years, or else have a fairly weak impact in terms of numbers of students strongly impacted and the effect sizes of the statistical gains.

Nevertheless, there is an empirical base for problem behavior prevention and social competence promotion interventions. A set of researchers has devoted its attention to quasi-experimental studies of programs, and their overall results show that the teaching of affective, cognitive, and behavioral skills can have at least short-term effects on health and behavior problems (Hamburg, 1990; National Mental Health Association, 1986; Price, Cowen, Lorion, & Ramos-McKay, 1988; Zins & Forman, 1988). Meta-analyses of these kinds of skills-based interventions have consistently shown that moderate effect sizes are obtained. Denham and Almeida (1987) found a relationship of $d = .78$ in 24 studies looking at the impact of intervention on the acquisition of social problem-solving skills, and $d = .58$ in 20 studies relating problem-solving skills to adjustment. In 10 studies looking at the direct mediation of intervention-related skills gains and adjustment, $d = .52$.

In a more recent meta-analytic study incorporating interventions teaching a wider range of social competencies, Schneider (1992) found that the overall $d = .89$. Some of his specific findings are of particular note. There were no instances, across 79 studies, of trained groups experiencing any negative impact. Similarly, no-treatment or placebo control groups were not found to experience consistent, significant gains. Findings for short-term studies seemed to be stronger than those from interventions that were more complex or of longer duration. Schneider (1992) had no explanation for this, but speculated that integrity of interventions is harder to maintain, particularly in field contexts, as they become longer or more procedurally involved. He pointed out that a shortcoming of most experimental and quasi-experimental studies to date was their lack of attention to details of implementation. This is an area that meta-analytic studies to date have addressed only in the most global ways, if at all.

From this base, researchers have turned to action research methods because of their considerable heuristic value in yielding information that informs interventions and promotes their being tailored to diverse populations and settings (Elias & Clabby, 1992). When judged by standards of traditional experimental methods, the application of action research for the purpose of developing and refining interventions may seem tenuous (Peterson, 1991). However, Peterson (1991) argues strongly that it is a fallacy and a tragedy to "wait" for science to find "answers" or "facts" before moving ahead to address pressing social issues and problems. More to the point, though, there are paradigmatic issues in that the role of contextualized knowledge is given great emphasis by action researchers and those who have worked in multiple sites and communities. This means that components that have been "validated" or "maximized" may be so only in certain contexts, or as part of configural combinations related to the content of the intervention, the delivery system, the recipients, and the sustaining factors in the surrounding environment. This is an issue of continuing controversy, as described by Elias (1991).

To illustrate the promise of the empirical warrant for social competence promotion efforts, the focus here is on programs that are reflective of vital multiyear, developmentally sensitive action research commitments. This is in keeping with Kuhn's (1970) and Rossi's (1978) perspectives on ways to examine innovations. They suggest an initial focus on examining exemplars of a particular paradigm – here, the social competence promotion paradigm – with gradual building of understanding by drawing information from the study of multiple examples in multiple contexts. Specifically, our focus is on social competence programs that have involved diverse target groups (from preschoolers through adolescents) and attempted to affect varied outcomes (e.g., peer relationships, delinquent behavior, substance use) to support the potential broad applicability of these efforts.

Results from quasi-experimental studies. Spivack and Shure (1974, 1988) evaluated a 2-year intervention in which teachers provided interpersonal-cognitive problem-solving skills training to low-income, African-American preschoolers and kindergartners. During Year 1, 10 nursery school teachers trained 113 children while 106 children were nontreatment controls. In Year 2, 131 remaining kindergartners were assigned to four groups: twice trained, nursery-trained only, kindergarten-trained only, and never-trained controls. All three training groups improved more than controls in problem-solving cognition (e.g., generating alternative solutions and consequences) and in teacher-rated classroom behavior.

Weissberg et al. (1981) evaluated the effects of a 42-lesson social problem solving curriculum with 563 urban and suburban second through fourth graders. Through role playing, videotape modeling, class discussion, and self-instructional exercises, teachers trained children in a six-step problem-solving process to apply to stressful social conflict situations. Following the formal training program, teachers conducted a weekly encore meeting during which problem-solving concepts were reviewed and applied to recent problems experienced by students. Program children improved more than controls on measures of cognitive and behavioral problem-solving skills. They also expressed greater confidence in their ability to deal effectively with interpersonal problem situations. Although training did not affect children's sociometric ratings, teacher ratings of adjustment reflected greater improvements for program children on shy-anxious behaviors, summed problem and competence behavior scores, and global ratings of likability and school adjustment.

With elementary school-aged students, Elias and Clabby (1989, 1992) have shown that students receiving a 2-year program designed to build self-control, group participation and social awareness, and social decision-making and problem-solving skills achieved skill acquisition and improvements on teacher ratings of behavior, sociometric indexes, and children's self-reported adjustment and ability to cope with everyday problem situations. When cohorts of students were followed into the middle school to see the impact of the social decision making and problem solving on their transition, it was found that students who had received the program in elementary school were better able to handle a range of stressors in the middle school environment than those who had not received training. Further, there was a relationship between the strength of the program received and the strength of observed effects: Those children receiving the full program had significantly better scores than those receiving a partial program, who in turn did significantly better than those students who did not receive any intervention (Elias et al., 1986). Finally, cohorts of students receiving the program in elementary school without any continuity in middle school were followed up in high school, up to 6 years after their exposure to the intervention. Children not receiving the program were characterized by higher rates of problem behaviors than experimental children. Interesting gender differences emerged, in that control boys had higher rates of self-destructive/identity problems, involvement with alcohol, and violent behavior to others, whereas control girls were characterized by the use of cigarettes or chewing tobacco and vandalism against parental property (Elias, Gara, Schuyler, Branden-Muller, & Sayette, 1991).

Rotheram-Borus (1988) examined the impact of a 24-session assertiveness training program with 343 children in grades 4 through 6. Children were assigned to one of three conditions: assertiveness training, an alternative treatment focusing on self-confidence training, and a no-treatment control group. Following assertiveness training, program children generated more assertive problem solutions and fewer passive and aggressive solutions than nonprogram children. In addition, teachers rated program children as better behaved and gaining higher achievement levels than the other groups. Furthermore, new classroom teachers also rated program children as higher in achievement 1 year later.

Working with middle school–aged youth, Weissberg and his colleagues have refined a social problem-solving approach to include a generalized thinking strategy (conveyed via a "stop light" model) that teaches students self-control, stress management, problem solving, decision making, and communication skills. Research into program effects indicated that the 421 urban adolescents receiving the program, relative to controls, gained in problem-solving skills, prosocial attitudes toward conflict resolution, teacher-rated impulse control and peer sociability, and self-reported delinquent behavior (Weissberg, Jackson, & Shriver, 1993). This research group has extended the application of the "stop light" framework to focused instruction in key target areas (e.g., use of tobacco, alcohol, and other illegal drugs). Working with both an urban and a suburban population, Caplan et al. (1992) reported broad gains in students' social adjustment and interpersonal effectiveness in both populations, when compared with controls. Specifically, gains were noted in constructive conflict resolution, impulse control, cognitive coping skills, and, most important, in reduced intentions to use drugs, hard liquor, and excessive amounts of alcohol.

Other projects targeted at specific substance use and problem behavior, such as the Life Skills Training program, have been developed to provide junior high school–aged children with largely targeted knowledge, motivation, and skills to resist influences to smoke (Botvin & Tortu, 1988). Based in social learning and problem behavior theories, the program looks at smoking as a link in a chain of behaviors likely to extend to the use of alcohol and other illegal substances. It combines specific training in social influence resistance (refusal skills and assertion skills) with more general training in prosocial skills such as stress management and problem solving. Some programs have added mass media programming and parent involvement components to the skills-focused classroom training (Pentz et al., 1989). A review of findings indicates that recipients of social influence approaches show significant reductions in the onset and prevalence of cigarette smoking, as well as marijuana and alcohol use, when compared with untreated controls (Ellickson & Bell, 1990; Hawkins et al., 1992; Rogers et al., 1989). However, there is evidence that findings are most consistent and enduring with regard to smoking and marijuana, and less so with regard to alcohol, probably because social norms against the use of alcohol are quite inconsistent. Unfortunately, there have been no studies to date that have been of sufficient duration that they have been able to follow up subjects into late adolescence or early adulthood to see the long-term effects on both substance use and substance abuse. Further, there is reason to expect not only gender differences, but also differences based on cultural background and neighborhood variables. Thus, much research remains to be done to understand the long-term impact of skills-based programs on the prevention of significant risk behaviors.

Another important project focus has been interventions that emphasize explicit schoolwide changes in governance as a complement to skills training approaches in the classroom. The Child Development Project (CDP) in San Ramon, California, seeks to produce a caring community in the classroom and elementary school by creating environments that foster self-determination, social competence, social connectedness, and moral guidance (Battistich, Elias, &

Branden-Muller, 1992; Solomon, Watson, Battistich, Schaps, & Delucchi, 1990). Walking into a CDP classroom, one will find students working in cooperative groups; discussing issues of social responsibility and prosocial values in their academic subjects, class meetings, and projects; actively helping their classmates, schoolmates, school environment, and the wider community; and participating in a discipline system that emphasizes their involvement in rule setting and in problem solving and deciding how disagreements are to be resolved. Schoolwide activities would reflect similar values, as would the operation of parent–teacher teams and the concept of "family homework." Data from a variety of studies, most of which have employed quasi-experimental designs, indicate that changes have been produced in social skills, social adjustment, classroom behavior, and, importantly, commitment to democratic values, as shown by balanced gains in self-assertion and in concern for others (Battistich et al., 1992).

The "Comer process" (1987), based on the work of James Comer at Yale University, is in essence a school site-based management approach that transforms the relationships among educators and parents so that there is a shared decision-making and responsibility base for an individual school. There are powerful radiating effects that this model generates, which Comer has described as a sense of empowerment that flows into the classrooms and touches the students, while also flowing out in the community and touching residents and service providers who interface with the school. Such processes seem to be especially welcome in inner-city areas. Initial evaluation results have found an impact on schoolwide levels of academic achievement and an invigoration of many parents and educators to participate in the educational system. Because research to date into school restructuring approaches has not been systematic or well coordinated across investigators and settings, these programs vary a great deal with regard to their classroom-centered skills-based emphasis. Indeed, so much effort goes into setting up and operating the management structure that some fear that the classroom component of the approach is given insufficient attention, thus leaving children without systematic access to targeted competence-building opportunities. Relatedly, these programs also have not been studied over a sufficient period of time to indicate their impact on problem behaviors.

Conclusions. Without doubt, the promise of the data on the exemplary programs just discussed must be tempered. The use of action research tends to be inconsistent with a microlevel experimental analysis of program components. There are many more facets of social competence and prevention programs that have not been examined, as compared with those which have been studied. However, studies of exemplars, despite their limitations, provide the best starting point from which to develop a science of promoting students' social competencies.

Operationalizing the processes and mechanisms of intervention-generated change: "Best practices" in school-based efforts

Perhaps the most exciting development in the field of social competence promotion is the attention being given to the science of interventions (Price et al., 1988; Zins & Forman, 1988; Zins & Ponti, 1990). Successful interventions are viewed as being theory driven, including both theories of the problem and theories of the intervention.

From our perspective, an intervention is best thought of as a strategy of influencing developmental trajectories and influencing the host organizations and the values and practices of professionals/professions and other individuals involved to facilitate the desired changes and sustain them, using an action research approach to monitor, evaluate, and modify the intervention in response to changes in the phenomena of interest and the ecological conditions. An intervention requires a knowledge of potential mediating influences, subgroup effects, change processes, and, perhaps most germane to our present considerations, a theory of the mechanisms and processes by which change can occur. These mechanisms – or, at least, interventionists' implicit views of them – are incorporated into the guidelines and procedures of interventions. Thus, rather than the traditional perspective of placing interventions into the domain of "practice," we believe that interventions embody – or should embody – theories of the problem and theories of change. As a corollary, then, one can derive information about mechanisms and processes of intervention from the "best practices" of exemplary projects and from replicated intervention findings linked to specific change procedures.

Thus, advancing knowledge concerning school-based promotion of social competence and prevention of problem behaviors requires that attention be paid to intervention design and procedures with the same care that is used to examine experimental procedures in laboratory research. As noted earlier, action research has been a valuable tool because of its implicit focus on intervention processes as well as outcomes (Elias & Clabby, 1992; Price et al., 1988; Weissberg et al., 1989). To provide an indication of how change processes are operationalized, this section presents an overview of the practices and considerations that (1) have guided the most successful social competence promotion programs and (2) have been touted by unsuccessful programs as factors that could have prevented their demise.

Key features of successful social competence promotion programs. Reviews of school-based programs – of varying degrees of effectiveness – designed to promote social skills, social competence, or positive health behaviors, or to prevent alcohol and other drug use, have yielded a set of factors associated with positive impact (e.g., Connell, Turner, & Mason, 1985; Consortium on the School Based Promotion of Social Competence, 1992; Elias & Clabby, 1992; G. Gottfredson & Gottfredson, 1985; Gresham, 1991; Walberg, 1986; Weissberg et al., 1989). Although it is beyond the scope of this chapter to provide a comprehensive description of these findings, the most reliably identified factors are included in Table 8.1.

To illustrate the linkage of factors representative of "best intervention practices" with operative mechanisms and processes, it will be useful to consider examples from several levels of factors. Leventhal, Prohaska, and Hirschman (1985) delineate several individual and peer group characteristics that have been associated with health risk behaviors, especially smoking. Similar to recent formulations by Lazarus (1991), they find that a combination of appraisal of a situation, goals for coping, and subjective indicators of goal attainment can delineate pathways leading toward or away from problem behaviors. For example, if peer pressure to join in problem behaviors is strong and peer acceptance is a highly valued goal, then enacting those

Table 8.1. *Factors associated with effective school-based social competence promotion programs*

Curriculum and instructional design factors
Focus on delivering specific skills at the appropriate developmental points
Teach specific skills for resisting negative social influences
Include both generic life skills and specific skills for prevention of specific
  behaviors [include a promotion and a prevention strategy]
Teach the coordination and integration of cognition, affect, and behavior
Include a peer leadership component at the upper grades
Have clear articulation with other existing subject areas, including some
  basic academic subject areas and health or family life education
Contain materials that are clear, up to date, and "user-friendly"
Ensure active student engagement through learning methods including
  modeling, role plays, performance feedback, dialoguing, and positive
  reinforcement

School and systemwide factors
Include programming of sufficient duration and intensity, ideally extending
  from grades pre-K to 12, and in a coordinated manner
Involve well-trained teachers or program deliverers who have an ongoing
  role in the host system
Design programs in a way that is acceptable to and reaches populations at
  risk and is coordinated with and linked to a continuum of services, including the school resource committee and special services and child study
  team services
Make provision to assess the integrity of the implementation
Demonstrate effects through a method of monitoring that includes indicators of implementation and goal-focused impact

School climate and norm structure factors
Evaluate the nature of norms for responding to misbehavior, victimization,
  and related violations of school rules, the degree to which these are
  shared among school staff and parents, and the extent to which they are
  consonant with the philosophy and approaches of a program
Determine the state of organizational readiness or health – indicated by
  such variables as teacher morale, school planning, decision making, and
  reward structures, articulated and shared school goals, willingness to
  adapt programs, and staff health – to see if the school is capable of implementing the program with fidelity and subsequently integrating it into
  other factors of the schooling experience

Table 8.1 (*cont.*)

Community factors
Include parent involvement and work to be completed at home, preferably
   involving parents
Show cultural sensitivity to the range of recipient student populations
   represented

---

behaviors is likely. If subjective distress is high and reduction of that
stress is a valued goal, then problem behaviors that might reduce that
distress are likely to occur. Other influences on problem behavior
patterns include the potency of symptom-based control and of conceptual control, in which an individual chooses to act in accordance with
a perceived benefit-to-cost ratio, what Rotter (1954) would have
termed a multiple approach/avoidance appraisal.

In essence, the mechanisms proposed by Leventhal et al. rely heavily on an interrelated series of appraisals about the nature of one's
immediate and long-term situation and the implications of certain
behaviors for one's self-perception and relationships in those time
frames. If we recall earlier discussion about social competencies and
characteristics associated with resilience, then it is clear that possessing problem-solving and learning-to-learn skills, a positive relationship, and the like will make it more probable that prosocial, healthy
decisions will be made. *A capacity for thoughtful reflection and appropriate interpersonal behavior in a context of positive relationships with competent individuals within a social structure filled with possibilities for valued
roles and involvement is a healthy antidote to risk.* These considerations
translate most directly into the curriculum and design factors in Table
8.1, as well as more generally to supportive factors in the external
environment.

Contributions by Cowen, Price, and others make it clear that simple solutions (and simple interventions) are unlikely to serve preventive or competence promotion purposes (Price et al., 1988). Many
skills are needed, some of which require complex programs with
periodic boosters over long periods of time, linked to developmental
trends; additionally beneficial is yoking the child and family components and anchoring them in a community context. Of course, this is

far more easily expressed than accomplished. But these mechanisms indicate the essential embeddedness of socialization processes and the necessity for successful interventions to have genuine embeddedness in enduring social environments. This is reflected in the school and systemwide factors, as well as community factors emphasizing the potency added by parent and cultural congruence with an intervention's goals and methods.

Yet another important consideration is the concept of readiness of change. Change does not occur according to the intervener's timetable. A program consisting of potent and validly conceived mechanisms and processes may not succeed because the host environments are not able to support those processes (Zins & Ponti, 1990). Thus, school climate and norm structure factors have been recognized as critical to intervention theory and practice. For example, program planners need to consider the idea of the resiliency/resistances balance within an organization as a way of operationalizing organizational readiness (Elias & Clabby, 1992). Among those markers of potent mechanisms and processes are the history of the organization's long-term response to innovations, the balance of new and experienced administrators, the overall history of the organization and the nature of its current trajectory, and the degree of articulation of goals and missions so that incoming programs can have benchmarks by which to create linkage and embeddedness.

It must be noted that the listing in Table 8.1 is not "systematic," but rather reflects those areas in which some reliable conclusions can be delineated. Indeed, the state of our overall knowledge base in the intervention area will be examined shortly. However, there is an additional focus that warrants explication because of the magnitude of the problem it represents. There is an unacceptable and seemingly growing number of students in the educational mainstream who can be thought of as being in at least moderate risk of future psychosocial dysfunction (as noted earlier). What facets of Table 8.1 are most salient to students at risk? These are the students whose status as disaffected, disillusioned, disconnected, or disruptive may not be accompanied by formal labels. Yet, to target a prevention or competence-enhancement program toward such students without taking into consideration the differences in their circumstances from students who are functioning at minimal risk would be a conceptual and practical error.

For example, there is debate about whether programs should be focused on at-risk groups or whether they should be designed to include all children. To a great extent, such issues are resolved in accordance with one's conceptualization of prevention and one's programmatic priorities. Considerations include the age of the children, the base rates of problem behaviors in the population, the developmental trajectory of a particular problem behavior, the history of effectiveness of a particular intervention, a costs–benefits analysis for the circumstances into which one is contemplating entering, and the possible effects of stigmatization.

Approaches such as multiple gate screening to select at-risk cases from the general population have not been sufficiently studied under a wide range of natural conditions (i.e., outside of the aegis of special projects with special funding and resources and often a limited time frame) to be able to reach cogent conclusions on their merits, as well as their merits relative to other preventive approaches. However, there is a sense that at-risk students will benefit from programs that are more intensive, more narrowly targeted, and of longer duration than those directed to students within the minimal risk category (Dryfoos, 1990; Schorr, 1988; Zigler & Berman, 1983). As interventions with at-risk children are likely to uncover significant problems that are beyond the ken of the classroom teacher and, regardless, that are inappropriate to address within the context of classroom-based group interventions (Elias, 1991), it is logical to expect that these children will require access to a system of triage into more individualized and "clinically" oriented services – akin to a multiple gate approach.

Further, in urban districts and other areas in which the concentration of moderate- and severe-risk students is relatively high, there are aspects of the school organization that provide an important context for addressing the needs of individual children. For example, research on victimization experiences in school – an occurrence that is highly related to rates of drug involvement, delinquency, dropping-out, and other forms of adolescent problem behavior and to which at-risk student are particularly prone – shows that these experiences are exacerbated by teachers with punitive attitudes, rules that are not perceived as fair, clear, or consistently enforced, and ambiguous responses to student misbehavior on the part of educators. In addition, there appears to be a linkage of victimization with lack of resources needed for teaching and with students' low levels of belief in conventional social rules (G. Gottfredson & Gottfredson, 1985). A moment's reflection is all that is needed to imagine the dynamic that is set up in such schools, as well as the difficulties faced by a social skills or other classroom-based intervention being introduced into such a disorderly environment.

An additional factor that cannot be disentangled from the risk status of the students is the risk status of school staff. The existence of a school environment characterized by low teacher morale, lack of teacher–administrator cooperation and communication, paucity of structures that foster teacher involvement in planning and decision making, ambiguous school goals and reward structures, and unclear role definitions severely hamper the capacity of a school to initiate and maintain programmatic innovations. This is especially true if staff resentment toward students is such that they do not believe that the most troublesome students are worth heroic staff toil and extra effort (Corcoran, 1985; D. Gottfredson, 1986; G. Gottfredson & Gottfredson, 1985).

These facts suggest that the effectiveness and durability of social competence promotion strategies and their capacity to reach children at risk can be meaningfully enhanced by expanding their focus to reach multiple risk and protective factors. The resulting multicomponent programs will be further enhanced if they reach across a variety of ecological levels and extend across multiple years, particularly those years during which protections against risk and reductions in risk factors may be most developmentally important (Elias & Branden, 1988). These multiyear, multicomponent, multilevel interventions are likely to call for changes in curriculum, instructional methods, school governance strategies, social relations within a school, extracurricular activities, and liaison between schools and their surrounding communities. Such far-reaching changes – which appear at this time to be necessary conditions for prevention of problem behaviors and promotion of social competence among at-risk students, and important for similar results with students at minimal risk – are unlikely to be accomplished through the mere training of school staff without organizational commitment to and follow-through in extensive professional development (Berman, 1981; Huberman & Miles, 1984).

Implications from the review of processes and mechanisms of intervention as contained in "best practices." As Table 8.1 implies, a curriculum may serve as the anchor of a program, but it is not itself sufficient to accomplish the goals of social competence promotion. Further, it should be clear that the principles of sound instruction are not unique to preventively oriented programs. Procedures for skill training used effectively in clinical and educational contexts all can be mobilized in the service of social competence promotion. However, the schoolwide and external factors listed in Table 8.1 suggest that the deceptive simplicity of classroom-based interventions disguises the necessity of their existing in a supportive organizational surround if they are to have strong and enduring effects. This information helps to provide an explanation of the limited effects of stand-alone interventions. When reflecting on the reasons for this problem, it is important to recall that even the most acclaimed intervention programs fall short on a number of the "best practices" outlined earlier. Like risk factors, it is entirely possible that lacking one "key program element" does a program little harm, but as the number of program gaps increases, the deleterious impact on the program takes on a multiplicative effect. Data from Commins and Elias (1991) suggest that factors related to school leadership and the balance of forces in the school for resiliency or resistance when responding to intervention initiatives are of particular importance in determining long-term program outcomes.

Indeed, whether focusing on children at moderate or high levels of risk or on the general population, a growing number of researchers are recognizing that an organizational perspective on intervention programs, their classroom features, the school environment, and the surrounding community must be incorporated into one's most basic thinking about school-based programs designed to promote social competence. The process of putting a program into place calls for involvement of the school and the broader school constituency in articulating primary needs and reflecting a range of cultural perspectives. There must be training in the program's philosophy and instructional technology and a commitment to instructional excellence and renewal, a skills focus, and a commitment to planning the program's developmental and long-range implementation and impact, as well as how it will be integrated with the overall educational mission and operation of the school, rather than being "added on." *Unfortunately, there are as yet no algorithms to provide a threshold for success or to provide an empirical warrant with regard to how these considerations can be jointly weighted or counterbalanced. The empirical warrant for well-designed social competence promotion does not extend to a detailed blueprint of how various helpful program elements must be arrayed.*

Despite these limitations, the press of social problems and tragic issues affecting children requires forward movement. The resilience paradigm simultaneously allows one to see what it is that puts so many youth at great risk for problem behaviors and negative outcomes of all types. Social competence promotion interventions are designed to address problem-solving and prosocial relationship skills, as well as the basic skills and expectancies needed to learn in school. They are directed toward providing basic skills for interpersonal effectiveness and sound psychosocial growth. But the ultimate outcomes will depend in large part on the strength of the social competence "signal" to the "noise" of environmental disruption. That is why a recent generation of social competence programs directs its attention not only to the individual program recipients but to the social, organizational, and community ecologies within which the interventions are embedded. It is an attempt to strengthen the "signal" while recognizing that efforts must be taken at a societal level to reduce the forces that threaten the resilient, adaptive capacity present in most children and environments.

The need for comprehensive, multiyear, multicomponent theoretical and intervention models

The concept of what is "necessary" to constitute an effective program has expanded against the expanding baseline of adversity; by increasing the scope of interventions, it is believed that relevant mechanisms will be activated through the operation of interrelated components that will lead to desired positive changes. From this perspective, it cannot be surprising that studies of so many stand-alone social skills interventions appear to be inconsistent with regard to their enduring effectiveness. Yet, it would not be bold to speculate that it is the (usually unassessed) influence of organizational-systemic and community factors that mediates the success of otherwise similar social skills programs.

In fact, these considerations have been noted in the community and preventive psychology literature, and in a way that incorporates the simultaneous operation of risk and protective factors. As summarized in the prevention equations or prevention formulas of Albee (1982) and Elias (1987), individual risk is heightened to the extent that the individual experiences stress and has physical handicaps, and is lowered to the extent that the individual possesses coping skills, perceives himself or herself as well supported, and has high positive self-esteem.

Elias (1987) pointed out that, in accordance with social learning theory, predicting individual risk would be improved by the use of sets of equations for the various situations and key settings one inhabits. The equations should reflect changes related to development, as well. Further, it is necessary to have a way of examining the risk likelihoods for populations and communities, not just for individuals. This macrolevel formula indicates that risk is increased as a function of increases in severity or frequency of *life stressors and risk factors in the environment;* risk is decreased to the extent to which protective factors are provided, in the form of *positive socialization practices in key socialization environments,* access to *social support and socioeconomic resources,* and *opportunities for positive relatedness and connectedness* of the kind that allows for prosocial bonding and the development of a sense of being valued and worthwhile.

Comprehensive, theoretical guidance of interventions appears to be necessary for clarifying program goals, clarifying the theoretical variables expected to bring about the ultimate desired state, guiding measurement of these variables, focusing intervention strategies on the theoretical variables of interest, providing an organizing framework to guide implementation as well as evaluation efforts, and enhancing communication about the design and effects of the program (Chen & Rossi, 1980, 1983; Elliott, 1979; Glaser, 1980; G. Gottfredson, 1984; Martin, Sechrest, & Redner, 1981; Wholey, 1987). Such theoretical perspectives will link program elements to theoretical variables in multicomponent, multiyear prevention programs directed toward factors related to the ultimate behaviors being targeted. Moreover, to increase the likelihood of powerful and enduring effects, preventive interventions must specify the linkages by which the proposed intervention is expected to reduce, eliminate, or mitigate exposure to risk. In short, prevention science requires the specification of linked hypotheses (i.e., theory) regarding how specific interventions are expected to reduce interaction with identified risk factors to prevent the development of a health or behavior problem. The following section presents two examples of comprehensive, theory-guided, multicomponent, multiyear social competence promotion efforts, evaluated with an action research orientation and quasi-experimental designs.

Adolescent health promotion via communitywide programs

Perry and Kelder (1992) propose a model of adolescent health promotion that has been utilized to organize the design and development of communitywide health programs for youth (as can be seen in Figure 8.1). The goal of these programs is to promote health, where health is conceptualized as having four interrelated domains: physical (referring to physiological functioning), psychological (referring to a subjective sense of well-being), social (referring to effectiveness in fulfilling social roles), and spiritual (referring to realization of individual potential and purpose) (Perry & Jessor, 1985). Within each of these four domains of health, outcomes of programs are identified in terms of prevalence of health-enhancing or health-compromising behaviors of the targeted populations. For example, a prevention program might seek a reduction in violent incidents at schools, a decreased school drop-out rate, or a decline in alcohol use.

The factors that influence the adoption and maintenance of health-related behaviors are derived from social-psychological theory (Bandura, 1977; Jessor & Jessor, 1977), and etiological research on adolescent problem behavior (Perry & Kelder, 1992). These conceptualizations have identified three levels of social-psychological risk factors that serve as the targets of intervention. These include environmental risk factors (such as role models, norms, opportunities, and social support), individual risk factors (such as levels of knowledge, values, self-efficacy, and functional meanings), and behavioral risk factors (such as social skills, intentions, existing repertoire, and reinforcements). The creative modification of these risk factors provides the basis for the content of health promotion programs.

The programs that are needed to change the risk factors identified include school-based curricula, peer leadership, school environmental modifications, parental involvement, community activities, environmental change, health-enhancing mass media, and public policies.

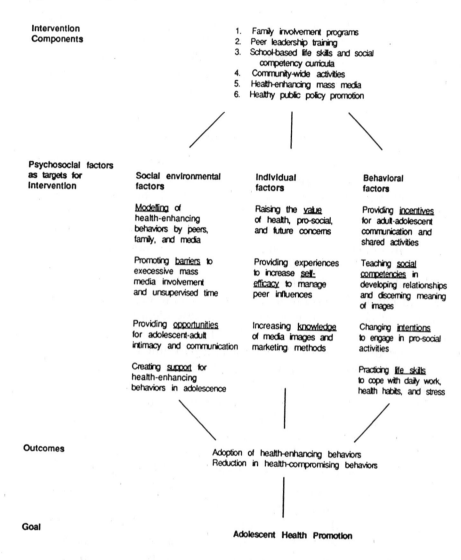

Figure 8.1.   A conceptual model of adolescent health promotion in the 1990s

Therefore, social competence promotion is an integral part of these health promotion efforts, as skills training is most efficiently and efficaciously delivered in or through the schools. Still, the addition of community-level programs augments change, particularly of environmental risk factors, of norms or role models or opportunities that exist outside of the school setting.

The opportunity to examine the potential of a school-based curriculum embedded in a communitywide program was available in the Minnesota Heart Health Program (MHHP). The MHHP is a research and demonstration project designed to reduce morbidity and mortality from cardiovascular diseases in three north-central U.S. communities. These communities took part in a six-year program designed to change eating, physical activity, and smoking habits. Cardiovascular risk factor screening of 70% of the adults, mass media promotional campaigns, environmental changes in grocery stores and restaurants, community quit-smoking contests, worksite programs, and community education were among the components of the MHHP (Blackburn et al., 1984; Mittelmark et al., 1986).

The Class of 1989 Study focused on a cohort of adolescents in one of the three MHHP education communities (Fargo, North Dakota–Moorhead, Minnesota) as well as the same-age cohort in the matched MHHP reference community (Sioux Falls, South Dakota). All students in both cohorts were originally surveyed in 1983, when they were in the 6th grade, and prior to the initiation of any of the larger MHHP efforts. These students were surveyed annually for 7 years until they graduated from high school in 1989. The students in Fargo-Moorhead, however, also took part in 5 years of peer-led behavioral health curricula from 1983 to 1987. These curricula also focused on the development of healthy eating, physical activity, and nonsmoking patterns. Details of these curricula are presented elsewhere (Perry, Klepp, & Sillers, 1989), but were primarily social skills–based and sought changes in key environmental, individual, and behavioral risk factors. In the 7th grade, all the students in Fargo–Moorhead in the Class of 1989 took part in the Minnesota Smoking Prevention Program (MSPP), a six-session curriculum designed to teach skills to identify and resist influences to smoke. MSPP had previously been successful in delaying onset of smoking, but only until the 10th grade (Murray, Pirie, Luepker, &

Pallonen, 1989). Therefore, the Class of 1989 Study examined the MSPP when it was augmented by 4 years of behavioral health curricula, peer leadership, and the activities of the larger MHHP. As is shown in Figure 8.2, the prevalence of smoking was significantly lower among Fargo–Moorhead students at every grade level, and still 40% lower at the end of 12th grade. The results are significant for both genders and with the school as the unit of analysis (Perry, Kelder, Klepp, & Murray, 1992). The Class of 1989 Study, then, provides an example of the potential enhancement of a school-based social competence curriculum (MSPP), which previously had demonstrated effectiveness for up to 3 years, when the program was embedded in a community where the norms, opportunities, and social support for nonsmoking were consonant with the process of change.

Use of the social development model to guide school and family change

The social development model (Hawkins et al., 1992; Hawkins & Weis, 1985) is an example of an integrated theory of prevention that has guided a longitudinal multicomponent prevention trial. An integration of control theory (Hirschi, 1969), social learning theory (Bandura, 1977), and social disorganization theory (Shaw & McKay, 1969), the social development model posits social bonding to family, school, positive peers, and neighborhood as a key protective factor. Bonding is thought to be important in regulating behavior because it provides motivation to live according to the standards held by the groups to which one is bonded. Four elements of social bonding have been shown to inhibit drug use and delinquency: strong attachment to parents (Brook, Brook, Gordon, Whiteman, & Cohen, 1990; Hundleby & Mercer, 1987; Jessor & Jessor, 1977); a high degree of commitment to schooling; active involvement in church activities (Schlegel & Sanborn, 1979; Wechsler & McFadden, 1979); and belief in the standards and norms and values of society (Akers, Krohn, Lanza-Kaduce, & Radosevich, 1979). In the social development model, attachment or emotional closeness, commitment or personal investment, and belief in the values of the social unit are seen as elements of the social bond.

The social development model hypothesizes that clear standards or

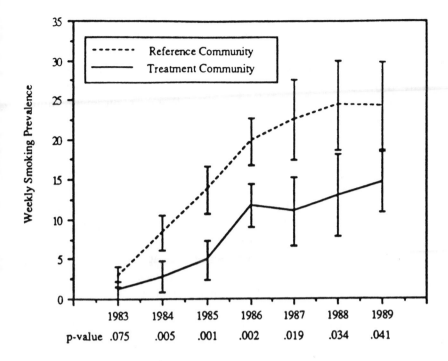

Figure 8.2. Smoking prevalence–cohort sample

norms for behavior represent a second protective factor against health and behavior problems. The model asserts that if children and adolescents are socialized in ways that promote bonding to family, school, and community and if these social units posit clear standards against behaviors such as precocious sexual activity, leaving school early, interpersonal violence, criminal activity, and tobacco, alcohol, or other drug use by children and adolescents, the incidence of these health and problem behaviors will be reduced. This represents an elaboration of the denominators in Albee's (1982) and Elias's (1987) prevention equations.

The social development model also hypothesizes protective developmental processes by which social bonding is built up. Three constructs are thought to interact in producing bonding: opportunities for active participation in the social unit, the individual's skills for effective participation, and the recognition provided for participation by the social environment. This specification of the elements of protective developmental processes suggests directions for prevention interventions across social units or domains. The model suggests that a common goal of preventive intervention with parents, teachers, child-care providers, and others responsible for children is to empower them to stimulate the development of bonding by involvement, stimulating the development of skills to participate effectively in family life, the classroom, and the peer group, and to recognize children for their efforts and performance.

Because the provision of opportunities for active involvement for young people is also an ingredient in the process of bonding, organizational change in school classrooms to promote cooperative learning and other active learning methods of instruction is suggested as a key element in program design. Similarly, there is value to interventions that encourage parents to become actively engaged with their children in learning and family work tasks. It also indicates the importance of promoting an organizational culture in which teachers and parents themselves feel committed to the task of implementing this model.

The social development model has guided the longitudinal prevention studies of Hawkins, Catalano, and their colleagues. In the Seattle Social Development Project, they tested a combination of preventive components to ascertain the cumulative effect of interventions seeking simultaneously to reduce risks in family, school, and peer domains. The interventions included parent training in family management skills to reduce risk factors, such as family conflict, early and persistent conduct problems, academic failure, poor and inconsistent family management practices, and permissive attitudes of family members toward children's alcohol or other drug use. Three distinct developmentally adjusted parent-training components were offered on a voluntary basis to parents when their children were in grades 1, 2, 3, 5, and 6. As in each intervention component, parents learned the importance of creating the conditions for strong family bonding: opportunities, skills, and recognition.

Teachers of children in the intervention condition in grades 1 through 6 learned methods of proactive classroom management, effective instruction, and cooperative learning to reduce risk factors of early and persistent conduct problems, academic failure, low degree of commitment to school. Through the use of these methods of instruction, teachers were encouraged to increase opportunities for active participation in learning as illustrated in cooperative learning groups, to teach skills for effective development lessons on classroom routines in the proactive classroom management segment, and to recognize and reinforce effort and improvement as illustrated in the mechanisms of effective teaching and the group reinforcement structures of cooperative learning. In addition, children in the intervention group received social competence training by their first-grade teachers using the *Interpersonal Cognitive Problem Solving* training program (Spivack & Shure, 1988).

The interventions were offered to children initially randomly assigned to experimental or control classrooms in eight schools serving high-crime neighborhoods of Seattle, though the study was later expanded. Children and parents in this study are being followed through their school careers. To date, observational data confirm greater use of intervention teaching practices in experimental classrooms than in control classrooms and parent-training attendance records show that 43% of parents of intervention students participated in parenting training (Hawkins, Catalano, and Associates, 1992). Following exposure to the combination of parent training, teacher training, and child training in social competence, intervention children from schools in high-crime neighborhoods in Seattle displayed lower rates of aggressive and self-destructive behavior by the end of grade 2 (Hawkins, Von Cleve, & Catalano, 1991), higher levels of bonding to family and school across the elementary grades, and lower rates of initiation of alcohol use and delinquent behavior by entry into grade 5 (Hawkins, et al., 1992) when compared with students in comparison classrooms. These results suggest the promise of theoretically guided interventions that include social competence promotion with other theoretically consistent preventive components that promote bonding to family, school, positive peers, and community.

It is noteworthy that intervention and control students did not differ following intervention in their norms or attitudes toward drug use. The intervention did not explicitly seek to address the protective factor or norms against drug use prior to grade 5. Although the results suggest that interventions to affect bonding, even without explicit attention to setting standards around drug use, may have protective power, it is likely that also encouraging the development of clear norms against drug use would further protect children against early drug use initiation.

An action agenda to address future issues

In this section, we attempt to identify those issues that we feel are most essential to progress in research, theory, and practice in the area of social competence promotion. Areas covered include the conceptual and methodological base of the work, the challenges of cultural diversity and the rise of violence in many societies, the need to think more in terms of service delivery systems than in terms of isolated interventions, and the education of current and future professionals to carry out and advance the kinds of approaches we believe to be necessary for genuine progress in the field.

More configural theories and methods

There is agreement among researchers that there are key gaps in our knowledge about social competence and its promotion. These questions are among those being raised most often: What are the longitudinal effects of social competence promotion efforts? How can translation of successful programs be made to diverse cultures and populations, particularly those not part of the demonstration samples? What factors mediate gains shown when prevention programs are effective? What differences are there in the operation of protective mechanisms in the face of various co-occurring risk factors? How does identity – or personal meaning – serve as a mediator of socialization messages related to health-enhancing and health-compromising behaviors? How can we more precisely define the interaction of various influences that are being uncovered in the literature? What are the best ways to assess the phenomena of interest? How can we use conventional means and recently developed techniques such as growth curve analysis to assess the process of change over time?

The work of Ianni (1989) leaves no doubt about the highly configural relationships one will encounter in any attempt to understand competence. For example, the way in which teenage pregnancy is viewed is subject to variation depending on type of community, religion, ethnicity, and gender of the parents with whom the teenager lives. Further, there is an important developmental shift in urban communities, such that there is much negative reaction to teen pregnancy but a corresponding degree of social reinforcement to being a teenage mother. However, as the child passes through infancy, both parent and child are assumed to be sufficiently competent and capable to cope with the situation on their own. Thus, support is withheld, given, and then withheld. However, community dynamics are such that the latter phase is both least visible and salient to the teenagers. From their perspective, they may be enduring the pregnancy as a rite of passage into respectful integration into the adult community. The reality is that the primary support system is likely to be the urban teens' own extended family, and they are unlikely to find easy access to health care, child-care assistance, or needed social services.

The prevention of violence and promotion of caring

It is our social forecast that the problem of enhancing youngsters' capacity for caring, nonviolent problem solving and for positive citizenship and the problem of minimizing school violence are among the most significant school-based and societal issues to be faced over the next decade. Epidemiological data show an increase in the problem of violence, especially among youth, through the 1980s. The early 1990s are likely to be remembered for the number of violent crimes involving guns in our nation's public schools. Work on a model of the etiology of caring, nonviolence, and school violence, incorporating demographic, social environmental, and personality factors that are both risk-increasing and protective in nature, as well as key related behavior such as bullying and sexual abuse, is becoming the focus of an increasing amount of research, writing, and funding. We anticipate advances in violence prevention and the promotion of domestic and foreign "peaceful coexistence" will come with a focus on social integration among high-risk children and families, training in social skills and citizenship skills with adolescents, and communitywide changes in norms, opportunities, and barriers to violence generated by collaborative communitywide projects and activities.

Moreover, it must be clear that social competence promotion and problem-behavior prevention programs are not substitutes for large-scale societal action directed at issues of poverty, health care, housing, and education. Relatedly, it cannot be assumed that legislative and even organizational-level mandates will necessarily translate into practices that will touch individual children in appropriate and effective ways. Ultimately, comprehensive interventions must not only operationalize processes and mechanisms that promote resilience but also translate them into ongoing, enduring service delivery systems that provide these processes and mechanisms with integrity.

Education in action research, the ecopolitical context of school-based social competence promotion, and dissemination

Training future researchers and scholars in the design, implementation, evaluation, and careful dissemination of social competence promotion action research projects requires a multidisciplinary perspective and a variety of skills for which many researchers have not been and are not being adequately prepared. The next generation of researchers – who will lead us to the third generation of programs – will need specific experiences with ongoing intervention programs in order to conduct the kind of research that will make advances. It is of particular importance that there be an increase in the pool of researchers and, especially, principal investigators, who are from culturally diverse backgrounds and who can lead projects into culturally diverse ecologies. This issue requires serious rethinking of current training efforts. Some models being developed in the field of professional psychology seem highly compatible with these directions and deserve much scrutiny (National Council of Schools of Professional Psychology, 1992; Peterson, 1991; Thomas & Elias, 1990).

Postscript

In moving to a developmental and process-oriented model that embraces the constructs of risk, protection, and resilience, the field of social competence promotion has integrated person-centered and environment-centered considerations and has forged a new unit of analysis for theory, research, practice, and policy. By taking a school-based focus, the field has acknowledged that it is context-sensitive and must be based in the reality of the settings in which people live, work, learn, and play, as well as in the reality of the settings that assist people when they have difficulties in adapting to their life circumstances. That we have learned this in a little over a decade is both remarkable and important, for we can now shape our efforts in ways that can have a greater impact on the lives of children, families, and communities. "At a time when the naysayers say nothing works, I am confident that we know a good deal more about school-aged children's and youth's problems and about what works than we did a 'decade plus one' ago. Such progress is satisfying" (Haggerty, 1990, p. 5). To this, we would add that this progress must also inspire us to continue the work begun, and to emphasize not only further increasing our knowledge, but putting that knowledge into effective, equitable practice.

References

Akers, R. L., Krohn, M. D., Lanza-Kaduce, L., & Radosevich, M. (1979). Social learning and deviant behavior: A specific test of a general theory. *American Sociological Review, 44,* 636–655.

Albee, G. (1982). Preventing psychopathology and promoting human potential. *American Psychologist, 37,* 1043–1050.

Bandura, A. (1977). *Social learning theory.* Englewood Cliffs, NJ: Prentice-Hall.

Battistich, V., Elias, M. J., & Branden-Muller, L. (1992). Two school-based approaches to promoting children's social competence. In G. Albee, L. Bond, & T. Monsey (Eds.), *Improving children's lives: Global approaches to prevention* (pp. 212–234). Newbury Park, CA: Sage.

Berman, P. W. (1981). Educational change: An implementation paradigm. In R. Lehming & M. Kane (Eds.), *Improving schools: Using what we know.* Beverly Hills, CA: Sage.

Berrueta-Clement, J. R., Schweinhart, L. J., Barnett, W. S., Epstein, A. S., & Weikart, D. P. (1984). *Changed lives: The effects of the Perry Preschool Program on youths through age 19.* Ypsilanti, MI: High/Scope Press.

Blackburn, H., Luepker, R. V., Kline, F. G., Bracht, N., Carlaw, R., Jacobs, D., Mittelmark, M., Stauffer, L., & Taylor, H. L. (1984). The Minnesota Heart Health Program: A research and demonstration project in cardiovascular disease prevention. In J. D. Matarazzo, J. A. Herd, N. E. Miller, & S. M. Weiss (Eds.), *Behavioral health: Handbook of health enhancement and disease prevention* (pp. 1171–1178). New York: Wiley.

Botvin, G. J., & Tortu, S. (1988). Preventing adolescent substance abuse through life skills training. In R. Price, E. Cowen, R. Lorion, & J. Ramos-McKay (Eds.), *14 ounces of prevention: A casebook for practitioners.* (pp. 98–110). Washington, DC: American Psychological Association.

Brook, J. S., Brook, D. W., Gordon, A. S., Whiteman, M., & Cohen, P. (1990). The psychosocial etiology of adolescent drug use: A family interactional approach. *Genetic, Social, and General Psychology Monographs, 116* (Whole No. 2).

Bush, P. J., Zuckerman, A. E., Theiss, P. K., Taggert, V. S., Horowitz, C., Sheridan, M. J., & Walter, H. J. (1989). Cardiovascular risk factor prevention in black schoolchildren: Two-year results of the "Know Your Body" program. *American Journal of Epidemiology, 129,* 466–482.

Caplan, M., Weissberg, R. P., Grober, J. H., Sivo, P. J., Grady, K., & Jacoby, C. (1992). Social competence promotion with inner-city and suburban young adolescents: Effects on social adjustment and alcohol use. *Journal of Consulting and Clinical Psychology, 60,* 56–63.

Chen, H. T., & Rossi, P. H. (1980). The multi-goal theory driven approach to evaluation: A model linking basic and applied social science. *Social Forces, 59,* 106–122.

Chen, H. T., & Rossi, P. H. (1983). Evaluating with sense: The theory driven approach. *Evaluation Review, 7,* 283–302.

Cherlin, A. J. (1988). *The changing American family and public policy.* Washington, DC: Urban Institute Press.

Cohen, C., & Naimark, H. (1991). United Nations Convention on the Rights of Children: Individual rights concepts and their significance for social scientists. *American Psychologist, 46,* 60–65.

Comer, J. P. (1987). New Haven's school–community connection. *Educational Leadership, 44* (March), 13–16.

Commins, W. W., & Elias, M. J. (1991). Institutionalization of mental health programs in organizational contexts: The case of elementary schools. *Journal of Community Psychology, 19,* 207–220.

Connell, D. B., Turner, R. R., & Mason, E. F. (1985). Summary of the findings of the School Health Education Evaluation: Health promotion effectiveness, implementation, and costs. *Journal of School Health, 55,* 316–323.

Consortium on the School-Based Promotion of Social Competence. (1991). Preparing students for the twenty-first century: Contributions of the prevention and social competence promotion fields. *Teachers College Record, 93,* 297–305.

Consortium on the School-Based Promotion of Social Competence (1992). Drug and alcohol prevention curricula. In J. D. Hawkins, R. F. Catalano, & Associates (Eds.), *Communities that care: Action for drug abuse prevention* (pp. 129–148). San Francisco: Jossey-Bass.

Corcoran, T. B. (1985). Effective secondary schools. In R. M. J. Kyle (Ed.), *Reaching for excellence: An effective schools sourcebook*. Washington, DC: U.S. Government Printing Office.

Costello, E. J. (1990). Child psychiatric epidemiology: Implications for clinical research and practice. In B. B. Lahey & A. E. Kazdin (Eds.), *Advances in clinical child psychology* (Vol. 13, pp. 53–90). New York: Plenum.

Cowen, E. L., & Work, W. C. (1988). Resilient children, psychological wellness, and primary prevention. *American Journal of Community Psychology, 16,* 591–608.

DeFriese, G., Crossland, C., MacPhail-Wilcox, B., & Sowers, J. (1990). Implementing comprehensive school health programs: Prospects for change in American schools. *Journal of School Health, 60,* 182–187.

Denham, S., & Almeida, M. C. (1987). Children's social problem solving skills, behavioral adjustment, and interventions: A meta-analysis evaluating theory and practice. *Journal of Applied Developmental Psychology, 8,* 391–410.

Dodge, K. A. (1986). A social information processing model of social competence in children. In M. Perlmutter (Ed.), *Cognitive perspectives on children's social and behavioral development* (pp. 77–125). Hillsdale, NJ: Erlbaum.

Dodge, K. A., & Feldman, E. (1990). Issues in social cognition and sociometric status. In S. R. Asher & J. D. Coie (Eds.), *Peer rejection in childhood: Origins, consequences, and intervention* (pp. 119–155). Cambridge: Cambridge University Press.

Dodge, K. A., Pettit, G. S., McClaskey, C. L., & Brown, M. M. (1986). Social competence in children. In *Monographs of the Society for Research in Child Development, 51* (2, Serial No. 213).

Dryfoos, J. G. (1990). *Adolescents at risk: Prevalence and prevention.* New York: Oxford University Press.

Elias, M. J. (1987). Establishing enduring prevention programs: Advancing the legacy of Swampscott. *American Journal of Community Psychology, 15,* 539–553.

Elias, M. J. (1990). Long-term social adaptation. In M. Green & R. Haggerty (Eds.), *Ambulatory pediatrics* (4th ed., pp. 64–68). Philadelphia: Saunders.

Elias, M. J. (1991). A multi-level action research perspective on stress-related interventions. In M. Colten & S. Gore (Eds.), *Adolescent stress: Causes and consequences* (pp. 261–280). Hawthorne, NY: Aldine de Gruyter.

Elias, M. J., & Branden, L. (1988). Primary prevention of behavioral and emotional problems in school-aged populations. *School Psychology Review, 17*, 581–592.

Elias, M. J., & Clabby, J. F. (1989). *Social decision-making skills: A curriculum guide for the elementary grades.* Rockville, MD: Aspen.

Elias, M. J., & Clabby, J. F. (1992). *Building social problem solving skills: Guidelines from a school-based program.* San Francisco: Jossey-Bass.

Elias, M. J., Gara, M., Schuyler, T., Branden-Muller, L., & Sayette, M. (1991). The promotion of social competence: Longitudinal study of a preventive school-based program. *American Journal of Orthopsychiatry, 61*, 409–417.

Elias, M. J., Gara, M., Ubriaco, M., Rothbaum, P., Clabby, J., & Schuyler, T. (1986). Impact of a preventive school problem-solving intervention on children's coping with middle-school stressors. *American Journal of Community Psychology, 14*(3), 259–275.

Ellickson, P. L., & Bell, R. M. (1990). Drug prevention in junior high: A multi-site longitudinal test. *Science, 247*, 1299–1305.

Elliott, D. S. (1979). Recurring issues in the evaluation of delinquency prevention and treatment programs. In D. Shichor & D. H. Kelly (Eds.), *Critical issues in juvenile delinquency.* Lexington, MA: Lexington Books.

Elliott, D. S., Huizinga, D., & Menard, S. (1989). *Multiple problem youth: Delinquency, substance abuse, and mental health problems.* New York: Springer-Verlag.

Felner, R., Lease, A., & Phillips, R. (1990). Social competence and the language of adequacy as a subject matter for psychology: A quadri-partite trilevel framework. In T. Gullotta, G. Adams, & R. Montemayor (Eds.), *Developing social competency in adolescence* (pp. 245–264). Newbury Park, CA: Sage.

Freedman, B. J., Rosenthal, L., Donahoe, C. P., Jr., Schlundt, D. G., & McFall, R. M. (1978). A social-behavioral analysis of skill deficits in delinquent and nondelinquent boys. *Journal of Consulting and Clinical Psychology, 46*, 1448–1462.

Gans, J. E., Blyth, D. A., Elster, A. B., & Gaveras, L. L. (1990). *America's adolescents: How healthy are they?* Chicago: American Medical Association.

Garmezy, N. (1985). Stress-resistant children: The search for protective factors. In J. E. Steveson (Ed.), *Recent research in developmental psycho-*

pathology (pp. 213–233). *Journal of Child Psychology and Psychiatry* (Book Supplement No. 4).

Garmezy, N. (1987). Stress, competence, and development: Continuities in the study of schizophrenic adults, children vulnerable to psychopathology, and the search for stress-resistant children. *American Journal of Orthopsychiatry, 57,* 159–174.

Glaser, D. (1980). The interplay of theory, issues, policy, and data. In M. W. Klein & K. S. Teilman (Eds.), *Handbook of criminal justice evaluation.* Beverly Hills, CA: Sage.

Gottfredson, D. C. (1986) *Creating effective urban public schools through researcher-practitioner collaboration.* Baltimore, MD: Johns Hopkins University Center for School Organizations of Schools.

Gottfredson, G. D. (1984). A theory-ridden approach to program evaluation: A method for stimulating researcher–implementer collaboration. *American Psychologist, 39,* 1101–1112.

Gottfredson, G. D., & Gottfredson, D. C. (1985). *Victimization in schools.* New York: Plenum.

Gresham, F. M. (1991). Conceptualizing behavior disorders in terms of resistance to intervention. *School Psychology Review, 20,* 9–22.

Haggerty, R. J. (1990). President's report: A decade plus one. In William T. Grant Foundation, *Annual Report 1990.* New York.

Hamburg, B. (1990). *Life skills training: Preventive interventions for young adolescents.* New York: Carnegie Council on Adolescent Development.

Hawkins, J. D., Catalano, R. F., & Associates (1992). *Community that cares: Action for drug abuse prevention.* San Francisco: Jossey-Bass.

Hawkins, J. D., Catalano, R. F., & Miller, J. (1992). Risk and protective factors for alcohol and other drug problems in adolescence and early adulthood. Implications for substance abuse prevention. *Psychological Bulletin, 112,* 64–105.

Hawkins, J. D., Catalano, R. F., Morrison, D. M., O'Donnell, J., Abbott, R. D., & Day, L. E. (1992). The Seattle Social Development Project: Effects of the first four years on protective factors and problem behaviors. In J. McCord & R. Tremblay (Eds.), *The prevention of antisocial behavior: Interventions from birth through adolescence* (pp. 139–161). New York: Guilford Press.

Hawkins, J. D., Von Cleve, E., & Catalano, R. F. (1991). Reducing early childhood aggression: Results of a primary prevention program. *Journal of the American Academy of Child and Adolescent Psychiatry, 30,* 208–217.

Hawkins, J. D., & Weis, J. G. (1985). The social development model: An integrated approach to delinquency prevention. *Journal of Primary Prevention, 6,* 73–97.

Hirschi, T. (1969). *Causes of delinquency.* Berkeley: University of California Press.

Huberman, M., & Miles, M. (1984). *Innovation up close: How school improvement works.* New York: Plenum.

Hundleby, J. D., & Mercer, G. W. (1987). Family and friends as social environments and their relationship to young adolescents' use of alcohol, tobacco, and marijuana. *Journal of Consulting and Clinical Psychology, 44,* 125–134.

Ianni, F. A. J. (1989). *The search for structure: A report on American youth today.* New York: Free Press.

Jason, L., Wine, A., Johnson, J., Warren-Sohlberg, L., Filipelli, L., Turner, E., & Lardon, C. (1992). *Helping transfer students: Strategies for educational and social readjustment.* San Francisco: Jossey-Bass.

Jessor, R., & Jessor, S. (1977). *Problem behavior and psychosocial development: A longitudinal study of youth.* Orlando, FL: Academic Press.

Kendall, P. C. (1991). Guiding theory for therapy with children and adolescents. In P. C. Kendall (Ed.), *Child and adolescent therapy: Cognitive-behavioral procedures.* New York: Guilford.

Kuhn, T. S. (1970). *The structure of scientific revolutions* (2nd ed.). Chicago: University of Chicago Press.

Lazarus, R. (1991). Cognition and motivation in emotion. *American Psychologist, 46,* 352–367.

Lerner, J. V., & Vicary, J. R. (1984). Difficult temperament and drug use: Analyses from the New York longitudinal study. *Journal of Drug Education, 14,* 1–8.

Leventhal, H., Prohaska, T., & Hirschman, R. (1985). Preventive health behavior across the life span. In J. Rosen & L. Solomon (Eds.), *Prevention in health psychology* (pp. 191–235). Hanover, NH: University Press of New England.

Martin, S. E., Sechrest, L. B., & Redner, R. (Eds.). (1981). *New directions in the rehabilitation of criminal offenders.* Washington, DC: National Academy Press.

Masten, A. S., Best, K., & Garmezy, N. (1990). Resilience and development: Contributions from the study of children who overcome adversity. *Development and Psychopathology, 2,* 425–444.

McFall, R. M. (1983). A review and reformulation of the concept of social skills. *Behavioral Assessment, 4,* 1–33.

Melton, G. B. (1991). Socialization in the global community: Respect for the dignity of children. *American Psychologist, 46,* 66–71.

Mittelmark, M. B., Jacobs, D. R., Carlaw, R. W., Finnegan, J., Jeffrey, R. W., Mullis, R. M., Pechacek, T. F., & Pirie, P. L. (1986). Community-wide prevention of cardiovascular disease: Education strategies of the Minnesota Heart Health Program. *Preventive Medicine, 15,* 1–17.

Murray, D. M., Pirie, P., Luepker, R. V., & Pallonen, U. (1989). Five- and six-year follow-up results from four seventh grade smoking prevention strategies. *Journal of Behavioral Medicine, 12,* 207–218.

National Advisory Mental Health Council. (1990). *National plan for research on child and adolescent mental disorders.* Washington, DC: National Institute of Mental Health.

National Commission on the Role of the School and the Community in Improving Adolescent Health. (1990). *Code Blue: Uniting for healthier youth.* Alexandria, VA: National Association of State Boards of Education.

National Council of Schools of Professional Psychology. (1992). *The core curriculum in professional psychology.* Washington, DC: American Psychological Association.

National Mental Health Association. (1986). *The prevention of mental-emotional disabilities: Report of the National Mental Health Association Commission on the Prevention of Mental-Emotional Disabilities.* Alexandria, VA.

Newcomb, M. D., Maddahian, E., & Bentler, P. M. (1986). Risk factors for drug use among adolescents: Concurrent and longitudinal analyses. *American Journal of Public Health, 76,* 525–530.

Pentz, M. A., Dwyer, J. H., MacKinnon, D. P., Flay, B. R., Hansen, W. B., Wang, E. Y. I., & Johnson, C. A. (1989). A multi-community trial for primary prevention of adolescent drug abuse: Effects on drug use prevalence. *Journal of the American Medical Association, 261,* 3259–3266.

Perry, C. L., & Kelder, S. H. (1992). Primary prevention of substance use. *Annual Review of Addictions Research and Treatment.* New York: Pergamon Press.

Perry, C. L., Kelder, S. H., Murray, D. M., & Klepp, K.-I. (1992). Community-wide smoking prevention: Long-term outcomes of the Minnesota Heart Health Program. *American Journal of Public Health, 82.*

Perry, C. L., Klepp, K.-I., & Sillers, C. (1989). Community-wide strategies for cardiovascular health: The Minnesota Heart Health Youth Program. *Health Education Research, 4* (1), 87–101.

Perry, C. L., & Jessor, R. (1985). The concept of health promotion and the prevention of adolescent drug abuse. *Health Education Quarterly, 12*(2), 169–184.

Peterson, D. R. (1991). Connection and disconnection of research and practice in the education of professional psychologists. *American Psychologist, 46,* 422–429.

Price, R. H., Cowen, E. L., Lorion, R. P., & Ramos-McKay, J. (Eds.) (1988).

14 ounces of prevention: A casebook for practitioners. Washington, DC: American Psychological Association.

Report of the Task Force on Education of Young Adolescents. (1989). *Turning points: Preparing American youth for the 21st century.* Washington, DC: Carnegie Council on Adolescent Development.

Rogers, T., Howard-Pitney, B., & Bruce, B. (1989). *What works? A guide to school-based alcohol and drug abuse prevention curricula.* Stanford, CA: Stanford Center for Research in Disease Prevention.

Rossi, P. H. (1978). Issues in the evaluation of human services delivery. *Evaluation Quarterly, 2,* 573–599.

Rotheram-Borus, M. J. (1988). Assertiveness training with children. In R. H. Price, E. L. Cowen, R. P. Lorion, & J. Ramar McKay (Eds.), *Fourteen ounces of prevention* (pp. 83–97). Washington, DC: American Psychological Association.

Rotter, J. (1954). *Social learning and clinical psychology.* Englewood Cliffs, NJ: Prentice-Hall.

Rutter, M. (1980). *Changing youth in a changing society.* Cambridge, MA: Harvard University Press.

Rutter, M. (1985). Resilience in the face of adversity: Protective factors and resistance to psychiatric disorder. *British Journal of Psychiatry, 147,* 598–611.

Rutter, M. (1987). Psychosocial resilience and protective mechanisms. *American Journal of Orthopsychiatry, 57,* 316–331.

Schlegel, R., & Sanborn, M. (1979). Religious affiliation and adolescent drinking. *Journal of Studies on Alcohol, 40,* 693–703.

Schneider, B. (1992). Didactic methods for enhancing children's peer relations: A quantitative review. *Clinical Psychology Review, 12,* 363–382.

Schorr, L. (1988). *Within our reach: Breaking the cycle of disadvantage.* New York: Doubleday.

Shaw, C. R., & McKay, H. D. (1969). *Juvenile delinquency and urban areas* (rev. ed.). Chicago: University of Chicago Press.

Simcha-Fagan, O., Gersten, J. C., & Langner, T. (1986). Early precursors and concurrent correlates of illicit drug use in adolescents. *Journal of Drug Issues, 16,* 7–28.

Solomon, D., Watson, M., Battistich, V., Schaps, E., & Delucchi, K. (1990, September). *Creating a caring community: A school-based program to promote children's sociomoral development.* Paper presented at the International Symposium on Research on Effective and Responsible Teaching, Fribourg, Switzerland.

Spivack, G., & Shure, M. (1974). *Social adjustment of young children.* San Francisco: Jossey-Bass.

Spivack, G., & Shure, M. (1988). Interpersonal cognitive problem solving. In R. Price, E. Cowen, R. Lorion, & J. Ramos-McKay (Eds.), *14 ounces of prevention: A casebook for practitioners* (pp. 69–82). Washington, DC: American Psychological Association.

Thomas, E., & Elias, M. J. (1990). Graduate training in community psychology: Integrating primary prevention into the training and repertoire of all professional psychologists and social workers. *Community Psychologist, 23,* 30–31.

Tuma, J. M. (1989). Mental health services for children: The state of the art. *American Psychologist, 44,* 188–199.

U.S. Department of Education. (1990). *Growing up drug free: A parent's guide to prevention.* Washington, DC.

Vartiainen, E., Pallonen, U., McAlister, A., & Puska, P. (1990). Eight-year follow-up results of an adolescent smoking prevention program: The North Karelia Youth Project. *American Journal of Public Health, 80,* 78–79.

Walberg, H. J. (1986). What works in a nation still at risk. *Educational Leadership, 44,* 7–11.

Waters, E., & Sroufe, L. A. (1983). Social competence as a developmental construct. *Developmental Review, 3,* 79–97.

Wechsler, H., & McFadden, T. (1979). Patterns of alcohol consumption among the young: High school, college and general population studies. In H. J. Blane & M. E. Chafez (Eds.), *Youth, Alcohol, and Social Policy* (pp. 39–58). New York: Plenum.

Weissberg, R. P., & Allen, J. P. (1986). Promoting children's social skills and adaptive interpersonal behavior. In B. A. Edelstein & L. Michelson (Eds.), *Handbook of prevention* (pp. 153–175). New York: Plenum.

Weissberg, R. P., Caplan, M., & Harwood, R. L. (1991). Promoting competent-enhancing environments: A systems-based perspective on primary prevention. *Journal of Consulting and Clinical Psychology, 59,* 830–841.

Weissberg, R. P., Caplan, M. Z., & Sivo, P. J. (1989). A new conceptual framework for establishing school-based social competence promotion programs. In L. A. Bond & B. E. Compas (Eds.), *Primary prevention and promotion in the schools* (pp. 255–296). Newbury Park, CA: Sage.

Weissberg, R. P., Gesten, E. L., Carnrike, C. L., Toro, P. A., Rapkin, B. D., Davidson, E., & Cowen, E. L. (1981). Social problem solving skills training: A competence-building intervention with second- to fourth-grade children. *American Journal of Community Psychology, 9,* 411–423.

Weissberg, R. P., Jackson, A. S., & Shriver, T. P. (1993). Promoting positive social development and health practices in young urban adolescents. In

M. J. Elias (Ed), *Social decision making and life skills development: Guidelines for middle school educators* (pp. 45–77). Gaithersburg, MD: Aspen.

Werner, E. E. (1989). High-risk children in young adulthood: A longitudinal study from birth to 32 years. *American Journal of Orthopsychiatry, 59,* 72–81.

Westchester County Social Competence in the Schools Task Force. (1990). *Promoting social development in elementary school children.* Westchester County, NY: Department of Community Mental Health.

White, B. (1988). *Educating the infant and toddler.* Lexington, MA: Lexington Books.

The White House. (1990). *National goals for education.* Washington, DC: National Commission on Excellence in Education.

Wholey, J. S. (1987). Evaluability assessment: Developing program theory. In L. Bickman (Ed.), *Using program theory in evaluation: New Directions for Program Evaluation* (no. 33). San Francisco: Jossey-Bass.

Zigler, E., & Berman, W. (1983). Discerning the future of early childhood intervention. *American Psychologist, 38,* 894–906.

Zill, N., & Schoenborn, C. A. (1990). Developmental, learning, and emotional problems: Health of our nation's children, United States, 1988. *Advance data from vital and health statistics* (No. 190). Hyattsville, MD: National Center for Health Statistics.

Zins, J. E., & Forman, S. (1988). Mini-series on primary prevention in the schools: From theory to practice. *School Psychology Review, 17*(4), 539–634.

Zins, J. E., & Ponti, C. R. (1990). Best practices in school-based consultation. In A. Thomas & J. Grimes (Eds.), *Best practices in school psychology – II* (pp. 673–694). Washington, DC: National Association of School Psychologists.

9

Intervention research: Lessons from research on children with chronic disorders

I. Barry Pless and Ruth E. K. Stein

In this chapter we examine interventions that aim to improve the psychological and social functioning of children at risk. One such group includes those who have, or have had, a chronic physical illness. The broad aim is to use interventions for this population as an example of what has been accomplished in intervention research generally, and to consider issues for future research.

Definitions and concepts

The definition of chronic illness is more complex than it may first appear. The most common is that used by the National Health Interview Survey, in which all conditions lasting longer than 3 months are designated as chronic (Wilder, 1972). This encompasses a very large range of disorders such as diabetes, asthma, hemophilia, cystic fibrosis, cerebral palsy, and muscular dystrophy.

Defining the term *maladjustment* can be equally arbitrary. In most studies, no clear distinctions are made between "emotional disorders," "behavioral disorders," or "psychosocial problems." Generally, the concept of maladjustment is defined operationally by the measures used including assessments of behavioral pathology, self-concept, and self-esteem; only rarely is there a formal clinical assessment of emotional disturbance. Moreover, morbidity is rarely measured at more than two points in time. Through the use of these definitions, the risk for secon-

I. Barry Pless is Professor of Pediatrics and Epidemiology at the Montreal Children's Hospital and Ruth E. K. Stein is Professor and Vice-Chairman of Pediatrics at the Albert Einstein College of Medicine.

dary emotional problems among children with chronic disorders has consistently been shown to be significantly greater than among children without such disorders and, consequently, they comprise a group who are clearly "at risk."

The term *intervention* as defined refers to "the set of actions that have the intent or effect of altering the course of, coming between, or interrupting future activities or processes" (*American Heritage Dictionary*, 1982, p. 672). Studying these alterations not only provides evidence of what works and what does not, but should also yield a better understanding of the processes that place children at increased psychological or social risk.

Thus, the interventions being considered are primarily those intended to prevent secondary disabilities, that is, to reduce the mental health morbidity of the children and their families. They include all those that alter or affect the risk of poor outcomes by protecting normal developmental processes in the face of stressful situations.

Intervention strategies and targets

Several aspects of the notion of intervention must be considered. Gordon describes three levels of interventions: *generalized* or universal interventions provided to everyone; *selected* interventions that are offered to a subset believed to be at risk; and *targeted* interventions directed to those at very high risk (Gordon, 1983). The nature of the problem and knowledge about whom to target, and when, influences the method of intervention chosen.

Accordingly, one way to think about interventions is to consider them in the context of a three-dimensional matrix that allows for combinations of target, type, and timing – who, what and when. "Who" refers to the target of the intervention: the child, parents, health care delivery system, or society. There are two components to the "what" dimension. The first relates to the nature of the actions involved and the second to what it is that needs to be modified. The first of these ranges from one-on-one counseling or psychotherapy to legislation or other social policy initiatives. The second aspect of the "what" dimension is the target behavior or aspect of the functioning of the child (or family) we seek to change. Here a somewhat arbitrary distinction is often made between physical functioning or, still more narrowly, treatment of the underlying disease, and psychosocial functioning. "When" refers to the timing of the intervention, and it is this dimension that permits a distinction to be made between therapeutic initiatives and those aimed at prevention.

In this chapter the terms intervention and treatment are used in the broadest possible sense. Our focus is on treatments that aim to improve the mental health and functioning of the child or the family and encompass all the combinations just described, with one important exception. Narrowly defined biomedical therapies, such as medications or surgery directed at biologic outcomes, are excluded. We do, however, consider some high-technology treatments because these may introduce a range of problems germane to the child's psychosocial functioning.

However, as stated, it is not our intention to evaluate biomedical interventions directly. There is a large literature assessing the efficacy of different forms of medical therapy (e.g., drugs or surgery), usually based on clinical trials. A smaller group of studies addresses the means by which this information is transmitted to, and adopted by others, both within and beyond the medical community (Lamas et al., 1992). In general we assume that conventional state of the art biomedical therapy is always available and affordable. While this is clearly not always the situation, and in spite of occasional spectacular successes, most chronic illnesses still cannot be prevented and medical therapy plays a limited role in modifying their impact on overall functioning of children. For some patients – for example, children with diabetes – it is possible that optimal therapy with perfect compliance effectively eliminates most symptoms and may sharply limit long-term physical sequelae. In many others, however, traditional medical therapy makes relatively little difference in functional outcome.

An intermediate category of interventions includes a variety of nonmedical services also intended to reduce the impact of the disorder on the child's functioning. For example, some psychological techniques may alter the presentation of a disease, such as attacks of asthma (J. Perrin, MacLean, & Perrin, 1989), or episodes of diabetic ketoacidosis (White, Kolman, Wexler, Polin, & Winter, 1984). In time these might be regarded as an extension of the "medical" approach. Unfortunately, therapy of this nature is rarely part of routine care for these children. Instead, the main strategy has been to develop programs that aim to prevent or modify the psychological consequences of the underlying condition.

Who is the target of the intervention?

Although the main target is, almost invariably, the child, it is important to note that the methods employed are not restricted to those involving the child alone. When the domain of primary interest involves psychosocial functioning, many strategies concentrate on parents, the whole family, the school, or the community. Thus, it is no longer reasonable to think of intervention only in terms of what happens in clinical settings, or in dyadic relationships between intervener and child.

What is the modality employed?

Clinicians usually think mainly in terms of the treatments provided for individual patients and, occasionally, for their families or patient groups. While this may include counseling provided by themselves or others such (clinical) interventions are only one component of the universe of maneuvers available. Many programs attempt to help children by involving groups of patients with similar problems, or their families.

Other interventions lie beyond the individual and groups in organizations, institutions, and policies whose programs may influence outcomes by bringing about social change. Such interventions have potential impact in both therapeutic and prevention roles.

The timing of interventions and their intent

The concept of intervention must also be widened to include prevention. In some respects, prevention could be viewed as one member of a family of interventions, distinguished only by their timing. While some would prefer to isolate work aimed exclusively at primary prevention and reserve the term intervention for techniques used to treat existing problems, this narrows the scope unreasonably. At a minimum, it seems appropriate to also consider secondary and tertiary prevention programs.

In a conventional clinical model, treatment (in this case what may be viewed as "psychotherapy" in the broadest sense) is offered only after the child becomes symptomatic. Emotional difficulties, if sufficiently distressing, alert the physician to seek assistance, usually from mental health colleagues. Treatment is then provided if such services are available and if the family agrees to accept help. However, there is still considerable reluctance to recognize and treat mental health problems, and among those with chronic illness, this reluctance occurs on the part of practitioners as well as families (Sabbeth & Stein, 1990).

In contrast, preventive programs are typically offered earlier, before the clinical need is apparent or before symptoms have become severe. This requires that they address a much larger target group – all those who may eventually have emotional problems. An alternative is to provide such preventive services at times of greatest stress, for example, at developmental transitions such as school entry or the onset of puberty.

The clinical and practical implications of treatment versus prevention differ greatly; both are equally important, although generally, preventive programs remain relatively neglected.

The need to identify risk factors

Because both therapeutic or preventive interventions are rarely available for all children who might need them, much research in the chronic illness-maladjustment area is based on the search for subgroups at greatest risk. To date, the extent to which some illnesses, in combination with other attributes or risk factors, generate significantly greater risks remains uncertain. Implicit in the search for risk factors is the notion that this will improve the ability to intervene effectively. This is so because the illness itself can rarely be prevented, and its biologic impact can only be diminished to a limited degree. Thus, one logical alternative is to seek ways to reduce risk by enhancing coping or reducing the stress of those viewed as most vulnerable or at highest risk.

While the search for risk factors has been the dominant theme of much of the research in this field for the past 3 decades, a fair conclusion is that the results have been largely disappointing. For example, the intuitive notion that severity of illness would help predict those at greatest risk for maladjustment has not been confirmed and some studies even conclude that it is those with intermediate levels of disability who are at greatest risk (e.g., McAnarney, Pless, Satterwhite, & Friedman, 1974). Others have proposed that visibility or the presence of socially stigmatizing disorders would be salient, but neither has been confirmed. The same is true for many other obvious candidates: age of onset, duration, or the nature of the disorder, especially with respect to the extent to which the central nervous system is involved. Here, too, some disagreement persists.

One of the few risk factors that appears to have been identified with some consistency is family function (Pless, Roghmann, Haggerty, 1972), but even this remains unconfirmed. In an important study by Rutter (1979), six family variables were significantly associated with subsequent psychiatric disorders: severe marital discord, low socioeconomic status, overcrowding or large family size, parental criminality, maternal psychiatric disorder, and the admission of the child into foster care. In another context Rutter (1977) suggested that, at least in the case of those with central nervous system disorder, such risk factors might be additive or multiplicative. A similar (but longer) list of what, in epidemiologic terms, might be viewed as risk factors were found to be predictive of IQ scores in a longitudinal study conducted in Rochester by Sameroff et al. (Sameroff, Seiffer, Barucas, Sax, & Greenspan, 1987). Both studies suggest that the effect of stressors or risk factors is cumulative: The more that are present, the greater the effect. Such findings provide guidance to the development of intervention programs, if some practical means can be found to eliminate all or some of these factors.

Others have noted that the epidemiology of chronic physical disorders is such that they occur with somewhat increased frequency among children who are also at higher risk for maladjustment because of another popular risk factor – poverty. Here the research support is generally more clear-cut but it is difficult to be certain whether it is poverty as such that constitutes the risk or other factors associated with it.

For example, the findings from the Ontario Child Health Survey of 3,294 randomly sampled children revealed that for those with a chronic disorder, the age- and sex-adjusted odds ratios for one or more psychiatric disorders was 2.1 (Cadman, Boyle, Szatmari, &

Offord, 1987). The odds ratio for those with a disorder accompanied by disability (e.g., some functional impairment) was, not unexpectedly, higher: 3.4. The increase in risk for neurotic disorders, social isolation, and low competence was notably high, especially for those with disability. In the face of poverty, these ratios increased still further.

In spite of such disturbing figures, the proportion of all child or adolescent psychiatric illness that would disappear if all chronic physical disorders were prevented or cured is only 9%. Accordingly, the reverse of the coin is equally interesting: The majority of children with these disorders appears to manifest no negative emotional consequences. This introduces the concept of resilience – one that will be considered in greater detail in the following section.

In summary, although children with a chronic physical disorder have higher than average mental health problems, it has not yet been determined definitively which factors place such children at increased risk for adverse emotional outcomes. And even if it were possible to identify these subgroups, it is not yet clear what kinds of interventions would be the most appropriate. Some convincing arguments favor various nonspecific approaches intended to enhance coping, but evidence of their success is limited. In all cases, the most promising approach depends on their being built on a sound theoretical model.

Theoretical considerations

Many approaches to children with these disorders are heavily influenced by the noncategorical school of thought (Pless & Pinkerton 1975; Stein & Jessop, 1982). This reflects the view that it is the chronicity of the disease and its characteristics or dimensions that matters most and that the nature of the specific disorder is much less important. Accordingly, the reader should not be surprised to discover that all the key studies reviewed in this chapter include a large variety of conditions.

The basis for this framework and the need to intervene to assist children with these disorders is based on the view that the presence of a chronic illness is a significant stressor – one that increases the demand for adaptation and coping.

A generic approach to intervention based on this notion draws on the views proposed by Kaplan and Cassel (1975). Their theory is based on the view "that susceptibility to a wide variety of diseases and disorders (including somatic as well as emotional and behavioral disorders) is influenced by a combination of exposure to psychosocial stressful situations and the protection afforded against these situations by adequate social supports" (p. 2). Accordingly, in recent years much interest has focused around the idea that enhancing social support might be part of the answer.

One attempt to follow this line of thinking is the development of support networks. These include parent and patient groups intended to give mutual support and assistance. However, surprisingly few studies have attempted to evaluate this strategy. Even if they were shown to have beneficial effects it seems unlikely that the results could be generalized because such groups are usually self-selected. Thus, those most likely to benefit may choose to become involved, whereas others in equal or greater need would not seek or accept help of this kind. Such problems of selective enrollment and its effects on the interpretation of these (and, indeed, all) intervention trials have been discussed by Stein, Bauman, and Ireys (1991).

The goal then is to examine interventions, broadly defined, aimed at enhancing the lives of children with chronic physical disorders and those of their families. Interest in these children arises from a large and still growing body of evidence that suggests they are at increased risk for a wide range of adverse life experiences. Much of the work focuses on psychosocial functioning of the child, but some studies are concerned with effects on other members of the family – parents and siblings – and still others on the impact on these children on society. Although in the past it was common to view the relationship between these illnesses and maladjustment as an example of the stress–coping paradigm, in recent years there has arisen an interest in risk, resilience, and development – an approach that may be viewed as the "flip side" of vulnerability.

Garmezy (1991) describes the construct as one "designed to represent a reality that many children exposed to . . . [stressful situations] continue to make positive adaptations to such stressors." He explains that "to speak of resilience does not necessarily reflect an imperviousness to stress. Rather, it is designed to reflect the capacity for recovery and maintained adaptive behavior that may follow initial retreat or incapacity upon initiating a stressful event." Garmezy adds, "Knowledge about these intriguing subgroups represents what is now termed resilience or stress resistance. However, these terms are not synonymous with invulnerability."

Evolving from this framework is a set of three propositions, each of which relates stress, personal attributes, and competence to maladjustment (Garmezy, Masten, & Tellegen, 1984). The first is referred to as the "compensatory model"; the second as the "challenge model" (in which limited amounts of stress are seen as a "potential enhancer" of competence); and the third is described as an "immunity-versus-vulnerability" model. In it, personal attributes are postulated as serving to dampen or increase the effects of stress.

Apart from this and other stress and coping models, a number of others have been proposed although most are simply variations on the main theme. For example, the approach proposed by Wallender et al. (Wallender, Varni, Babani, Banis, & Wilcox, 1989) also views the combined effects of risk and resistance factors as serving to produce either competence or maladjustment. In contrast, Shontz (1971) treats physical disorders as moderating variables (i.e., those that alter typical relationships between other sets of factors common to healthy children).

Others, such as LaGreca (1990), observe that most previous studies fail to place sufficient emphasis on some aspects of existing models. Specifically, LaGreca argues that more attention must be paid first, to the role of peers in disease adaptation and treatment management and, second, to those aspects of the illness or its treatments that affect social functioning. Although her report tends to ignore methodologic shortcomings in many of the studies reviewed, few would disagree with her conclusions that future studies should pay more attention to the factors cited here. It is also easy to agree that there is a need to incorporate assessments of specific social behaviors and disease-related tasks in future studies; to consider developmental issues; and, increasingly, to use longitudinal designs.

Controversy about theoretical models does, however, highlight a common problem in research involving interventions. The theoretical models in most studies of psychological or social risk are complex, poorly understood, or inconsistently applied. Each of these has implications for the design and implementation of interventions. They also affect their evaluation, and the level of conclusions that can be drawn when interventions fail to achieve their intended effects. This is a topic to which we will return at the end of this chapter.

Broad-based social interventions

Before we consider social interventions, it is important to acknowledge that it is extremely difficult to evaluate them objectively. Conventional procedures based on, for example, epidemiologic principles, can rarely be applied in this setting. Texts devoted to estimating the effects of social interventions (Judd & Kenny, 1981; Weiss, 1972) rely on the same basic principles as are used in conventional epidemiologic research. When opportunities for some form of quasi experimentation are sharply limited, only case studies remain as a basis for evaluation. Nonetheless, these social interventions may be of such importance that they cannot be ignored just because they are difficult to measure. Accordingly, it is unreasonable to adopt any single set of evaluation criteria to assess what has been accomplished, especially in this domain.

Public policy interventions

We focus first on interventions in the public policy arena and consider several examples from recent national activities in the United States. A series of major legislative and judicial actions in the United States have created important changes in the range of services and procedures for providing services to children with chronic disorders.

PL 94-142, the Education for All Handicapped Children Act, obligates local communities to provide educational services to those with special educational needs, as well as to those who are at risk of having such difficulties if they lack access to special services. Further, the law requires that the education be provided through public financing and in the least restrictive environment. This was the first major public mandate to insure education access for large numbers of students "at risk."

The law has important ramifications for children with chronic physical disorders. It mandates many services, but it does not insure consistency across individual jurisdictions in the manner in which these mandates are implemented (Singer & Butler, 1987). For example, although medical treatments are theoretically available in school, the law does not insure that children will uniformly receive such treatment in the school. In some school systems in the United States children still cannot receive medications. Nor does the legislation require schools to provide easy transition from home instruction to school instruction in situations in which there are frequent health-related absences. Nevertheless, the net effect of this legislation has been a dramatic increase in early identification and access to improved educational services for many children, but because of the flaws described in its implementation it falls short of the goal intended.

Another effect of this legislation, and the later amendments to the act in PL 99-457, is to change the professional personnel responsible for the at-risk population. Until the adoption of PL 94-142, the major agent for the management of children with a chronic disorder was the physician. (Although physicians were never seriously involved in addressing educational issues, it was widely assumed that in providing truly comprehensive care at least some of these would be addressed.) The first of these two legislative acts shifted the responsibility to the educational community. Furthermore, the later legislation, PL 99-457, provided that the lead agency be determined by each state. Thus, it changed the balance of responsibilities. In some cases, in David Mechanic's terms, this served to partially demedicalize some aspects of the care of these children. Although intended to assure that *someone* is responsible, it places the medical providers in a less central role, and sometimes they serve as consultants. Further, there is no mechanism to insure that the communication bridges necessary for optimal coordination of care will be built or maintained.

A second major legislative initiative involves the Omnibus Reconciliation Act (OBRA) of 1989. This legislation redefined the responsibility for Title V programs (Children with Special Health Needs Programs) making each state responsible for *systems* of care, including the coordination and monitoring of care for all children with special health care needs. It also mandates a community-based and family-centered approach. This is a radical departure from the Title V programs of the past, which were not system-based and which produced an inconsistent patchwork of services and standard-setting activities. Moreover, OBRA 1989 required that 30% of Title V Maternal and Child Health Bureau funds be earmarked for the subpopulation of children with special health needs.

A final policy initiative to be considered is the U.S. Supreme Court Decision in *Sullivan v. Zebley* (1990). This decision overturned the Social Security Administration's regulations for qualifying children for Supplemental Security Income (SSI) benefits as too restrictive. It held that children should be eligible for SSI if their functioning was sufficiently impaired, irrespective of their ability to qualify on the basis of any single diagnosis on a list. (It is noteworthy that the Court used the language of a William T. Grant Foundation Consortium paper in its ruling.) The decision has already led to over 200,000 additional children qualifying for SSI benefits. Further, in most states this has led, directly or indirectly, to having many more children qualify for Medicaid, as well as a number of other service benefits or entitlements. In addition, it means that almost a half-million applicants who have been denied benefits since 1982 are now being reconsidered for retroactive benefits (Perrin & Stein, 1991).

Health service, insurance, and parental leave

In addition, there is a wide range of state-level initiatives that address changes in health care delivery, insurance mechanisms, and parental leave policies. All of these public policy initiatives affect the lives of children with chronic disorders in a substantial way and it is reasonable to assume that they will influence their overall well-being and adjustment.

Yet virtually none of the initiatives has been subjected to careful evaluation, and the few outstanding examples of attempted evaluations, such as the Collaborative Study (Butler et al., 1985; Butler, Singer, Palfrey, & Walker, 1987; Singer & Butler, 1987), have been geared more to assess implementation, rather than their impact on developmental or behavioral outcomes. It is more the rule than the exception that there is little direct interaction between the research community's evaluative or theoretically driven research activities and the implementation of public initiatives such as these, which may actually overwhelm the effects of most smaller-scale interventions.

Nonlegislative forces

The same is true of the dramatic nonlegislative forces that are currently changing the financing of health care services. Although, for example, the Rand Corporation's assessment has examined the effect of different insurance alternatives on health outcomes generally, virtually none of the conclusions can be extrapolated to the population of children with special health needs (Anderson, Brook, & Williams, 1991; Valdez et al., 1985). What little evidence there is suggests that the move towards health maintenance organizations may offer few benefits and many liabilities for this group of children (Horowitz & Stein, 1990; Schlesinger, 1986).

Other influences are those related to changing patterns of service within health care establishments. These include changes brought about within the profession with respect to manpower or the delivery of services. Major changes have resulted from the emergence of expensive technologies and their application to a wide range of clinical problems. These often dictate the state of the art of care as, for example, when it became standard practice to move high-risk mothers to hospitals that have tertiary-care nurseries. One consequence is that children who are technology-dependent as a result of being born prematurely would be more likely to survive. They would, however, for the most part, be separated geographically from their home communities. The effect of this on their long-term development is only now being assessed. As standards of care change, the research community is conducting intervention research on a moving stage – one on which both the questions and the subjects are changing.

Another category of intervention that should be considered, is the more indirect effects of social and economic forces. For example, the changing economic climate, increasing numbers of single-parent families, child-care alternatives, and their ability or willingness to accommodate the needs of children with ongoing health conditions may all have critical effects. Here, too, the effects of these forces may be far more important than the molecular processes we are attempting to understand and influence at the clinical level.

It is worth noting again that unlike more typical therapies, the targets of these intervention efforts focus on systems, rather than individuals. Some are geared to specific service sites (e.g., hospitals or schools) and others to communities as a whole. Because of the nature of these targets, as has been stated, it may prove virtually impossible to apply rigorous scientific criteria to evaluate their effects. At best, we are often left with inferring their effects from quasi-experimental data.

Finally, it is important to consider the effects of medical technology itself in the care and treatment of the underlying physical disorders. New treatments, such as home dialysis or portable ventilators, bring with them the opportunity for changing both biological and psychological outcomes. They may increase the psychological burden on families in exchange for physiological improvement. As these boundaries redefine the nature of our research questions, they inevitably change the platform on which research is conducted. It is against this background that other manipulations and interventions must be assessed.

Clinical interventions

In 1986 a critical appraisal of studies describing the risk that chronic disorders confer for maladjustment was published (Nolan & Pless, 1986). This was later expanded to include the relatively few studies that describe interventions addressed to this problem (Pless & Nolan, 1991). More recently a meta-analytic approach was also used to examine this body of research (Lavigne & Faier-Routman, 1992). All the findings confirm the presence of significant risk for various kinds of emotional disturbance in the presence of a chronic illness.

Throughout many of these studies, the investigators searched for specific psychiatric outcomes and for clear predictors of these outcomes. The former proved fruitless (Pless & Nolan, 1991), whereas some analyses from the meta-analytic study suggest that "when considered as sets, disease/disability variables, child variables, and family/parent variables each make statistically significant contributions to the prediction of maladjustment." Unfortunately, as was stated in the section on risk factors, this conclusion is not widely supported by the findings of others.

Accordingly, the main cause of emotional problems among these children is still assumed to be the existence of any condition that is chronic. Nevertheless, many studies continue to search for more specific attributes that further define the risk in this population. Such indicators may derive from demographic characteristics of the child, biologic factors, personal susceptibility, or from a consideration of the social or medical environment. Each of these has been examined in detail elsewhere and the findings need not be repeated here. In general, while the yield from this body of work has been intriguing, few findings are sufficiently clear-cut to permit the identification of clinical subgroups with the precision needed to serve as a basis for more efficient intervention strategies.

This body of work is pertinent to a consideration of interventions because a full understanding of these determinants would undoubtedly stimulate the construction of targeted therapeutic or preventive programs. Only when we know with reasonable certainty the prevalence and relative potency of these or other risk factors can focused approaches become feasible. Without such knowledge tactics are necessarily global, and this may partly explain why the reviews failed to identify more than a handful of intervention studies of significant scope or magnitude.

In the first two reviews, considerable attention was paid to the research designs and less to the types of maladjustment studied. Only a few of the reports used a cohort design, or were true population-based prevalence surveys. Fewer still were experimental or quasi experimental. Most studies were cross-sectional or case series. Despite the paucity of studies with powerful designs, however, most reach the same conclusion: "that a causal relationship exists between chronic disorders and emotional problems" (Pless & Nolan, 1991).

The sections that follow summarize findings from several of the principal studies involving interventions aimed at the prevention of these problems. Although a few make reference to support groups, many are based on identifying someone to serve as a "therapist" whose goal is to offer therapy, counseling, or nonspecific support to the child or family. Others rely on educational or training approaches. To some extent the results arrive at what appear to be different conclusions regarding the efficacy of the services provided but in the concluding section an attempt is made to resolve these seeming discrepancies. The descriptions that follow are based in part on the report by Pless and Nolan (1991), and thereafter, we offer some examples of targeted clinical studies.

Global clinical interventions

Family counselors. Several studies by Pless and Satterwhite grappled with the problem of how to effect positive change in the emotional status of children with chronic illnesses (Pless & Satterwhite, 1972; Pless & Satterwhite, 1975a). Their novel approach employed nonprofessional ("lay") persons ("middle-aged, middle-class women") who were trained to act as child and family advocates and counselors. The intervention was prompted by findings from a study of a random, population-based sample of 209 chronically ill children (with disorders of many types) that disclosed a striking need for many forms of assistance. These included "explanations about the nature of the child's illness; the utilization of various supportive, professional, and para-professional workers; effective coordination of existing services; help with behavioral and educational problems; and above all, the therapeutic benefits to the mother of a sympathetic listener" (Pless & Satterwhite, 1975b).

As a result, six counselors – women from 32 to 51 years of age, all with their own families, and all with a university education – were chosen to provide the intervention over a 1-year period. They received five 6-hour training sessions and worked an average 10 hours per week, each with 8 families. Approximately 55% of their time was spent providing education, counseling, and psychotherapy. The evaluation included 42 control families with chronic illnesses who received standard services. Assignment was random, following stratification on a measure of family functioning. Pretest and posttest evaluations used a battery of paper-and-pencil behavioral measures to construct an overall index. Using this measure, 60% of those in a counseled group showed improvement in their psychological status compared with only 41% of controls. The remainder in each group showed deterioration. It is of interest that the amount of improvement was greatest in low-risk (i.e., fewer problem) families.

Based on these favorable results, this service was subsequently adapted for several specialty clinics and, though not objectively evaluated, was described as "successful." In spite of these encouraging findings, the counselor program has never been replicated, although a similar strategy, also using nonprofessional women, was used to help prevent child abuse. To our knowledge this intervention has not been implemented elsewhere for children with chronic disorders. In part this may be because it is difficult to find a mechanism for paying nonprofessionals from conventional hospital budgets but, as will be discussed later, reasons for nonadoption are more complex.

Pediatric Ambulatory Care Treatment Study (PACTS). In the PACTS study over 200 children with a wide range of chronic disorders were randomly allocated to receive either a comprehensive home care program or standard care (Stein & Jessop, 1984). The former provided coordination of care by a pediatrician and nurse practitioner and sought to foster patient independence and maximize adjustment through the provision of a broad range of primary care services using a combined biomedical and psychological approach. The intervention continued for a minimum of 6 months. Pretest and posttest data were collected on three occasions – baseline (prerandomization), 6 months, and 12 months. The measures employed included the Personal Adjustment and Role Skills Scale (PARS II) for children 5 and over, and the Psychiatric Symptom Index for mothers. After adjusting for pretest scores, home care subjects did significantly better at 6 months on both child and maternal measures, but the results were less impressive at 12 months. The adjusted mean PARS total scores for the standard and home care groups at 6 months were 65.9 and 69.4 respectively, compared with 65.4 and 68.7 at 12 months. In a subsequent report, however, the investigators provide further evidence for the efficacy of this intervention (Stein & Jessop, 1991). At an average of 5 years following randomization, the 49 subjects available for retest on the PARS II yielded results with large and statistically significant scores favoring those who had received the PACTS program. Using ANCOVA, the adjusted posttest means were 67.0 for the standard care children versus 74.5 for those in the home care group. This offers gratifying evidence for the pronounced, enduring, and measurable benefit of comprehensive psychosocial care for these children. Another finding from this study was that the greatest benefit was derived by those whose illness burden was small and whose coping resources were low. As the authors note, this suggests "that the conventional priority of allocating intervention resources to the medically most burdensome cases may not always be maximally beneficial" (Jessop & Stein, 1991). Again, in spite of the clear positive findings, there has been little evidence that the PACTS strategy has been adopted elsewhere.

Social workers. A study was conducted in Montreal to evaluate the effectiveness of social workers in this domain (Nolan, Zvagulis, & Pless, 1987). After children with many different chronic illnesses were stratified by illness type, they were randomly assigned to experimental or control groups, and those in the intervention group then further randomly assigned to one of four social workers for 6 months. These received counseling and support services intended to enhance self-concept and minimize family stress. Effectiveness was assessed principally by comparing, among other measures, changes in scores on the Child Behavior Checklist (CBCL) before the intervention with those 6 months after the intervention. An additional study, seeking possible "lag effects," was conducted after a further interval of 18 months.

At none of the time points, however, were there any statistically significant differences in favor of the experimental group on the CBCL or any of the secondary measures used. Although the help of the social workers was warmly received by most families, it is likely that they were ineffective when assessed objectively, either because the period of intervention was too brief or because the nature of the services needed was not well suited to professionals accustomed to "crisis intervention" situations.

The McGill Nursing Trial. In view of the latter concerns, a similar trial was conducted using nurses as interveners (Pless et al., 1993). The specific goal was to determine whether nurses, all of whom were trained in a program whose orientation is characterized as "unique" (the McGill model) (Gottlieb & Rowat, 1987), would be able to modify the psychosocial adjustment of children with a chronic illness and/or to enhance the parenting competence or self-esteem of the mother. The subjects were 4- to 16-year-olds with a wide variety of chronic disorders drawn from nine hospital specialty clinics. Consenting families were interviewed, and baseline measures administered. Subjects were then stratified by clinic and assigned randomly to intervention or control groups. Within clinic strata, intervention subjects were further randomly assigned to one of three nurses who then provided supplementary services over the succeeding 12-month period. Control subjects received routine services of the specialty clinic, as required. At the conclusion of the study a second, blinded interview took place and the battery of measures was readministered. An additional questionnaire assessed the parent's perception of the service provided and, to further understand the changes that occurred, in-depth interviews were also conducted with a selected subsample in the intervention group.

The three nurses selected had been oriented within a preventive model that focused on developing the child's self-esteem, building family resources, facilitating family functioning, and enhancing access to other professional services. Criteria were established to ensure that all subjects received a basic and uniform level of support. This consisted of a 12-month intervention period, an initial home assessment, one home visit within the first 3 months, one home visit during the last 3 months, and monthly phone calls. As well, all received any additional contacts they required.

Several outcomes were considered. The primary outcome measure was the Child Behavior Checklist (CBCL). Others included the Master Family Assessment Device (FAD); the Goldberg Health Index to assess maternal well-being (anxiety and depression); the Personal Adjustment and Role Skills Scale (PARS III); the Abidin Parental Stress Index (PSI); and Harter's Perceived Competence Scale.

The results indicate that while the nurses did not seem particularly effective in improving scores on the CBCL, they were somewhat effective in reducing the number with deteriorating scores – that is, they had greater success in a preventive as opposed to therapeutic role. Following ANCOVA, in which pretest scores were included as covariates, the F-ratio for posttest PARS III scores was 6.8 ($p < .01$) while for CBCL Sum T scores it was only 0.6 (NS). For children with CBCL scores that were abnormal at the outset (i.e., within the "clinical" range), the program's effectiveness was evident in the greater number of scores that improved and the fewer that worsened.

These results provide modest support for concluding that the intervention positively influenced psychosocial functioning. Unfortunately, no similar benefits were found for maternal competence or self-esteem. And, although it was postulated that the intervention would exert both a therapeutic and preventive effect, only the latter was found. In the intervention group, 3.9% of children exhibited a change in behavioral problems from age-appropriate levels to the clinical range over time, compared with 8.6% of the controls.

To what extent may these findings be related to changes in self-concept? On the younger version of the Perceived Competence Scale, the mean score of the intervention group deteriorated on the peer acceptance subscale, although this was not consistent with the results from the PARS III peer relation subscale, and on the older version of Harter's measure there were, again, no significant differences between group mean change scores. Thus a further question is how much might the changes be attributable to effects on the mothers? Unfortunately, the nurses' effect on maternal competence and self-esteem, as measured by the PSI, also failed to show any significant differences.

PIRC Studies. The Preventive Intervention Research Center for Child Health (PIRC) at the Albert Einstein College of Medicine has implemented and evaluated several interventions to prevent mental health problems in children with serious ongoing health conditions and their families. Three programs, LEAP, STEP, and TEEN, all focus on developmental transitions, based on the view that these are important times of increased risk for children with physical disorders. Each program is characterized by high participation rates, low attrition, and excellent fidelity.

The Low Birthweight Evaluation and Assessment Program (LEAP) is a randomized controlled trial of a hospital-based preventive intervention for mothers who have given birth to very low birthweight infants (< 1,700 grams). The goals are to (1) prevent psychiatric disorder among mothers of these very premature infants; (2) enhance developmental outcomes of the infants; (3) facilitate healthy maternal–infant interaction; (4) prevent "vulnerable child" syndrome; and (5) maintain the infant in medical follow-up to permit the identification of physical or developmental problems that may result from prematurity.

To achieve this the program provides support, educational guidance, and coordination of care through the intensive involvement of a nurse intervener (NI). The NI approaches eligible new mothers within 48 hours of the birth to provide information about the Neonatal Intensive Care Unit (NICU), and to offer emotional support. She helps mothers identify the many people in the NICU and how they are involved in the care of her baby. The NI works with the mother and infant for 2 years, offering six standard "modules" of information and guidance that focus on the infant's growth and development. She also is available to mothers "on demand" to answer questions, provide support, and to be with them during medical or family crises.

Preliminary results suggest that mothers receiving the intervention are less anxious than control mothers, and that among treated mothers those who were more emotionally disturbed initially improve the most. Further, the intervention group mothers demonstrate more adaptive feeding interactions at 6 months' corrected gestational age.

STEP, "Sharing the Experience of Parenting," is a randomized trial of a home-based intervention for mothers of children 5 to 8 years of age whose children have chronic health problems, such as asthma, diabetes, spina bifida, and sickle cell disease. The goals are to (1) prevent mental health problems in the mothers, (2) reduce behavioral problems in the children, and (3) enhance mothers' confidence and competence in dealing with their children. Lay interveners who have themselves successfully raised children with such problems were trained to deliver this 1-year supportive intervention to mothers as part of a parent-to-parent network. The intervention consists of intensive interaction between the intervener and mother around a set of standardized topics identified through qualitative interviews with mothers (e.g., parenting and discipline, school issues, dealing with the health care system, getting through hard times). The interveners meet face-to-face with mothers and have extensive telephone contact between visits. They provide information, affirmation of the mother's skills, and emotional support. Three times a year a "family event" is held, with food, entertainment, and time for sharing issues and concerns. These events include all family members of intervention mothers. Three hundred sixty families have been enrolled in the study in three cohorts and 95% of the first cohort have completed the third round of data collection. Mothers in the intervention group have shown improved self-efficacy and self-esteem, and less stress compared with control mothers (Ireys, Silver, Stein, Bencivenga, & Koeber, 1991).

The "Teen Education and Employment Network" (TEEN) is a

randomized controlled trial of the effectiveness of a two-part preventive intervention for high-risk adolescents with serious ongoing health conditions. It targets 14- to 17-year-old Bronx youths, and offers a 13-session social skills training program followed by a 4-month job internship in a community facility in a "helping" position. The goals are to (1) prevent psychological disorders among these adolescents, (2) enhance independence and future orientation, (3) increase self-esteem and perceived competence, and (4) enhance employability.

To achieve this, the program helps adolescents to acquire concrete social, listening, and problem-solving skills, to enhance self- and other-awareness, and to build a peer community. Subjects are paid for their participation in the training and graduates are offered a paid job internship for 4 months, 10 hours per week. Most are placed as homework helpers with younger children in community facilities, as geriatric visitors, as peer counselors in an adolescent pregnancy program, and in day-care centers working with young children. Retention at 1 year after the intervention is over 90% and there is evidence of significant improvement in self-esteem and some decreases in mental illness symptoms, as measured by the Behavior Symptom Inventory (Coupey, Bauman, Lauby, Koeber, & Stein, 1991).

Condition-Specific Clinical Interventions

A preliminary review of interventions targeted at specific chronic disorders indicates that since 1980 there were fewer than 20 such reports. For the most part, the designs were extremely weak. Many suffered from insufficient numbers to yield results that are statistically meaningful and many more employed questionable measures. The most consistent important weakness was the absence of randomized assignment of the modality of "therapy" being assessed. In addition, many studies failed to address the psychosocial issues adequately, if at all. The latter shortcoming in particular may be attributed to the fact that many of these studies were led by subspecialists whose main concern was the reduction of physical morbidity.

In the section that follows, the studies selected are not intended to comprehensively represent this body of literature. They are chosen simply to illustrate the range of issues being considered as well as the strengths and weaknesses of this genre of research.

For example, a recent, small, focused trial examined the efficacy of an educational intervention by computer to assist children with asthma (Ruben et al., 1986). The goal was to change how children manage their disease and thus decrease morbidity. An interactive computer game – Asthma Command – was tested on children with and without asthma between 7 and 12 years of age. It addressed four basic principles of management: recognition of symptoms, use of medications, use of the emergency room, and encouraging school attendance. The game simulates 1 day in each season, and to obtain high scores, it forces children to use their knowledge to maneuver through the obstacles presented.

The results indicate improvement in knowledge about the disease, behavior related to its management, and a trend toward the reduction of medical visits for acute attacks. Whether these findings will translate into improved physical morbidity and better psychosocial functioning remains to be seen. However, a review (Howland, Bauchner, & Adair, 1988) of the impact of asthma education programs on the morbidity generated by the disease, as reported in 13 studies, concludes that none showed favorable outcomes. Numerous methodologic criticisms permitted only the cautious conclusion "that some programs do reduce health care utilization among those children with more severe disease." Furthermore, no specific reference is made to possible effects on psychosocial functioning despite the fact that many speculated that with improved understanding would come a sense of greater control, which, in turn, would influence adaptation.

These omissions are the rule, not exceptions. Even many presumably "comprehensive" interventions fail to address social and emotional functioning. For example, in an attempt to assess the impact of a "comprehensive home and ambulatory program" also intended to improve pediatric asthma management, involving randomized assignment of 95 children ages 6 through 16 years, the results only include a reduction in school absenteeism and improved small airway function, as well as better use of metered aerosol medications (Hughes, McLeod, Garner, & Goldloom, 1991). Although the authors note that "more study than control families reported that their asthmatic child took responsibility for . . . asthma management," it is disappointing that the study did not include an attempt to assess the impact this might have on emotional adjustment.

The problem also exists when similar studies are conducted by psychologists. In a randomized trial involving 32 families of adolescents with juvenile onset diabetes (Satin, LaGreca, Zigo, & Skyler, 1989), the effects of various forms of family intervention and parent simulation techniques were assessed. Subjects in one intervention group showed significant decrements in hemoglobin A1 (a measure of diabetic control), whereas those in both intervention groups had more positive perceptions of "a teenager with diabetes" when compared with controls. These subjects reportedly maintained improved care patterns at 6-month follow-up, but, again, there is no mention of effects on psychosocial functioning as such.

The few apparent exceptions frequently arise in nonexperimental studies. For example, Varni, Wilcox, and Hanson (1988) assessed what they refer to as the "mediating effects" of social support on children with rheumatoid arthritis. However, the design is cross-sectional and the study simply involved including measures of social support provided by family and peers into the analyses after adjusting for disease activity. It was found that family support significantly predicted both internalizing and externalizing behavior problems, accounting for a surprisingly high proportion of variance (22%). Although findings such as these may be pertinent when considering the design of prevention programs for children with chronic disorders, the data fail to provide direct evidence of what would happen in a planned intervention.

Two much more convincing studies have recently been published. While both address prematurity – a problem that is not usually considered to be a chronic disorder as such – the sequelae of prematurity, especially very low birth weight, are clearly pertinent. The first is the Infant Health and Development Program (Gross, 1990). This large-scale clinical trial was established to evaluate the efficacy of a comprehensive early intervention in reducing the developmental and health problems of low-birth-weight infants. Its strength lies both in its size, with 985 infants studied at eight sites; its design, which included randomization to intervention and control groups; careful blinding; and the choice of outcome measures. The latter included a measure of cognitive development (the Stanford-Binet); several measures of health status; and, of greatest relevance to this chapter, a measure of behavioral competence – the Child Behavior Checklist. All were administered at 36 months corrected age.

While both groups received the same set of follow-up services, those in the experimental group also received home visits, the child attended a development center, and the parents participated in group meetings. The home visits occurred weekly in the first year and then biweekly. They included the provision of health and developmental information and family support as well as two curricula: One had games and activities for the parent to use with the child to enhance cognitive, linguistic, and social development, and the other involved a systematic approach to the management of problems identified by the parents. Center attendance 5 days a week began at 12 months of age, and permitted the staff to implement the learning activities introduced in the home visits. The parent groups also began at 12 months and were held bimonthly. They provided information and an opportunity for social support.

With respect to the adjustment outcome, the mean score in the follow-up (control) group was 47.2, compared with 43.7 in the intervention group. This difference represents an effect size of $-.18$, which is statistically significant ($p = .006$). This apparently small difference represents an adjusted odds of having an abnormal score (>63) of 1.8 for those in the control group. It is also of interest that higher scores were associated with several baseline variables (certain sites; being black or Hispanic; being male; and lower maternal age and education level). Nevertheless, controlling for these still revealed a significant intervention effect and, notably, only significant interaction – with maternal education. This suggested that the behavioral benefits of the intervention were only demonstrable among less educated mothers.

Richmond (1990) refers to this as a "pioneering" study, not only because of the important results achieved, but also because of the successful application of state-of-the-art design and implementation components. Although he identifies several important additional questions that remain to be answered, including how long the improvements persist and those most likely to benefit from the intervention, he is convinced the findings will have critical policy implications – especially so since the cost of the intervention was not prohibitive.

The second major study also illustrates a critical methodologic point – the importance of considering a developmental phenomenon that may account for "sleeper or lag effects." As the authors explain, "Because important cognitive and behavioral outcomes may not be measurable until later and/or because the effects on transactional patterns may be cumulative over long periods, proper evaluation of interventions . . . may have to continue into developmental periods well beyond those in which the intervention occurs" (Achenbach, Howell, Aoki, & Rauh, 1993). In this study and intervention, the Mother–Infant Transaction Program (MITP), was "designed to optimize caretaking interactions by enhancing mothers' adjustment to their [low-birth-weight] infants." This program was implemented by a nurse in the NICU who "worked with the mother and baby in seven daily sessions during the week prior to the baby's discharge from the hospital, plus four home sessions at 3, 14, 30, and 90 days after discharge." The sessions encouraged the mothers' confidence and comfort with the baby by providing modeling, demonstration of care, verbal instructions, and practical experiences. Clearly, this is much simpler and less intense than the trial described previously.

Although both studies were designed as randomized trials, and both focused on low-birth-weight infants, another important difference is the much smaller number of subjects involved – 40 in each of three groups: low-birth-weight experimental (LBWE) and control (LBWC), and a normal-birth-weight comparison group. It may be that the smaller samples in part account for the delay before significant effects were evident. Overall, the behavior of the children in the LBWE group was rated as superior to that of those in the LBWC group by teachers using the Teacher Report Form.

It must be restated that these few examples are intended only to illustrate the type of work frequently seen in disease-specific studies. A few are better with respect to both design and measures, but many are worse. Not surprisingly, few of the results are sufficiently compelling to prompt their replication or extension in other chronic disorders. Thus, the noncategorical approach, and the studies described that have adopted it, appears to offer the best hope for further advances in this endeavor.

A developmental perspective

When applied to children and adolescents, much of the foregoing only makes sense when seen in a developmental context. The central feature of all phenomena that relate to children is the dynamic background of developmental change. It is what makes research in this area so challenging, because findings are rarely independent of age and stage. Accordingly, it is entirely possible that strategies that appear highly effective in one age group will be found to be ineffective in another. Under these circumstances, in studies that cover a wide age range, the net result may appear unimpressive and, indeed, may be interpreted as negative or nonsignificant. Unfortunately, few intervention studies are sufficiently large to permit the effects in each age group to be examined separately.

Although the notion that developmental stage may be an essential mediator of intervention effects is a compelling consideration, its salience is likely to vary greatly depending on the nature of the intervention. In other words, some programs may be highly age-dependent, whereas others are not. For example, peer counseling is probably only feasible among teenagers, whereas parent support groups should have few, if any, age boundaries.

Implementation issues and other challenges

As has been stated, most efforts in this field are therapeutic, whereas those of greatest interest in this chapter may be conceptualized as preventive interventions. In the latter context, and perhaps less evidently in the former as well, the main unresolved issue is the lack of replication or widespread adoption of those that appear to be of value. A number of explanations for this failure need to be considered, beginning with cost–benefit considerations because, in spite of the rhetoric surrounding prevention, the relative effectiveness of prevention as opposed to intervention is not known.

It is not even clear what steps are needed to insure that the results of evaluation studies are widely known. Although there was much interest in the 1960s in what was called the "sociology of diffusion" of innovations, this issue is now less evident. Bridging the gap is more challenging in the case of prevention strategies, which rarely involve economic benefits, than it is in the case of treatment. As a rule, therapy involving medications is brought to the attention of physicians (and, occasionally, parents and children as well) by pharmaceutical companies seeking to profit from their investment. There is no known parallel for preventive measures, or even for therapies that involve few, if any, economic incentives.

The failure to adopt programs whose value has been demonstrated convincingly by randomized trials should not lead to the conclusion that such trials are a waste of resources. On the contrary, it is the many studies that fail to adopt this design, or others that approximate it, that may be wasteful. Promoting adoption is complex, and scientific merit alone appears to play a relatively minor role. It is, however, important to acknowledge that the absence of replication may be a deterrent. Sensible scientists and clinicians are likely to be cautious about adopting a program whose value has been demonstrated only once, no matter how convincing the data appear to be. Unfortunately, it is difficult to persuade imaginative investigators to replicate someone else's work, and it is often equally difficult to have such work funded or published. Instead, what is often found are studies that are, in essence, "variations on a theme." For example, many key elements in the studies described in the previous (noncategorical) section include ingredients from the pioneering family counselor study, which, in turn, derives from the early work of Kaplan and Cassel (1975). And, it is noteworthy that it is in work built on these elements that the most consistent positive results are found.

It may also be that some of the reluctance to implement programs more widely arises from the general failure to discover many genuine risk or protective factors. Although the importance of the family in both respects seems reasonably well established, this alone does not permit a subgroup of the population at risk, all with chronic disorders, to be easily identified and thus make the provision of the intervention more cost-effective.

Another part of the problem appears to arise from the mind–body duality, and this may extend into social and health policy. Expenditures on high-technology interventions (the body part) are much easier to "sell," to the public, politicians, and other physicians, than are prevention programs of almost any kind. A skeptical interpretation of this duality is that innovations in technology generate income (for some), whereas social and psychological interventions are costly and rarely profitable. Linked to this is the general reluctance, particularly in the United States in the present political climate, to support social engineering solutions to health problems. In one sense this is paradoxical. The United States is well ahead of many other countries in introducing legislation such as that described in an earlier section, despite its heralded opposition to state interference in family matters. It may be that the case for going the next step and adopting "molecular solutions" such as PACTS or the Family Counselor program, or elements of PIRC, has not been made forcefully enough. It is more likely, however, that other factors account for the failure to adopt these promising solutions.

One such factor may be questions of "turf." Whose responsibility is it to promote social interventions or prevention programs? In the case of children with chronic disorders, this broad issue has been examined only at the clinical level. Most children with these disorders have a primary physician but as a rule a subspecialist expert in the biologic aspects of the disorder is consulted to confirm the diagnosis and to provide the specialized aspects of care. If it were appreciated fully that these children are at considerable risk for socioemotional problems, whose responsibility is it to provide whatever interventions may be available? It appears that few specialists accept this responsibility (Pless, Satterwhite, & Van Vechten, 1978), and those in hospital settings, especially teaching hospitals, may be even less inclined to do so. Although this may appear paradoxical (because academics should be most knowledgeable about, and responsive to, scientific evidence), the fact remains that few specialists are themselves inclined to provide even the most elemental form of intervention – counseling. Instead, the family is referred to other health professionals: psychologists, psychiatrists, social workers, and, in some settings, nurses. Ideally, this arrangement may be viewed as "shared care"; more cynically it may also be viewed as "dumping" a difficult problem into the laps of others.

From the perspective of these "others," the scene may appear quite different. Social workers, for example, may judge that such problems "belong" to them and that the physician has little or no role to play. In the context of the growing struggle of nursing as a profession for greater autonomy, a similar, perhaps more powerful, argument is often made. In essence, the view expressed is that, unlike physicians, who have been trained to concentrate only on the patient, modern nurses are oriented to seeing these children in the context of the family, and even more broadly, in a dynamic sociocultural dimension. Much of present day nurse training is devoted to these principles and they form the basis of at least one part of the struggle for control of these patients and their families.

The overriding problem may well be, as Haggerty (1991) has stated,

that much of the care of children with chronic disease today is done in subspecialty clinics in major medical centers, where attention is less likely to be given to the psychological needs of these children and their families. The unsettled question is whether we should meet these needs by setting up and organizing services for care of children with chronic illness in general (chronic diseases) clinics and in private practices, with strong input from nurses, psychologists, social workers, using the subspecialists primarily as consultants; or whether adding these psychosocial services to the subspecialty clinics is a better method. In several medical centers, the latter approach has been developed, especially for children with multi-system disorders, such as spina bifida, or with neuromuscular diseases, such as muscular dystrophy.

Most pediatric services in the U.S., when they have provided these additional services, have done so by a team of multidisciplinary care-givers in medical centers and have focused on social services, counseling, and coordination. . . .

The jury is still out on how best to provide these . . . services, and it would seem advisable to experiment with several different types of organized care, accompanied by careful evaluation.

Finally, a variation on the "turf" interpretation may shed some light on what appears to some to be the continued, unwarranted emphasis on risk and pathology, as opposed to health or resilience. Garmezy (1991) suggests that resilience research has been so neglected because of "the segregation of our sciences. Psychiatry is focused on both the development and the description of psychopathology while developmental psychology and developmental biology have fixed their agendas on normative development. The potential linkage of these and related disciplines (e.g., neurobiology and the neurosciences, behavioral and molecular genetics, personality study, and sociology) lies in the study of both normative and non-normative development. This emergent field is known as developmental psychopathology."

An agenda for further research

Clearly, one of the most important unresolved questions is that pertaining to the identification of risk and protective factors. Finding answers may require much larger samples than those customarily used in this area of research, as well as new conceptual models or new ways to incorporate those that now seem most promising. It will also be necessary to consider further the nature of help being provided. If it becomes possible to target high-risk subgroups among those with chronic disorders, what are really the best interventions that might be offered?

The most direct response is some type of psychotherapy for those who are clearly disturbed. Although aside from concerns about access and resources few would dispute the desirability of providing mental health services to these children, solid evidence of the efficacy of any form of psychotherapy is still lacking. Furthermore, as Furman and Ahola (1989) remind us, there is an astonishing scarcity of studies that examine the *adverse* effects of psychotherapy and it is "theoretically conceivable that [it], whether individual, group therapy, or family therapy, may actually sometimes cause harm."

As an alternative, despite the caveats articulated by Rutter (1982), solid arguments continue to be made in favor of various nonspecific, preventive programs. As has been shown, evidence in favor of their effectiveness is encouraging but tentative. Although the model – that illness acts to the detriment of mental health by increasing stress, for the child, the family, or both – remains compelling, it has only led to a few specific interventions. If the cause of the stress cannot be modified in any direct fashion, one popular alternative is to seek new ways to enhance coping, for example, by fostering social support networks. This model is also consonant with that proposed by Rutter (1987) in his description of mechanisms that contribute to psychosocial resilience. In the end, however, the field seems wide open for new ideas about intervention based on any of the models described.

Accordingly, an important consideration is the further exploration of the theoretical base for such interventions. Recent papers by Bauman, Stein, and Ireys (1991a, 1991b) suggest some principles for multilevel assessment of theoretical, conceptual, operational, and implementation models that can enhance both the power of the research being conducted and improve the potential for successful transfer and replication of effective interventions to test their generalizability.

Another issue for the research agenda of the future is a more balanced evaluation of medical interventions, their technologies, and their collective impact. Specifically, the psychosocial impact of these technologies remains to be determined. This is an important consideration at a time when resources are being shifted toward high technologies in such a dramatic manner, because this shift affects the appropriation of resources for other aspects of health care delivery including mental health services.

The considerations outlined here, taken together, frame a much needed "intervention science." By this we mean that beyond determining what is helpful in reducing risk, we also need to understand the processes being altered and how to maximize their effectiveness across sites and situations (Bauman et al., 1991a). It requires as well that more attention be paid to the range of outcomes of interest. Until recently, there were few data that showed interventions to be effective by any criteria. As this science improves, deciding which outcomes are important becomes more of a consideration. Intervention research should distinguish between administrative, programmatic, proximal, and distal outcomes on the one hand, and on the other, between clinical and statistical effectiveness. It should also distinguish between effectiveness, efficacy, and efficiency criteria (Bauman et al., 1991b). It certainly must consider the possibility that a given intervention may have different short- and long-term effects on different domains or on different members of the family (child vs. parent), some of which may even prove harmful. An objective approach to the values placed on these trade-offs is urgently needed.

Finally, there is also a need to be cognizant of the prevailing double standard in research. It is evident that different criteria are applied to psychological and social interventions than to biomedical interventions. The latter are often allowed to continue without being held to any absolute or relative standard, so long as they hold out the potential prospect of improving survival or quality of life. Cost is rarely an issue in their widespread adoption. In contrast, social interventions are, for the most part, required to be stringently evaluated when introduced deliberately, and rarely evaluated when done through political or administrative processes. In the light of such difficulties, future research in this area will not be easy. Those with influence must become receptive not only to the need for high quality studies in this extremely important domain but also to their inherent difficulty and complexity.

References

American Heritage Dictionary (2nd college ed., p. 672). Boston, MA: Houghton Mifflin Company.

Achenbach T. M., Howell, C. T., Aoki, M. F., & Rauh, V. A. (1993). Nineyear outcome of the Vermont intervention program for low birth weight infants. *Pediatrics, 91*(1), 45–55.

Anderson, G. M., Brook, R., & Williams, A. (1991). A comparison of costsharing versus free care in children: Effects on the demand for office-based medical care. *Medical Care, 29*, 890–898.

Bauman, L. J., Stein, R. E. K., & Ireys, H. T. (1991a). A framework for conceptualizing interventions. *Sociological Practice Review, 2*, 241–251.

Bauman, L. J., Stein, R. E. K., & Ireys, H. T. (1991b). Reinventing fidelity: The transfer of social technology among settings. *American Journal of Community Psychology, 19*: 619–639.

Butler, J. A., Singer, J. D., Palfrey, J. S., & Walker, D. K. (1987). Health insurance coverage and physician use among children with disabilities: Findings from probability samples in five metropolitan areas. *Pediatrics, 79*, 89–98.

Butler, J. A., Winter, W. D., Singer, J. D., & Wenger, M. (1985). Medical care use and expenditure among U.S. children and youth: Analysis of a national probability sample. *Pediatrics, 76*, 495–507.

Cadman, D., Boyle, M., Szatmari, P., & Offord, D. R. (1987). Chronic illness, disability, and mental and social well-being: Findings of the Ontario Child Health Study. *Pediatrics, 79*, 805–813.

Coupey, S. M., Bauman, L. J., Lauby, J. L., Koeber, J. R., & Stein, R. E. K. (1991). Mental health effects of a social skills intervention for adolescents. *Pediatric Research, 29*(4) Pt. 2 (April), 3A.

Furman, B., & Ahola, T. (1989). Adverse effects of psychotherapeutic beliefs: An application of attribution theory to the critical study of psychotherapy. *Family Systems Medicine, 7,* 183–195.

Garmezy, N. (1991). Resilience in children's adaptation to negative life events and stressed environments. *Pediatric Annals, 20,* 460–466.

Garmezy, N., Masten, A. S., & Tellegen, A. (1984). The study of stress and competence in children: A building block for developmental psychopathology. *Child Development 55,* 97–111.

Gordon, R. S., Jr. (1983). An operational classification of disease prevention. *Public Health Reports, 98,* 107–109.

Gottlieb L., & Rowat, K. (1987). The McGill model of nursing: A practice-derived model. *Advances in Nursing Science, 9,* 51–61.

Gross, R. T. (1990). The infant health and development program. Enhancing the outcomes of low-birth weight, premature infants: A multisite randomized trial. *Journal of the American Medical Association, 263*(22) 13, 3035–3042.

Haggerty, R. J. (1991). *William T. Grant Foundation Annual Report.* New York.

Horowitz, S. M., & Stein, R. E. K. (1990). Health maintenance organization vs. indemnity insurance for children with chronic illness. Trading gaps in coverage. *American Journal of Diseases of Children, 144,* 581–586.

Howland, J., Bauchner, H., & Adair, R. (1988). The impact of pediatric asthma education on morbidity: Assessing the evidence. *Chest, 94,* 964–969.

Hughes, D. M., McLeod, M., Garner, B., & Goldloom, R. B. (1991). Controlled trial of a home and ambulatory program for asthmatic children. *Pediatrics, 87,* 54–61.

Ireys, H. T., Silver, E. J., Stein, R. E. K., Bencivenga, K., & Koeber, C. (1991). Evaluating a parent support program for mothers of chronically ill children. *American Journal of Diseases of Children, 145,* 397.

Jessop, D. J., & Stein, R. E. K. (1991). Who benefits from a pediatric home care program? *Pediatrics, 88,* 497–505.

Judd, C. M., & Kenny, D. A. (1981). *Estimating the effects of social interventions.* Cambridge: Cambridge University Press.

Kaplan, B. H., & Cassel, J. C. (1975). *Family and health: An epidemiological approach* (pp. 1–4). Chapel Hill: University of North Carolina.

LaGreca, A. M. (1990). Social consequences of pediatric conditions: Fertile area for future investigation and intervention? *Journal of Pediatric Psychology, 15,* 285–307.

Lamas, G. A., Pfeffer, M. A., Hamm, P., et al. (1992). Do the results of randomized clinical trials of cardiovascular drugs influence medical practice? *New England Journal of Medicine, 327,* 241–247.

Lavigne, J. V., & Faier-Routman, J. (1992). Psychological adjustment to pediatric physical disorders: A meta-analytic review. *Journal of Pediatric Psychology, 17*(2), 133–157.

McAnarney, E., Pless, I. B., Satterwhite, B., & Friedman, S. (1974). Psychological problems of children with juvenile rheumatoid arthritis. *Pediatrics, 53*, 523–528.

Nolan, T., & Pless, I. B. (1986). Emotional correlates and consequences of birth defects. *Journal of Pediatrics, 109*, 201–216.

Nolan, T., Zvagulis, I., & Pless, I. B. (1987). Controlled trial of social work in childhood chronic illness. *Lancet, 2*, 411–415.

Perrin, J. M., & Stein, R. E. K. (1991). Reinterpreting disability: Changes in supplemental security income for children. *Pediatrics, 88*(5), 1047–1051.

Perrin, J. M., MacLean, W. E., & Perrin, E. C. (1989). Parental perception of health status and psychologic adjustment of children with asthma. *Pediatrics, 23*, 26–30.

Pless, I. B., Feeley, N., Gottlieb, L., Rowat, K., Dougherty, G., & Willard, B. (in press). A randomized controlled trial of the effects of a nursing intervention with children with chronic physical disorders. *Pediatrics.*

Pless, I. B., & Nolan, T. N. (1991). Revision, replication and neglect – research on maladjustment in chronic illness. *Journal of Child Psychology and Psychiatry, 32*(2), 347–365.

Pless, I. B., & Pinkerton, P. (1975). *Chronic childhood disorder: Promoting patterns of adjustment.* Chicago: Yearbook Medical Publishers.

Pless, I. B., Roghmann, K. J., & Haggerty, R. J. (1972). Chronic illness, family functioning and psychological adjustment: A model for the allocation of preventive mental health services. *International Journal of Epidemiology, 1*, 271–277.

Pless, I. B., & Satterwhite, B. (1972). Chronic illness in childhood: Selection, activities, and evaluation of non-professional family counselors. *Clinical Pediatrics, 11*, 403.

Pless, I. B., & Satterwhite B. (1975a). Chronic illness. In R. J. Haggerty, K. J. Roghmann, I. B. Pless (Eds.), *Child health and the community* (pp. 78–94). New York: Wiley.

Pless, I. B., & Satterwhite, B. (1975b). The family counselor. In R. J. Haggerty, K. J. Roghmann, & I. B. Pless (Eds.). *Child health and the community* (pp. 288–302). New York: Wiley.

Pless, I. B., Satterwhite, B., & Van Vechten, D. (1978). Division, duplication and neglect: Patterns of care for children with chronic disorders. *Child Care, Health and Development, 4*, 9–19.

Richmond, J. (1990). Low-birth-weight infants. Can we enhance their development. *Journal of the American Medical Association, 263*(22), 13, 3069–3070.

Ruben, D. U., Leventhal, J. M., Sadock, R. T., Letovsky, E., Schotland, P., Clemente, I., & McCarthy, P. (1986). Educational intervention by computer in childhood asthma: A randomized clinical trial testing the use of a new teaching intervention in childhood asthma. *Pediatrics, 77*, 1–10.

Rutter, M. (1977). Brain damage syndromes in childhood: Concepts and findings. *Journal of Child Psychology and Psychiatry, 18*, 1–21.

Rutter, M. (1979). Protective factors in children's responses to stress and disadvantage. In M. W. Kent, & J. E. Rolf (Eds.), *Primary prevention of psychopathology: Vol. 3. Social competence in children* (pp. 49–74). Hanover, NH: University Press of New England.

Rutter, M. (1982). Prevention of children's psychosocial disorders: Myth and substance. *Pediatrics, 70*, 883–894.

Rutter, M. (1987). Psychosocial resilience and protective mechanisms. *American Journal of Orthopsychiatry, 57*, 316–331.

Sabbeth, B., & Stein, R. E. K. (1990). Mental health referral: A weak link in comprehensive care of children with chronic physical illness. *Journal of Developmental and Behavioral Pediatrics, 11*, 73–78.

Sameroff, A. J., Seiffer, R., Barucas, R., Sax, M., & Greenspan, S. (1987). IQ scores of four-year-old children: Stoical environmental risk factors. *Pediatrics, 79*, 343–350.

Satin, W., LaGreca, A. M., Zigo, M. A., & Skyler, J. S. (1989). Diabetes in adolescence: Effects of multifamily group intervention and parent simulation of diabetes. *Journal of Pediatric Psychology, 14*, 259–275.

Schlesinger, M. (1986). On the limits of expanding health care reform: Chronic care in prepaid settings. *Milbank Memorial Fund Quarterly, 64*, 189–215.

Shontz, F. C. (1971). Physical disability and personality. In W. S. Neff (Ed.), *Rehabilitation psychology* (pp. 33–74). Washington, DC: American Psychological Association.

Singer, J. D., & Butler, J. A. (1987). The education for all handicapped children act: Schools as agents of social reform. *Harvard Educational Review, 57*, 125–152.

Stein, R. E. K., Bauman, L. J., & Ireys, H. T. (1991). Who enrolls in prevention trials? Discordance in perception of risk by professionals and participants. *American Journal of Community Psychology, 19*, 603–617.

Stein, R. E. K., & Jessop, D. J. (1982). A noncategorical approach to chronic childhood illness. *Public Health Reports, 97*, 354–362.

Stein, R. E. K., & Jessop, D. J. (1984). Does pediatric home care make a difference for children with chronic illness? Findings from the pediatric ambulatory care treatment study. *Pediatrics, 73,* 845–853.

Stein, R. E. K., & Jessop, D. J. (1991). Long term mental health effects of a pediatric home care program. *Pediatrics, 88,* 490–496.

Sullivan v. *Zebley,* 88-1377 (U.S. Supreme Court, 20 Feb. 1990).

Valdez, R. B., Brook, R. H., Rogers, W. H., Ware, J. E., Keeler, E. B., Sherbourne, C. A., Lohr, K. N., Goldberg, G. A., Camp, P., & Newhouse, V. P. (1985). Consequences of cost-sharing for children's health. *Pediatrics, 75,* 952–961.

Varni, J. W., Wilcox, K. T., & Hanson, V. (1988). Mediating effects of family social support on child psychological adjustment in juvenile rheumatoid arthritis. *Health Psychology, 7,* 421–431.

Wallender, J. L., Varni, J. W., Babani, L., Banis, H. T., & Wilcox, K. T. (1989). Family resources as resistance factors for psychological maladjustment in chronically ill and handicapped children. *Journal of Pediatric Psychology, 14,* 157–174.

Weiss, C. H. (1972). *Evaluation research: Methods for assessing program effectiveness.* Englewood Cliffs, NJ: Prentice-Hall.

White, K., Kolman, M. L., Wexler, P., Polin, G., & Winter, R. J. (1984). Unstable diabetes and unstable families: A psychosocial evaluation of diabetic children with recurrent ketoacidosis. *Pediatrics, 73,* 749–755.

Wilder, C. (1972). Limitation of activity and mobility due to chronic conditions, United States, National Health Interview Survey. *Vital Health Statistics, 10*(96).

10

Stress research: Accomplishments and tasks ahead

Michael Rutter

When the topic of stress, coping, and resilience was reviewed a decade ago in *Stress, Coping, and Development in Children* (Garmezy & Rutter, 1983), the paucity of research on effects in childhood, as compared with that in adulthood, was noted. A key issue at that time was whether the associations found in later life held similarly for the early years and, if there were differences, what these variations might be due to. Questions were asked about what made particular events stressful to the individual, in the sense that they elicited psychological and physiological responses, and also with respect to creating a risk for psychopathology (see Garmezy, this volume, chap. 1). The importance of individual differences in susceptibility was emphasized and questions were asked as to what was involved in resilience and in successful coping with stress and adversity. Attention was drawn to the fact that apparently negative experiences could be either sensitizing or steeling in their effects (meaning that a vulnerability to later stressors could be either increased or decreased). It was argued that there was a need to consider stress and coping processes at several levels – social, psychological, and neurochemical. It made little sense to think of reducing everything to, say, a neurochemical level. Rather, each level provided a different and complementary perspective; an integration across levels was required in order to understand the mechanisms and processes involved. The social meaning of experiences was important, and many needed to be considered in interactional terms; nevertheless, it was necessary to determine how the

Michael Rutter is Honorary Director of the MRC Child Psychiatry Unit, Institute of Psychiatry, London.

processes that began in a social context led to intraorganismic changes. It was notable both that the book ended by drawing attention to some crucial methodological issues and that there was very little discussion of interventions designed to improve the way that children dealt with stress experiences.

Accomplishments during the past decade

Since that time, the field has moved on in very important ways, as discussed in the earlier chapters of this volume. Each chapter highlights many specific findings of interest and importance, but in turning to the ways in which research into stress, coping, and resilience needs to move forward in the years to come, it may be useful to draw attention to some broad themes that span the various specific chapters.

Evidence on risk in childhood

During the past 10 years, evidence has steadily accumulated that negative events and experiences are indeed associated with psychopathology in childhood (Goodyer, 1990), the findings showing many parallels to those in adult life. Thus, it is clear that there are significant risks associated with bereavement (see Clark, Pynoos, & Goebel, this volume, chap. 4), with divorce and remarriage (see Emery & Forehand, this volume, chap. 3), with chronic physical disorders (see Pless & Stein, this volume, chap. 9), with both man-made and natural disasters (Yule, 1994), and with a broader range of events that appear to carry long-term psychological threat (Goodyer, 1990). Nevertheless, the research findings have also been important in their indication that a focus on isolated life events is not the most appropriate way of viewing most stressors (Rutter & Sandberg, 1992). Thus, for example, it is apparent that the psychopathological risks associated with divorce stem as much from the family patterns that precede and follow the breakup of the parental marriage as from the breakup itself (see Emery & Forehand, this volume, chap. 3). Similarly, the risks associated with bereavement are a consequence of the parental illness that preceded the death and the range of sequelae that sometimes follow the death of a parent (see Clark et al., this volume, chap. 4). The grief of the surviving parent, the continuing absence of the parent who died, and the effects on parental care may all be involved in the risk process. As Clark et al. put it, it is the aggregated *accumulation* of events over time that contributes to the emergence of psychological resilience or vulnerability in individual cases (see also Garmezy & Masten, 1994).

Conceptual and methodological issues

As well summarized by Gore and Eckenrode (this volume, chap. 2), there is now a much better appreciation of the conceptual and method-ological issues involved in risk research. Some of these concern gains in understanding of the possible confounding factors that need to be taken into account, and some concern improved methodologies for using epidemiological and longitudinal research strategies to test hy-potheses about causal mechanisms (see Rutter, in press). In many ways, however, the most important advances involve an appreciation of the need to take into account the various different mechanisms involved in person–environment interactions (see Wachs & Plomin, 1991) and in individual differences in perceptions of stress situations (Grych & Fincham, 1990), stress-buffering mechanisms (Jenkins & Smith, 1990; Masten et al., 1988; Rutter, 1991a), and indirect chain reactions over time (Rutter, 1989a; Rutter & Rutter, 1993). At one time, there tended to be an assumption that, because negative life events provoked or precipitated the onset of psychiatric disorder, they necessarily involved an increase in developmental discontinuities. It is now clear that assumption is unwarranted. The biological "norm" is neither continuity nor discontinuity, neither change nor stability (Rutter, 1994a). Both are expected and both require explanation. Depending on circumstances, negative life experiences may either accentuate preexisting psychological characteristics, be they adaptive or maladaptive, or alter them. However, the former is more common than the latter (Caspi & Moffitt, 1993).

Mediating mechanisms

Initial concepts of stress induced by psychosocial experiences focused on the adaptations required when major life changes were involved (Holmes & Rahe, 1967). During the 1970s there was a major reap-praisal of this concept through the work of Paykel (1974, 1978), who noted the importance of differentiating between desirable and undesirable life changes; of Lazarus (Lazarus & Launier, 1978), who emphasized the role of cognitive appraisal of the events; and of G. Brown and Harris (1978, 1989), who showed the need to take into account the social context of life events in order to assess the psychological threat to the individual. These were important advances, but during the 1980s and early 1990s, there have been significant moves toward a greater specification of the mediating mechanisms involved in the risk processes associated with psychosocial experiences that carry an increased risk of psychopathology. The range of processes that are being considered may be illustrated through several examples. Thus, it has been shown that parental loss includes a quite heterogeneous range of experiences, only some of which carry long-term psychopathological risks. Also, although the loss of a parent through death is associated with grief reactions, some of which lead into psychiatric disorder, the long-term risks are very small as compared with those associated with parental separation or divorce (Kendler, Neale, Kessler, Heath, & Eaves, 1992). Moreover, the long-term risks are a function of the impaired parental care and family functioning that may follow parental death, rather than the death itself as an acute event (Harris, Brown, & Bifulco, 1986; see also Clark et al., this volume, chap. 4).

The long-term risks associated with divorce, by contrast, have been well substantiated (Cherlin et al., 1991; Kendler et al., 1992; Kuh & MacLean, 1990). On the other hand, longitudinal studies have clearly indicated that the psychopathology is often evident before the divorce (e.g., Block, Block, & Gjerde, 1986), with the main risk stemming from parental conflict (Amato & Keith, 1991), rather than the event of divorce itself. We have also had to give up the idea that divorce necessarily brings parental conflict to an end. Follow-up studies have indicated that, all too often, conflict persists and, moreover, the extent to which children are caught up in this conflict is an important factor in determining the degree of psychopathological risk (Buchanan, Maccoby, & Dornbusch, 1991). Marked individual differences in children's response to parental divorce have been noted in all investigations but it is only relatively recently that there have been systematic studies examining why this is so even with children within the same family (Grych & Fincham, 1990). It is not just a matter of some families having more conflict than others, although that is undoubtedly an important consideration (Hetherington, Cox, & Cox, 1978), but also that siblings within the same family differ in their perceptions of family conflict (Monahan, Buchanan, Maccoby, & Dornbusch, 1993), doubtless in part because of the variations in the ways in which the conflict impinges on them and affects their relationship with their parents.

Not surprisingly, physical child abuse has been found to be a substantial risk factor (Skuse & Bentovim, 1994). Within the childhood age period, it carries an increased risk of aggressive behavior and, in adulthood, it is associated with an increased risk of serious parenting difficulties and abusive behavior to the victim's own children (Rutter, 1989b; Widom, 1989). However, the mechanisms by which the experience of abuse leads to aggressive behavior have been unclear. An important longitudinal study by Dodge and his colleagues (Dodge, Bates, & Pettit, 1990; Weiss, Dodge, Bates, & Pettit, 1992) has shown that social cognition may play a key mediating role in this process. Harsh parental discipline was associated with child aggression, in part directly, and in part via an effect on maladaptive social processing (with a tendency to a hostile attentional bias, aggressive solutions to interpersonal problems, and inattention to relevant social cues).

Puberty in girls provides another example. Several studies have shown it to be associated with a substantial increase in dieting and other eating problems (Alsaker, in press; Attie & Brooks-Gunn, 1992; Petersen & Leffert, in press). The evidence, however, indicates that the key factor is not the development of secondary sexual characteristics but, rather, the accumulation of fat that tends to accompany it. The extent to which this occurs is, in addition, a function of attitudes to body shape and weight that prevail in the community at the time. It is pertinent to note that, although this seems to be the way in which abnormal eating behavior begins, somewhat different factors (associated with personal and interpersonal difficulties) play a greater role in the maintenance of eating problems (Attie & Brooks-Gunn, 1989).

Unusually early puberty in girls is also associated with an increase in norm-breaking behavior (Stattin & Magnusson, 1990). In this case, the mechanisms seem to be somewhat different. The Stockholm longitudinal study findings indicated that the increase in norm-breaking behavior was found only in those early-maturing girls who associated with an older peer group. The stimulus may have been physiological but the mediation seemed to be social-psychological. This mechanism was confirmed in the Dunedin longitudinal study (Caspi, Lynam, Moffit, & Silva, 1993; Caspi & Moffitt, 1991). The New Zealand data, however, yielded two additional features: the effect was evident only in coeducational and not all-girls schools, and the effect was most evident in girls who were already showing some disruptive behavior.

In each of these examples (and in others that could have been mentioned), progress has been made in moving from a broadly based risk indicator to something that is much closer to the mediating mechanism. It will be appreciated that the question is not one of finding the "basic" cause but rather of gaining an understanding of the mechanisms *over time* that may be involved. In most cases this involves a series of linked processes, rather than just a single crucial operation.

Range of psychopathological consequences

Virtually all clinical and epidemiological studies have shown the very high degree of comorbidity between supposedly different psychiatric disorders in childhood and adolescence (Achenbach, 1991; Caron & Rutter, 1991; Zoccolillo, 1992). Some investigators have argued from these, and other similar findings, for a global concept of "problem behavior" (Jessor, Donovan, & Costa, 1992) rather than the making of diagnostic differentiations. However, although clearly there is a need to understand the mechanisms involved in comorbidity (see Compas & Hammen, this volume, chap. 7), the effects of stress may not be quite the same with respect to different types of psychopathology (see Gore & Eckenrode, this volume, chap. 2). On the other hand, it is certainly evident that it is important to examine a wide range of psychopathology when considering the effects of negative life events and experiences. For example, in an attempt to focus more on the positive aspects of resilience, some investigators have argued for a focus on social competence rather than the absence of psychopathology (Luthar & Zigler, 1991). It may indeed be desirable to study the development of social competence, but Luthar's (1991) findings indicated that children who appeared resilient in terms of the presence of social competence were often nonresilient when judged in terms of the presence of emotional disturbance. It is evident that any adequate study of resilience is going to need to encompass both the presence of positive features and the absence of negative ones.

In recent years, the concept of posttraumatic stress disorder has become very fashionable with respect to children's responses to adverse experiences, as well as adults' reactions. The earlier literature had suggested that children's responses to disasters, and other overwhelmingly stressful events, differed in some respects from those of adults (Garmezy & Rutter, 1985). It is important that investigations during the past few years that have included more detailed interviews with the children themselves have shown that many of the characteristic qualities of posttraumatic stress disorder as seen in adults (such as numbing, flashbacks, and preoccupation with the event) occur in children as well as adults (Yule, 1994). The finding is important in alerting us to the need to include coverage of these (and other related) phenomena when examining children's responses to negative life experiences. However, as the earlier chapters of this volume indicate, the form of psychopathological reactions to negative life experiences is very far from confined to the particular syndrome known as posttraumatic stress disorder. Moreover, it is not as yet clear whether these features are commonly found in relation to more everyday negative life experiences (as distinct from catastrophic disasters) and, equally, it is not known whether posttraumatic stress disorder constitutes a distinct syndrome with qualitative differences from other psychiatric disorders, or rather whether it provides a "coloring" to a range of syndromes that arises from the fact that they were precipitated by some acute, grossly stressful, occurrence.

Developmental considerations and long-term effects

Over the years, there has been a marked, and important, shift in the ways in which developmental considerations have been conceptualized. At one time, there was a general view that pre-school children were markedly *less* vulnerable than older children to the effects of brain damage (Rutter, 1982, 1993), and were markedly *more* vulnerable to psychosocial stressors (see critique by Clarke & Clarke, 1976).

It is now clear that neither generalization is warranted. Age is not a unitary phenomenon and a correlation with age does not in on of itself provide any explanation in terms of mechanisms (Rutter, 1989c). There are some ways in which young children are more vulnerable and some ways in which they are less vulnerable, and it is necessary to go on to look at the processes involved in the varied range of observed age effects. Similarly, by analogy with the phe-nomenon of imprinting in birds, it was assumed that there were important critical periods in human development. As it became ap-parent that the phenomenon of imprinting was by no means as fixed as was once thought (Bateson, 1966, 1990), and as the misleading nature of analogies with imprinting became clear (Rutter, 1991b), the concept of critical periods went out of fashion and came to be rejected by many investigators.

In recent times, the pendulum has to some extent swung back. Although the old-style concept of fixed critical periods has proved untenable, the notion of sensitive periods in development has much more validity. There are well-established examples in both the psycho-social and somatic arenas of experiences that have a more marked effect (or a different type of effect) at some ages than others, and which have surprisingly long-lasting consequences extending even into adulthood (Bock & Whelan, 1991). Thus, it is well demonstrated that visual experiences in early life play a key role in the development of the visual cortex of the brain. It is because of that effect that children whose strabismus (squint) is not corrected in early life are left permanently without binocular vision. The extent to which there are comparable features in other psychological functions remains un-certain. However, it is striking that institutional care for the first few years of life is associated with differences in the pattern of peer relationships at 16, even when the children return to a family setting for most of their upbringing (Hodges & Tizard, 1989a, 1989b). More-over, quite unlike other psychopathological consequences, this effect seems to be independent of home circumstances in later childhood and adolescence.

Recent findings have also been surprising in showing, apparently, that maternal depression in the first year of a child's life is associated with significant cognitive impairment, although depression after that time period does not have this effect (Cogill, Caplan, Alexandra,

Robson, & Kumar, 1986; Murray, 1992). The finding has been evident in three separate studies so far but all samples have been fairly small and there is still a need for a larger-scale study that takes better account of confounding variables. Nevertheless, there remains the important suggestion of a possible sensitive period effect.

It certainly cannot be claimed that research has provided an understanding of the mechanisms involved in either age-specific susceptibilities or long-term effects. However, what the empirical evidence has done is open up both issues in ways that indicate that the phenomena may have greater validity than was hitherto supposed. Clearly there is a need to investigate the varied range of mechanisms involved.

Group differences

At one time, social scientists were inclined to see poverty and social disadvantage as key causal influences on childhood psychopathology. Accordingly, many social scientists played a major advocacy role in urging governments to take action to relieve disadvantage and poverty and to remove gross social inequities. There is, of course, every reason to take active steps to improve the circumstances of children who are being reared in conditions that fall well below anything that could be regarded as acceptable. There is no need to invoke psychopathological risks to argue the case for social and political action. Nevertheless, it has become increasingly clear that the association between poverty/social disadvantage and psychopathology is nowhere near as clear-cut as was once assumed. Thus, Nettles and Pleck (this volume, chap. 5) draw attention to the evidence that although African-Americans show higher rates of some psychosocial disorders, they show lower rates of others (such as suicide and depression). They rightly emphasize that it is a serious mistake to equate any ethnic minority group with poverty and disadvantage (because there is huge heterogeneity in the living circumstances of all). However, one might have supposed that the tendency for a higher proportion to experience poverty and social disadvantage would be accompanied by an increased risk for all forms of psychopathology. It is important, therefore, to note that is not so.

The evidence from trends over time is even more striking. Over the course of this century, and especially during the period since World War II, there has been a general increase in living standards in most industrialized countries. At least until the past decade, this has also been associated with a reduction in social inequities. This reasonably consistent trend toward improved living conditions *has* been associated with marked benefits in physical health, as indicated by a falling infantile mortality and a rising life expectancy (Marmot & Smith, 1989). By contrast, and against most people's expectations, there has not been any parallel trend for a reduction in psychopathological disorders in young people (Rutter & Smith, in press). Indeed, to the contrary, there is evidence that greater affluence and improved living conditions have been accompanied by an *increase* in some forms of psychopathology or psychosocial disorder. Thus, although suicide rates in old people have come down, suicide rates in adolescents and young adults have gone up; crime rates have risen markedly; drug and alcohol problems have become more frequent; and probably depressive disorders, too, have become more prevalent in young people.

These findings provide an important warning not to mistake risk indicators for risk mechanisms. On the whole, at any one point in time, poverty and social disadvantage *are* accompanied by an increased risk of psychopathology. The secular trend data, however, are persuasive in showing that it is most unlikely that the risk mechanism lies in either poverty or poor living conditions per se. Rather, the evidence suggests that the effect comes about because poverty is, in turn, associated with family disorganization and breakup, which are rather nearer to the relevant risk mechanisms.

Intervention

Unlike its predecessor a decade ago (Garmezy & Rutter, 1983), this volume has been able to point to evidence on interventions designed to help children and families cope better with stress circumstances, some of which appear to bring real benefits. Elias and Weissberg (this volume, chap. 8) summarize what is known on school-based interventions, and Pless and Stein (this volume, chap. 9) do the same with respect to interventions involving children with chronic physical disorders. The research provides a variety of good leads on possible elements in the interventions that are associated with effective promotion of social competence, but so far the range of interventions is limited and the findings do not provide a clear indication of the risk and protective mechanisms that are involved.

Research tasks for the future

Overall liability to disorder

Most of the adult literature on the effects of negative life events has focused on temporal connections with the onset of some form of disorder (G. Brown & Harris, 1989). The evidence is convincing that this association is valid and reflects a causal connection. However, most psychiatric disorders are recurrent or chronic. Thus, this is clearly so with conduct disorders, which show a high degree of persistence into adult life (Robins, 1978; Zoccolillo, Pickles, Quinton, & Rutter, 1992); it is the case with depressive disorders, where there is a high rate of recurrence in adult life after depression in childhood (Harrington, Fudge, Rutter, Pickles & Hill 1990): and, contrary to earlier assumptions, the rate of recurrence is also relatively high with anxiety disorders (Keller et al., 1992; Last, Perrin, Hersen, & Kazdin, 1992). Accordingly, the question of whether life events and experiences influence the overall liability to psychopathological disorder is necessarily a more important question than whether life events influence the timing of the onset of one particular episode. A further issue with respect to psychiatric disorders in childhood is that it seems that, in most cases, there is no one clear date of onset (Rutter & Sandberg, 1992). Rather, the typical picture is one of multiple onsets with an episodic worsening of disorder, or a gradual accumulation of symptomatology. The examination of the temporal conjunction of life events and onset of disorder provides a most useful research tool to examine possible causal connections. However, there is still a need to examine the associations with overall psychopathological risk and to find ways of testing whether the association represents a causal link. In order to have an adequate measure of psychopathology, it is clear that multiple informants and multiple time-points are highly desirable (Rutter & Pickles, 1990). That is because studies have been unanimous in showing relatively low correlations between parent and teacher reports and fluctuations over time.

What is the risk mechanism?

Far too much research into psychosocial risk factors has been content to stop at the point of identifying risk variables. There is no shortage of data on such variables and we know a good deal about the identification of risks. What we know much less about is how these risk mechanisms operate. Inevitably, that means that we are in a weak position when designing interventions to prevent or treat disorders. Moreover, there is a considerable danger that wrong actions may be taken because we misidentify the aspects of the risk situation that provide the risk. Thus, for example, this was evident in the flush of enthusiasm that followed Bowlby's (1951) report on maternal deprivation and which led to recommendations that mothers should not go out to work and that group day care was inevitably damaging to children (Baers, 1954; World Health Organization, 1951). Subsequent research has been clear in showing that neither maternal employment nor group day care as such are important risk factors (Rutter, 1991b); it is the quality of child care and the continuity in parenting that matter, rather than whether the mother remains full-time at home. Similarly, as already noted, the main psychopathological risks associated with parental divorce stem from the conflict rather than the breakup of the parental marriage as such. Or, again, the main long-term psychopathological risks associated with parental death derive from the family consequences rather than from the event of parental loss on its own. In each of these cases, we have moved somewhere nearer the risk mechanism, but there is quite a long way to go before we fully understand the processes.

However, there are some important leads available on at least some of the issues that require further exploration. For example, it is evident that there is a very strong overlap between acute negative life events and chronic psychosocial adversities, with the main risks seeming to be associated with the latter rather than the former (Sandberg et al., 1993). The message is clear that it is necessary to study the interplay between acute and chronic life experiences, and not to treat acute events as if they arose out of the blue.

Behavior genetic findings have also been important in their implication that nonshared environmental effects are much stronger, on the whole, than shared ones (Plomin & Daniels, 1987). That is to say, differences within families seem to be more influential than differences between families. At first sight that is a very surprising suggestion because of the extensive evidence that familywide variables such as family discord, or parental mental disorder, or family disorganization carry substantial psychopathological risks. It is important to appreciate that the genetic evidence does not mean that these experiences are unimportant. Rather, the implication is that many familywide experiences impinge differently on different children in the same family (Rutter, 1994 b). For the most part, children are actively engaged with their own social environment and are not simply passive recipients of positive and negative stimuli. There is evidence that when parents are depressed and irritable they do not act in a hostile or critical manner to an equal extent with all their children (Rutter, 1978). Very frequently, there is a tendency to pick on or to scapegoat one particular child. As already noted, too, children's involvement in, and perceptions of, parental conflict vary, even when they live in the same home (Monahan et al., 1993). It may also be the case that, with chronic negative experiences, it is more important that one child is systematically treated worse than others, than that the overall conditions in the family as a whole are not very good (Dunn & Plomin, 1990).

It would be a mistake to neglect shared family influences, for clearly they are important when dealing with environmental extremes and also with certain forms of psychopathology, such as conduct disorder and delinquency (DiLalla & Gottesman, 1989; Plomin, Nitz, & Rowe, 1991). Nevertheless, the clear indication is that we need to move away from considering risk experiences in a global fashion as if they impinged in the same way on all children in the family. Instead, the focus should be on differences between siblings and on the specifics of each child's interaction with the family and the social environment more generally (see Hoffman, 1991).

Testing of causal mechanisms

The past few years have seen some serious challenges to the usual assumption that variables that look "environmental" involve risks that are necessarily environmentally mediated. Thus Plomin (1994; Plomin and Bergeman, 1991) has gathered together the genetic evidence indicating that there is a significant genetic component to a wide range of risk variables that have ordinarily been assumed to operate environmentally. These include features such as acute life events, lack of social support, qualities of parent–child interaction, television viewing, and so on. It has been argued, on this basis, that some of these risks reflect genetic mediation and not environmental mechanisms. Undoubtedly, the challenge needs to be taken seriously (Rutter, 1994c). The evidence, although limited, is clear-cut that there are indeed significant genetic components in many supposedly environmental measures. This arises as an understandable consequence of passive gene–environment correlations. Many environmental risk factors reflect people's behavior of one kind or another and insofar as that behavior involves any kind of genetic influence, the "environmental" variable will be in part genetically determined. Thus, for example, parents of superior intelligence will differ from parents who are mentally handicapped in the environments that they provide for their children. Similarly, parental mental disorder is associated with risk environments (Rutter, 1989d) but obviously it also reflects the genetic factors implicated in mental disorders.

This finding should not just be taken as a warning not to assume that effects are environmentally mediated just because the variable "looks" environmental. The specifics are also relevant. For example, Plomin and his colleagues (Plomin, 1994; Plomin, McClearn, Pedersen, Nesselroade, & Bergeman, 1989) have shown that the genetic component of the HOME measure of family environment was not a function of parental IQ. That raises important questions about what are the parental qualities that lead to variations in the home environment provided for children. Similarly, the evidence from several studies has indicated that the genetic component in parental warmth is greater than that in parental control (Plomin, 1994). A likely implication is that the latter is more open to influence by the child's behavior. Or, again, Kessler et al. (Kessler, Kendler, Heath, Neale, & Eaves, 1992) showed that social support was in part shaped by genetic factors. The evidence also indicated that there was a true environmentally mediated association between lack of support and depression but also that some of that association was not due to support per se but rather to the genetic or environmental factors that influence success in developing friendship networks. Studies examining gene–environment correlations are still few and far between but what is apparent already is that evidence of this kind will be useful in gaining a better understanding of environmental risk factors. It is important to note, however, that the fact that a variable is in part genetically determined does not necessarily mean that its effects are genetically mediated. It is quite possible for a variable to be strongly influenced by genetic factors but nevertheless to have effects that are environmental in their transmission. It should be added, too, that the evidence by no means points to a strong genetic component in most environmental measures. For the most part, only some 10% to 50% of the variance is genetically determined.

Scarr (1992; Scarr & McCartney, 1983) has put forward a somewhat different argument with respect to her proposal that there are strong active and evocative gene–environment correlations. What this suggests is that, to a very substantial extent, people shape and select their own environments. The evocative effect comes about because children's behavior evokes responses from other people and active effects arise through people choosing the social settings with which they engage. Furthermore, it is argued that the individual characteristics that are driving experiences are strongly genetically influenced. Her theory is provocative in its implications but, as Plomin (1994) pointed out, there is a lack of direct supporting evidence that genetic effects are actually influential to an important extent in the way that Scarr suggested. The matter has been so little investigated up to now that the issue must remain open. On the other hand, there is a good deal of evidence that individual characteristics are associated with marked effects on variations in environmental risk. This important point is discussed further.

The challenge to provide rigorous tests of the supposed causal effect underlying associations between negative life experiences and psychopathology does not only derive from genetic studies. There is a very important need to use research designs that provide the necessary tests. For obvious reasons, very few psychosocial risk factors can be studied under controlled conditions in the experimental laboratory. Nevertheless, that definitely does not mean that causal hypotheses cannot be tested (see Rutter, in press). Farrington (1988) has argued for the strength of longitudinal research designs in which within-individual change can be examined in relation to changes in the hypothesized risk variable, and Rutter (in press) has drawn attention to the power of reversal designs and of dose–response relationships. By reversal, all that is meant is that if the occurrence of the hypothesized risk variable leads to an increase in psychopathology, in most circumstances it should follow that the removal of that risk variable should also be associated with a reduction in psychopathology. This has been demonstrated in relation to the effects of unemployment (Rutter, 1994b) and the causal inference is much strengthened by that finding. By dose–response relationship, it is meant that if the effect is truly causal, in ordinary circumstances one would expect that the risk will go up in parallel with the strength of the risk exposure. Thus, if engagement in family conflict is truly involved in the causal processes leading to psychopathology, the risk should rise in relation to the severity of conflict and the degree of children's involvement in it. There are a variety of other ways in which epidemiological data can be used to test causal hypotheses (see Rutter, in press a) but most rely on some sort of "natural experiment" in which variations in the pattern of risk variables can be used to determine which particular feature is associated with variations in psychopathological risk.

Individual differences in vulnerability to stress

As the various chapters of this volume indicate, we know surprisingly little about individual differences in vulnerability to stress and clearly their investigation remains an important item on the research agenda. Barr, Boyce, and Zeltzer (this volume, chap. 6) outline findings indicating that psychobiological reactivity is likely to play a key role in such individual differences. The matter certainly warrants further systematic investigation. Barr et al. note the example of the physiological/psychological characteristic of behavioral inhibition which, if stable over time, is associated with an increased risk of anxiety disorders (Hirshfeld et al., 1992). It is clear from both human and animal studies (Suomi, 1991) that this feature is mainly evident in challenge or stress situations. It seems reasonable to hypothesize, therefore, that the risk features associated with the characteristic may be mediated through an effect on an increased vulnerability to stress. However, that suggestion has not been tested directly up to now. It should be noted that, although this appears to be an important risk variable for anxiety disorders, it also appears to be a protective factor against conduct disorders (Lahey, McBurnett, Loeber, & Hart, in press). Children with persistent conduct disorders have been found to be physiologically underreactive to experimental stress situations (Magnusson & Bergman, 1990), although such disorders show quite a strong association with chronic psychosocial adversity. It is clear that the risk and protective functions of the characteristic are not yet understood.

Genetic factors may also be implicated in individual differences in vulnerability to stress and adversity. Thus, a variety of studies have shown that the genetic vulnerability to adult crime is more likely to result in actual criminality if there is additional exposure to environmental risk factors such as institutional care in infancy, multiple temporary family placements, and an adverse environment in the adoptive home (Cloninger & Gottesman, 1987).

In many ways, the most surprising omission from the list of variables that have been well studied in relation to individual differences in vulnerability to stress concerns subclinical levels of psychopathology. There is evidence that, in relation to a range of life changes such as early puberty, parenting, and unemployment, the individuals who are most likely to act adversely are those already showing some emotional or behavioral difficulties (Caspi et al., 1993; Rutter & Rutter, 1993). It is, perhaps, not an unexpected finding but the mechanisms remain uncertain.

There are very striking sex differences in patterns of psychopathology (Earls, 1987) and there have been suggestions that this may be a function of differences in vulnerability to stress. The evidence on this point is rather contradictory and inconclusive (Zaslow 1989). Even if the gender differences in vulnerability in childhood remain uncertain, however, there are some well-replicated differences in adult life. The most striking of these concerns the fact that marriage appears to have an important protective function in males, but if anything a vulnerability effect in females (see, e.g., Bebbington, Tennant, & Hurry, 1991; Gove, 1978). Of course, before it can be assumed that the difference between married and single people is truly a function of the protective effect of marriage, it is necessary to make certain that the difference does not stem from the prior characteristics of individuals who do and who do not get married. Certainly, there are such differences. For example, a U.K. study showed that those who received special education and also those who went to university were less likely than others to get married (Kiernan, 1988). However, it is not known whether such features explain the apparent sex difference in the buffering role of marriage.

In the volume in stress and coping a decade ago (Garmezy & Rutter, 1983), attention was drawn to the fact that one set of stress experiences could either increase or decrease vulnerability to later stress experiences. Although it is clear that is indeed the case, we know remarkably little about what differentiates these two contrasting sequelae of stress. It has been argued that the key may lie in whether, in some sense, individuals cope successfully with the stress. If they do, the experience may be steeling, but, if they do not, the reverse may be the case. However, there is little systematic evidence on whether this is so. There is growing evidence that the characteristic of making active plans in relation to key life transitions and challenges may be an important factor fostering resilience – through a variety of mechanisms, including a reduction in exposure to stress situations (Clausen, 1991; Quinton & Rutter, 1988; Rutter, Champion, Quinton, Maughan & Pickles, in press). There is reason to suppose that this is an important ingredient in successful coping (see Elias & Weissberg, this volume, chap. 8), and clearly this is a variable that warrants further study. However, hard evidence on its role in relation to differences in vulnerability to stress is distinctly thin at the moment.

Individual differences in risk exposure

In many ways the most important issue that has emerged over the last decade concerns the crucial need to consider the reasons for individual differences in risk exposure (Rutter & Rutter, 1993). It is obvious that there are huge differences in people's experiences of environmental risk. Some people experience a whole host of negative experiences of various kinds, whereas others seem to go through life relatively untroubled by serious stress or adversity. Although it has long been obvious that this was so, the matter has received surprisingly little attention from psychosocial researchers. Yet, there are important leads on why this might be the case. Thus, the behavior of individuals is important in terms of its effects on how other people behave toward them and in terms of the overall risk environments experienced. This is evident in both short-term and long-term studies. In the short term, both experimental and naturalistic studies have shown that aggressive children tend to elicit an increased rate of aggressive responses from other people (Dodge, 1980). In part, this is a consequence of the direct effects of the individual's own behavior, but studies have also shown that there are effects that result from the reputations that people bring with them (Hymel, Wagner, & Bulter, 1990). In Robins's (1966) classic long-term follow-up study of antisocial children into adult life showed that they experienced a much increased rate of a wide range of negative experiences, such as unemployment, lack of social support, rebuffs from friends, poverty, and broken marital relationships. The Gluecks' follow-up of delinquent boys showed much the same thing (Sampson & Laub, 1993), as did Champion's (Champion, Goodall & Rutter, submitted) follow-up of a sample of inner London children. It is readily appreciated that the negative behavior of antisocial youngsters elicits negative reactions in other people and that those reactions serve to bring about negative experiences in an unfortunate continuing vicious cycle. Similarly, there are negative consequences of teenage pregnancy that may make life in the years that follow more difficult for the women involved (Furstenberg, Brooks-Gunn, & Morgan, 1987). The notion that people select and shape their own experiences conveys a somewhat misleading picture of active choice. Many of these effects arise through a lack of positive choice rather than definite decision making. Nevertheless, however it comes about, it is clear that people's own behavior does much to shape their experiences.

Genetic factors may play some role in this. Twin studies have shown that there is a genetic component to some sorts of negative life events (Kendler, Neale, Heath, Kessler, & Eaves, 1991; McGuffin, Katz, & Rutherford, 1991), and a familial tendency to experience life events was reported in one study (McGuffin, Katz, & Bebbington, 1988).

In addition to these personal factors, it is also apparent that societal influences over which the individual has no control also play an important part. For example, the comparison of children in inner London with children living on the Isle of Wight showed that the former had a rate of psychiatric disorder that was some twice as high (Rutter, Cox, Tulping, Berger, & Yule, 1975). A detailed analysis of the findings indicated that the main explanation for this was the increased rate of family difficulties associated with life in the metropolis (Rutter & Quinton, 1977). There are important geographical differences in various forms of psychopathology (Quinton, 1994; Reiss, in press), although the mechanisms involved remain obscure.

Racial discrimination is also associated with marked differences in negative life experiences. For example, in both the United States and the United Kingdom, unemployment rates are much higher in young blacks than in young whites. The British data show that this ethnic difference remains just as strong even after educational qualifications have been taken into account (White & McRae, 1989). Although racial discrimination is illegal, it is clear that it continues to operate in fields of employment and housing (C. Brown, 1984) as well as in more personal individual encounters.

Much of the focus in thinking about prevention has been on people's responses to negative life experiences. However, it may be even more useful to focus on the factors involved in the determination of why some people have more than their fair share of such negative experiences. For this reason, among others, the investigation of individual differences in environmental risk exposure remains a high priority.

Carry forward of stress effects

As already noted, there is evidence that, in some circumstances, there may be a very long-term carry forward of the sequelae of stress and adversity in early childhood. To some extent it seems that this represents a persistence of psychopathological consequences and to some extent it appears to reflect a resulting increased vulnerability to later stress and adversity. However, surprisingly little is known of the mechanisms involved; yet a substantial range of possibilities exists (Rutter, 1989a). These extend from (1) possible neural effects, as are evident in studies of visual deprivation in infancy (Blakemore, 1991); (2) neuroendocrine effects as have been shown in animal studies of acute physical stress (Hennessy & Levine, 1979); and (3) linkages by which one form of adversity predisposes to another (Quinton & Rutter, 1988) to (4) cognitive variables such as self-esteem, self-efficacy, and internal working models of relationships (Bretherton, 1987; Harter, 1983; Rutter & Rutter, 1993). Certainly, it is clear that all of us think about the experiences that we undergo and develop mental sets about them. It is quite plausible that these cognitive sets play a major role in the carry forward of experiences. However, systematic data to test whether that is the case are largely lacking. Here, then, is another item on the research agenda.

Interventions

Finally, as already noted, there is a need for the exploration, and testing, of the effectiveness of a wider range of interventions. Up to now, most have focused on helping individuals develop better coping or social problem-solving styles (see Elias & Weissberg, this volume, chap. 8). However, it is clear that this is far from the only way in which preventive interventions can be conceptualized. For example, there is good evidence that the overall social characteristics of schools have an important effect on pupils' behavior and scholastic attainments (Maughan, 1994; Mortimore, in press). There have been some attempts to intervene in schools in a way designed to improve overall school efficacy (e.g. Comer, 1991), but such interventions have been few and far between and so far they lack rigorous evaluation. Similarly, although we know that there are marked area differences in rates of psychopathology and in rates of stress experiences, there is a paucity of attempts to intervene at the community level (Reiss, in press). Of course, to a substantial extent this reflects the fact that we lack an understanding of the mechanisms involved in community influences but investigations to determine what those are would be most valuable. There is also a certain amount of evidence suggesting that participation in youth organizations may also be beneficial (Quinn, in press), but once more rigorous evaluations are lacking and we do not know which features of participation in youth organizations are protective. The media are known to exert some influence on young people's behavior, especially when their effects pull in the same direction as influences in the home (Wartella, in press). However, it is not known whether the media may be harnessed to aid people's coping with stress and adversity.

Family planning, in its broadest sense, also has an important role. The United States has one of the highest teenage pregnancy rates in the developed world and it is apparent that this is a consequence of a lack of availability of contraceptives (Hayes, 1987). As unwanted pregnancies during the teenage period bring with them quite a string of stresses and adversities, this would seem to be an important area where action is indicated. There is also a variety of situations known to carry substantial risks where appropriate interventions might reduce the hazards for the children. For example, this would seem to apply in the case of parental mental disorder (Rutter, 1989d). At present, most psychiatrists treating adult patients do not give a high priority to a consideration of what is happening with the care of the children. Perhaps, if this was picked up as a serious issue requiring action, the risks might be reduced.

So far, there is not the evidence to indicate which of these various avenues of intervention carries the greatest potential for benefits. However, what is clear is that there is a substantial range of ways in which the prevention of the ill effects of stress and adversity might be tackled. What is needed now is a systematic exploration of the most promising of these possibilities, together with a testing of the effects of well-planned interventions.

Conclusions

As indicated in the introduction to this chapter, there has been very substantial progress in the understanding of stress, coping, and resilience in childhood and adolescence. As is often the case, the findings that have resulted from systematic research have forced a reconceptualization of the issues. With the exception of a few unusual circumstances, stress effects are no longer seen as what happens when an individual encounters some acute negative life event that arises *de novo*. There is now a much greater appreciation that few life events are random occurrences. Rather, they need to be seen as the outcome of what has gone before. An adequate understanding of such experiences involves an appreciation of how individual differences in environmental risk exposure arise. Also, however, it is apparent that very few apparently acute events are truly acute in their effects. The main risks derive from negative events that are part of chronic or recurrent adversities. The key event (such as bereavement or divorce) constitutes a useful risk indicator, but the risk mechanisms involve a more complex range of happenings both before and after the event. It is also clear that it is seriously misleading to see events simply impinging on individuals who are passive recipients of environmental forces. Rather, people actively engage with their environment, and the ways in which they do so play a major role in determining whether their experiences are risky or protective in their effects. The study of individual differences in vulnerability to stress remains a research priority, as it was a decade ago, and now, as indicated then, the question needs to be tackled at both the individual and social interactional levels. Another shift in focus concerns the need to move from studying life events in terms of provoking or precipitating the onset of a single episode of disorder to investigating their role in relation to an overall liability to disorder as shown over time.

Finally, future research will have to pay even more attention to the need for rigorous testing of hypotheses about causal mechanisms. In that connection, it will be important to make use of genetic strategies. That is not because genetic factors are likely to be important in stress reactions (although it is possible that they may turn out to be so) but rather because it is only through the use of genetic strategies that environmental hypotheses can be put thoroughly to the test (Rutter, 1994c). The polarization of nature and nurture now has a distinctly old-fashioned and outdated feel to it. The future lies in studying the interplay between the two and, in that connection, stress, coping, and resilience occupy center field.

References

Achenbach, T. M. (1991). "Comorbidity" in child and adolescent psychiatry: Categorical and quantitive perspectives. *Journal of Child and Adolescent Psychopharmacology, 1,* 271–278.

Alsaker, F. (in press). Timing of puberty and reactions to pubertal change. In M. Rutter (Ed.), *Psychosocial disturbances in young people: Challenges for prevention.* Cambridge: Cambridge University Press.

Amato, P. R., & Keith, B. (1991). Parental divorce and the well-being of children: A meta-analysis. *Psychological Bulletin, 110,* 26–46.

Attie, I., & Brooks-Gunn, J. (1989). Development of eating problems in adolescent girls: A longitudinal study. *Developmental Psychology, 25,* 70–79.

Attie, I., & Brooks-Gunn, J. (1992). Developmental issues in the study of eating problems and disorders. In J. H. Crowther, S. E. Hobfoll, M. A. P. Stephens, & D. L. Tennenbaum (Eds.), *The etiology of bulimia nervosa: The individual and familial context,* (pp. 35–58). Washington DC: Hemisphere.

Baers, M. (1954). Women workers and home responsibilities. *International Laboratory Review, 69,* 63–80.

Bateson, P. (1966). The characteristics and context of imprinting. *Biological Reviews, 41,* 177–211.

Bateson, P. (1990). Is imprinting such a special case? *Philosophical Transactions of the Royal Society of London, 329,* 125–131.

Bebbington, P. E., Tennant, C., & Hurry, J. (1991). Adversity in groups with an increased risk of minor affective disorder. *British Journal of Psychiatry, 158,* 33–40.

Blakemore, C. (1991). Sensitive and vulnerable periods in the development of the visual system. In G. R. Bock & J. Whelan (Eds.), *The childhood environment and adult disease* (pp. 129–154). Chichester: Wiley.

Block, J. H., Block, J., & Gjerde, P. F. (1986). The personality of children prior to divorce: A prospective study. *Child Development, 57,* 827–840.

Bock, G. R., & Whelan, J. (Eds.) (1991). *The childhood environment and adult disease.* Ciba Foundation Symposium No. 156. Chichester: Wiley.

Bowlby, J. (1951). *Maternal care and mental health.* Geneva: World Health Organization.

Bretherton, I. (1987). New perspectives on attachment relations: Security, communication, and internal working models. In J. D. Osofsky (Ed.), *Handbook of infant development* (2nd ed., pp. 1061–1100). New York: Wiley.

Brown, C. (1984). *Black and white Britain: The third PSI survey.* London: Heinemann.

Brown, G. W., & Harris, T. O. (1978). *Social origins of depression: A study of psychiatric disorder in women.* London: Tavistock.

Brown, G. W., & Harris, T. O. (1989). *Life events and illness.* New York: Guilford.

Buchanan, C. M., Maccoby, E. E., & Dornbusch, S. M. (1991). Caught between the parents: Adolescents' experience in divorced homes. *Child Development, 62,* 1008–1029.

Caron, C., & Rutter, M. (1991). Comorbidity in child psychopathology: Concepts, issues and research strategies. *Journal of Child Psychology and Psychiatry, 32,* 1063–1080.

Caspi, A., Lynam, D., Moffitt, T. E., & Silva, P. A. (1993). Unravelling girls' delinquency: Biological, dispositional, and contextual contributions to adolescent misbehavior. *Developmental Psychology, 29,* 19–30.

Caspi, A., & Moffitt, T. E. (1991). Individual differences are accentuated during periods of social change: The sample case of girls at puberty. *Journal of Personality and Social Psychology, 61,* 157–168.

Caspi A., & Moffitt, T. E. (1993). When do individual differences matter? A paradoxical theory of personality coherence. *Psychological Inquiry, 4,* 247–271.

Cherlin, A. J., Furstenberg, F. F., Chase-Lansdale, P. L., Kiernan, K. E., Robins, P. K., Morrison, D. R., & Teitler, J. O. (1991). Longitudinal studies of effects of divorce on children in Great Britain and the United States. *Science, 252,* 1386–1389.

Clarke, A. M., & Clarke, A. D. B. (1976). *Early experience: Myth and evidence.* London: Open Books.

Clausen, J. S. (1991). Adolescent competence and the shaping of the life course. *American Journal of Sociology, 96,* 805–842.

Cloninger, C. R., & Gottesman, I. I. (1987). Genetic and environmental factors in antisocial behavior disorders. In S. A. Mednick, T. E. Moffitt, & S. A. Stack (Eds.), *The causes of crime: New biological approaches* (pp. 92–109). Cambridge: Cambridge University Press.

Cogill, S., Caplan, H., Alexandra, H., Robson, K., & Kumar, R. (1986). Impact of postnatal depression on cognitive development in young children. *British Medical Journal, 292,* 1165–1167.

Comer, J. (1991). The Comer School Development Program. *Urban Education, 26,* 56–82.

DiLalla, L. J., & Gottesman, I. I. (1989). Heterogeneity of causes for delinquency and criminality: Lifespan perspectives. *Development and Psychopathology, 1,* 339–349.

Dodge, K. A. (1980). Social cognition and children's aggressive behavior. *Child Development, 51,* 1386–1399.

Dodge, K. A., Bates, J. E., & Pettit, G. S. (1990). Mechanisms in the cycle of violence. *Science, 250,* 1678–1683.

Dunn, J., & Plomin, R. (1990). *Separate lives: Why siblings are so different.* New York: Basic Books.

Earls, F. (1987). Sex differences in psychiatric disorders: Origins and developmental influences. *Psychiatric Developments, 1,* 1–23.

Farrington, D. P. (1988). Studying changes within individuals: The causes of offending. In M. Rutter (Ed.), *Studies of psychological risk: The power of longitudinal data* (pp. 184–199). Cambridge: Cambridge University Press.

Furstenberg, F. F., Jr., Brooks-Gunn, J., & Morgan, S. P. (1987). *Adolescent mothers in later life.* Cambridge: Cambridge University Press.

Garmezy, N., & Masten, A. (1994). Chronic adversities. In M. Rutter, E. Taylor, & L. Hersov (Eds.), *Child and adolescent psychiatry: Modern Approaches* (3rd ed., pp. 191–208). Oxford: Blackwell Scientific.

Garmezy, N., & Rutter, M. (Eds.). (1983). *Stress, coping, and development in children.* New York: McGraw-Hill.

Garmezy, N., & Rutter, M. (1985). Acute reactions to stress. In M. Rutter & L. Hersov (Eds.), *Child and adolescent psychiatry: Modern approaches* (2nd ed., pp. 152–178). Oxford: Blackwell Scientific.

Goodyer, I. M. (1990). *Life experiences, development and childhood psychopathology.* Chichester: Wiley.

Gove, W. B. (1978). Sex differences in mental illness among adult men and women: An evaluation of four questions raised regarding the evidence on the higher rates of women. *Social Science and Medicine, 12B,* 187–198.

Grych, J. H., & Fincham, F. D. (1990). Marital conflict and children's adjustment: A cognitive-contextual framework. *Psychological Bulletin, 108,* 267–290.

Harrington, R., Fudge, H., Rutter, M. Pickles, A., & Hill, J. (1990). Adult outcome of childhood and adolescent depression. I. Psychiatric status. *Archives of General Psychiatry, 47,* 465–473.

Harris, T. O., Brown, G. W., & Bifulco, A. (1986). Loss of parent in childhood and adult psychiatric disorder: The Walthamstow Study 1. The role of lack of adequate parental care. *Psychological Medicine, 16,* 641–659.

Harter, S. (1983). Development perspectives on the self-system. In E. M. Hetherington (Ed.), *Socialization, personality and social development: Vol. 4. Mussen's Handbook of Child Psychology* (4th ed., pp. 275–385). New York: Wiley.

Hayes, C. D. (Ed.). (1987). *Risking the future: Adolescent sexuality, pregnancy, and childbearing* (Vol. 1). Washington, DC: National Academy Press.

Hennessy J. W., & Levine, S. (1979). Stress, arousal and the pituitary-adrenal system: A psychoendocrine hypothesis. In J. M. Sprague & A. N. Epstein (Eds.), *Progress in psychobiology and physiological psychology* (pp. 133–178). New York: Academic Press.

Hetherington, E. M., Cox, M., & Cox, R. (1978). The aftermath of divorce. In J. H. Stevens, Jr., & M. Matthews (Eds.), *Mother–child, father–child relations*, Washington, DC: NAEYC.

Hirshfeld, D. R., Rosenbaum, J. F., Biederman, J., Bolduc, E. A., Faraone, S. V., Snidman, N., Reznick, J. S., & Kagan, J. (1992). Stable behavioral inhibition and its association with anxiety disorder. *Journal of the American Academy of Child and Adolescent Psychiatry, 31*, 103–111.

Hodges, J., & Tizard, B. (1989a). IQ and behavioural adjustment of ex-institutional adolescents. *Journal of Child Psychology and Psychiatry, 30*, 53–75.

Hodges, J., & Tizard, B. (1989b). Social and family relationships of ex-institutional adolescents. *Journal of Child Psychology and Psychiatry, 30*, 77–97.

Hoffman, L. W. (1991). The influence of the family environment on personality: Accounting for sibling differences. *Psychological Bulletin, 110*, 187–203.

Holmes, T. H., & Rahe, R. H. (1967). The social readjustment rating scale. *Journal of Psychosomatic Research, 11*, 213–218.

Hymel, S., Wagner, E., & Bulter, L. (1990). Reputational bias: View from the peer group. In S. R. Asher & J. D. Coie (Eds.), *Peer rejection in childhood* (pp. 156–186). Cambridge: Cambridge University Press.

Jenkins, J. M., & Smith, M. A. (1990). Factors protecting children living in disharmonious homes: Maternal reports. *Journal of the American Academy of Child and Adolescent Psychiatry, 29*, 60–69.

Jessor, R., Donovan, J. E., & Costa, F. M. (1992). *Beyond adolescence: Problem behavior and young adult development.* Cambridge: Cambridge University Press.

Keller, M. B., Lavori, P. W., Wunder, J., Beardslee, W. R., Schwartz, C. E., & Roth, J. (1992). Chronic course of anxiety disorders in children and adolescents. *Journal of the American Academy of Child and Adolescent Psychiatry, 31*, 595–599.

Kendler, K. S., Neale, M. C., Heath, A. C., Kessler, R. C., & Eaves, L. J. (1991). Life events and depressive symptoms: A twin study perspective. In P. McGuffin & R. Murray (Eds.), *The New Genetics of Mental Illness* (pp. 146–164). Oxford: Butterworth-Heinemann.

Kendler, K. S., Neale, M. C., Kessler, R. C., Heath, A. C., & Eaves, L. J. (1992). Childhood parental loss and adult psychopathology in women: A twin study perspective. *Archives of General Psychiatry, 49*, 109–116.

Kessler, R. C., Kendler K. S., Heath, A., Neale, M. C., & Eaves, L. J. (1992). Social support, depressed mood, and adjustment to stress: A genetic epidemiologic investigation. *Journal of Personality and Social Psychology, 2,* 257–272.

Kiernan, K. E. (1988). Who remains celibate? *Journal of Biosocial Science, 20,* 253–263.

Kuh, D., & MacLean, M. (1990). Women's childhood experience of parental separation and their subsequent health and socioeconomic status in adulthood. *Journal of Biosocial Science, 22,* 121–135.

Lahey, B. B., McBurnett K., Loeber, R., & Hart, E. L. (in press). Psychobiology of conduct disorders. In G. P. Sholevar (Ed.), *Conduct disorders in children and adolescents: Assessments and intervention.* Washington, DC: American Psychiatric Press.

Last, C. G., Perrin, S., Hersen, M., & Kazdin, A. E. (1992). DSM-III-R anxiety disorders in children: Sociodemographic and clinical characteristics. *Journal of the American Academy of Child and Adolescent Psychiatry, 31,* 1070–1076.

Lazarus, R. S., & Launier, R. (1978). Stress-related transactions between person and environment. In L. A. Pervin & M. Lewis (Eds.), *Perspectives in interactional psychology* (pp. 287–327). New York: Plenum.

Luthar, S. S. (1991). Vulnerability and resilience: A study of high-risk adolescents. *Child Development, 62,* 600–616.

Luthar, S. S., & Zigler E. (1991). Vulnerability and competence: A review of research on resilience in childhood. *American Journal of Orthopsychiatry, 61,* 6–21.

Magnusson, D., & Bergman, L. R. (1990). A pattern approach to the study of pathways from childhood to adulthood. In L. Robins & M. Rutter (Eds.), *Straight and devious pathways from childhood to adulthood* (pp. 101–115). Cambridge: Cambridge University Press.

Marmot, M. G., & Smith, G. D. (1989). Why are the Japanese living longer? *British Medical Journal, 299,* 1547–1551.

Masten, A. S., Garmezy, N., Tellegen, A., Pellegrini, D. S., Larkin, K., & Larsen, A. (1988). Competence and stress in school children: The moderating effects of individual and family qualities. *Journal of Child Psychology and Psychiatry, 29,* 745–764.

Maughan, B. (1994). School influences. In M. Rutter & D. Hay (Eds.), *Development through life: A handbook for clinicians.* Oxford: Blackwell Scientific.

McGuffin, P., Katz, R., & Bebbington, P. (1988). The Camberwell collaborative depression study: IV. Depression and adversity in the relatives of depressed probands. *British Journal of Psychiatry, 152,* 775–782.

McGuffin, P., Katz, R., & Rutherford, J. (1991). Nature, nurture and depression: A twin study. *Psychological Medicine, 21,* 329–335.

Monahan, S. C., Buchanan, C. M., Maccoby, E. E., & Dornbusch, S. M. (1993). Sibling differences in divorced families. *Child Development, 64,* 152–168.

Mortimore, P. (in press). The positive effects of schooling. In M. Rutter (Ed.), *Psychosocial disturbances in young people: Challenges for prevention.* Cambridge: Cambridge University Press.

Murray, L. (1992). The impact of postnatal depression on infant development. *Journal of Child Psychology and Psychiatry, 33,* 543–561.

Paykel, E. S. (1974). Life stress and psychiatric disorders. In B. S. Dohrenwend & B. P. Dohrenwend (Eds.), *Stressful life events: Their nature and effects* (pp. 139–149). New York: Wiley.

Paykel, E. S. (1978). Contribution of life events to causation of psychiatric illness. *Psychological Medicine, 8,* 245–253.

Petersen, A., & Leffert, N. (in press). What is special about adolescence? In M. Rutter (Ed.), *Psychosocial disturbances in young people: Challenges for prevention.* Cambridge: Cambridge University Press.

Plomin, R. (1994). *Genetics and experience.* Thousand Oaks, CA: Sage.

Plomin, R., & Bergeman, C. S. (1991). The nature of nurture: Genetic influences on "environmental" measures. *Behaviour and Brain Sciences, 14,* 373–427.

Plomin, R., & Daniels D. (1987). Why are children in the same family so different from one another? *Behavioral and Brain Sciences, 10,* 1–15.

Plomin, R., McClearn, G. E., Pedersen, N. L., Nesselroade, J. R., & Bergeman, C. S. (1989). Genetic influence on adults' ratings of their current family environment. *Journal of Marriage and the Family, 51,* 791–802.

Plomin, R., Nitz, K., & Rowe, D. C. (1991). Behavioral genetics and aggressive behavior in childhood. In M. Lewis & M. Miller (Eds.), *Handbook of developmental psychopathology* (pp. 119–134). New York: Plenum.

Quinn, J. (in press). Positive effects of participation in youth organizations. In M. Rutter (Ed.), *Psychosocial disturbances in young people: Challenges for prevention.* Cambridge: Cambridge University Press.

Quinton, D. (1994). Cultural and community influences. In M. Rutter & D. Hay (Eds.), *Development through life: A handbook for clinicians.* Oxford: Blackwell Scientific.

Quinton, D., & Rutter, M. (1988). *Parenting breakdown: The making and breaking of inter-generational links.* Aldershot: Averbury.

Reiss, A., Jr. (in press). Community influences on adolescent behavior. In M. Rutter (Ed.), *Psychosocial disturbances in young people: Challenges for prevention.* Cambridge: Cambridge University Press.

Robins, L. (1966). *Deviant children grown up.* Baltimore: Williams and Wilkins.

Robins, L. (1978). Sturdy childhood predictors of adult antisocial behaviour: Replications from longitudinal studies. *Psychological Medicine, 8,* 611–622.

Rutter, M. (1978). Family, area and school influences in the genesis of conduct disorders. In L. Hersov, M, Berger, & D. Shaffer (Eds.), *Aggression and antisocial behaviour in childhood and adolescence* (pp. 95–113). *Journal of Child Psychology and Psychiatry* (Book Series No. 1). Oxford: Pergamon.

Rutter, M. (1982). Developmental neuropsychiatry: Concepts, issues and problems. *Journal of Clinical Neuropsychology, 4,* 91–115.

Rutter, M. (1989a). Pathways from childhood to adult life. *Journal of Child Psychology and Psychiatry, 30,* 23–51.

Rutter, M. (1989b). Intergenerational continuities and discontinuities in serious parenting difficulties. In D. Cicchetti & V. Carlson (Eds.), *Child maltreatment* (pp. 317–348). New York: Cambridge University Press.

Rutter, M. (1989c). Age as an ambiguous variable in developmental research: Some epidemiological considerations from developmental psychopathology. *International Journal of Behavioural Development, 12,* 1–34.

Rutter, M. (1989d) Psychiatric disorder in parents as a risk factor for children. In D. Shaffer, J. Philips, & N. B. Enzer (Eds.), *Prevention of mental disorders, alcohol and other drug use in children and adolescents, OSAP Prevention Monograph 2* (157–189). Rockville, MD: Office for Substance Abuse Prevention, U.S. Department of Health and Human Science.

Rutter, M. (1991a). Psychosocial resilience and protective mechanisms. In D. Cicchetti, K. Nuechterlien, & S. Weintraub, (Eds.) *Risk and protective factors in the development of psychopathology* (pp. 181–214). New York: Cambridge University Press.

Rutter, M. (1991b). A fresh look at "maternal deprivation." In P. Bateson (Ed.), *The development and integration of behaviour* (pp. 331–374). Cambridge: Cambridge University Press.

Rutter, M. (1993). An overview of developmental neuropsychiatry. In F. M. C. Besag & R. T. Williams (Eds.), *The Brain and Behaviour: Organic Influences on the Behaviour of Children.* Special issue. *Educational and Child Psychology, 10,* 4–11.

Rutter, M. (1994a). Continuities, transitions and turning points in development. In M. Rutter & D. Hay (Eds.), *Development through life: A handbook for clinicians.* Oxford: Blackwell Scientific.

Rutter, M. (1994b). Concepts of causation: Tests of causal mechanisms and implications for intervention. In A. Petersen & J. Mortimer (Eds.), *Psy-*

chosocial disturbances in young people: Challenges for prevention. Cambridge: Cambridge University Press.

Rutter, M. (1994c) Genetic knowledge and prevention of mental disorders. Background paper for P. J. Mrazek & R. J. Haggerty (Eds.), *Reducing risks for mental disorders: Research strategies for prevention.* Committee for Prevention of Mental Disorders, Institute of Medicine, Washington, DC.

Rutter, M., Champion, L., Quinton, D., Maughan, B., & Pickles, A. (in press). Origins of individual differences in environmental risk exposure. In P. Moen, G. Elder & K. Luscher (Eds.), *Perspectives on the ecology of human development.* Ithaca: Cornell University Press.

Rutter, M., Cox, A., Tupling, C., Berger, M., & Yule, W. (1975). Attainment and adjustment in two geographical areas. I. The prevalence of psychiatric disorder. *British Journal of Psychiatry, 126,* 493–509.

Rutter, M., & Pickles, A. (1990). Improving the quality of psychiatric data: Classification, cause and course. In D. Magnusson & L. R. Bergman (Eds.), *Data quality in longitudinal research* (pp. 32–57). Cambridge: Cambridge University Press.

Rutter, M., & Quinton, D. (1977). Psychiatric disorder – ecological factors and concepts of causation. In H. McGurk (Ed.), *Ecological factors in human development* (pp. 173–187). Amersterdam: North Holland.

Rutter, M., & Rutter M. (1993). *Developing minds: Challenge and continuity across the lifespan.* Harmondworth: Penguin; New York: Basic Books.

Rutter, M., & Sandberg, S. (1992). Psychosocial stressors: Concepts, causes and effects. *European Child and Adolescent Psychiatry, 1,* 3–13.

Rutter, M., & Smith D. (Eds.). (in press). *Psychosocial disorders in young people: Time trends and their causes.* Chichester: Wiley.

Sampson, R. J., & Laub, J. H. (1993). *Crime in the making: Pathways and turning points through life.* Cambridge, MA: Harvard University Press.

Sandberg, S., Rutter, M., Giles, S., Owen, A., Champion, L., Nicholls, J., Prior, V., McGuiness, D., & Drinnan, D. (1993). Assessment of psychosocial experiences in childhood: Methodological issues and some illustrative findings. *Journal of Child Psychology and Psychiatry, 34,* 879–897.

Scarr, S. (1992). Developmental theories for the 1990s: Development and individual differences. *Child Development, 63,* 1–19.

Scarr, S., & McCartney, K. (1983). How people make their own environments: A theory of genotype → environmental effects. *Child Development, 54,* 424–435.

Skuse, D., & Bentovim, A. (1994). Physical and emotional maltreatment. In M. Rutter, E. Taylor, & L. Hersov (Eds.), *Child and adolescent psychiatry: Modern approaches* (3rd ed., pp. 209–229). Oxford: Blackwell Scientific.

Stattin, H., & Magnusson, D. (1990). *Pubertal maturation in female develop-ment.* Hillsdale, NJ: Erlbaum.

Suomi, S. J. (1991). Early stress and adult emotional reactivity in rhesus monkeys. In G. R. Bock & J. Whelan (Eds.), *The childhood environment and adult disease* (pp. 171–188). Chichester: Wiley.

Wachs, T. D., & Plomin, R. (Eds.). (1991). *Conceptualization and measurement of organism–environment interaction.* Washington, DC: American Psycho-logical Association.

Wartella, E. (in press). Media and the problem behaviors of adolescents. In M. Rutter & D. Smith (Eds.), *Psychosocial disorders in young people: Time trends and their causes.* Chichester: Wiley.

Weiss, B., Dodge, K. A., Bates, J. E., & Pettit, G. S. (1992) Some conse-quences of early harsh discipline: Child aggression and a maladaptive social information processing style. *Child Development, 63,* 1321–1335.

White M., & McRae, S. (1989). *Young adults and long-term unemployment.* London: Policy Studies Institute Publications.

Widom, C. S. (1989). Does violence beget violence? A critical examination of the literature. *Psychological Bulletin, 106,* 3–28.

World Health Organization, Expert Committee on Mental Health. (1951). *Report on the second session 1951.* Geneva: WHO.

Yule, W. (1994). Post traumatic stress disorders. In M. Rutter, E. Taylor, & Hersov (Eds.), *Child and adolescent psychiatry: Modern approaches* (3rd ed., pp. 392–406). Oxford: Blackwell Scientific.

Zaslow, M. J. (1989). Sex differences in children's responses to parental divorce. II. Samples, variables, ages and sources. *American Journal of Orthopsychiatry, 59,* 118–141.

Zoccolillo, M. (1992). Co-occurrence of conduct disorder and its adult outcomes with depressive and anxiety disorders: A review. *Journal of the American Academy of Child and Adolescent Psychiatry, 31,* 547–556.

Zoccolillo, M., Pickles, A., Quinton, D., & Rutter, M. (1992). The outcome of conduct disorder: Implications for defining adult personality disor-der. *Psychological Medicine, 22,* 971–986.

Appendix A
Multidisciplinary consortia
(Membership as of May 1992)

Consortium on Adolescent Bereavement

David Balk, Ph.D., Kansas State University
David Brent, M.D., Western Psychiatric Institute and Clinic
David Clark, Ph.D., Rush-Presbyterian-St. Luke's Medical Center
Barry Garfinkel, M.D., University of Minnesota
Madelyn S. Gould, Ph.D., M.P.H., Columbia University
Emily Harris, M.D., Langley Porter Psychiatric Institute
Gerald Koocher, Ph.D., Children's Hospital, Boston
Elliott Kranzler, M.D., Columbia University
Robert Pynoos, M.D., M.P.H., University of California, Los Angeles
Elizabeth Weller, M.D., Ohio State University
Ronald Weller, M.D., Ohio State University

Consortium for Research on Black Adolescence

Patricia Bell-Scott, Ph.D., University of Geogia
Carol J. Carter, Ph.D., Central Connecticut State University
Joyce E. Everett, Ph.D., Smith College of Social Work
Patrick C. McKenry, Ph.D., Ohio State University
Saundra Murray Nettles, Ph.D., Johns Hopkins University
Joseph H. Pleck, Ph.D., Wellesley College
Howard R. Ramseur, Ph.D., Massachusetts Institute of Technology
Ronald L. Taylor, Ph.D., University of Connecticut

Consortium on Chronic Illness in Childhood

Laurie Bauman, Ph.D., Albert Einstein College of Medicine
Dennis Drotar, Ph.D., Cleveland Metropolitan General Hospital

Steven Gortmaker, Ph.D., Harvard School of Public Health
John Leventhal, M.D., Yale University
Paul W. Newacheck, Ph.D., University of California, San Francisco
Ellen Perrin, M.D., University of Massachusetts Medical Center
James Perrin, M.D., Massachusetts General Hospital
I. Barry Pless, M.D., Montreal Children's Hospital
Ruth E. K. Stein, M.D., Albert Einstein College of Medicine
Deborah Klein Walker, Ed.D., Massachusetts Department of Public Health
Michael Weitzman, M.D., Rochester General Hospital

Consortium on Depression in Childhood and Adolescence

William Beardslee, M.D., Judge Baker Children's Center
Jeanne Brooks-Gunn, Ph.D., Columbia University
Bruce Compas, Ph.D., University of Vermont
Norman Garmezy, Ph.D., University of Minnesota
Constance Hammen, Ph.D., University of California, Los Angeles
Nadine Kaslow, Ph.D., Emory University
Helen Orvashel, Ph.D., Nova University
Anne Petersen, Ph.D., University of Minnesota
Arnold Sameroff, Ph.D., University of Michigan
Stephen Suomi, Ph.D., National Institute of Child Health and
    Human Development

Consortium on the Development Psychobiology of Stress

Ronald Barr, M.D., Montreal Children's Hospital
W. Thomas Boyce, M.D., University of California, San Francisco
Christopher Coe, Ph.D., University of Wisconsin
Richard Davidson, Ph.D., University of Wisconsin
Candice Feiring, Ph.D., University of Medicine and Dentistry of New Jersey
Megan Gunnar, Ph.D., University of Minnesota
John Jemerin, M.D., University of California, San Francisco
Michael Lewis, Ph.D., University of Medicine and Dentisty of New Jersey
Stephen Porges, Ph.D., University of Maryland
Mary Schneider, Ph.D., University of Wisconsin
Carol Worthman, Ph.D., Emory University
Lonnie Zeltzer, M.D., University of California, Los Angeles

Consortium on Divorce and Children

Gene Brody, Ph.D., University of Geogia
Kathleen Camara, Ph.D., Tufts University
Andrew Cherlin, Ph.D., Johns Hopkins University
Robert Emery, Ph.D., University of Virginia
Rex Forehand, Ph.D., University of Georgia
Frank Furstenberg, Jr., Ph.D., University of Pennsylvania
E. Mavis Hetherington, Ph.D., University of Virginia
Eleanor Maccoby, Ph.D., Stanford University
Robert Mnookin, Ph.D., Stanford University
Joanne Pedro-Carroll, Ph.D., University of Rochester
Donald Wertlieb, Ph.D., Tufts University
Nicholas Zill, Ph.D., Westat, Inc.

Consortium on the School-based Promotion of Social Competence

Kenneth A. Dodge, Ph.D., Vanderbilt University
Maurice J. Elias, Ph.D., Rutgers University
Denise C. Gottfredson, Ph.D., University of Maryland
J. David Hawkins, Ph.D., Social Development Research Group
Leonard A. Jason, Ph.D., DePaul University
Philip C. Kendall, Ph.D., Temple University
Cheryl L. Perry, Ph.D., University of Minnesota
Mary Jane Rotheram-Borus, Ph.D., Columbia University
Roger P. Weissberg, Ph.D., University of Illinois, Chicago
Renee Wilson-Brewer, Ph.D., Education Development Center, Inc.
Joseph E. Zins, Ed.D., University of Cincinnati

Consortium for Research Involving Stress Processes

Deborah Belle, Ph.D., Boston University
David Dooley, Ph.D., University of California, Irvine
John Eckenrode, Ph.D., Cornell University
Susan Folkman, Ph.D., University of California, San Francisco
Susan Gore, Ph.D., University of Massachusetts, Boston
Ian Gotlib, Ph.D., Northwestern University
Benjamin Gottlieb, Ph.D., University of Guelph
Ronald Kessler, Ph.D., University of Michigan
Joan Liem, Ph.D., University of Massachusetts, Boston

Nan Lin, Ph.D., Duke University
Peggy Thoits, Ph.D., Vanderbilt University
Robert Weiss, Ph.D., University of Massachusetts, Boston
Donald Wertlieb, Ph.D., Tufts University
Blair Wheaton, Ph.D., University of Toronto

Name index

Abel, E. L., 10
Achenbach, T. M., 14, 228, 229, 230, 233, 234, 255, 342, 359
Adair, R., 339
Adam, T., 249
Adams, M. R., 196
Addy, C., 244
Ader, R., 191
Adrian, C., 244
Ahola, T., 347
Akers, R. L., 300
Albee, G., 296, 301
Alexandra, H., 361
Alkon-Leonard, A., 197
Allen, J. P., 279
Allen, W., 147
Allgood-Merten, B., 239, 240, 241
Allison, P. D., 74, 78
Alloy, L. B., 249
Almeida, M. C., 281
Alpert-Gillis, L. J., 88, 90
Alsaker, F., 358
Altschul, S., 104
Amato, P. R., 68, 74, 78, 81, 82, 83, 85, 89, 357
Ambonetti, A., 123
American Association of University Women, 161
American Heritage Dictionary, 318
American Psychiatric Association, 106, 114, 228
Anand, K. J. S., 190, 202, 205, 206
Anders, T. F., 201

Anderson, E., 168
Anderson, E. R., 82
Anderson, G. M., 329
Anderson, J. C., 235, 243
Anderson, J. E., 200
Anderson, J. T., 196
Andrews, J., 253
Aneshensel, C., 50
Angold, A., 227, 243
Anthony, E. J., 8, 10, 11
Antonovsky, A., 184
Aoki, M. F., 342
Armistead, L., 84, 88
Aronoff, M. S., 241
Arthur, B., 103
Asarnow, J. R., 244
Aseltine, R. H., Jr., 29, 51
Ashley, L., 200
Askenasy, A. R., 186
Asmussen, L., 33
Asterita, F., 187
Atkeson, B. M., 74, 81
Attie, I., 358
Austin, A. W., 166
Aynsley-Green, A., 205

Babani, L., 325
Bachen, E. A., 195
Bachman, J., 52, 151
Baers, M., 365
Baker, L., 227
Baldwin, A., 11
Baldwin, C., 11

Subject index

conduct disorder comorbidity, 237–8
continuity-discontinuity issue, 228–9
course of, 244–5
covariation and comorbidity, 225–58
developmental issues, 239–41
diagnosis of, and development, 240
differential vulnerability in women,
    23–4
family occurrence, 247
family processes, 251–2
features of, 239–41
gender differences, 239
grief overlap, 121–3
incidence, 242–3
intervention, 252–4
life events association, 364
pharmacotherapy, 252–3
psychological processes, 248–50
recurrence, 364
risk factors, and comorbidity, 245–
    52, 257
depressive syndrome
covariation, 234
identification of, 228
descending pain pathways, 208–9
desipramine, 253
developmental factors
and children of divorce, 82–3
contextual model, 26
critical period theory, 361
and depression, 239–41
and intervention evaluation, 342
as intervention mediator, 342–3
research in, 13–15
and risk taking, blacks, 172
sensitive period theory, 361–2
and vulnerability, 360–1
developmental psychopathology, 14–15,
    347
developmental tasks, 48–9
developmental transitions
gender differences in impact of, 34
planning for, 371
dexamethasone suppression test, 127
diabetes intervention, 340
difficult temperament, 83–4, 92–3
dimensional models, 323–4, 342–3
divorce effects, 64–93
demography, 66

developmental vulnerability model, 48
economic distress, 67–8, 89
hidden distress, 77–9
long-term risks, 357–8
and nonresidential parent, 67–8
parental conflict as risk factor, 72–3,
    85–6, 357–8
parental loss comparison, 108, 118–
    21, 157
and parental psychopathology, 71–2
prospective studies, 75–6
and residential parent, 69–71
resilience factors, 79–93
see also children of divorce
divorced fathers, 68–9, 87
divorced mothers
economic consequences, 67–8
parenting skills, 86–7
relationships with children, 69–71
dose-response relationship, risk, 369
dreams
and parental loss, 113
and witness to violent death, 125
drop-outs, 150, 162, 169–70
drug abuse
black adolescents, 153–4
school-based interventions, 284–5
DSM-III-R
depression definition, 228
pathological grief definition, 114, 122
Duke Epidemiologic Catchment Area
    Study, 124
dysthymic disorder, 236

easy temperament, 92–3
eating disorders, and puberty, 358
economic considerations, intervention,
    343–4
economic stress
and divorce, 67–8, 89
and parental death, 118–19
Education for All Handicapped Chil-
    dren Act, 326–7
educational expectations, 160–1
educational level, mothers, 341
educational opportunity
black adolescent resilience, 159–60,
    168
teenage mother resilience, 159–60